AF529126

Introduction to Bioeconomics

Introduction to BIOECONOMICS

Dr. I. Sundar
Associate Professor of Economics
Directorate of Distance Education
Annamalai University,
Tamil Nadu, India

GLOBAL RESEARCH PUBLICATIONS
NEW DELHI (INDIA)

First Published - 2011

ISBN: 978-81-89630-08-9

Published by

GLOBAL RESEARCH PUBLICATIONS
4830/24, 1st Floor, Ansari Road
Darya Ganj, New Delhi-110002 (India)
Phone : 23245225. Fax : 91-11-23272135
E-mail: globalresearchpublications@gmail.com, grpindia@vsnl.net

Contents

Preface

Bioeconomics in terms of Biological Economics is exactly what has been developed for the study of these *Bioeconomical* events and their interactions through the synthesis of the sciences of life and the sciences of society for a better understanding of their causes. *Bioeconomics* is a paradigmatic shift in the study of problems that arise in the interface of Biology and Economics. In this sense the human economic system may be considered as an extension of its biological system and as such it must be founded on the concept of entropy and its activity must therefore, be subject to entropy law. This is a scientific foundation for biophysical distinction between the human economic process based on chrematistics and nature's economic process based on exchange of materials and recycling. Bioeconomics deals with many interactions rather than their interrelations and as such it is much more encompassing than other interdisciplinary fields such as Ecological Economics. Furthermore, since these interactions are often non-linear their elucidation requires knowledge that is truly interdisciplinary

Bioeconomics—a emerging of views on biology and economics—on the one hand invites the "export" of situational logic and sophisticated optimization developed in economics into biology. On the other hand, human economic activity and its evolution, not least over the past few centuries, may be considered an instance for fruitfully applying ideas from evolutionary biology and Darwinian theory. Since many of the features of the paradigmatic change that were introduced into the sciences by Darwinism may be desirable for economics as well, the question whether the Darwinian revolution can be a model to introduce a new paradigm in economic theory is explored.

Biological and economical activities are among the most important human endeavours while conservation, cooperation and coevolution are the rules in the biological world. The domain of economical activity is dominated by an abuse of biological resources, competition and mismanagement. *Bioeconomics,* by integrating the evolutionary principles of Biology required for the long-term survival of human species with the socioeconomic principles necessary for the short-term well-being can advance the survival instinct so essential for the sustainability of humanity.

This book aims at developing an understanding of utilization of biological resources in production of goods and services based on theoretical and practical knowledge. This book provides students with an overview of the fundamental concepts of bio-economic issues and theories related to sustainable utilization of biological resources such as the biophysical economics, fisheries economics, marine economics, aquaculture economics, economics of biodiversity, economics of biotechnology, environmental economics, ecological economics and resources economics and their interrelationship among them in inter disciplinary in perspective. This book also demonstrates the use of economic tools for decision-making on bio-economic models. It explores the terminology, conventions, procedures and planning policy applications. It also covers a number of contemporary bio-economic issues and programmes.

This book is organized in 12 chapters. The first chapter deals with bio-economics-basic concepts and meaning with reference to evolutionary biology and evolutionary economics. The second chapter discusses the development of economics and biosciences focusing on Darwin theory of evaluation and steady state economics. The third chapter narrates evolution and development of economics. The fourth chapter is biological adaptation in human societies. It discusses bio-economic analysis of Darwin theory. The fifth chapter discusses biophysical economics in terms of application of physical principles in economic theory. The sixth chapter deals with Economics of biodiversity. It makes an analysis of theory of economic instruments in valuation of biological resources. The seventh chapter makes a detailed discussion on economics of bio-pesticide. The eighth chapter discusses bio-economic analysis of aquaculture with reference to fish culture. The ninth chapter makes a discussion on marine bio-economics. It deals with valuation of marine resources, and marine ecosystem, selfish aquaculture, economic potential for offshore aquaculture. The tenth chapter examines the economics of biotechnology with reference to application of economic measures in valuation of property rights of biological resources. The eleventh chapter makes an analysis of sustainable development. It deals with concept theme, dimensions of sustainable development, sustainable community and sustainable development approaches in India. The last chapter makes a detailed discussion on sustainable society. It examines the trans disciplinary pollution control policy instruments, socially sustainable economic growth and sustainable trade system.

I express my sincere gratitude to our revered Vice Chancellor Dr. M. Ramanathan and Dr. S.B. Nageshwara Rao, Director, Directorate of Distance Education, Annamalai University who have been the source of constant inspiration in my academic and research endeavor. I express my sincere gratitude to Dr. N. Malathi, Professor and Head, Department of Economics for her motivation in writing this book. I also thank profusely Dr. D. Namasivayam, Professor and Head Economics Wing, Directorate of Distance Education, Annamalai University for his constant encouragement in my academic and research career.

It is with heart and soul that I thank Shri. S.K. Jha, Proprietor Serials Publications, New Delhi for evincing a keen interest in publishing this book.

Dr. I. Sundar

1

Bio-Economics Concept and Meaning

BIOECONOMICS

A progressive branch of social science that seeks to integrate the discipline of economics and biology for the sole purpose of creating theories a better job of explaining economic events using a biological basis and vice versa. The proponents of bioeconomics believe that the same patten can be seen in biological evolution can be applied to stock market behavior, as many of the same "causal interactions" and "survival elements" found there as well as in nature. Bioeconomics is the study of the dynamics of living resources using economic models. It is an attempt to apply the methods of environmental economics and ecological economics to empirical biology. Bioeconomics applies optimal control methods to mathematical models using environmental and ecological elements for resource protection issues relating to resource economics. Bioeconomics is the science determining the socioeconomic activity threshold for which a biological system can be effectively and efficiently utili without destroying the conditions for its regeneration and therefore its sustainability.

Bioeconomics is closely related to the early development of theories in fisheries economics, initially in the mid 1950s by Canadian economists Gordon (1954) and Anthony Scott (1955). Their ideas used recent achievements in biological fisheries modeling, primarily the works by Scha (1957) on establishing a formal relationship between fishing activities and biological growth through mathematical modeling confirmed by empirical studies, and also relates itself to ecology and the environment and resource protection. These ideas developed out of the multidisciplinary fisheries science environment in Canada at the time. Fisheries science and modeling developed rapidly during a productive and innovative period, particularly among Canadian fisheries researchers of various disciplines. Population modeling fishing mortality were introduced to economists, and new interdisciplinary modeling tools became available for the economists, which made it to evaluate biological and economic impacts of different fishing activities and fisheries management decisions.

The main area of interest is the investigation and clarification of the interactions that occur at the interface of the socioeconomic and biological system. They occur when the socioeconomic system in its daily activity impacts the biological system and gives rise to such phenomena as global warming, depletion of the ozone layer and others. It goes without saying that these interactive phenomena that are moreover complex and are of uncertain nature have serious repercussions for the human enterprise. Economics has not really dealt with the concepts of uncertainty and irreversibility as economists cannot make up their minds that humanity is definitely and irreversibly destroying the foundation of life: killing the goose that lays the golden egg.

- Bioeconomic activity is the closest approximation of the human socioeconomic enterprise to the economy of nature because it has the biological support functions incorporated in its theoretical foundation: mimicking nature's biological processes of conservation, regeneration and recycling and as importantly for allowing the biological temporalities to run their course and not to be interfered with.
- The human socioeconomic system, especially since the industrial Revolution, has been dominated by two tendencies:

- The Exponential Growth Model: exponential population growth requiring exponential economic growth based on the exponential utilization of biological resources.
- The Comparative Advantages Model: developed industrial countries importing cheap biological resources especially fossil fuels from underdeveloped countries and exporting luxury items at exorbitant prices to them. This type of trade would be o.k. if undeveloped countries were paid the real price (value) for their resources. However, these models are facing a challenge which is of the psychological nature brought about by technology: How to overcome the old mentality of paying, and receiving, more money for doing extra work with the new mentality of paying, and receiving, more money for doing less work. This is due to the political imperative of having continuous economic growth by encouraging maximum production and consumption in order to have full employment
- This means that in time there will be less need for the conventional type of work. This is where a type of socioeconomic activity based on the bioeconomic principles comes into its own; namely Economics of the Third Way.
- This is the bioeconomic business activity, which is an integrating matrix encompassing both conventional as well as unconventional type of work and whose lapidary is a model based on cooperation competition, solidarity and trust and both quantity and quality in contrast to the neoclassical capitalist market economy based only on competition, quantity and lack of trust.

The classical economic belief that the biological system is not a capital stock and that the biological resources are either infinite or are at best substitutable has done great damage to our thinking in relation to the planetary system and also in relation to our lifestyle as far as our methods of production and consumption are concerned. Furthermore, it must be appreciated that humanity is an integral part of the biospheric system and its development and evolution must proceed in unison with that of the biological system; that is they have to coevolve.

The dynamics of the biological system is changing drastically due to the prevalent anthropocentric attitude which has to change to a biocentric one if the serve linear impact of the globalised economic system on the non-linear biospheric system is to be reversed now and to be avoided in the future. Moreover, the biocentric attitude is essential for the enhancement of the coevolution of the biological system with the human socio-economic system an towards a harmonious and sustainable mode of existence. To achieve this sustainable existence the human socio-economic system will have to be transformed from a plundering capitalist system ignorant of the biological limits to economic growth and the intrinsic value of nature to a system whose activities will be adjusted to the socio-economic realities and more so to the biospheric realities of depletion of biological resources and severe environmental contamination.

The disciplines developed to resolve the interactive problems have not been very successful although each has contributed a little to extend our understanding. The main reasons for incomplete success have been that these problems are interactive, accumulative and complex and therefore there is a need for interdisciplinary investigation that would be encompassing of all these factors. Bioeconomics, Biological Economics [Mohammadian, 1980] is an innovative discipline developed with biocentric and coevolutionary perspectives in mind. It is a paradigmatic shift in the study of Economics by means of a thorough and complete synthesis between Biology and Economics to provide solutions for the uncertain and accumulative Bioeconomical problems facing humanity. Taking advantage of the vast accumulated knowledge of Biology and extending it to Economics would make available the necessary tools to tackle the complex an interactive problems present at the interface of the human biological and economic activity systems.

BIOECONOMICS: SYNTHESIS OF BIOLOGY AND ECONOMICS

In the past several decades new disciplines have been proposed to alleviate some gross weaknesses of the economic theory. Resource Economics [Pearce and Turner, 1990] was the first and has attempted to account for the scarcity of the biological resources and their true market value. This has evolved to Environmental Economics [Pillet and Murota, 1987] taking into account what the economists have called 'externalities' that is the negative impacts of economic activity on the environment and which are outside the sphere of classical economic theory. Ecological Economics [Constanza, 1989] has been the most recent attempt in order to enlarge this field of study and to complete the missing links by studying in addition in order to enlarge this field of study and to complete the missing links by studying in addition the relationships between the many aspects of the economy and the total environment in which it operates. The appearance of new problems such as the global warming and the depletion of the ozone layer has brought to light the theoretical defects of the classical and neo-classical economic theories in relation to the biosphere. To provide solutions for these problems an innovative and holistic methodology based on interdisciplinarity [Mohammadian, 1997] is required that could guarantee a coherent response to the biospheric problematique and to ensure planetary sustainability.

Bioeconomics is an attempt in this direction and pursues the symbiosis of economic activity with that of the biological activity in a coevolutionary manner for the mutual benefit of both. It makes possible a better understanding of not only the interrelations but more importantly the interactions between the economic variables and the biologic ones acting in the planetary system. Also, the discipline of Bioeconomics will be useful to clarify the systemic and evolutionary factors necessary for ensuring the sustainability of the planetary activities in its biotic and abiotic entirety [Mohammadian and Jimenez, 1998). In addition, it is quite possible that we will understand more fully how biological systems with such vast diversity have coevolved and continue to do so for the benefit of all. It should be obvious that this knowledge will be very useful for the coevolutionary development of the human economic system in a contaminated biosphere on the way to total depletion of its biological resources.

The economic rationality must interlock with the biological rationality thus adjusting the logic of the economic to the logic of the biologic. Certain market economic activities and modes of operation resemble that of biology and the Darwinian evolution through competition for survival, selection and adaptation allows to amplify the conceptual and theoretical foundation of Economics. But this should not lead to a new macroeconomic determinism dominated by "egoistic genes" of the economic agents that only wish to maximize profits and utility of their productive units i.e companies or that of the consuming units (H. economicus). However, it should be appreciated that cultural evolution is much more rapid than the biological evolution and humankind has the capacity to learn to face the challenges in order to coevolve towards biological and socio-economic systems of more complexity and maturity.

Therefore, a new vision is needed now to put into context the human economic development and the development of all forms of life in general on a sustainable foundation thus avoiding the reductionist-mechanistic outlook and as such to renew the ethical principles and the value system in relation to nature. This should help us to delve deeply into the essence of the structural and dialectical interactions between the economic sphere (econosphere), the social (sociosphere), the technological (technosphere) and the biological (biosphere) within a united biospheric system of cognition and learning.

The post-industrial globalised economic system should explore the biological organization a the foundation of the economic management and it should inscribe to the biosphere because "if all products of the biosphere cannot be reduced to the market place however, all products of the market belong t the biosphere and are subject to biological laws" [Passet, 1979]. Likewise human beings must intervene in all economic activities as part and parcel of nature, means, agents and final objective and since these activities develop in a living environment which it impacts and interactions are produced, therefore the logic of the economic must be integrated into the logic of the biologic. The Bioeconomic paradigm attempts a drastic change in the investigation of these problems by studying the interactions in the economy-biology interface with an interdisciplinary, intersectorial and holistic methodology in order to confront the global problems in their dynamics of actions, reactions and interactions between the realm of economy and the realm of biology.

The weakness of the orthodox paradigms of the market economy becomes quite evident if we appreciate the intrinsic scarcity of the biological resources and the impossibility of sustainable management from the viewpoint of the market duet to its emphasis on limited time scale. The market treatment of biological resources and services as 'free goods' shows great contradictions, ethical ignorance and absence of rationality. Bioeconomics would make it possible then to speak of the logic of the living from a "super-organism" perspective: the planet, Gaia with the capacity for homeostatic regulation of the environment and of the conditions necessary for life [Lovelock, 1990]. Therefore, from the Bioeconomic point of view and in accordance with the autopoeitic theory of living systems [Maturana and Varela, 1972] the human economic activity system has certain characteristics to render it a quasi-living system in the sense that it is able to self-organise and coevolve within the planetary system. This, in essence, is the logic of Bioeconomic paradigm because it transcends the objectives of quantification and monetization in order to aspire to those of quality and humanization without the necessary for permanent artificial assistance from the human system. This is possible only when the economic process is biologically sustainable; in short only when it becomes Bioeconomic.

BIOECONOMIC DEVELOPMENT AND COEVOLUTION

Bioeconomics is a synthetic and interdisciplinary methodology that makes it possible to investigate the interactions that present themselves at the biology-economy interface. These interactions will also have to be studied both at the temporal as well as spatial scale in a holistic and integrated manner. In this way, it is hoped to develop a Bioeconomic model with scientific rigour to be useful as a model for coevolutionary development.

Coevolution is a dynamic process that functions as a series of reciprocal responses between two interactive and evolving systems. The human economic system is totally dependent upon the biological system and both are very interactive. The human species, contrary to other animal species, not only uses but also constructs and transforms its natural environment that as a result is in a constant process of change; that is to say that nature is transformed and is re-created. Also, as actions are reciprocal and interactive nature also impacts the human species that consequently is changing and therefore, the planet as a whole nature and humanity is being transformed from a state of being to a state of becoming [Prigogine, 1980] with grave repercussions for nature itself and for the humankind in particular.

Although interactions between the human economic system and the biological system have been generally positive and productive it is also true that in many cases they have been unfavourable and have resulted in coevolutionary cases that have been very damaging for the planetary system. A very outstanding example is the case of human ignorance of the danger sings emanating from the impact of human economic activity associated with the global warming, the depletion of the ozone layer and others. Also, there have resulted from this unfavourable coevolution national and regional conflicts with grave consequences or the biospheric system [Mohammadian, 1996]. These conflicts, all of them resulting from unfavourable coevolutionary interactions, have their origin in the human psyche and therefore, it is essential to affect a drastic transformation to change to a more biocentric attitude and a less anthropocentric one. However, it is also true that the direct causes of these conflicts are to be found in the over-exploitation of the biological system by the socio-economic system of competition, production and consumption that is for ever more complex technologically and as a result loses its capacity for profiting from the potential of development generated by the coevolutionary process. To take the first steps toward a sustainable society to be founded on conservation and coevolution it is necessary to appreciate the errors of our culture based on the supremacy of humankind and its commercial inclination for wastefulness and abuse of biological resources. There must be something drastically wrong with a culture that in the name of improving the quality of life is finishing with its own biological capital, contaminating its own 'home' and thus endangering its own survival.

Consequently, Bioeconomics with its inherent coevolutionary perspective founded upon the cultural and traditional knowledge of bioeconomic systems evolved during millenniums can facilitate a model of coevolutionary development with optimum management of human and biological resources. In other words, Bioeconomics is the scientific discipline and the coevolutionary process is a functional tool available to put the theory of Bioeconomics at the service of coevolutionary development.

BIOECONOMIC DEVELOPMENT AND ENTROPY

It is important to always remember that human beings are an integral part of nature and at the summit of evolution while nature itself is inherent in humanity as a species and by which it is subdued and controlled. The result of this control is the industrial civilization which through the international economic system is endangering the self-regeneration of nature, its self-purification and self-organisation. But, also it must be realized that the human economic system cannot function beyond the physical limits of the biological system and indefinite economic growth is impossible within a closed biospheric system. Therefore, an optimum scale for economic growth must be defined in relation to the global biological system and the flows of matter and energy are to be precisely defined in regards to entropic limitations.

The concept of entropy and the irreversibility of the biological processes leading to the qualitative degradation of matter and energy has been manifested eloquently by Georgescu-Roegen who buries once and for all the mechanistic dogma of the orthodox economic paradigm and brings to light the inviability of a permanent stationary state in a finite biospheric system [Georgescu-Roegen 1971].

The evolution of exosomatic techniques of ever-increasing complexity has amplified humanity's biological evolution for obtaining low-entropy matter and energy and thus spreading its domination over the biosphere. This has resulted in the disproportionate exploitation of biological capital with the concomitant division of the planet in two extremely rich and extremely destitute halves. Therefore, the entropy law is affecting humanity in both the biological activity system and in its economic activity system thus causing significant social conflicts. But the evolution of techniques for the continuous exploitation of the biological capital is confronting socio-economic limitations in that the transformations required for the optimal use of these techniques are becoming more expensive, more time-consuming and in need of organizations that would lead to more bureaucracy thus limiting development of a sustainable society.

However, the evolutionary process has had a very positive effect on the biosphere and from humanity's perspective it can be said that during its evolutionary period entropy has decreased; in other words the evolutionary process has been negentropic. Of-course this does not mean that the biological system is defying the entropy law; far from it, the universe in its totality is entropic. Then we are faced with the question: how has the biological system produced and maintained order while confronted with the insurmountable entropy trap? This is where the biological knowledge of Bioeconomic paradigm based on the theory of "dissipative structures" [Prigogine and Glansdorf, 1971] can enlighten us through a deep understanding of the feedbacks and interactions between the biological process and the economic process. It is, therefore, from the vantage point of entropy and irreversibility of biological processes that another of the important scientific principles of Bioeconomics is introduced.

New scientific theories such as the non-linear thermodynamic theory of open systems, the theory of complexity and the theory of dissipative structures could help to clarify to a great extent the theoretical basis for a human economic system operating in a state far from equilibrium and resulting in low entropy. It would be possible by means of dissipative structures to account for the paradox in the concept of entropy observed in a physical system and in a biological system. Entropy in a physical system signifies waste and disorder but order and stability in a biological system and the loss of matter and energy becomes the means for development and evolution to a higher and more complex level of existence. Therefore, it should theoretically be possible to think of a new economic system in the form of a bioeconomic system characterized by dissipative structures and structural coupling that would make it possible for such a system to operate in a quasi-cognitive state and with minimum entropic degradation. There is no conceivable way that the human economic system can be rendered sustainable if the entropy level is not at lest reduced. If there is no other environment but our biosphere with which the resulting entropy can be exchanged then a Bioeconomic activity system based on the concept of dissipative structures could be a possible solution. Furthermore, it would be possible to understand why the human economic system, through its best activity indicator the stock exchange, from time to time exhibits such erratic behaviour that completely baffles the economists.

A BIOECONOMIC MODEL FOR SUSTAINABILITY

The economic process directed by the market forces does not possess an inherent function for sustainability and what is more the market sensibility is not conscious of an economic development process which in addition to being competitive it also has to be sustainable biologically optimums and it probable that none of them could guarantee sustainability of the economic system.

To find equilibrium between the economic optimum and the biologic optimum together with the maximum well-being and sustainable conditions of life are the basic objectives of the Bioeconomic model. However, it is necessary to emphasise two relevant aspects: the first has to do with the degree of sustainability and the ethical burden relative to the conservation of the biological capital and the values assigned to it. The second aspect has to do with the scale of economy, its functioning as an open system and the limitations of the thermodynamic laws.

The concept of sustainability may be expressed as multifunctional, in short, it could be said that there exist three functions. The first, as a basic support of life and human activities, is the biological. The second, of a productive character, is the techno-economical and the third is the socio-cultural; all of them are interdependent and interactive and they are all implicated in the ethical dimension and are compromised with biosphere (bioethics). Also, they are all essential for rendering human progress and well-being sustainable in a manner that is biologically productive, environmentally benign, economically viable and socially just. Nevertheless, different level of actions could be established according to the degree of dominance of each function. In this manner an efficient sustainable development process will respond to a vision that is predominantly biocentric, that is conservationist, that will establish an economic subsystem limited by the exigenecies of the biological system for optimizing flows of matter and energy in the productive process. Moreover, the maintanence of the biological capital is essential because in reality it cannot be substituted by the manufactured capital produced by the economic system of the humankind and also the environmental damage resulting from the process of production would be limited. On the contrary, a less efficient process of sustainable development is accompanied by a technocentric vision which is less conservationist and where limits imposed by the biological system are less strict. This would allow the substitution of the biological capital by the manufactured capital by accepting the belief that the biological system makes no real contribution to the economic productive process and any increase in productivity results from advances in science and technology. This, of-course, is completely false and is made quite clear by the theory of Bioeconomic development having its roots in the undeniable importance of the biological system and its resources for the economic activity. Also, Bioeconomic development does not suffer from the oxymoron nature of 'sustainable economic development' achieved through growth and can ensure economic development that is amenable to both quantitative and qualitative interests of the present and future generations by dematerialization of the economic productive process and by disengaging the human economic activity from the severe environmental degradation with which it has been associated for so long.

According to the Bioeconomic development model the perfect substitution of different forms of capital cannot be taken for granted. Some biological goods and services viz biogeochemical cycles are essential for the maintenance of life support systems and cannot be replaced. However, there exist some biological assets that although they could be considered not essential for the human well-being nevertheless they are essential for human survival or for that of other species. Presumably these 'vital' assets such as the atmosphere, the ozone layer and others could be classified in a sub-division under "critical natural capital" and are practically not substitutable [Pearce and Turner, 1990].

The Bioeconomic model also emphasizes the value of the biological system in response to humanity's performance and the fact that it enjoys an intrinsic value necessary for its vital functions which exceed individual desires or even that of human existence or the existence rights of other species. These are all integral parts of the Bioeconomic model of human sustainable development and should take precedent over market regulatory mechanisms optimizing the process of economic development. According to the biological theory of cognition [Maturana, 1970] and the system concept a human being as a living system is a cognitive system and the process of life is a cognitive process. A living system responds to its environment by continuous changes which transform its reactions and behaviour through cognition by means of "structural coupling" [Maturana and Varela, 1987]. The significance of this for human sustainable development should be obvious as it is quite possible that the economic activity by structurally coupling with the biological activity, that is by means of continuous interactions and structural changes, becomes a quasi-cognitive system in the form ofa Bioeconomic system and therefore the human economic development process is rendered more efficient in its production and less entropic in the utilization of biological resources, in short, more sustainable. Paraphrasing the statement "to live is to know"

BIO-ECONOMICS AND SUSTAINABLE DEVELOPMENT

Bioeconomics and sustainable development is a little that covers the interactions of the natural environment with the economic process under the target of sustainable development. The concept of the Ecologically Sustainable Economic Development (ESED) emerged in the publications of the World Conservation Strategy as a policy framework to combat the environmental decay afficting our planet, a decay mainlyowed to the increasing pollution and the alarming surge in the extraction of natural resources. The ESED has grown in popularity since the publication of the Burntlandreport (WECD, 1987). In it, the ESED is defined as "the development that meets the need of present generations without compromising the ability o the future generations to meet their own needs" or as "a pattern of social and structural economictrans formations which increase the benefits available in the present without jeopardizing the likely potentials for similar benefits in the future" (WECD, 1987).

From these definitions it is patently clear that the ESED sets a meaningful social target which, however, requires further elaboration in order to assume an operational dimension. A somewhat more precise definition, addressing policy issues, can be found also in the Bruntland report: "in essence sustainable development is a process of change in which the exploitation of resources, the direction of investments, the orientation of technological development and institutional change are all in harmony and enhance both current ad future potentials to meet human needs and aspirations" (WECD, 1987). All three definitions share a common trait: the needs of present and future generations should be potentially fulfilled without trade-offs between fulfillment of present generations needs and fulfillment of future generations needs.

The word "potentially" applies exclusively for the needs of future generations that cannot be brought under scrutiny at present since the preferences of future generations have not arisen as yet, and consequently, are unknown to us; therefore the only readily available strategy would be to waive, for the time being, the potential for fulfillment of the needs of future generations, irrespective of the shape these needs may assume. Two different scientific approaches are widely known as "strong" and "weak" sustainability. "Strong" sustainability views the needs of future generations as independent of the needs / preferences of present generations maintains that any needs arising at and belonging to a future period may have to be formulated in a manner entirely Tracing operational conditions for the ecological sustainable economic development independent of the way present needs/ preferences are currently formulated. After all, the needs and preferences of future generation may take a different shape than that assumed by the needs and preferences of present generations may take a different shape than that assumed by the needs and preferences of present generations or even be wholly irrelevant to them. In this context, a rational policy should aim at eliminating the boundaries that stifle the formulation and fulfillment of future generations needs and preferences. As a result the "strong" sustainability approach asserts that the ESED, offering itself as a rational policy, must, eliminate those boundaries whose cause may lie in advanced environmental degradation and inexorable exploitation of natural resources. For, once these calamities have gathered momentum, they decrease the potential welfare that generations in times to come may have. With that consideration mind, Christensen outlines sustainable development as the development ensuring the existence of the natural environment, which acts as a basis for human welfare.

EVOLUTIONARY BIOLOGY AND EVOLUTIONARY ECONOMICS

A major motivation for biologists to explore evolution further was the fact that some phenomena of evolution have still not been explained satisfactorily. Among them is the so called Darwin's dilemma since this problem had already raised by Darwin himself. The question is: How can complex organs or parts of the body like an eye, a limb or a wing be the result of a gradual selection process? An eye, for example, is a complex system of a lens, a retina, tissue, nerves and so on. If an eye is indeed the product of gradual selection, it has not developed as a whole, and all of a sudden. There must have been intermediate forms with which the individual organism was not only viable but which were also selected since according to Neo-Darwinism, every intermediate form, including incomplete ones, must have shown a selective advantage. It is obvious, then, that this explanation of the emergence of complex new structures was not satisfying. It was shown that this deficiency of Neo-Darwinism lies in its disregard of the rules of transformation from genotype to phenotype. Neo-Darwinism concentrates on two research areas: genetic and phenotypic evolution, implicitly assuming that the sphere in between genetic evolution and phenotypic evolution is not relevant and not knowing whether the genetic changes responsible for big changes in form were the same as for small variations within species. Thus, Neo-Darwinism was blamed for only explaining what body forms can be maintained in organismal evolution, but not what forms are generated. It was reasoned that mutations only produce small variations from what already exists but do not create new forms and mutations are often the result of negative impacts such as radiation and hence they destroy more than they create. In addition, selection is a mechanism that can only work on what already exists.

Thus, a theory of how completely new organs, structures and body plans come into existence was still lacking.

This scientific challenge has given rise to a rather new research program called Evolutionary Developmental Biology or informally "EvoDevo") which combines two research areas which had existed quite independently until roughly 1990: developmental biology and evolutionary biology. Developmental biology deals with the development of organisms and ontogenetic rules of the development of forms and structure, in particular the origin and evolution of embryonic development. EvoDevo seeks to extend this research in concentrating on interdependencies between ontogenesis and evolution, in particular the analysis of causal relationships between embryonic and evolutionary processes. One of the main questions posed by EvoDevo is: Does developmental embryonic evolution bias the produced phenotypic variations or constrain certain paths of evolution?

Some exponents of EvoDevo have concentrated on physical processes that guide how cells organize organs and tissues. The stickiness, elasticity, and chemical reactions within and between cells affect the body plan of an organism. Since body plans have internal inertia, evolution is not completely arbitrary, but works around these stable body plans. Consequently, there is a multitude of development constraints. Neo-Darwinism implicitly assumes that genetic and morphological variation and evolution are highly positively correlated. However, results in molecular genetics show that this is not the case and even from the complete knowledge of the genome, one cannot infer the anatomy of an organism. The ontogenetic formation of morphological structures is not determined by genes only but is due to an interdependent activity of genes, cells, tissue and external factors. Epigenetics is the study of heritable changes in the phenotype or gene expression caused by non-genetic mechanisms. In a wider sense it refers to all mechanisms other than changes in the underlying DNA-sequence that influence the embryonic development. Epigenetics can hence be interpreted as a counter- reaction to the dominance of genetics in Neo-Darwinism.

One of the discoveries of EvoDevo in contrast to Neo-Darwinism has been that the same or similar organs and structures in different animals such as eyes, limbs, hearts, legs, wings etc. have not been "invented repeatedly from scratch", which means they would have emerged from distinct changes in the number and sequence of genes. Instead, similar organs and structures have "evolved by modification of some ancient regulatory networks under the command of the same master gene or genes". In other words, common and very old genes or master genes have existed latently in the genome of all animals for a very long time since early evolution, and they are the reason for similar body plans and organs in very different animals in different branches of the genealogical tree. Genes that code for body plans are called Hox-genes. These old and complex genes are activated in embryonic development. Hox-genes together with transcription factors proteins that bind to DNA and turn transcription on or off and signaling pathways communicating cells lead to traveling proteins that induce changes in the cell and in gene expression are considered to be elements of a genetic tool box. Similar sets of Hox-genes and sometimes even identical single genes can produce a variety of body plans because the genetic tool box has been differently combined by the function of genetic switches viz promoters, enhancers. Genetic switches are regions of DNA that are typically located near the genes upstream on the same strand of DNA, and they can turn genes on and off reacting to transcription factors specialized signal proteins. Genetic switches allow the same tool kit genes to be used differently and thus are a central factor in the creation of variety. Thus, these genetic switches are considered to be the "key actors" in embryonic development and evolution. Though the discovery of Hox-genes was important, it came out that it is not a single Hox-gene that is responsible for one new organ or structure but groups of gene switches and proteins build networks that regulate the formation of whole organs and structures. Changes in genetic switches trigger a shifting in the zones of hox-genes and thus are responsible for all kinds of changes in the body form, including the creation of new species. Thus, not the invention of new Hoxgenes caused evolution but the genetic switches triggered by ecological conditions worked on the genetic tool kit. According to this view, natural selection is not responsible for the creation of new body forms but determines only which forms are actually been realized.

Kirschner and Gerhart argue on similar lines with their hypothesis of facilitated variation. They say organisms restrain some components of their phenotype from certain changes whereas on the other hand, other components are released for change. Restricted elements are called "conserved core components" and they consist of a sequence of several protein components. These core components have remained relatively intact through time, and have not been subject to gradual change but rather to discontinuous waves of change. Specific features of these core processes make them robust and flexible, e.g. weak regulatory linkage, modularity, and compartmentalization. These features have not changed in the course of time but have provoked regulatory. The greatest amount of change is not due to changes within core components but due to regulatory changes of core processes. Among these regulatory changes are changes in the date, place, amount, and circumstances of gene expression, cell signaling, the role of Hox genes in embryonic development, the program for developing extremities etc. As a result of these regulatory changes core components are used in new combinations and in a different amount at other times in other places. Under the new conditions the flexible core components might show different performance and new phenotypes. Carroll argues in the same line: "At an anatomic level, multifunctionality and redundancy are keys to understanding the evolutionary transitions in structures" and Müller states "(T) the new tenets by EvoDevo may be called "emergence" and "inherency". Core components are adaptive, and have been selected due to their robustness in embryonic development and anatomic stability. Consequently, phenotypes which have emerged from regulatory modifications of core components are presumably less lethal, more viable and better adapted than completely new phenotypes. In this way variation is facilitated and accelerated. Organisms combine a limited number of components to transform a small amount of random mutations into new phenotypic forms. However, organisms and not mutations are the protagonists in the realization of concrete body forms. This view also stresses the existence of established and approved components for innovation.

It is well known that genomes consist of DNA with coding sequences genes in the narrow sense and DNA with non-coding sequences, also called "dark matter of the genome". In the last decades it has emerged that in the non-coding sequences–the larger part of the genome–specific elements, called "transposable elements" or transposons can change the structure of the genome, including changes to germ cells. Transposable elements can double single genes or groups of genes; they can reorganise genes by combining them differently, and they can change the local position of genes the reason why they are sometimes also called jumping genes and thus bring genes under the control of other genetic switches. These phenomena can be interpreted as a form of "self-organization" of the genome but they also include the possibility of the creation of new genes. The activity of the transposable elements is under the control of the cell, which according to some biologists is considered to be a cognitive entity. The cell in turn is under the impact of ecological conditions. The cell has several possibilities to exert an impact on the activity of transposable elements. It can create new transposable elements, or can control and even restrict their activity. In the latter case, the deactivation of transposable elements–a mechanism that is called RNA-interference because it blocks or destroys RNA molecules–exerts stability in the phenotype of an organism when there is no drastic change in the ecological conditions. However if, on the contrary, radical and lasting ecological changes prevail the organism gives information to the cells which - through the weakening of the RNA interference and easing of the control of transposable elements - in turn induces a creative process of reorganisation of the genome. From these findings some biologists have concluded that changes to the genome are not mainly a consequence of random point mutations, but are due to reactions of the cell, which responds to radical and stressful changes in the ecological conditions, in the form of nuclear radiation, contact with varmints, extreme diet, water scarcity, injuries etc. According to this view, speciation has primarily arisen from radical changes in the genome which in turn was mainly induced by eruptive activations of the transposable elements.

Furthermore, an analysis of the genome of several species has shown that mutations are unevenly distributed. It seems that the cell has the capacity to allow only some parts of the genome to be subject to mutations, mainly those parts that have been duplicated by transposable elements whereas Hox-genes and other important sequences are less subject to mutations. In other words, the original Hox-genes have been retained, whereas the copied genes have been released for change, e.g. for the reorganisations of mutations. The conclusion to be drawn here is that mutations are not completely random and that the cell shows a high capacity to control the genomic architecture.

One of the most surprising new findings in the new research areas was the discovery that changes in the environment can exercise a permanent influence on the gene regulation and gene expression and through this mechanism heritable changes in the phenotype can be induced. These mechanisms can take place in the form of epigenetic inheritance or in form of RNA-interference. Typically, changes in the environment induce chemical modifications of the DNA, which turn a gene on or off. This process does not represent a mutation but it exerts effects similar to a mutation and hence constitutes an epigenetic mark that can be passed on to the next generation. This epigenetic inheritance is a sensation because it questions one of the dogmas of Neo-Darwinism, the so called Weismann barrier according to which hereditary information moves only from germ cells to somatic cells and not vice versa. However, according to epigenetic inheritance changes in somatic cells can indeed induce changes in germ cells. Epigenetic inheritance can even considered to be Lamarckian since gene regulation and gene expression react to environmental stimuli and the phenotypic results can last for generations. For example, it has been found that extreme diet during gestation can change epigenetic patterns of the descendants and new traits arise that can last for generations and also affect fertility. It should be mentioned that in contrast to mutations epigenetic marks are reversible but like mutations they can be subject to selection. Though epigenetic inheritance has been confirmed in countless experiments and recent studies rather confirm than refute it, whether it represents an evolutionary principle is still an open question - even in the progressive research community which challenges Neo-Darwinism.

In another research branch, a multitude of findings in the last decades suggest that co-operation is an important principle of evolution, in particular in the creation of new species. For example, in early evolution eukaryotik cells came into existence because archaea-cells imported bacteria and let them become part of their cells so called endosymbiosis. This important evolutionary step was a precondition for the evolution of animals and humans and cannot be explained with Neo-Darwinian principles, but only with co-operation. Furthermore, it has been widely recognized that in the early stages of evolution but also in more recent times not only gene transfer from one generation to the next vertical gene transfer took place but also massive horizontal gene transfer, i.e. gene exchanges between individuals of completely different species. Transposable elements transposons or "jumping genes" can transfer genes from the genome of one organism into the genome of another organism. This phenomenon was an important creative factor of recombination. For example, mammals took over genes from viruses, and today it is known that more than 220 genes in the human genome come from horizontal gene transfer. The empirical evidence of horizontal gene transfer also implies that phylogenetic trees have to be reconsidered in the sense that they no longer have to be presented as linear lines that branch out but as networks of lines branching out. In this view, evolution is no longer considered to be linear but reticulate. Since phenomena like endosymbiosis, horizontal gene transfer as well as gene duplication, recombination of genes, and changes in the regulation of genes have played a considerable role in the creation of variety, it is argued that the role of point mutations in the creation of new species has been overestimated by Neo-Darwinism.

With regard to macro-evolution, it has been generally acknowledged also in Neo-Darwinism that it is characterized by periods of stasis in which changes in the genomes were minor. Furthermore, extensive paleontological studies provide more and more evidence that the incidence of species disappearance is mainly due to punctual mass extinctions, such as volcanism, mega-ice ages, etc. Consequently, natural selection appears not to be the predominant cause of species disappearance and on the makro-level randomness is still an evolutionary factor.

RECENT DEVELOPMENTS IN EVOLUTIONARY BIOLOGY: ASSESSMENT

In this section the question is addressed of how biologists have assessed the recent findings, before turning to its relevance for economics. The research program of EvoDevo has led to a complete change of the view of how complex biological systems evolve. Already in 1994 Gerd B. Müller wrote: "Of course, Neo-Darwinist theory has in its core statements been confirmed, and generally been accepted But then: "The inclusion of internal 'organismic' factors would not only mean an extension of the synthetic theory but would amount to a paradigm shift". Müller (1994) argues that in Neo- Darwinism the only forces that give evolution a direction are external factors whereas in a system theory of evolution variations would be considered to be dependent on internal factors, namely the path-dependent rules of embryonic development.

Another representative of EvoDevo, Sean B. Carroll says: "First, It is asserted that Evo Devo constitutes the third major act in a continuing evolutionary synthesis. Evo Devo has not just provided a critical missing piece of the Modern Synthesis

- embryology - and integrated it with molecular genetics and traditional elements such as paleontology. The wholly unexpected nature of some of its key discoveries and the unprecedented quality and depth of evidence it has provided toward settling previously unresolved questions bestow it with a revolutionary character". However, Carroll does not see any contradiction with the main principles of Neo-Darwinism.

Kirschner and Gerhard see their theory of facilitated variation as a supplement to and completion of Darwin's. They also raise the question of whether their theory can contribute to the understanding of social, political or technical elements. Subsequent to some careful suggestions in the form of analogies, they conclude that at least their proposition provokes other metaphors than those of Social Darwinism. They suggest that history in general is not only the product of selection determined by external factors and competition but also the structure and capacity of societies and organizations to evolve, to adapt and to renew.

Some of the presented research results are acknowledged by Neo-Darwinism and are then often interpreted as an exception, e.g. in the case of horizontal gene transfer. In other cases the same discovery leads Neo- Darwinists and Non-Neo-Darwinists to converse interpretations. For example, in a standard textbook on evolution one can still read "The genes of most transposable elements do not contribute to development or function of the host organism; rather, they encode only proteins essential for replication and transposition of the retroelement itself. They are an example of a selfish genetic element, or 'selfish gene'". To Bauer genes cannot be interpreted as egoistic since they are under the control of the cell and not autonomous. Bauer claims: "Genes and respectively genomes follow three basic biological principles : co-operation, communication and creativity". In Bauer's understanding of evolution, selection plays a role, but only in the sense of a tautology: Individual organisms which are nonviable cannot survive and those which are not propagable will not reproduce themselves.

Though it is definitely too early to give a conclusive appraisal of the recent findings in evolutionary biology, the least one can say is that a thorough reassessment of the significance of chance, mutations and selection in biological evolution is inevitable. The most interesting question concerns the role of selection as an evolutionary principle. Most of the representatives of the recent research findings would agree that the predominance of natural selection is one of the weakest elements of Neo-Darwinism until recently, even in Neo-Darwinism because of the findings of genetic drift (Senglaub 1998, 574) the statement "no evolution without selection" was no longer be maintained. But according to new findings some Neo-Darwinists argue that genetic drift can no longer be considered to be crucial for speciation. Instead they emphasize the significance of natural selection: "Nobody really doubts that most of the body parts have been formed by selection". It is obvious that in Neo-Darwinism natural selection has not really lost importance. This is different in the research areas presented here. In EvoDevo and in some branches of genetics and molecular biology the significance of natural selection is obviously pushed back. Instead, internal factors and regulatory changes in the creation of new species as well as mass extinctions in the distinction of species are emphasized.

It can be concluded that the recent findings in biology outside the mainstream suggest a shift away from random mutations, competition, selection, towards cooperation, regulation, networks, self-organisation and path-dependency. In particular and contrary to Neo-Darwinism some findings in evolutionary biology suggest that amongst others (1) mutations are not completely random and variety is not only triggered by mutations (2) selection is not the predominant evolutionary factor in the modification of species, the origin of new species and the extinction of species (3) the systemic character of the genome including phenomena of co-operation, self organization and communication have been underestimated also in the generation of novelty (4) there is more and more evidence on discontinuous evolution.

The presented research programs in biology have in common the fact that their representatives do not reject Neo-Darwinism completely, all of them being convinced of evolution and the principle of common descent. It should also be stressed that the research finding presented above are generally confirmed and accepted. Yet, the overall assessement and interpretation with respect to Neo-Darwinism is quite controversial. Some say they are still satisfied with Neo-Darwinism, others suggest an extension of Neo-Darwinism or even a new evolutionary synthesis and "some say it's time for Modern Synthesis (Pennisi, 2008,). Only a minority - among them the German medical researcher Joachim Bauer - have declared "the end of Darwinism" (Bauer 2008).

The variety of theoretical approaches in biology can also be viewed in a broader context. In the philosophy of science it is argued that, since 1970, in science in general, and not only in biology, there has been a tendency from a monolithic towards a pluralistic understanding of science. In biology, this would imply that Neo- Darwinism will not be substituted but be supplemented by a range of distinct alternative approaches. This would be, by the way, a very similar development to that of economics.

CONSEQUENCES FOR EVOLUTIONARY ECONOMICS

We have seen that at present there is a pluralism of scientific interpretations of evolution: Traditional Neo-Darwinist interpretations go along with new ones which explicitly break with Neo-Darwinism without denying common descent and without completely rejecting the role of random genetic modification and selection. This pluralism cannot be denied. What makes an assessment for economists really difficult is that those biologists who have come up with the new concepts and principles do not agree on the significance of these new findings and their relation to the mainstream paradigm of Neo-Darwinism.

One reason why biological scientists draw different conclusions from the new findings is not so much grounded in professional controversies but rather due to the implications of the research results for the social and cultural life in the human societies we actually live in. For example, Carroll's motivation to adhere to the random variation-selection-paradigm is to support teaching in biological evolution based on scientific results and to provide a multitude of arguments against Creationism and Intelligent Design (Carroll 2006). Considering the anti-Darwinian and anti-evolutionary movements of Creationism and Intelligent Design it could be noted that it seems to be too difficult for scientists - mainly in the U.S. - to make clear to the public that in the scientific community there is unanimity that evolution has definitely taken place but a controversy on how it has taken place. In a non-scientific public discussion a scientific discipline viz evolutionary biology that is not united in the explanation of its main research object (evolution) is much weaker than one that adheres to traditional principles. In addition, critics of Neo - Darwinism risk. Consequently, most of the biologists in the profession strive to avoid this dispute. This is not the case for Bauer. His goal to stress the role of co-operation and communication in evolution is - according to his own statement - in order to demonstrate that the idea of egoism as a central evolutionary principle as well as the consideration of living beings as machines is not based on solid scientific research. He argues that this is important to acknowledge since concepts like those of egoistic genes generate anthropological models that have negative consequences for the way we actually live in human societies.

Although not all scholars of evolutionary economics are inclined to resort to theories in biology, there are two arguments as to why these recent findings in evolutionary biology should be of interest to the scientific community of evolutionary economists: (1) For those evolutionary economists who have always found that the fact of evolution in general is more inspiring than the theory, new findings in evolutionary biology will still have effects but only indirect ones. Theories always influence mental attitudes and the way studies are conducted and empirical results are looked at. As Zimmerli put it: "Each scientific theory sediments into human consciousness in a way that its theorems are eventually considered to be elements of reality". (2) In biology, critics of Neo-Darwinism argue that mainstream biology is very much shaped by mechanical physics and economics, and that, in general, beings are considered to be machines not living systems. Thus, the danger in evolutionary economics is that in resorting to Neo- Darwinism indirectly all the mechanical aspects this research area has intended to avoid are re-imported. One of the common characteristics of biology and economics – in contrast to physics – is that they deal with living organisms. Consequently, in evolutionary economics one of the crucial questions should be: What are the main properties of living systems? In the past, the influences of theories of evolutionary biology on economics were manifold and can be summed up by different heuristic strategies, some of which will be hinted at in the following.

An important way in which biology has had an influence on economics was by the methodological device of analogies. It is widely acknowledged that analogies in sciences can have important heuristic functions and they are used as a method to build new hypotheses. It should be emphasized that the method of analogy in science as such cannot be criticized. In particular it cannot be argued that the analogy is inadequate because some characteristics, elements or relations from the original theory in one science do not correspond with those of the destination theory in another science because it is the essence of the analogy that not all aspects match. Thus, the statement that an analogy is inadequate or useful, or more general, good or bad, is illegitimate since the analogy is a method and not the correspondent, counterpart or equivalent itself. The problem with these kinds of analogies is that they might become a justification in the sense that without further arguments, studies or proves the findings from one science are directly transferred to another science. Analogies hence run the risk of starting a life on their own without being reassessed and verified. This holds in particular for analogies based on the variationetention- selection paradigm. Theories based on these analogies often fail to study whether the principles of variation, retention and selection are indeed the core principles of evolution in economic reality and whether omitting specific economic, social and cultural factors is a proper approach.

Furthermore, since the explanation of biological evolution is undergoing a reassessment, in which the traditional core principles of evolution, such as blind mutation and selection, lose significance although as argued above, they do not become completely irrelevant, concepts like Generalized Darwinism are probably no longer up to date. As has already been argued by Cordes (2006), Generalized Darwinism does not even take into account all those principles that mainstream biologists consider to be essential principles of Darwin's theory. For example, the principles of descent and of speciation are not chosen to belong to Generalized Darwinism. Buenstorf (2006,) states that since Generalized Darwinism turned the heuristic frame into an ontological fact subjects that are not covered by the assumed three core principles of evolution are excluded from examination, e.g. certain forms of learning and knowledge transfer. It is further argued that Generalized Darwinism does not take into account the principles of co-operation and self-organization. Though the representatives of Generalized Darwinism concede that to explain evolution sufficiently "auxiliary" principles are required Why are co-operation and selforganization not considered as core principles of Generalized Darwinism and what are the selection criteria that make the difference between core and auxiliary principles of evolution?

As mentioned above not all evolutionary economists are inclined to let themselves be inspired by theories of biological evolution. In particular, analogies and concepts like Generalized Darwinism bear the danger of neglecting specific human, social and economic aspects of evolution and, in addition, their explanative power is rather humble. Not only economic crises like the one we are actually in should remind us that there is still much to learn about human behaviour and economic systems. Thus, instead of looking for common principles with other scientific disciplines we argue in favour of concentrating more on the specific characteristics of human, social and economic evolution. This kind of analysis can acknowledge that human beings have animal bodies and hence are to a certain extent subject to biological evolution. However, in addition, the evolution of societies and economies follows certain rules and norms some of which are at least in part the result of deliberate decisions and are not subject to biological evolution. The continuity hypothesis is, for example, a heuristic strategy which is in line with these requirements.

2

Development of Economics and Biosciences

ECONOMICS AND NATURAL SCIENCE

There has been no revolution in economic science, and there is not likely to be any. The question we have really to determine is how we can make the best use of the accumulated knowledge of past generations, and to do that we must look more closely into the economic science of the 19th century. Among the natural sciences, ecology was a "late bloomer." People interested in biology described natural environments and contemplated how biological systems developed historically, but such empirical descriptions were not combined with systemic thinking until the second half of the 19th century. Thus our story starts with economics.

The "physiocrats," a group of French social philosophers writing in the mid 18th century, were the first school of economics. They believed that the universal laws of physics hence the school's name extended their grand rule in some yet to be identified way to create a natural social order. This social order was made up of people with sovereign rights entitled to the produce of their labor. According to the physiocrats, real economic activity consisted of working the land. Food wholesalers, processors, and retailers were simply living off the fruits of others and their take should be minimized. The belief that natural law determines social order has taken many forms since the physiocrats and inevitably generates controversy. The physiocrats never identified how the laws of physics applied to economic systems, but their insistence on treating individuals as sovereign entities, like atoms, in the tradition of key liberal social philosophers such as Hobbes and Locke who assumed that society is merely the sum of its individuals, has stayed with mainstream economics ever since. While subsequent economists never discovered how the laws of physics ruled economies, they did duplicate the pattern of thinking of mechanics in their conception of market interactions. Adam Smith initiated this pattern of reasoning.

ADAM SMITH AND THE INVISIBLE HAND

Adam Smith (1723–1790), widely recognized as the founder of modern economics, was a moral philosopher. While economics since Smith has assumed a heavy scientific gloss, critical ethical issues have always been embedded in its theory. And the key ethical issue has always been whether the pursuit of individual greed can be in the interest of society as a whole. Smith reasoned that if two people who are fully informed of the consequences of their decision choose to enter into an exchange, it is because the exchange makes each of them better off. Appealing to Judeo-Christian images of God, Smith invented the metaphor of the "invisible hand," arguing that markets induce people to behave for the common good *as if* they were guided by a higher authority.

Modern economics typically continues to assume that society is simply the sum of its individuals, the social good is the sum of individual wants, and markets automatically guide individual behavior to the common good. By the end of the 19th century, the market model had been formalized mathematically and it turned out to be the same mathematics as used by Newton for mechanical systems. This atomistic view of individuals and mechanistic view of a social system contrasts sharply with the more organic, or ecological, view that community relations define who people are, affect what they want, facilitate collective action, and have a historical continuity of their own. While Adam Smith was a moral philosopher, his economics made morality less important. For most of human history, people's sense of identity has come through living within a community and its moral precepts.

Today, this is increasingly less important among either the materially wealthy or aspirants to material wealth and may indeed account for their frequent visits to the psychiatrist. Among the multiplicative factors affecting environmental degradation, the role of materialism and its relation to moral behavior is rarely discussed and is in need of broader, more serious scientific and public discourse.

The growth of individualism and materialism associated with modernity and the consequent decline in community and concern with moral conduct are not Adam Smith's fault, but he played a decisive role in setting up the reasoning that justified individual greed. In an age when Europeans and North Americans were rebelling against the tyranny of church and state and social philosophers were building theories from the individual up to the society rather than from society down to the individual, Adam Smith argued that markets link individual greed to the common good without coercive social institutions. And ever since Smith, the critical question, if too rarely discussed, has been whether markets really do this as well as he believed. One glaring contradiction is that the economic model of society argues that individual behavior supports the common good while simultaneously arguing that communities are not needed because markets will provide for the common good. The issues of market and community are being addressed at the end of the twentieth century by a variety of scholars who argue that communities are necessary at different geographic scales to define the social good, adapt the social order, and manage environmental systems.

The cleric-turned-economist Thomas R. Malthus (1766–1834) explained the prevalence of war and disease as secular, material phenomena rather than as acts of God. He argued that human populations were capable of increasing exponentially and would do so as long as sufficient food and other essentials of life were available. He further hypothesized that people could expand their food supply arithmetically through new technologies and expansion into new habitats. Given the potential for geometric increases in population and only arithmetic increases in food supply, population periodically surpasses food supply (Figure 1). At these times, Malthus argued, people would ravage the land, go to war over food, and succumb to disease and starvation. Human numbers would consequently drop to sustainable levels whence the process would repeat. This basic model from economics is still widely used today by biological scientists.

Thomas Malthus and Population Growth

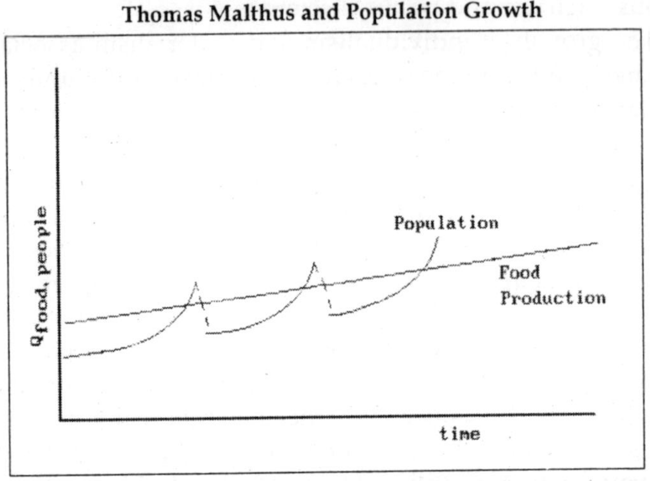

Figure 1: Thomas Malthus' Model of Population Growth and Collapse.
(*Source:* Authors)

Malthus' model is beguilingly simple and consequently demographic history never quite supports it precisely. Yet periodically in specific places, Malthus' model has been confirmed, and history may yet confirm it globally. Few question whether population must ultimately be stabilized in order to sustain human well-being at a reasonable level. The expansion of human populations into previously unpopulated or lightly populated regions, the intensity with which firewood is collected, and the push to increase food production through modern agrochemical, monocultural techniques, so harmful to biodiversity, are driven over the long run by population increase. The continued rapid rate of population growth in the poorest nations threatens to keep them poor while diminishing the possibilities that the people of these nations will ever be able to consume at levels comparable to people in the rich nations using current modern technologies without vastly accelerating environmental degradation.

Malthus' model has become a part of human consciousness, making it difficult to contemplate, let alone discuss, the issues of population and its effects on the environment without his framing becoming central to the discussion. The success of Malthus' model stems from its simplicity, but the dynamics of population growth and how people depend on the environment are much more complex than the model suggests. Thus, while Malthus provided us with a powerful model, its simplicity restricts its usefulness for policy making beyond the obvious prescription that fewer people would probably be better for sustainability than more people.

In addition to his influence on economic and demographic thought, Malthus had an enormous influence on other key intellectual figures. Both Charles Darwin and Alfred Russell Wallace credited Malthus with providing them the key insight that led them to the theory of natural selection. Marx developed many of his views in opposition to Malthus. Even John Maynard Keynes (1883–1946) was influenced by Malthus' theory and incorporated it in a theory of underconsumption, inventory buildups, and the business cycle.

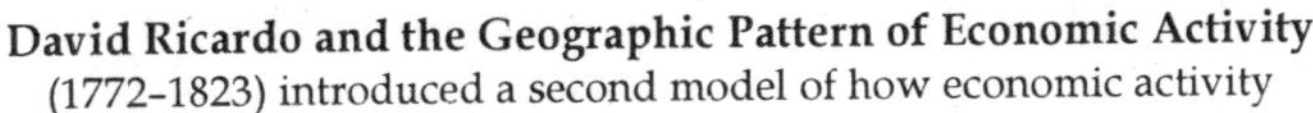

David Ricardo and the Geographic Pattern of Economic Activity
(1772–1823) introduced a second model of how economic activity

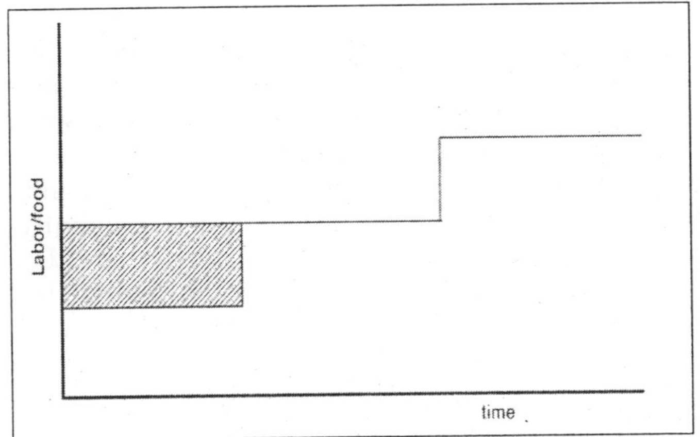

Figure 2: Ricardo's Explanation of Rent, Represented by the Shaded Area

David Ricardoelates to the environment, not because he was concerned with environmental degradation or human survival, but rather because he wished to justify why landlords received a rent from land ownership. Ricardo argued that people would initially farm the land that produced the most food for the least work labor per unit of food, the y-axis of Figure 2. As population increased, farming would *extend* to less fertile soils requiring more labor the extensive margin. Food prices would have to rise to cover the cost of the extra labor on the less fertile land. This means that the initial land would earn a rent, a return above production cost, indicated by the shaded area in Figure 2. Higher food prices, in turn, would also induce a more *intensive* use of labor on the better land the intensive margin. This model indicates how increasing population drives people to farm in previously undisturbed areas and how higher food prices lead to the intensification and, in modern agriculture, to the greater use of fertilizers and pesticides on prime agricultural lands. This model also gives us insights into how fluctuations in food prices can result in the periodic entry and exit of farmers on the extensive margin and in shifts in farming practices on the intensive margin. Ricardo's model of how agricultural activities are patterned on the land in response to population growth and changes in food prices is critical to our understanding of the complex interrelations between human survival and ecological life-support systems.

Ricardo's model of resource use patterns is similar to how those in the earth sciences think about the use of mineral resources. Petroleum geologists and mineralogists often presume, just as Ricardo did, that the best quality resources are used first even though history shows that a significant portion of the best quality resources are frequently not discovered until poorer quality resources have already been used. The models of Malthus and Ricardo led to classical economics being called the "dismal science." The carrying capacity limits of Malthus' model and the lower quality of the next available resources in the model of Ricardo conflicted with the beliefs in progress which were so prevalent during the 19th century. The Ricardian theory of differential rent also had dismal distributive consequences since an increasing share of the total product of the land went to landlords. These models are now touted by environmental scientists concerned about population growth, excessive consumption, and environmental degradation, and argued against by mainstream economists. During most of the twentieth century, economists built new models with different assumptions in combinations that support beliefs in unlimited material progress.

SADI CARNOT, RUDOLF CLAUSIUS, AND THERMODYNAMICS

Sadi Carnot (1796–1832) founded thermodynamics with his classic 1824 study of the efficiency of steam engines, *Reflections on the Motive Power of Fire*. Carnot was the first to recognize that the amount of work that could be extracted depended on the temperature gradient between the source and sink. He effectively identified what were to become formalized as the laws of thermodynamics by Rudolf Clausius (1822–1888) a quarter century after Carnot's death. The first law of thermodynamics states that energy can neither be created nor destroyed. The second law, also known as the entropy law, states that the amount of energy available for work in a closed system only decreases with use. The laws of thermodynamics are frequently invoked in the construction of models of ecosystems and have been extended to models of human-environment interactions as well.

The second law effectively makes physics the dismal science for it states that the total useful energy in the universe, the amount of work remaining that can be done is constantly declining. Since any action requires energy, any activity today is at the expense of potential activity in the future. What hope is there for progress in a constantly degrading universe? This question has been pursued again and again for well over a century. Whether and how it is resolved depends on how fast the entropy of the universe is increasing and just how far into the future we are concerned. An important point to remember, however, is that the Earth is an "open" system, and even if the entropy of the universe is increasing, the entropy of Earth may be declining by a smaller amount, of course. The study of the thermodynamics of open, non-equilibrium systems came much later.

CHARLES DARWIN AND THE EVOLUTIONARY PARADIGM

Charles Darwin (1809–1882) was influenced by the economic arguments of Malthus as he began thinking about the question: why are there so many different types of plants and animals? After years of observing the natural and human-dominated ecosystems of his time most notably as a naturalist aboard the H.M.S. Beagle on its voyage around the world in 1831–1836 and thinking about this question, he arrived at what, to him, seemed the only possible explanation. His answer, which has come to be a cornerstone of modern biology and ecology, was that species evolve by the processes of adaptation and natural selection. Population pressure, associated with the ability of species to expand their numbers to the carrying capacity of their environment, favored the survival of those individuals with the particular characteristics that made them more effective at reproducing themselves.

Darwin waited until late in his professional career to publish his findings. His On the Origin of Species by Natural Selection was first published in 1859 when the author was 50. In the same year, by the way, as Karl Marx's *Critique of Political Economy* Darwin was immediately attacked by those holding what was then the mainstream view of "divine creation." The evolutionary paradigm continues to be attacked to this day by those espousing "creationism," but, in spite of its gaps, no other theory possesses anything approaching the explanatory power of evolution. Since Darwin's day, the paradigm of evolution has been tested and broadly applied to both ecological and economic systems as a way of formalizing our understanding of adaptation and learning behaviors in nonequilibrium dynamic systems. The general evolutionary paradigm posits a mechanism for adaptation and learning in complex systems at any scale using three basic interacting processes: 1) information storage and transmission; 2) generation of new alternatives; and 3) selection of superior alternatives according to some performance criteria.

The evolutionary paradigm is different from the conventional mechanical paradigm of economics in at least four important respects: 1) evolution is path dependent, meaning that the detailed history and dynamics of the system are important; 2) evolution can achieve multiple equilibria; 3) there is no guarantee that optimal efficiency or any other optimal performance will be achieved due in part to path dependence and sensitivity to perturbations; and 4) "lock-in" survival of the first rather than survival of the fittest is possible under conditions of increasing returns. While, as Arthur notes, "conventional economic theory is built largely on the assumption of diminishing returns on the margin in terms of local negative feedbacks," life itself can be characterized as a positive feedback, self-reinforcing, autocatalytic process and we should expect increasing returns, lock-in, path dependence, multiple equilibria, and suboptimal efficiency to be the rule rather than the exception in economic and ecological systems.

In biological evolution, the information storage medium is the genes, the generation of new alternatives is by sexual recombination or genetic mutation, and selection is performed by nature according to a criterion of "fitness" based on reproductive success. The same process of change occurs in other ecological, economic, and cultural systems, but the elements on which the process works are different. For example, in cultural evolution the storage medium is the culture in terms of the oral tradition, books, film, or other storage medium for passing on behavioral norms, the generation of new alternatives is through innovation by individual members or groups in the culture, and selection is again based on the reproductive success of the alternatives generated, but reproduction is carried out by the spread and copying of the behavior through the culture rather than biological reproduction. One may also talk of "economic" evolution, a subset of cultural evolution dealing with the generation, storage, and selection of alternative ways of producing things and allocating that which is produced.

Evolutionary theories in economics have already been successfully applied to problems of technical change, to the development of new institutions, and to the evolution of means of payment.

For large, slow-growing animals like humans, genetic evolution has a built-in bias toward the long run. Changing the genetic structure of a species requires that characteristics in terms of phenotypes be selected and accumulated by differential reproductive success. Behaviors learned or acquired during the lifetime of an individual cannot be passed on genetically. Genetic evolution is therefore usually a relatively slow process requiring many generations to significantly alter a species' physical and biological characteristics. Cultural evolution is potentially much faster. Technical change is perhaps the most important and fastest evolving cultural process. Learned behaviors that are successful, at least in the short term can be almost immediately spread to other members of the culture and passed on in the oral, written, or video record. The increased speed of adaptation that this process allows has been largely responsible for *Homo sapiens'* amazing success at appropriating the resources of the planet. As already mentioned, humans now directly control from 25 to 40% of the total primary production of the planet's biosphere and this is beginning to have significant effects on the biosphere, including changes in global climate and in the planet's protective ozone shield.

Thus the costs of this rapid cultural evolution are potentially significant. Like a car that has increased speed, humans are in more danger of running off the road or over a cliff. Cultural evolution lacks the built-in long-run bias of genetic evolution and is susceptible to being led by its hyper-efficient short-run adaptability over a cliff into the abyss. Another major difference between cultural and genetic evolution may serve as a countervailing bias, however. As Arrow has pointed out, cultural and economic evolution, unlike genetic evolution, can at least to some extent employ foresight. If society can see the cliff, perhaps it can be avoided. While market forces drive adaptive processes, the systems that evolve are not necessarily optimal, so the question remains: what external influences are needed and when should they be applied in order to improve an economic system via evolutionary adaptation? The challenge faced by ecological economic systems modelers is first to apply the models to gain foresight, and then respond to and manage the system feedbacks in a way that helps avoid any foreseen cliffs. Devising policy instruments and identifying incentives that can translate this foresight into effective modifications of the short-run evolutionary dynamics is the challenge.

JOHN STUART MILL AND THE STEADY-STATE

John Stuart Mill (1806–1873) was the son of social philosopher James Mill (1773–1836), who also wrote on economics. Mill is important for having expanded on the linkages between individual behavior and the common good suggested by Adam Smith, arguing that competitive economies had to be based on rules of property use and a sense of social responsibility that favored the common good. At the same time, he argued that competitive markets were essential to freedom. As a social philosopher seriously concerned with liberty, Mill also wrote on the immorality and waste of human productive talent that resulted from the subjugation of women by men. While his concern with subjugation of women was perhaps too instrumentally based, he neither saw material prosperity as an end in itself nor foresaw that continuous growth in material well-being was possible. Mill was one of the first economists to plead for conservation of biodiversity, or against the conversion of all natural capital into man-made capital. Mill envisioned economies becoming mature and reaching a steady-state in which people would be able to enjoy the fruits of their earlier savings, or material abstinence, which had been necessary for the accumulation of industrial capital. The idea that economies would reach a steady-state was both consistent with the Newtonian view of systems so dominant at the time and consistent with natural phenomena. Inceasing growth is not observed in nature, and relatively steady-states rather than random change are perceived as "natural." Herman Daly builds on Mill and argues for a steady-state economy where flows of resources into production and of pollutants back to the environment are kept at a steady level. The steady-state metaphor has become critical to finding common ground for achieving sustainable development.

KARL MARX AND THE OWNERSHIP OF RESOURCES

Karl Marx (1818–1883) addressed, among his multiple critiques of capitalism, how the concentration of land and capital among a small portion of society affected how economies worked. There is an extensive collection of literature written by scholars influenced by Marx. Some of this literature addresses the sustainability of development and how the ownership of resources affects the path of development. Neoclassical models also readily show how resource ownership affects resource use. However, for a variety of political reasons, this facet of the neoclassical model was ignored in the West during the Cold War. Indeed, in the United States, economists who were concerned with the *distribution* of ownership of resources were politically disempowered through their association with a central concern of Marx. Western neoclassical economists, including resource and environmental economists, addressed questions of the *efficient allocation* of resources, leaving the initial distribution of resources among people as a given, not to be questioned. We now recognize that the initial distribution of rights to resources and to the services of the environment is critically important to resource and environmental conservation and the prospects for sustainability.

It has long been known that how economies allocate resources to different ends depends on how resources are distributed among people, that is, whether they are owned by or otherwise under the control of different people. Peasants or others who work land and interact with biological resources owned by someone else have little incentive to protect them. Landlords can only counteract this lack of incentive by diverting their own labor or that of managers under them from other productive activities and employing it to monitor and enforce their interests in protection. This diversion of human potential would not be necessary with a more equal distribution of control. Furthermore, especially wealthy landlords may have little interest in protecting any particular land or biological resource for their descendants when they hold land in such abundance that their foreseeable descendants are certain to have an adequate share.

To illustrate why distribution is important, imagine two countries with identical populations and identical resources allocated by perfect markets. In the first country, rights to resources are distributed between people approximately equally, people have similar incomes, and they consume similar products, perhaps corn, chicken, and cotton clothing. In the second country, rights are concentrated among a few people who can afford luxury goods such as beef, wine, caviar, fine clothes, and tourism, while those who have few rights to resources, living nearly on their labor alone, consume only the most basic of goods like rice and beans. In each country, markets efficiently allocate resources to the production of products, but how land is used, the types of products produced, and who consumes them depend on how rights to resources are distributed. For different distributions of rights, the efficient use of resources is different.

Within the 20th-century global discourse on development policy, many have argued that economic injustices within nations as well as between nations have limited the development options of poor nations and thereby, in the long run, those of the rich as well. Similarly in the late 20th century global environmental discourse, many argued that environmental injustices and the international ecological order limit the possibilities for conservation. The vast majority of the people on the globe still consume very little. The poor are poor for two reasons. First, they do not have sufficient long-term access to resources to meet their ongoing material needs. Second, they are well aware that others consume far more than they do, that their poverty is relative, and rightfully strive to improve their own relative condition. Striving to meet their material needs and aspirations without long-term secure access to adequate resources, the poor have little choice but to use the few resources at their disposal in an unsustainable manner. The poor, excluded from the productivity of the fertile valleys or fossil hydrocarbon resources controlled by the rich are forced to work land previously left idle because of its fragility and low agricultural productivity: the tropical forests, the steep hillsides, and arid regions.

An environmental justice movement addresses why the poor and people of color bear a heavy share of the environmental costs of development. The poor and people of color are more likely to live near waste disposal sites and more likely to work in polluted environments. This movement also speaks to the excessive material and energy consumption of the wealthy 20–30% of the world's population made up of the middle classes and rich in the northern, industrialized nations as well as the elite in middle income nations and in some poorer ones. The rich consume the bulk of the resources and account for many of our environmental problems the global access to resources by the rich means that many of the environmental impacts of their consumption decisions occur at a great distance, beyond their view, beyond their perceived responsibility, and beyond their effective control. The relationships between unequal access to resources, the unsustainability of development generally, and the loss of biodiversity in particular were major themes of the United Nations Conference on Environment and Development held in Rio de Janeiro in June 1992. Rich peoples and political leaders of northern industrialized countries generally have understandably had some difficulty participating in this discourse and even greater difficulty participating in the design of new global institutions to address the role of inequity in environmental degradation.

Our understanding of the environmental consequences of concentrated ownership and control are rooted in economic thinking, especially that of Karl Marx. Questions of equity are extremely important to the process of environmental degradation and to the possibilities for sustainable development. The occupation and ecological transformation of the Amazon have been partly driven by the concentration of the ownership of land in the more productive regions of Amazonian nations and partly driven by the economic power and hence political influence of the rich that has enabled them to obtain subsidies to engage in large-scale land speculation or cattle ranching. The ongoing efforts to establish international agreements on the management of biodiversity and climate change have been repeatedly forestalled by debates over the ownership and control of resources. But it is not simply a debate over fairness. The structure of the global economy and how specific economies interact with nature in the future will depend on which nations—the nations of origin or of the Northern commercial interests, the likely discoverers of new uses for heretofore unused species—receive the "rent" from resources. Marx and his followers in communist countries have made a negative contribution to the allocative efficiency problem, even while highlighting issues of just distribution. Their ideological rejection of rent and interest as necessary prices, and their insistence on a labor theory of value that neglected nature's contribution were responsible for much of the environmental destruction in communist countries.

W. STANLEY JEVONS AND THE SCARCITY OF STOCK RESOURCES

W. Stanley Jevons (1835–1882) contributed initially to meterology, logic, induction, and statistics while also making contributions to economics. He was one of the pioneers of the marginal utility theory of value. However, of more interest to ecological economics is his recognition of the critical importance of energy, which in his day meant coal. It was his argument that the British economy and the success of the empire were dependent on coal, a rapidly dwindling resource that brought him notoriety as an economist and a chair in political economy. He subsequently contributed to the mathematical formalization of economics The *Theory of Political Economy*, 1871, continued to write on the philosophy of science *The Principles of Science*, 1874, and speculated on the relationship of sunspots and financial crises (published in *Investigations in Currency and Finance*, 1884).

ERNST HAECKEL AND THE BEGINNINGS OF ECOLOGY

While ecology has been said to have its roots in the Greek science of Hippocrates, Aristotle, and Theophrastus, or in the 18th-century natural history of Linnaeus and Buffon, or in Darwin and Wallace's evolutionary biology, ecology as a named science did not emerge as a "self-conscious" discipline with its own name until Ernst Heinrich Haeckel (1834–1919) first used the word penology in 1866. Practitioners began to use this term in the last decade of the 19th century, Eugenius Warming (1841–1924) published the first ecology text in 1895, and the first formal ecological societies formed during the second decade of the 20th century. Thus, as a practical and practiced science, ecology is a 20th-century phenomenon. In 1870 Haeckel produced the first full-fledged definition of ecology: By ecology we mean the body of knowledge concerning the economy of nature—the investigation of the total relations of the animal both to its inorganic and to its organic environment including above all, its friendly and inimical relations with those animals and plants with which it comes directly or indirectly into contact—in a word, ecology is the study of all those complex interrelations referred to by Darwin as the conditions of the struggle for existence.

Thus, even in this initial definition of the field, a deep conceptual relationship with economics is evident. Ecology was, in Haeckel's words, the study of the economy of nature. Economics, conversely, can be thought of as the ecology of humans. But historically the science of ecology evolved out of biology and ethology the science of animal behavior and thus had very different intellectual roots than economics. In practical terms, ecology became the study of the economy of that part of nature that does not include humans. Since Haeckel's early definition, many other interpretations of the definition of ecology proliferated based on changing areas of interest and emphasis. When there was a focus on animal populations, ecology was "the study of the distribution and abundance of animals". Later, when ecosystems became a major focus, ecology was: "the study of the structure and function of ecosystems". But what has remained at the core is the relationship of organisms to their environment as the dominant species of animal on the planet, *Homo sapiens* and its relationship to its environment is obviously central to the scope of ecology by any of its various definitions.

Thus, from the very beginning of ecology as a science, there have been continuing attempts to incorporate humans and the social sciences. Most of these attempts, unfortunately, did not get very far. The tendency in the social sciences was to consider humans somehow outside the laws and constraints that applied to other animals and ecologists were not persistent or effective enough in their attempts to extend ecological thinking to *Homo sapiens*. As McIntosh points out if human factors are beyond ecological consideration, what then is human ecology? It is not clear whether ecology will expand to encompass the social sciences and develop as a metascience of ecology. The alternative is a more effective interdisciplinary relationship between ecology and the several social sciences. Ecological economics can be seen as an attempt to build this more effective interdisciplinary relationship as a bridge to a truly comprehensive science of humans as a component of nature that will fulfill the early goals of ecology.

ALFRED J. LOTKA AND SYSTEMS THINKING

Alfred J. Lotka (1880–1949), was trained as a physical chemist, but his broad interests in chemistry, physics, biology, and economics led to a far-reaching synthesis of these fields together with thermodynamics in his 1925 book, *Elements of Physical Biology*. Lotka was the first to attempt an integration of ecological and economic systems in quantitative and mathematical terms. He viewed the whole world of interacting biotic and abiotic components as a system, where everything was linked to everything else and nothing could be understood without an understanding of the whole system. He also stressed the importance of looking at systems from an energetic point of view.

Lotka's work was grand in scope and, although recognition was slow in coming, it eventually influenced both noted ecologists like E. P. Odum and H. T. Odum and economists like Paul Samuelson, Henry Schultz, and Herbert Simon. Lotka's work was clearly in the synthetic, transdisciplinary spirit of the 19th century, but was coming at a time when the disciplines had already started to fragment. Lotka was not a professional scholar until late in his career, and his isolation from the pressures of the academic disciplines probably allowed him to more easily achieve and maintain his broad perspective. While Lotka is probably best known for his equations describing two-species population dynamics which were simultaneously discovered by Vito Volterra and have come to be known as the Lotka-Volterra equations, these equations occupied only two pages of his 1925 book. His more important contributions from the perspective of ecological economics were his attempts to treat ecology and economics as an integrated whole, exhibiting nonlinear dynamics and constrained and structured by flows of energy. He attempted to model quite explicitly the economy of nature, and developed a general evolutionary approach to this problem. But since he was interested in systems, not just species and populations, he developed systems criteria to drive evolution. What has come to be known as "Lotka's energy principle" or "Lotka's power principle" posited that systems survive by maximizing their energy flow, defined as the rate of effectively using energy, or power. In single species populations this reduced to the usual criterion of reproductive success, but his formulation allowed the generalization to all systems, from simple chemical systems to biological, ecological, and economic systems. These ideas presaged the development of general systems theory.

A.C. PIGOU AND MARKET FAILURE

Arthur C. Pigou (1877–1959) formally elaborated how costs and benefits that are not included in market prices affect how people interrelate with their environment. An externality is a phenomenon that is external to markets and hence does not affect how markets operate when in fact it should. Consider, for example, pesticide use in agriculture and the associated loss of biodiversity. In Figure 3 below, S_0 illustrates the willingness of farmers to supply food at different prices. As the price of food increases (the y-axis), the quantity of food (the x-axis) that farmers are willing to supply increases. D is the demand curve illustrating the willingness of people to purchase greater quantities of food at lower prices. The market clears, in the sense that the quantity supplied equals the quantity demanded, at the price P_0 and quantity Q_0.

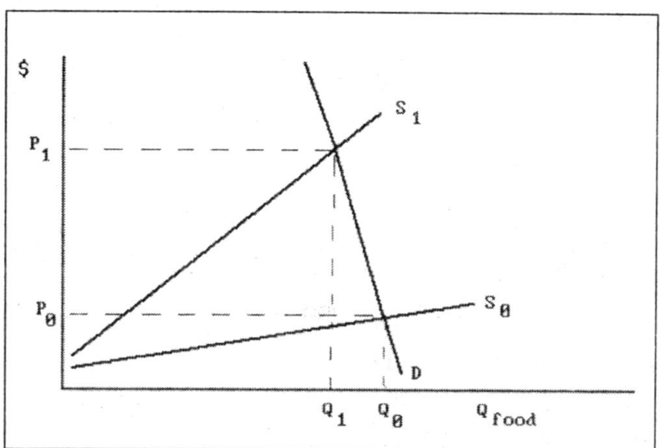

Figure 3: Market Distortions Due to an External Cost

Now imagine that we could measure, for example, the value of biodiversity lost through pesticide use and add this to the cost of pesticides. The higher cost of pesticides would reduce the quantity of food that farmers could produce at any given price, shifting the supply curve to S_1, the price of food to P_1, and the quantity of food supplied and demanded to Q_1. By internalizing the cost of lost biodiversity through farmers' decision to use pesticides, we internalize a cost that was previously external to the market and thus affect how the market operates. Following the logic of Pigou and numerous environmental economists since, biodiversity is not protected adequately because its value is not included in the market signals that guide the economic decisions of producers and consumers and thereby the overall operation of the economic system. The logic of market failure has led economists, and increasingly biologists as well, to argue that the critical environmental resources need to be incorporated into the market system.

One way of doing this is to grant to private individuals the sole rights to use particular environmental resources. This individual then both reaps the economic benefits from using the resource now but also may benefit through conserving the resource for use at a later date. This means consumers will pay a higher price, reflecting the costs of managing the species in a more sustainable manner. It is important to keep in mind, however, that incorporating species into the market system may not result in their conservation and indeed could even accelerate their extinction. Species within the market system, for example, will not be conserved if their value is expected to grow at less than the rate of interest unless other controls are also put on their harvest.

The processes of biodiversity loss also interact with each other in a larger, reinforcing process of positive *feedbacks*. The degradation of any particular area increases the economic pressure on other areas. The loss of woody species through climate change reduces the possibilities for carbon fixation and reduces the opportunities to ameliorate further climate change. To bring a system into equilibrium, negative feedbacks are needed. Economics helps us see how biodiversity is decreasing because so few genetic traits, species, or ecosystems have market prices, the negative feedback signals that equilibrate market economies. In market systems, prices increase to reduce the quantity demanded when supplies are low and prices drop to increase the quantity demanded when supplies are high, keeping demand and supply in equilibrium. The problem, economists argue, is that most genetic traits, species, and ecosystems are being lost because they do not have prices acting as a negative feedback system to keep use in equilibrium with availability. When individuals of the species become fewer, there is no increase in price to decrease the quantity used. By putting economic values on species and through various ways including them in market signals, biodiversity loss would be reduced. Furthermore, the economic explanation and solution is systemic. Unlike bioreserves, which reduce human pressures on species within the protected area but typically increase them beyond it, including the value of biodiversity in the price system would beneficially affect decisions in every sector of the economy.

Biologists also find the idea that we need to know the economic values of species compatible with their own understanding that if the true value of species to society were understood, more species would be conserved. Clearly, if we knew the value of biological resources, we would be in a better position to manage them more effectively. And, to the extent these values could be included in the market system, markets themselves could assist in the conservation of biodiversity. The situation can frequently be improved through amending market signals. At the same time, it is important to remember that market values only exist within a larger system of values, which for many people include the preservation of nature for ethical or religious reasons. Even when species cannot be better conserved through the market, knowing their economic value can help convince people and their political representatives that the species deserves protection. Environmental valuation can also improve how we analyze the benefits and costs of development projects that affect biodiversity. Techniques for valuation include determining people's willingness to pay to maintain diversity through questionnaires and through analyses of their expenditures to observe interesting environments and particular species.

While several techniques for estimating the value of the environment are proving interesting, valuation is by no means an easy task and estimates should be used cautiously. A major difficulty is related to the systemic nature of economics, ecosystems, and the process of environmental degradation. Market systems relate everything to everything else. When the price of oil changes, for example, the price of gasoline changes, the demand and hence the price of products that use gasoline such as automobiles changes, the demand for and hence the price of coal changes, and so on. Prices bring markets to equilibrium and their flexibility is essential to this task. Similarly, the "right" price for a given species or ecosystem will depend on the availability of a host of other species or ecosystems with which they are interdependent as well as with other species and ecosystems that may be substitutes or complements in use. To think that a species or ecosystem has a single value is to deny both ecosystem and economic system interconnections. Nevertheless, environmental valuation can assist us in understanding at least the minimal importance of ecological services and conveying this understanding to the public to improve the political process of finding common ground.

HAROLD HOTELLING AND THE EFFICIENT USE OF RESOURCES OVER TIME

Harold Hotelling (1895–1973) developed a model of efficient resource use over time that helps us understand how resources are exploited over time and the conditions under which conservation or depletion occurs. Hotelling reasoned that the owner of mineral resources had two options: that of extracting the resource and putting the profits in the bank where they would earn interest, and that of leaving the resource in the ground to appreciate in value. The owner would choose the

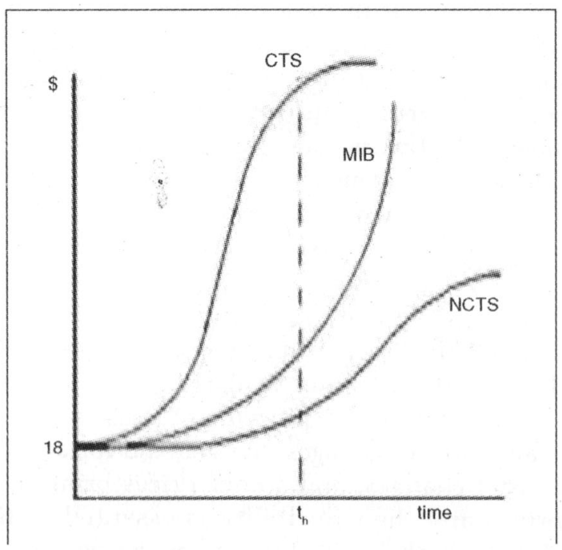

Figure 4: Commercial and Noncommercial Tree Growth and Harvest Time

first option unless the potential profits that could be earned from mining the resource in the future were increasing in value at a rate faster than the rate of interest. If this were the case, then it made sense to leave the resource in the ground. He then reasoned that, under particular conditions, a mining industry consisting of competitive resource owners would behave such that resources in the ground would increase in value at the rate of interest, for this would be the condition under which resource owners would be indifferent between mining and not mining a little more. If this condition were not met, they would all mine more if they could earn more by putting their revenues in the bank, or mine less if they could earn more by leaving the resource in the ground. Expectations about the future are critical in Hotelling's model, and are embodied in the expected interest rate and expected future price of the resource.

Clearly the level of the interest rate affects how biological resources are managed and hence the rate and direction of ecosystem transformation and species extinction. Any species or ecosystem that cannot be managed at a level such that it is generating a flow of services at a rate greater than the rate of interest "should" be depleted (Figure 4). Since even many economists find exploitation to extinction rather crass, there has been considerable interest in whether the interest rate produced by private capital markets reflects the social interest and whether, when these interests are factored in, a social rate of interest would not be significantly lower than the private interest rate. Might private capital markets work imperfectly, generating rates of interest that are too high and hence leading to excessive biodiversity loss? There are good reasons to expect that lower interest rates would favor the conservation of biodiversity, though there are situations when this would not be the case. Low interest rates allocate investments from the fastest growing projects, but increase the total number of projects that are worth investing in. Thus, low interest rates favor conservation in terms of their effects on allocation, but in terms of their scale-increasing effect they work against conservation. This has not been simply an academic argument.

The World Bank now realizes how its own evaluation policies have hastened biodiversity loss and, in part for this reason, has a policy of not financing the transformation of natural forest habitat.

ECONOMICS AND ECOLOGY SPECIALIZE AND SEPARATE

Every profession lives in a world of its own. The language spoken by its inhabitants, the landmarks familiar to them, their customs and conventions can only be learnt by those who reside there. By the end of the 19th century the trend to increasing specialization and professionalization in science was well under way, and economics as a profession became more and more popular. What has come to be called the "reductionist" paradigm was beginning to hold sway. This paradigm assumes that the world is separable into relatively isolated units that can be studied and understood on their own, and then reassembled to give a picture of the whole. As the complexity of science increased, this was a very useful idea, since it allowed dividing up the problem into smaller, more manageable pieces that could be attacked intensively. Chemists could study chemistry without being distracted by other aspects of the systems they were studying. Also, the rapid increase in the sheer number of scientists that were actively working made it necessary to organize the work in some way, and the disciplinary structure seemed a logical and useful way to do this. But once university departments were set up in the various disciplines, internal reinforcement systems came to reward only work in the discipline. This rapidly led to a reduction in communication across disciplines and a tendency for the disciplines to develop their own unique languages, cultures, and ways of looking at the world. In economics, this led to a growing isolation from the natural resource (or land) component of the classical triad of land, labor, and capital, and with it a growing isolation from the natural sciences. Economics departments began to reward theory more highly than applications and the discipline as a whole attempted to pattern itself on physics, which was probably the most successful example of the advantages of the disciplinary model of organization.

This trend continued in the early through mid-20th century and, by the time of the renewed environmental awareness of the 1970s, economics had become highly specialized and abstracted away from its earlier connections with the natural environment. Textbooks at the time barely mentioned the environment and concentrated instead on the microeconomics of supply, demand, and price formation and the macroeconomics of growth in manufactured capital and GNP. At the same time, economics was becoming absorbed with professionalization. As A. W. Coats noted: At least since the marginal revolution of the 1870s, mainstream economists have sought to enhance their intellectual authority and autonomy by excluding certain questions which were either sensitive such as the distribution of income and wealth, and the role of economic power in society or incapable of being handled by their preferred methods and techniques, or both. These are precisely the questions which are emphasized by their professional and lay critics and, more recently, by many economists who cannot be dismissed by their professional colleagues as either ignorant or incompetent.

The story in ecology is somewhat different. It is significant to noted, ecology is a much younger science, and it has always been more explicitly pluralistic and interdisciplinary. But its roots were in biology and the trend in biology was much the same as in other areas of science. The initial split into botany and zoology was followed by further specialization into biochemistry, biophysics, molecular biology, and so on. In ecology itself there was something of a split between the population ecologists Robert MacArthur concentrated on individual populations of organisms, and systems ecologists E. P. and H. T. Odum focused on whole ecosystems. But this split never got to the point of separation into distinct departments and disciplines, although many academic programs took on a decided flavor in one direction or the other.

Through all of this, ecologists, more so than any other discipline, have maintained communication across most of the natural sciences. To study ecosystems, one has to integrate hydrology, soil science, geology, climatology, chemistry, botany, zoology, genetics, and many other disciplines. The dividing line for ecologists has been at a particular species: *Homo sapiens*. Even though Haeckel's original definition explicitly included humans, and many ecologists have argued and worked to operationalize this integration, for the vast majority of active ecologists, the study of humans is outside their discipline, left to the social sciences. Indeed, most ecologists looked for field sites as remote from human activities as possible to conduct their research. Ecological economics is an attempt to help rectify this tendency to ignore humans in ecology, while at the same time rectifying the parallel tendency to ignore the natural world in the social sciences.

THE REINTEGRATION OF ECOLOGY AND ECONOMICS

Ecology and economics have been pursued as separate disciplines through most of the 20th century. While each has certainly borrowed theoretical concepts from the other and shared patterns of thinking from physics and other sciences, each has addressed separate issues, utilized different assumptions to reach answers, and supported different interests in the policy process. To be sure, individual scholars kept trying to introduce the issues addressed by natural science into economics, but they were systematically rejected by economists as a group. Indeed, in their popular manifestations as environmentalism and economism, these disciplines became juxtaposed secular religions, preventing the collective interpretation and resolution of the numerous problems at the intersection of human and natural systems. Ecological economics arose during the 1980s among a group of scholars who realized that improvements in environmental policy and management and protecting the well-being of future generations were dependent on bringing these domains of thought together. Numerous experiments with joint meetings between economists and ecologists were held, particularly in Sweden and the United States, to explore the possibilities of working together. Meanwhile, there was also growing discontent with the deficiencies in the system of national accounts that generates measures of economic activity such as gross domestic product, while ignoring the depletion of natural capital through the mining of resources such as petroleum and through environmental degradation. Economists and ecologists joined to encourage the major international agencies to develop accounting systems that included the environment. Buoyed by such initial efforts, the International Society for Ecological Economics (ISEE) was formed during a workshop of ecologists and economists held in Barcelona in late 1987, and the journal, *Ecological Economics*, was initiated in 1989. Major international conferences of ecologists and economists have been held since then, many ecological economic institutes have been formed around the world, and a significant number of books have appeared with the term ecological economics in their titles.

Ecological economics is not a single new paradigm based in shared assumptions and theory. It represents a commitment among economists, ecologists, and others, both as academics and as practitioners, to learn from each other, to explore new

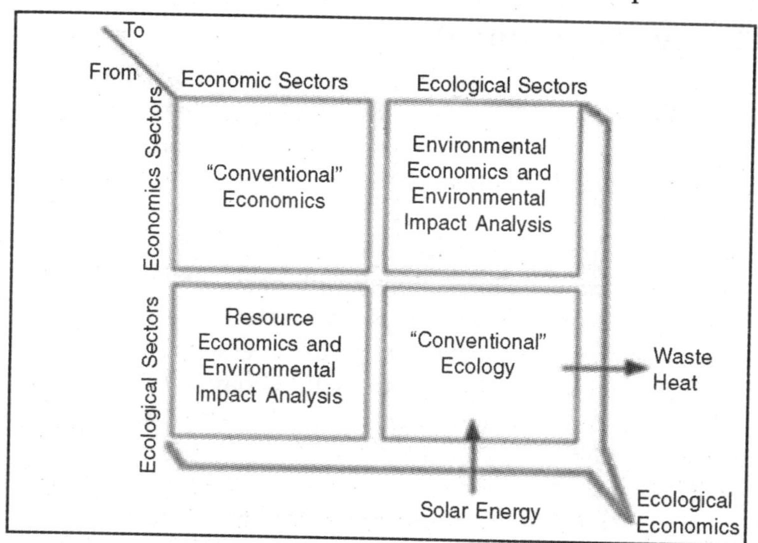

Figure 5: Relationship of Domains of Ecological Economics and Conventional Economics and Ecology, Resource and Environmental Economics, and Environmental Impact Analysis

patterns of thinking together, and to facilitate the derivation and implementation of new economic and environmental policies. To date, ecological economics has been deliberately conceptually pluralistic even while particular members may prefer one paradigm over another. One way of looking at it is to view ecological economics as encompassing economics and ecology and their existing links in the form of resource and environmental economics and environmental impact analysis as shown in Figure 5. Ecological economists are rethinking both ecology and economics by, for example, extending the materials balance and energetic paradigm of ecology to economic questions, applying concepts from economics to better understand the nature of biodiversity, and arguing from biological theory how natural and social systems have coevolved together such that neither can be understood apart from the other. Today's ecological economists are indebted to particular scholars who, though they have been predominantly ecologists or economists themselves, have maintained and demonstrated the advantages of a transdisciplinary approach.

GENERAL SYSTEM THEORY

Systems analysis is the study of systems that can be thought of as groups of interacting, interdependent parts linked together by complex exchanges of energy, matter, and information. There is a key distinction between "classical" science and system science. Classical science is based on the resolution, or reduction, of phenomena into isolatable causal trains and the search for basic, "atomic" units or parts of the system. Reductionist approaches are appropriate if the interaction between the parts is nonexistent, weak, or essentially linear so that they can be added up to describe the behavior of the whole. While these conditions are met in some physical and simple chemical systems, they are almost never met in more complex living systems. A "living system" is characterized by strong, usually nonlinear, interactions between the parts. Such complex feedbacks make resolution into isolatable causal trains difficult or impossible and also mean that small-scale behavior cannot simply be "added up" to arrive at large-scale results. Of course, this has not prevented scientists from assuming that living systems can be reduced to causal trains and isolatable parts, but this also explains why disciplinary environmental science and economics has produced inappropriate policies and management schemes.

Some scientists have long addressed the difficulties of working with complex systems. Ludwig von Bertalanffy, however, is especially credited with advancing the formal study of systems through a paper he wrote in 1950. This paper drew the attention of others who then chose to explore the field together. In *General System Theory* (1968), von Bertalanffy and his cohorts argued that similar patterns of interaction could be found in quite different systems and ventured the argument that once these basic patterns were understood, all systems could be understood. While this has not proved to be the case, one participant of the general system theory group, Kenneth Boulding, produced a series of books drawing parallels between economic and ecological systems, inspired other potential ecological economists in their formative years, and then helped in the founding of ecological economics as a formal effort.

OPEN-ACCESS RESOURCE MANAGEMENT AND COMMONS INSTITUTIONS

When nature can be divided into separate properties that are individually owned, the owners have an incentive to use the property carefully so that they can continue to use it in the future. When nature cannot be so divided and many people use the resource together, problems can arise. Resources used by multiple users without rules governing their use will be overexploited. Both traditional and modern societies typically develop rules for the use of resources held in common. A. C. Pigou addressed the problem of collective resource use in the 1920s and subsequent economists have developed formal models. The phenomenon did not become widely understood, however, until it was popularized in an article in *Science* magazine written by Garret Hardin, titled "The Tragedy of the Commons". The problem Hardin addressed is more accurately referred to as "open access" resources rather than "common property." Common ownership is not in itself a tragedy since many resources have been successfully managed as commons.

Open access can develop through the destruction of common institutions regulating the use of resources used jointly by people, leading to tragic consequences. Societies in transition between traditional and modern form frequently experience the tragedy of over use when neither traditional nor modern forms of common control prevail. Similarly, resources for which access is difficult to restrict, such as on frontiers beyond the control of governments, in the open sea, and wildlife that crosses national boundaries, are frequently overexploited. The absence or destruction of institutions regulating commons has led to the extinction of diverse species and the genetic impoverishment of many.

H. Scott Gordon formulated the problem of open-access resources as shown in Figure 6. Imagine an open-access fishery with total costs and total revenues from fishing effort as shown. Profits or rents from the fishery are maximized at level of effort

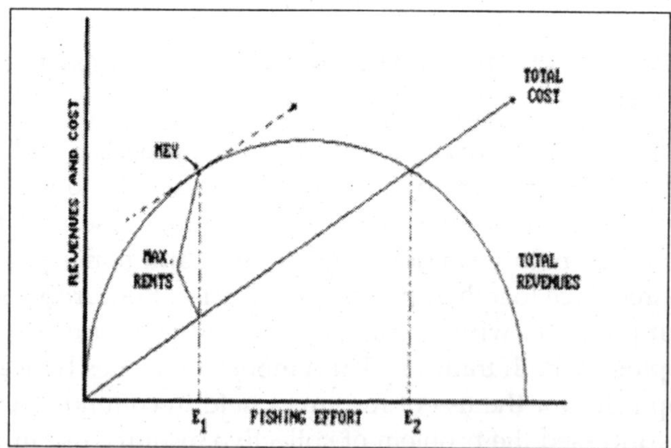

Figure 6: Excessive Fishing Effort Occurs in an Open-access Fishery because Existing Fishermen expand their Effort and New Fishermen enter the Fishery Beyond Level E_1, the Point of Maximum Profit. Each Fisherman Continues to make a Profit by Increased fishing up to level E_2, where the Total Revenues equal Total Costs. Further Fishing beyond this point is Economically Counterproductive because Costs exceed Revenues

E_1 but with unrestricted access, people would put more effort into fishing until the level E_2 was reached where no rent would be earned from fishing and no one would consider additional fishing worth the effort since costs would now be greater than revenues. Since more fish are caught at greater levels of effort, overfishing is more likely to occur in an open-access fishery than in a fishery managed as a commons. To the extent that biodiversity is manifested as different genetic traits, species, and ecosystems that cannot be owned by individuals and incorporated in market systems, we need common management institutions to conserve biodiversity for our descendants. At the end of the 20th century, international biodiversity agreements began to be formulated and implemented. In some cases, traditional common property institutions for the protection of biodiversity can be maintained in the face of modernization. In other cases, new institutions will be needed. Common property institutions may be communal, regional, national, or global. The health of institutions at all of these levels will be critical to conserving biological diversity and ecosystem integrity. For this reason, commons institutions are central to the work of many ecological economists. Similarly, it is now well understood that the global climate-regulating system is a common resource in need of common management institutions. For centuries, industrializing nations have dumped carbon dioxide, a by-product of fossil fuel combustion, and other greenhouse gases into the atmosphere without regard for their impacts on the climate system as a whole. Commons institutions for the management of the global climate system are in the process of being agreed to and implemented.

While Garret Hardin as a biologist "discovered" a phenomenon long understood by economists, Hardin was able to convey the larger meaning of the phenomenon to a broad audience and awake natural scientists to the importance of institutions for environmental management. His article is still one of the most frequently found among the readings for environmental courses. Hardin, by crossing disciplines and demonstrating the significance to policy of economics and ecology used together, contributed to the rise of ecological economics.

ENERGETICS AND SYSTEMS

In the year 1971 two influential books were published by two authors who did not yet know of each other, one a noted ecologist and one a noted economist. The books were very different in style and in many other ways, but both books were about energy, entropy, power, systems, and society and both can be said to have made a major contribution to setting the stage for ecological economics. One was Howard T. Odum's *Environment, Power, and Society* and the other was Nicholas Georgescu-Roegen's *The Entropy Law and the Economic Process.* Nicholas Georgescu-Roegen (1906–1994) was born in Romania, trained in mathematical statistics in France, assumed academic and government positions in his native country, and fled to the United States after World War II to become an economist, working with Professor Joseph Schumpeter at Harvard. His contributions to the further mathematical refinement of standard neoclassical economics in the areas of utility and consumer choice, production theory, input–output analysis, and development economics were honored by his being designated a Distinguished Fellow of the American Economic Association. He is most noted, however, for his contributions in the area of entropy and economics, which still stir considerable controversial discussion among economists.

Georgescu-Roegen argued that all economic processes entail the use of energy and that the second law of thermodynamics, the entropy law, clearly indicates that the available energy in a closed system can only decline. Like others before him, he also noted the parallel between the degradation of the availability of energy and the degradation of the order of materials. Economic processes entail using relatively concentrated iron resources, for example, which are then further concentrated through the use of energy, but ultimately end up being dispersed as rust and waste, less concentrated than the original iron ore. Biodiversity degradation can also be thought of as a parallel problem. New technologies do not "create" new resources, they simply allow us to degrade energy, material order, and biological richness more rapidly. Critics have argued that the entropy law is not important because the earth is not a closed system. It receives sunlight daily and is expected to continue to do so for another several billion years. Yet modern industrial economies are fueled by fossil hydrocarbons, accumulations of past solar energy which are clearly limited, while current solar energy is of limited flow and of relatively low concentration.

Georgescu-Roegen's message is controversial, in part, because it conflicts with beliefs in progress that are still strongly held by economists. The message is also difficult to interpret because it does not inform us how quickly we need to make the transition from stock energy resources to flow energy resources. In this sense, we simply need to look at resource constraints as well as the ability of the global system to absorb carbon dioxide and other greenhouse gases; the entropy law itself does not provide additional information. The entropy law, however, does provide a strong bass beat to the sirens being sounded by scientists studying climate change, biodiversity loss, and soil degradation. Nicholas Georgescu-Roegen not only motivated one of his students, Herman Daly, to address the long-term human predicament but also inspired many others to ponder the various ways the entropy law helps us understand irreversibility, systems and organization, and our options for the future.

The hourglass analogy can be extended by considering the sand in the upper chamber to be the stock of energy in the sun. Solar energy arrives to earth as a flow whose amount is governed by the constricted middle of the hourglass that limits the rate at which sand falls. Suppose that in ancient geologic ages some of the falling sand had gotten stuck against the inner surface of the bottom chamber, but at the top of the bottom chamber, before it had fallen all the way. This becomes a terrestrial dowry of low entropy, a stock that we can use up at a rate of our own choosing. We use it by drilling holes in it through which the trapped sand can fall to the bottom of the lower chamber. This terrestrial source of low entropy can be used at a rate of our own choosing, unlike the sun whose energy arrives at a fixed flow rate–we cannot "mine" the sun to use tomorrow's sunlight today, but we can mine terrestrial deposits and in a sense use up tomorrow's petroleum today.

There is thus an important asymmetry between our two sources of low entropy. The solar source is stock abundant, but flow limited. The terrestrial source is stock limited, but flow abundant temporarily. Peasant societies lived off the solar flow; industrial societies have come to depend on enormous supplements from the unsustainable terrestrial stocks. Reversing this dependence will be an enormous evolutionary shift. Georgescu-Roegen argued that evolution has in the past consisted of slow adaptations of our endosomatic organs heart, lungs, etc. which run on solar energy. Now evolution has shifted to rapid adaptations of our exosomatic organs cars, airplanes, etc. that depend on terrestrial low entropy. The uneven ownership of exosomatic organs and the terrestrial low entropy from which they are made, compared to the egalitarian distribution of ownership of endosomatic capital, was for Georgescu-Roegen the root of social conflict in industrial societies.

Howard T. Odum was born in Durham, North Carolina in 1924, the son of Howard W. Odum, a noted sociologist. H.T. Odum was a meteorologist in the American tropics during World War II, received an A.B. in Zoology from the University of North Carolina in 1947, and a Ph.D. from Yale University in 1951, under ecologist G. Evelyn Hutchinson. He has been concerned with material cycles and energy flow in ecosystems and he produced one of the first energy flow descriptions of a complete ecosystem in his famous study of Silver Springs, Florida. He also contributed heavily to his brother Eugene P. Odum's influential textbook, *Fundamentals of Ecology*, first published in 1953. This textbook was the standard in ecology for several decades and helped to establish several important ecological concepts, both in the profession and in the public consciousness. In particular, the concept of the ecosystem was fully developed and was quantified using units of energy and material flows.

In addition to his father and Hutchinson, H. T. Odum was influenced in his thinking by Lotka and von Bertalanffy, and he was concerned with many of the same problems as Georgescu-Roegen. His approach was broader than Georgescu-Roegen's, however, and went beyond economics and thermodynamics to include systems in general, from simple physical and chemical systems to biological and ecological systems to economic and social systems. In *Environment, Power, and Society* he laid out a comprehensive integration of systems with energy flow used as the integrating factor. He even developed his own symbolic language similar in intent and use to Forrester's systems dynamics symbols to help describe and model the common features of systems. This language was both an indispensable aid to the initiated practitioner in helping to understand systems concepts and a barrier to outsiders gaining access to these same concepts.

Odum's work on energy flow through systems and dynamic modeling of systems spawned, or at least paralleled and encouraged, an immense amount of work by his students and others ranging from input–output studies of energy and material flow in ecological and economic systems to dynamic simulation models of whole ecosystems and integrated ecological economic systems. Probably the most concise and complete treatment of the application of many of H. T. Odum's ideas to ecological economics is the 1986 book by C. A. S. Hall, C. Cleveland, and R. Kaufmann titled *Energy and Resource Quality: The Ecology of the Economic Process.*

SPACESHIP EARTH AND STEADY-STATE ECONOMICS

Kenneth Boulding's classic "The Economics of the Coming Spaceship Earth" set the stage for ecological economics with its description of the transition from the "frontier economics" of the past, where growth in human welfare implied growth in material consumption, to the "spaceship economics" of the future, where growth in welfare can no longer be fueled by growth in material consumption. This fundamental difference in vision and worldview was elaborated further by Daly in recasting economics as a life science—akin to biology and especially ecology, rather than a physical science like chemistry or physics. The importance of this shift in "pre-analytic vision" cannot be overemphasized. It implies a fundamental change in the perception of the problems of resource allocation and how they should be addressed. More particularly, it implies that the focus of analysis should be shifted from marketed resources in the economic system to the biophysical basis of interdependent ecological and economic systems.

Daly further elaborated on this theme with his work on "steady state economics" which worked out the implications of acknowledging that the Earth is materially finite and nongrowing, and that the economy is a subset of this finite global system. Thus the economy cannot grow forever at least in a material sense and ultimately some sort of sustainable steady state is desired. This steady state is not necessarily absolutely stable and unchanging. Like in ecosystems, things in a steady-state economy are changing constantly in both periodic and aperiodic ways. The key point is that these changes are bounded and there is no long-term trend in the system. Daly's work in steady-state economics can be seen as one of the direct antecedents of ecological economics.

ADAPTIVE ENVIRONMENTAL MANAGEMENT

In the late 1970s, Canadian ecologist C. S. Holling became director of the International Institute for Applied Systems Analysis (IIASA). His earlier work on spruce budworm outbreaks in northern boreal forests had led him to a complex and dynamic view of ecosystems that eventually took over from the more "equilibrium" concepts that had held sway earlier. Adaptive environmental management redraws conventional boundaries by integrating science and management. Holling realized that laboratory and controlled field experiments on parts of ecological systems could not be aggregated to an understanding of the whole.

Adaptive environmental management has proved to be an effective approach to understanding and managing complex, changing systems with large uncertainties. While this approach emerged out of ecology and its application to management, it has tremendous implications for social organization. Environmental managers, people in associated communities, and those in the broader public who are especially interested in environmental issues should question, assist in the monitoring, and share in the learning.

COEVOLUTION OF ECOLOGICAL AND ECONOMIC SYSTEMS

One of the strongest barriers to the union of economics and ecology has been the presumption that ecological and economics systems are separable and do not need to be understood together. Economists think of economic systems as separate from nature, while the vast majority of natural scientists think of natural systems as apart from people. Indeed, social scientists generally have thought that all social phenomena are culturally determined. When natural scientists do consider social phenomena, they "naturally" look to natural law to explain it.

Evolutionary ecologists Paul Ehrlich and Peter Raven first alerted the scientific community to the importance of coevolution between species. The niche to which species evolve has most frequently been described as a fixed, physical niche. With the characteristics of the niche fixed, evolution acquires a direction, and evolutionary stories usually entail the species

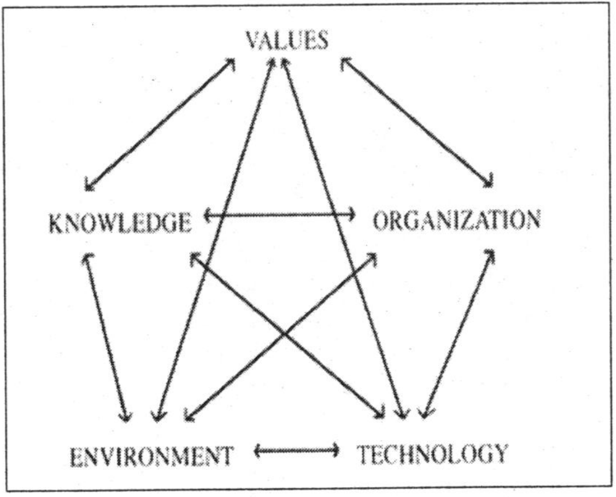

Figure 7: The Coevolutionary Development Process

progressively fitting the characteristics better and better. Hence evolutionary stories are frequently stories of progress, with human evolution providing the ultimate story of progress. Coevolution simply acknowledges that the characteristics of a species' niche at any one time are predominantly other species and their characteristics. Hence, the characteristics of any one species are selected in the context of the characteristics of other species and vice versa; species coevolve. Even as evolutionary direction and the analog to Western beliefs in progress are lost, coevolution helps explain why species fit together into ecosystems while at the same time species and ecosystems continue to change.

Norgaard illustrates how understanding the coevolutionary process can help us to understand how natural and social systems interconnect and change. From this, he suggests new directions for social organization to enhance environmental sustainability, social justice, and human dignity. Consider development as a process of coevolution between knowledge, values, organization, technology, and the environment (Figure 7). Each of these subsystems is related to each of the others, yet each is also changing and affecting change in the others through selection. Deliberate innovations, chance discoveries, and random changes occur in each subsystem that affect, through natural selection, the distribution and qualities of components in each of the other subsystems. Whether new components prove fit depends on the characteristics of each of the subsystems at the time. With each subsystem putting selective pressure on each of the others, they coevolve in a manner whereby each reflects the other. Thus everything is coupled, yet everything is changing.

Environmental subsystems are treated symmetrically with the subsystems of values, knowledge, social organization, and technology in this coevolutionary explanation of development. New technologies, for example, exert new selective pressures on species, while newly evolved characteristics of species, in turn, select for different technologies. Similarly, transformations in the biosphere select for new ways of understanding the biosphere. For example, the use of pesticides induces resistance and secondary pest resurgence, selecting both for new pesticides and for more systematic ways of thinking about pest control. Pests, pesticides, pesticide production, pesticide institutions and policy, how we understand pest control, and how we value chemicals in the environment demonstrate an incredibly tight and rapid coevolution in the second half of this century. In the short run, people can be thought of as interacting with the environment in response to market signals or their absence. The coevolutionary model, however, incorporates longer-term evolutionary feedbacks. To emphasize coevolutionary processes is not to deny that people directly intervene in and change the characteristics of environments. The coevolutionary perspective puts its emphasis on the chain of events thereafter, and how different interventions alter the selective pressure and hence the relative dominance of environmental traits which, in turn, select for values, knowledge, organization, and technology and hence subsequent interventions in the environment.

While the coevolutionary perspective treats changes in the various subsystems symmetrically, let us use this model to address technology in particular. People have interacted with their environments over millennia in diverse ways, many of them sustainable over very long periods, many not. Some traditional agricultural technologies, at the intensities historically employed, probably increased biological diversity. There is general evidence that traditional technologies, again at the level employed, included biodiversity-conserving strategies as a part of the process of farming. Technology today, however, is perceived as a leading culprit in the process of biodiversity loss. Modern agricultural technologies override nature, but do so only locally and temporarily. They do not "control" nature. Pesticides kill some pests, solving the immediate threat to crops. But the vacant niche left by the pest is soon filled by a second species of pest or the original pests evolve resistance, pesticides drift to interfere with the agricultural practices of other farmers, and pesticides and their by-products accumulate in soil and groundwater aquifers to plague production and human health for years to come. Each farmer strives to control nature but creates new problems beyond his or her farm and in subsequent seasons for others. Because of all the new problems created beyond the individual farm in space and time, preharvest crop losses due to pests since World War II have remained around 35% while pesticide use has increased dramatically.

New technologies that work with natural processes rather than override them are sorely needed. During the past two centuries, technologies have largely descended from physics, chemistry, and, at best, microbiology. Ecologists and evolutionary biologists were never given the opportunity to systemically review such technologies, nor is it clear that our ecological and evolutionary understanding are sufficient to review them adequately now. A few agricultural technologies, such as the control of pests in agriculture through the use of other biologicals, have descended from ecological thinking. But research and technological development in biological control was nearly eliminated with the introduction of DDT in agriculture after World War II. Research on and development of agricultural technologies requiring fewer energy and material inputs eventually received considerable support in industrial countries after the rise in energy prices during the 1970s and the farm financial crises in the United States during the early 1980s. Support for agroecology, for technologies based on the management of complementarities between multiple species including soil organisms, however, is still minimal. Learning how to use renewable energy sources will be long and difficult since most of our knowledge has developed to capture the potential of fossil energy. Our universities and other research institutions are still structured around disciplinary rather than systemic thinking, and public understanding of the shortcomings of current technologies and possibilities for ecologically based technologies is weak. Scientists and technologists reproduce themselves and their institutions through direct control and education; hence science and technology sometimes respond slowly to changes in the social awareness of environmental problems.

From the coevolutionary perspective, we can see more clearly how economies have transformed from coevolving with their ecosystems to coevolving around the combustion of fossil hydrocarbons. In this transformation, people have been freed from the environmental feedbacks on their economic activities that they experienced relatively quickly as individuals and communities. The feedbacks that remain, however, occur over longer periods and greater distances and are experienced collectively, even globally, by many peoples making them more difficult to perceive and counteract. By tapping into fossil hydrocarbons, Western societies freed themselves, at least for the short to medium term, from many of the complexities of interacting with environmental systems. Coevolution occurred around fossil hydrocarbons. Tractors replaced animal power, fertilizers replaced the complexities of interplanting crops that were good hosts of nitrogen-fixing bacteria with those which were not, and pesticides replaced the biological controls provided by more complex agroecosystems. Furthermore, inexpensive energy meant crops could be stored for longer periods and transported over greater distances. Social organization coevolved around these new possibilities very quickly. Each of these accomplishments was based on the partial understanding of separate sciences and separate technologies. This coevolutionary explanation of the unsustainability of modern societies then is simply that development based on fossil hydrocarbons allowed individuals to control their immediate environments for the short run while shifting environmental impacts, in ways that have proven difficult to comprehend, to broader and broader publics ultimately to the entire global polity and on to future generations. These more distant impacts can select on our social organization as we realize their long-term and global implications and choose to respond in advance, or they can select directly as they are experienced in the future.

The coevolutionary perspective helps one to see that the problem of humans interacting with their environment is not simply a matter of establishing market incentives or appropriate rules about the use of property. Our values, knowledge, and social organization have coevolved around fossil hydrocarbons. Our fossil fuel-driven economy has not simply transformed the environment, it has selected for individualist, materialist values; favored the development of reductionist understanding at the expense of systemic understanding; and preferred a bureaucratic, centralized form of control that works better for steady-state industrial management than for the varied, surprising dynamics of ecosystem management. And the coevolutionary framing highlights how our abilities to perceive and resolve environmental problems within the dominant modes of valuing, thinking, and organizing are severely constrained.

THE ROLE OF NEOCLASSICAL ECONOMICS IN ECOLOGICAL ECONOMICS

After all of this description of alternative paradigms, it is important to reiterate that ecological economics is methodologically pluralistic and accepts the framework of analysis of neoclassical economics along with other frameworks. Indeed, neoclassical market analysis is still an important pattern of thinking within ecological economics. There are, however, differences between patterns of thinking and how the patterns are used with particular assumptions. We have already emphasized that most neoclassical economists assume that technological advance will outpace resource scarcity over the long run and that ecological services can also be replaced by new technologies. Ecological economists, on the other hand, assume that resource and ecological limits are critically important and are much less confident that technological advances will arise in response to higher prices generated by scarcities. This difference in worldview, however, does not prevent neoclassical and ecological economists from sharing the same pattern of reasoning.

There is another way in which neoclassical and ecological economists differ even while using the same patterns of thinking. It is observed that neoclassical economists have chosen to ignore how the initial distribution of rights to resources affects how markets subsequently allocate resources between end products and consumers. They have chosen to ignore this relationship since World War II largely for two reasons. First, Karl Marx focused on questions of the distribution of power, and the "other" side of the Cold War, the former USSR, China, and other nations, invoked Marx's name to rationalize their approach to social relations and development. In the West, especially the U.S. during the 1950s, questioning the distribution of power was effectively an act of disloyalty. But neoclassical economists also had a second rationale for ignoring equity in the initial distribution of rights to resources. Growing economies could avoid the political difficulties of redistribution by making everyone better off. This became an important argument for increasing the rate of economic growth even in the countries that were already rich.

Concern over sustainability has led to new concerns with equity in an era when Cold War politics have become history. Clearly, sustainability is a matter of transferring assets to future generations. This is a question of equity between generations. To understand sustainability using neoclassical economic reasoning, the distribution of resources between generations, or intergenerational equity, must be central. But sustainability is not simply a matter of intergenerational equity. In a world of very rich and very poor, asset transfer between generations is likely to be at less than a sustainable level. The very rich can be so rich that they do not worry about their progeny having enough. The very poor, on the other hand, can be so poor that each generation has to exploit resources and degrade environmental systems merely to subsist. For many ecological economists, these extremes characterize the world we live in and account for much of the unsustainability. The extremes internationally between rich and poor nations also make it very difficult to reach international understandings on managing the global commons. So sustainability is also a matter of intragenerational and international equity. The conventional stance of neoclassical economists remains that economic growth will provide the conditions to resolve these inequities. But there have been two generations of economic growth since the international development programs were established after

World War II, and inequality has increased. Thus the conventional stance is wearing a little thin and is increasingly questioned.

There is yet a third reason why neoclassical economists historically have not included distribution in their arguments. Once distribution is taken into consideration, there are many possible efficient market allocations depending on how rights to resources are distributed between people. Since World War II, however, economists have undertaken analyses of the costs and benefits of alternative public projects and other public decisions so as to advise legislatures and public agencies as to which project or decision is best. The Neoclassical economics cannot determine whether one distribution of resources between people is better than another. Moral criteria must be invoked and the decision must be made politically. But political decision making is more typically driven by the existing distribution of power than by moral discourse. To a large extent, economists were asked to undertake cost-benefit analysis in order to offset the politics of power. Economists see themselves as acting more in the public interest than the politicians responding to power and pressure groups.

The realization that economics must work with a more democratic politics complements another research style emerging within ecological economics. Acknowledging that economists need to understand ecology and vice versa further opens the door to asking whether anyone can possibly be excluded from sharing in the search for sustainability. Surely, to the extent that social and ecological systems differ from place to place, local, experiential knowledge will be essential to implementing specific solutions.

INCREASED EFFICIENCY AND DEMATERIALIZATION

Entrepreneurs and consumers have always had an incentive to get more from less. At the same time, when an individual uses less, he or she typically reaps only a portion of the benefits because of the numerous ways we are connected through ecosystems. Furthermore, choosing to use less must frequently be done collectively through developing new technologies, changing infrastructure such as that which supports automobile use over public transit, and adjusting the rules of the game for all.

A group of ecological economists are documenting the prospects for "dematerialization" at the Wuppertal Institute for Climate, Environment, and Energy in Germany. Their arguments parallel those of Lovins while also picking up on Herman Daly's argument that we need to stabilize the rate of material throughput in the economy. They have calculated the material input per unit of service for numerous consumption goods. Researchers at Wuppertal think material flows can be reduced by as much as a factor of 10. All of this may seem remote from an ecological management perspective, but the counterargument is that we are so far from a level of flow consistent with natural fluxes where management is even possible that the first step is massive reduction in human-induced material flows.

ECOSYSTEM HEALTH

To a considerable extent to date, while whole ecosystems have been protected, only individual species have been managed. Models have been derived from principles of population biology that suggest how, for example, Douglas fir trees or salmon can be harvested sustainably. But trees and the salmon do not thrive apart from other species and a myriad of other factors that affect ecosystem behavior. For this reason, efforts to manage individual species using these models have proven amazingly ineffective. In light of both broader concerns with maintaining ecosystems per se and the failures of individual species models, a group of ecologists and social scientists joined together in the early 1990s to study and promote the concept of ecosystem health and launched the journal *Ecosystem Health* in 1995. The ecologists are using the term "ecosystem integrity" to make new bridges between biology and policy. "Conservation biology" emerged as a field during the 1980s among biologists who were not content to simply study the decline of biodiversity and became intent on saving species from extinction. These multiple efforts include scientists who participate in ecological economics as well. They are all examples of groups of scientists who are using science effectively to new ends by shedding the old assumptions about how knowledge fits together and affects progress.

ENVIRONMENTAL EPISTEMOLOGY

The field of philosophy that studies how we think we can learn "truth" is known as epistemology. Clearly, if *Homo sapiens* is so special because the species is smarter than other animals, then the special problems we have gotten ourselves into relative to other animals must in some sense also be related to how we think. And if we believe that science has indeed driven the technological, and even to some extent the institutional, changes that are behind development, then how we know things scientifically must also be partly responsible for the environmental consequences of development. In this sense, the environmental crises of the latter half of the 20th century are challenging the underlying premises of the dominant forms of Western science. To argue that separating economics from ecology is a mistake, a dominant premise of ecological economics, is to make an epistemological statement. Realizing this, several ecological economists have explored the history and philosophy of science to directly understand how environmental crises have developed. One of the dominant premises of Western science, for example, has been the idea that nature behaves in a predictable manner according to universal principles that once discovered are applicable everywhere. If nature, however, is evolving and, furthermore, has evolved differently in different places, then the expectation that there can be a "physics" of nature can lead people to make a good number of mistakes. If it is such basic premises that are at the root of our crises, then it would be most effective to tackle them directly before trying to create new ways of understanding.

POLITICAL ECOLOGY

It is significant to observe that Karl Marx has had an important influence on the social sciences. Besides focusing our attention on power and inequity, Marx has helped us keep our attention on history. The environmental crises of the latter half of the 20th century have stimulated new critiques of capitalism and development by Marxist anthropologists, economists, historians, and sociologists. From these critiques, a new field known as political ecology has emerged. Again, the overlap of participants between political ecology and ecological economics is strong. While most of the arguments with respect to equity made in ecological economics are formally neoclassical, the concern with equity complements research in the area of political ecology on power, poverty, and environmental transformation using Marxian frames of analysis. In ecological economics, we are beginning to see the two historically separate strands of economic thought used to inform each other.

3

Evolution and Development of Economics

In biology, where the main examples of interactors are proteins, cells, and organisms, the relevant instructions are contained in genomes. The trials with them–such as mutations and recombinations–are considered random, as no use of information relevant to their eventual success has been found. In the social sciences, where interactors may be exemplified by different social and economic organizations–from small groups to entire economies and societies–the relevant instructions are contained, as explained in more detail below, in institutional rules. The trials with their changes need not be entirely random: some information on their eventual effects may be acquired from practice and or theory, and used in making these trials. But as this information is, and for a foreseeable future appears to remain, far from perfect, even these trials must at least partly be random, made with the help of some irrelevant inputs. Many of them are therefore also likely to be errors, requiring what may labeled as Darwinian selection before a successful variant of institutional rules can be found and retained.

ENVIRONMENTS

Each interactor faces certain environments: nature and possibly other interactors, which may be its competitors and/or collaborators, either independent or fellow agents of a higher-level interactor. The environments contain the resources–materials, energy, and information–which the interactor needs in order to form, develop and function according to its instructions. The conditions for obtaining the needed resources imply the success criteria for testing interactors' performance. In generous environments the conditions are easy to meet and the tests are easy to pass: a wide variety of interactors can succeed and thus allow a wide variety of instructions to be selected and retained. But in hard environments, where the needed resources are difficult to obtain, the variety of successful interactors is narrow. Successful instructions–among all the feasible instructions that the more or less random evolutionary experimenting can try–are there rare if they exist at all, and may require long experimenting before any of them is found.

All this brings to light the important point that in general, Darwinian evolution is only satisficing–and not, as it is sometimes wrongly claimed, optimizing. It does not seek maximum efficiency, only eliminates what the environmental success criteria evaluate as excessive inefficiencies. In hard environments, where even small inefficiencies are excessive, satisficing of course does converge to optimizing. But if the environments are more generous, instructions may prescribe and their interactors exhibit many useless and wasteful ornaments, and yet both be approved of as successful. Why an interactor needs materials and energy significantly differs from why it needs information: the former, to have a range of possibilities to act, and the latter, to know which of these possibilities to choose. This implies two success conditions: (A) the materials and energy that it possesses and/or is able to obtain must allow at least one of the possibilities to lead to success; (B) the information that it possess and/or is able to obtain must allow at least one of the successful possibilities to be found. Condition (A) is harder: if it is not met, no success is possible. But if (B) is not met, success is only unlikely: the interactor may still go ahead and try its chance with the help of some random or otherwise irrelevant inputs. Of course, the more of the relevant information is missing, the less likely it is to succeed.

But there is a more fundamental precondition: to obtain from environments and effectively use any resources, each interactor must already be equipped with a minimum of corresponding resources, including tools, energy, and information. Its effective uses of resources are thus doubly constrained: by their availability in its environments, and by its equipment for finding them, obtaining them, and using them. Sufficiently sophisticated interactors may have the ability, due to sophisticated instruction in their information equipment, to use parts of the obtained resources for developing their equipments, and thus allowing more of the available resources to be obtained and used in the future. Importantly, however, this process can never start from zero. At any moment, the actual equipment constrains all uses of resource, including those for its own development. Hence, as can be deduced by simple recursive reasoning, no interactor can start as an empty box–a blank slate, or tabula rasa–that environments might equip at their will. Each must begin with some intrinsically own initial equipment, which determines how the obtaining and using of resources from environments may start, and sets ultimate limits to how far, in the most generous environments, its may potentially continue.

In biology, as noted, the key initial equipment of an organism resides in its genome, which determines how the organism can start using environmental inputs for its development, and sets limits to what extent, in the most favorable environments, it could potentially develop. What is the initial equipment of an economy, and how it limits the economy's development potential. They are easy to interpret in terms of standard theories of capital and investment. And many problems with information equipments are easy to understand by all the users of personal computers, who know that every information processing needs pre-existing information equipment in the form of suitable hardware and software. But one information problem is less easy: how can any information equipment form and develop by itself, without some pre-existing information equipment of an intelligent designer? It is this problem that only some form of Darwinism appears able to solve. To get a handle on it, it is necessary to adopt a very broad perspective on information and carefully clarify all the terms used.

INFORMATION, DATA, AND INSTRUCTIONS

Information problems are of prime importance for social scientists simply because different humans and their different societies differ much less in the materials of which they are made and in the energy they need for living than in the ways in which the materials and the uses of energy are shaped. All existing individuals and all existing societies can thus be seen as outcomes of choices from wide ranges of alternatives that the materials and energy available make equally feasible. What determines which specific individuals and which specific societies will form and how they will develop–and indeed that they will be human individuals and human societies, and not individuals and societies of other species–is therefore above all the information used for guiding these choices.

To comprehend information problems in their entirety, the notion of "information" must first be given a sufficiently broad meaning to include both the information that interactors may receive and process and the one with which they need to be equipped. It appears best to follow the main lines of the quantitative theories of information that define it in relation to choice situations. Here, however, it will not be necessary to quantify information exactly: this would require a number of simplifying and therefore doubtful assumptions, and might mislead attention from primary problems to secondary mathematical subtleties. The following rough definition will suffice:

Information for an interactor is what helps it to choose an alternative from a set of two or more feasible alternatives one that meets its internal success criterion–e.g. maximizing its objective function or satisficing its norm. The information can be carried by an event chosen by nature or other interactors from a set of two or more possible events. Given the interactor's choice set and success criterion, the more choice alternatives there are and the fewer of them would be successful, the more information the interactor needs to find one of these. If some of this information is missing and the choice must nevertheless be made, the information deficit must be covered from irrelevant, possibly random events. The higher the deficit, the more likely the chosen alternative will fail.

Thus, importantly, what is information depends on the interactor considered, and not on the environments. Objectively, these only produce physical events, such as electromagnetic waves or air vibrations, which can contain information only to the extent to which the interactor is equipped, in addition to the material means needed for perceiving them, with information on how to use them. Otherwise physical states and events are nothing more than physical states and events. To distinguish the information processed from the information equipment for processing it, it is suitable to call the former "data" and the latter "instructions." But these are only roles, not permanent properties: data in one choice problem may become instructions in another choice problem, or vice versa. Automatic computer programming and the programming of learning offer clear examples: in both cases, instructions are used for elaborating other instructions, and these thus play, while being elaborated, the roles of data.

The term "instruction" is closely related to the one of "program." We agree with the increasingly accepted view that human behavior is program-based, and thus admits that the information equipment of an interactor may also be said to consist of programs. Like in computer programming, instructions are seen to be elements of programs, and programs are seen to be specifically organized chains or networks of instructions.

There are two reasons why we focus on instructions rather than programs. One is diplomatic: as interactors are meant also to include humans, describing these as instructed sounds better than describing them as programmed. The second reason is factual: such a detailed focus is necessary clearly to see that one program may combine instructions of different origins. But, to include humans, both terms must be interpreted more broadly than in ordinary computer programming (although advanced computer programming can also embrace these broad interpretations). In particular, programs must be seen also to govern purposeful behaviors, learning, searching, discovering, innovating, and creating. Instructions must therefore include norms and/or objectives, feedback loops, and prescriptions for generating random or otherwise arbitrary trials and for identifying and eliminating the committed errors.

As opposed to usual computer programming, where one instruction determines just one operation, instructions must be admitted, as in ordinary languages, to be possibly less sharp, determining only a more or less large subset of feasible actions. A simple, but for social scientists important example is the choice of a move in a game: the rules of the game are more or less broad instructions telling the players which moves are permissible, and the players must then use their own internal instructions to specify which of the permissible moves they choose. The choice of a specific action may thus be understood as a result of cooperation of several instructions. They may be viewed as gradually narrowing constraints, eliminating larger and larger parts of a given choice set, until only one choice alternative is left. Considering the total quantity of information needed to specify this alternative, each of these instruction can be seen to supply some of it, and all of them all of it. This includes even the cases when not all of the relevant information is available. Then, as noted, to obtain the total needed to proceed with the choice, some of the instructions must prescribe uses of random or otherwise irrelevant steps.

All this makes it clear that the above-mentioned initial equipment, which each interactor needs to start receiving and using inputs from environments, must contain specific initial instructions telling it how to do so. The sophisticated interactor which is able to use some of these inputs for improving itself - in other words, to learn, and possibly even learn to learn - must contain specific initial instructions also for developing these abilities. The general principle behind all this is that each information processing - be it a relatively simple use of data for immediate decisions or complex learning of new instructions for future uses - requires some pre-existing instructions.

ONE-LEVEL EVOLUTION AND DEVELOPMENT

Both the evolution of instructions and the development of interactors may possibly take place at several levels: some interactors may act as instructed agents forming and developing a larger interactor while being themselves formed and developed first, consider just one level. This can be represented as follows: Assume a set of agents, internally instructed for certain associative and functional behaviors, and certain environments implying certain success criteria. The task of evolution is to find additional instructions that could guide the agents to form, develop a make function large in a variety of alternative ways, o by enough the one accorde ere must be some evolutionary memories in which successful instruct are interactor, able to succeed in these environments.

But evolution is sometimes impossible and sometimes unnecessary. Three cases must be distinguished: (a) the environments are so harsh and/or the agents so little able that no ways of instructing them can help; (b) the environments are so tolerant and the agents' internal instructions are so complete that they self-organize into a successful larger interactor automatically by themselves; (c) the agents are able to self-organize which only few will produce a successful larger interactor. It is only in (c) that evolution is both needed and possible. In (a), no larger successful interactors can form at all, and in (b), all of them are automatically successful without any evolution. But (b) can be seen an extreme case of (c). In general, the instructions guiding the agents come there from two sources - inherent, and supplied by evolution. There may therefore be many variants of (c) which differ in the proportion of the two. Case (b) can then be regarded as the extreme (c) in which all the instructions are inherent and none is supplied lution.

Conceptually, the existence of such a proportion is clear. But empirically, it is difficult to measure it, so that opinions may differ on what it is. Thus, concerning the evolution of life, traditional Darwinians belittle, if not entirely neglect, the inherent instructions and believe that only those supplied by evolution are significant.

Considering (c) as the only case in which a Darwinian evolution may work, there are three more conditions that must be met to allow this evolution actually to work and eventually to succeed. First, there must be a feasible variety of sets of tentative instructions with which trials can be made and which contains, possibly as a very small sub-variety, some successful ones. Second, the agents' internal instructing must enable them to receive and actually follow such instructions. Third, the must be some evolutionary memories in which successful instructions can be retained. If all these conditions met, one-level evolution and development can be understood to unfold as follows: (1) Without full information about the consequences, the evolution tentatively picks a combination of instructions and supplies it to the agents. (2) With the help of their internal instructions, the agents receive this combination, join it to their internal instructions, and, guided by both, try to form, make function, and develop a larger interactor. (3) If such an interactor forms and develops.

If out of all possible combinations of instructions, only very few are successful, it may take a long time, with many repetitions of these steps, before the evolution happens to pick one of them. The time is possible to shorten if many parallel experiments can be conducted simultaneously. But extensive uses of this possibility appear limited to the biochemical experimenting in the evolution of life. In socioeconomic evolution, considered in more detail below, the number of parallel experiments is much more limited. This evolution must therefore proceed mainly by series of successive experiment

MULTILEVEL EVOLUTION AND DEVELOPMENT

To show how evolution and development can work at more than one level, it suffices to clarify two neighboring level will then by possible to clarify by simple recursive reasoning. At level (I), assume again a set of agents, internally instructed for certain associative and functional behaviors, and environments implying certain success criteria. Consider again case (c), in which the agents, to be able to form and develop successful larger interactors, need to complement their internal instructions with additional instructions supplied by evolution. But now the environments are more adverse: the larger interactors can succeed only if they are able further to self-organize at level (II) into an even larger successful interactor – possibly called "group" or "societors as "small," "mid-sized" and "large." This makes the task of the evolution more difficult. Its instructions must now enable the small interactors to form and develop mid-sized interactors that will not only succeuals, but will moreover be able to form and develop large successful interactors. The key to understanding multilevel evolution is to realize that that level (I) evolution, to attain such a double success, can employ two alternative strategies, for w are "complete instructing" and "instructing for a higher-level evolution."

Complete instructing means that the evolution must endow the small interactors with all the instructions that they need to form and develop mid-sized interactors so precisely that these from the beginning contain all the instructions needed for the forming and developing of a large successful interactor. This strategy turns level (II) into case (b): the mid-sized interactors can self-organize into a successful large interactors by themselves, so thát no level (II) evolution need, nor can, take place. This strategy may also be described as "one level of evolution or even require environ (II) and may also be described as "two levels of evolving and eveloping of a sophisticated brain, without which no such evolution could take place. This strategy may also be described as "one level of on with two levels of development."

Note that this is the strategy of virtually all biological evolution, where it is extended to "one level of evolution with many levels of development." The evolution produces genomes which may completely instruct the forming and developing of a high hierarchy of completely instructed interactors – from proteins and cells to organisms and virtually all of societies of organisms. For instance, even the forming of an ant society is completely instructed by the ants' genomes. Not to be confused by the possible adaptability and flexibility of such societies, it is important to keep in mind that complete instructing need not be, and usually is not, closed deterministic programming: it may all ments more or less to contribute to the development at all levels.

Instructing for a higher-level evolution means that the mid-sized interactors do not receive from the small ones all the instructions they need to form and develop a large successful interactor. Instead, they receive instructions for seeking the missing instructions themselves, by own trial-and-error experimenting – in other words, by conducting level (II) evolution. This strategy repeats case (c) at level ution with two levels of development." Note that not to endow the mid-sized interactors with all the need instructions for the forming and developing of a successful large interactor, and make them instead search for the missing instructions themselves, does not diminish the amount of instructions they need. On the contrary, this amount is larger. This apparent paradox is immediately clear to all the computer programmers who know that programming a computer for performing a certain task needs a shorter program than programming it for finding out how to perform this task by itself. Compare also the complete genomic instructing of ants with the human genomic instructing for a higher-level evolution, which must include instructions for the formid

FROM GENERAL DARWINISM TO A CONCEPTUAL MODEL OF ECONOMIC CHANGE INTERACTORS AND INSTRUCTIONS IN ECONOMICS

Like in all social sciences, the smallest interactors in economics are human individuals, but attention is narrowed to their behaviors as economic agents – meaning, as usual, their ways of using scarce resources. But it must be kept in mind that this includes the forming, running and developing of economic organizations, and making these organizations evolve. Economic organizations of different sizes and tightness – from small and tightly organized households, workshops, and bureaus to large and more loosely organized national economies and supranational economic unions – are the larger interactors. For most of present purposes, it will suffice to consider two of their levels: (I) firms and government agencies, and (II) national economies.

That a market economy is regarded as an organization may need to be explained, as organizations are often defined as entities pursuing objectives, while markets are often viewed as orders which do not do so. The point is that markets do not indeed pursue the objectives of any of their participants, but they are automatic regulation devices with feedback loops that make them aim at certain states, and may thus be regarded "as if" they had objectives of their own. That these objectives may differ from those of their participants is precisely what raises problems for policy-for instance, a market economy may stubbornly aim at maintaining a lower growth and a higher unemployment than what all of its agents would wish it to do. The instructions of an economic organization are its "institutional rules," possible to visualize as the rules of a game. Each institutional rule constrains and thus shapes, but typically does not fully determine, the behaviors of the organization's members, and through these behaviors influences the organization's form, development and performance. According to their origins, institutional rules fall into formal, designed and imposed by certain top agent(s)-such as legislators in economies, or owners of firms-and informal, spread from anonymous innovators by spontaneous imitations-such as perhaps first clearly described by Hayek (1967). The effective institutional rules of most of economic organizations are mixtures of both.

While each organization has its own institutional rules, the same rules may be used in different organizations-for instance, different firms may use the same rules of corporate governance, or different national economies may use the same property rights. The rules of a higher level constrain the variety of permissible rules of the subordinate levels-for instance, the corporate law of a national economy constrains the variety of permissible rules of corporate governance within its firms. The behaviors of individuals of constrained by the rules of all organizations of which they are members-for instance, the behaviors of a firm's owners and employees are constrained both by the internal rules of the firm and by the overall rules of the entire economy. Under these constraints, their actual behaviors are determined in detail by their internal idiosyncratic instructions. They may respect an institutional rule voluntarily, if it coincides with some of their internal rules–such as a law that coincides with some of their moral norms–and/or because its violations are sanctioned.

Important constraints also work in the opposite direction. The internal instructions of individuals imply in part their motivations interms of utility, values and in part their cognitive abilities, including abilities to learn more or less bounded rationality, talents). Both impose constraints on what institutional rules they may be able to understand and willing to respect. While the constraint of will may be softened by increased incentives and/or sanctions, the constraint of understanding is harder. This appears to be why individuals of exceptionally bounded rationality may have difficulties with respecting even simple rules, while some highly intricate rules could not be properly understood by anyone.

Like interactors in general, economic organizations also form, function, develop and evolve–although most economists, with the exception of economic historians, usually assume that national economies are already formed, and consider initial forming only for smaller organizations within them. The main point of applying SGD to economics is to put institutional rules in the center, and use them to split the processes of economic change into development and evolution. The development of an organization consists of entry and exit of its agents and changes in their positions, relationships and behaviors - which leads in an economy to the forming and developing of markets, firms, and government agencies–all of this under the constraints of its actual institutional rules. The evolution consists of changes of these rules.

In principle, this split is simple, but in detail, it may cause difficulties that need to be clarified. First, it is only relative to the organization considered. An typical example is the evolution of rules of firms that is part of the development of the economy under its constant rules–such as the evolution of corporate governance of specific firms taking place under the constraints of a constant corporate law of the economy. Second, the distinction is more difficult to see in economics than in biology. There, evolution and development proceed at very different speeds, which makes it easy to distinguish one from the other: an organism can usually fully develop with a virtually constant genome, while the evolution of genomes is much slower, spanning over many generations of fully developed organisms. In contrast, the development of an economic organization and the evolution of its institutional rules often proceed at more comparable speeds, and may even be closely interwoven.

The closeness of the two speeds also increases the difficulties of judging the effects of different institutional rules on their organization. Some institutional rules may not have enough time to demonstrate their full development potential, as they may be changed before the development under their guidance comes anywhere close to maturity. And newly evolved institutional rules may not be given the opportunity to start with a new organization, but must do with the already formed and more or less developed organization left to them by their predecessors. This may prolong the time they need to show what they can achieve, as much of the previous development may has to be undone before the development under their guidance may start taking off. But none of these difficulties refutes the logic of the distinction. They only require careful attention to fine points in order to get the distinction right in concrete situations.

THE DEVELOPMENT OF AN ECONOMIC ORGANIZATION

An organization forms and develops by self-organizing of its members, which is based on their associative behaviors, instructed by its institutional rules. Some individuals may, and usually do, play more important roles than others–such as industrial entrepreneurs creating firms, or politicians organizing government agencies. But the roles of others are never entirely negligible: virtually all members more or less importantly contribute, positively or negatively, to how the self-organizing will unfold and the organization thus develop. To avoid all superficial analogies with the development of organisms, it is important to realize the differences, which mainly stem from differences between their respective basic agents–molecules in organisms and human individuals in economic organization. Most important are two: the former are internally instructed for more complex behaviors, and are more heterogeneous less standardized, than the latter. The higher complexity of human behaviors limits the possibilities of institutional rules to help: they cannot guide individuals as precisely as genomic instructions can guide molecules. Just like the rules of a game, they may only set more or less broad limits and leave individuals free to choose their behaviors within these limits. But then, the individuals are also less informed on how to behave, and must therefore use more of trial-and-error experimenting to find this out, than the molecules.

Moreover, as this complexity includes abilities to learn and adapt, the development of human organizations is complicated by additional feedback loops – such as the often discussed path-dependence–that change individual behaviors in function of the development, and this then changes its speed and/or direction in function of the behavioral changes. The heterogeneity implies that the development of an economic organization must solve more problems than the development of an organism. There, thanks to the highly standardized molecules, it is relatively easy for genomic instructions to make it sure–possibly with some minor trial-and-error experimenting– that molecules of guaranteed qualities will play the right roles within cells, and cells of guaranteed qualities will occupy the right positions within the organism. In contrast, the individuals who are to form and develop the organization may be of very different and in advance unknown talents, which raises the problems of recognizing their talents, designing their positions, selecting the right individuals for the right positions, and keeping the positions and the individuals adjusted to each other over time. All these problems must be solved, under the guidance of the organization's institutional rules, by the individuals' self-organizing, which must therefore involve much more of trial-and-error experimenting than the development of an organism. Examples of the developmental errors are the tried designs and the tried assignments of positions within the organization that turn out to cause serious inefficiencies undermining the organization's success–such as a too difficult job assigned to an insufficiently talented individual. The such errors may and do happen makes the success of the development strongly depend on the organization's internal selection - how precise, severe, and fast this selection is in detecting them and eliminating them -which in turn depends on the organization's institutional rules. But note well what is often overlooked: such an internal development selection, shaped by the organization's institutional rules differs from the external evolutionary selection imposed by environments–such as nature, competing organization, or a higher-level organization of which the organization may be a member–on which more below.

THE EVOLUTION OF ECONOMIC ORGANIZATIONS

An economic organization evolves, as noted, by changing its institutional rules–and thus changing its ways of functioning and developing, including its development potential. To see why the right actors for this central evolutionary role are institutional rules, consider the two main alternative views of socioeconomic change in which this role is given to other notions: to routines by Nelson and Winter (1982), and to memes by Dawkins (1976, 1982). Institutional rules turn out to occupy an advantageous middle ground between the two. They form a subset of memes, as only some memes, in addition to replicating from mind to mind, also instruct the minds on how to form, develop and make function organizations. Routines form a subset of theirs, as only some institutional rules may be so constraining that they prescribe individual behaviors step by step.

Why the middle ground is best can be explained as follows. The notion of memes is too broad, possibly corresponding to the entire genome of a multicellular organism, including the non-instructing "junk," but not to genes, which, in addition to replicating, instruct the protein synthesis, and thus crucially contribute to the organism's forming, functioning and developing. The notion of routines is too narrow, as routines do not really correspond to what the members of an organization have in common: many parts of many routines are specific to individuals, hidden in their idiosyncratic tacit knowledge. Moreover, both have the disadvantage of being less tangible than institutional rules. Memes are more difficult to identify because of the enormous variety and heterogeneity of the ideas that may spread from mind to mind. Routines are more difficult to identify because so many parts of them are tacit. In contrast, many institutional rules are clearly written laws, regulations, or charters. As demonstrated by ethnologists and organizational theorists, even the unwritten rules, such as informal social and cultural norms, can often be clearly identified and mapped.

The evolution of institutional rules, like the biological evolution of genomes, is also a kind of trial-and-error experimenting, structured according to Campbell (1965) into variety, selection, and retention here definitely not "replication". But it differs from biological evolution in several important respects. One is that the variety originates in two types of sources - formal and informal - corresponding to the two types of institutional rules. Another difference is that the tentative picking of the institutional rules to be tried - as, for instance, in the design of an economic reform - need not be, as noted, entirely random. Although far from perfectly informed, it may be helped by relevant learning, or hindered by false religious or ideological beliefs. Another important difference is that the performance tests of economic organizations, which determine the fate of their institutional rules, involve an extra success criterion. In addition to being tested for their coping with environments, as organisms are, economic organizations are moreover tested for their coping with their own members.

A comparison with an ant society may again illustrate. For the evolutionary success of the ants' genomes, this society only needs to be efficient enough to obtain all the needed resources from its environments, but they run no risk of being rejected by dissatisfied ants. In contrast, the institutional rules of an organization, to succeed in their evolution, must moreover make themselves and the outcomes to which they lead sufficiently acceptable, possibly with the help of feasible enforcement, to its members. Because of this extra success criterion, the evolution of institutional rules can be retarded by repetitions of cycles of political and economic crises: institutional rules that lead to economic efficiency, and thus allow their organization successfully to cope with its environments, may be disliked and politically rejected by the members, while the politically preferred institutional rules may cause inefficiencies that throw the organization into a deep economic crisis, and be thus made unsustainable by the environments. What appears to be the only way to prevent an unhappy end, in which some of the crises would grow into a catastrophe, is double learning: humans must learn which institutional rules can make their organizations efficient enough not to cause too deep economic crises, and then learn to like, or at least tolerate and respect, such rules, not to cause too deep political crises.

MULTILEVEL EVOLUTION AND DEVELOPMENT IN ECONOMICS

Much about several levels of economic evolution and development can be understood. The small interactors can be interpreted as individuals, the large interactor as their national economy, and the mid-sized interactors as their smaller organizations–such as firms and government agencies. The instructions involved are in the individuals' genomes, in the internal institutional rules of their organizations, and in the overall institutional rules of the entire economy. But there are three special points that should be noted. First, to avoid confusion, it is important to keep in mind that the processes involved may switch names from evolution to development, and vice versa, depending on the level considered. The already noted example is the evolution of the institutional rules of firms that is part of the development of the economy.

Second, compared to the "two levels of evolution with two levels of development". There is one more level of development. Level zero, which has again no evolution, as human genomes are assumed constant, now involves the important development of human behaviors by extensive learning and adapting, for which these genomes provide rich initial instructing. It was already noted that human learning and adapting may complicate the development of economic organizations by feedback loops already at one level. It is rather obvious that many more such loops may complicate their development and evolution at several levels. Here, however, it is only possible to note that the present conceptual framework can recognize them and make room for them, without examining them in detail. Third, the inter-level relationships that appear to require most attention in economic practice are those involving performance tests, success criteria, and selection. The main principle is that the institutional rules of an organization whose performance is severely tested by environments must transmit, to remain selected and retained, much of this severity to the internal performance tests and selection criteria for its members. Thus, for example, the institutional rules of an economy whose performance is tested in severe international competition must transmit much of this severity, together with its selection consequences, to the performance testing of its firms, and their internal institutional rules must transmit much of that severity, together with its selection consequences, to the performance testing of their employees, to begin with their managers. In details, this principle may require qualifications due to well-known aspects of human psychology - such as the existence of limits to the pressure that can make individuals perform better rather than worse–but here also these details must be left aside.

GROUP SELECTION

The issue of group selection is perhaps the clearest this issue is still highly controversial and reputed for being difficult to understand, while the framework can explain it quite easily. First, the framework makes the simple but essential point that groups are interactors, and cannot therefore be units of selection. It points out that groups are formed, developed and made function by their individual members who share and respect what are for each group its specific institutional rules, and that it is only these rules that can be selected and lastingly retained in some evolutionary memory. Group themselves may keep changing in many ways–their members may come and go, and they may even voluntarily dissolve. They can therefore be only units of testing of their institutional rules: their performance is tested according to certain success criteria, and if they succeed, it is their rules that are selected and lastingly retained– e.g., written down or remembered by some of its former members. They may then be used by similar individuals for the forming and developing of similar, similarly successful groups.

A complication is that the institutional rules of a group can only be a limited part of all the instructions that govern individual behaviors. To recall, the members must first of all possess some internal instructions that enable them to form groups in general, and according to the institutional rules of a specific group in particular. In consequence, there are several types of group selection, which differ in the proportion and the origins of the initial instructions, and in the variety of the institutional rules that these instructions allow the members to adopt. To avoid confusion, at least three types of groups must be distinguished: (i) groups formed instinctively by animals without social learning–such as the earlier considered ant society; (ii) independent groups of humans–such as a tribe living in the wilderness; (iii) groups of humans within a larger society. In a type (i) group, all its institutional rules are part of their members' genomes, which leave no room for any alternatives. Whatever might be called "group selection" must therefore be an inseparable part of the biological evolution of these genomes.

In a type (ii) group, all the initial instructions of its members are also part of their genomes. But, being humans, the genomes enable them extensively to learn and adapt, so that the variety of institutional rules that they are able to adopt is consequently large although not unlimited. The responsibility for the performance of such a group is shared by its institutional rules and the genomes of its members, both of which thus also are, at their respective evolutionary levels, the targets of the selection. In a type (iii) group, the initial instructions of its members, in addition to those contained in their genomes, moreover include the institutional rules of the larger society - such as its cultural including religious norms, and its legal framework. These rules may crowd out much of the variety of institutional rules of groups that the members of the society can possibly adopt. This shifts some of the responsibility for groups' performance to the institutional rules of the society, which thus become a third target of the selection. That these rules are indeed co-responsible can be seen by considering that the forming of groups is easier, and they have more chances to succeed, in some cultures and under some laws than in other cultures and under other laws. That human genomes are co-responsible for the performance of human groups and societies may not be immediately clear and calls therefore for explanation. The point is that the genomes may indeed matter only little for how humans actually behave, but they are fully responsible for the variety of behaviors that their bearers, when instructed by different institutional rules, might possibly learn. This responsibility becomes critical if the success of a group or a society requires individual behaviors that do not belong to this variety - such as behaviors that are more altruistic or more rational than what the genomes allow their bearers to learn.

NEW QUESTIONS THAT HELP BRING TOGETHER DIFFERENT FIELDS OF ECONOMICS

There are three relatively new fields of economics to which the framework is most closely related, although so far they have themselves kept rather separated from each other: cognitive economics, institutional economics, and evolutionary economics. In addition to accommodating most of their actual questions and answers, the framework raises for them a few new questions that may help bring them together. For cognitive economics, the main new questions are: (1) What is reasonable to assume about the genomically given abilities of humans to learn and adopt different institutional rules, and thus adapt to different types of economies and societies? (2) What is reasonable to assume about the bounds of human rationality and about the inequalities of their distribution in society?

Question (1) inquires into the limits of what may be called "universal social grammar," a sister notion to the genomically given universal grammar that determines and limits the abilities of humans to learn languages, compellingly argued to exist by Chomsky. Its answer is important for questions about the evolution of institutional rules and about the possibilities of influencing this evolution by reform policies.

The answer to question (2) is important for two questions about the development of an economy: (a) To how high complexity may its top jobs be allowed to develop without overtaxing the cognitive abilities of its even most talented individuals? (b) How sharp selection must be institutionalized to find for the top jobs the most talented individuals, or at least protect these jobs from incapable ones? The point here is that the smaller the rationality inequalities, the less sharp selection is needed, and vice versa. Institutional economics is directly concerned with the questions about the evolution of institutional rules and the possibilities of their reforms, which have been explored from its side by several authors. The new question for this economics is: What are the effects of different institutional rules on the self-organizing of individuals, through them on the formation, the development and evolution of production organizations, and ultimately on the development of an entire economy?

This question demands institutional economics to extend attention from its usual focus on transaction costs and other incentives to the dynamics of industrial change. Incentives undoubtedly remain important, but this dynamics strongly depends also on other, by institutional economists so far less explored factors–such as the freedom of entry and the tradability of ownership of firms, needed for allowing a rich variety of entrepreneurial trials, and the effectiveness of the selection by market competition, needed for enforcing precise and rapid elimination of the committed errors. The basic idea for analysis is that the institutional rules which allow a rich variety of entrepreneurial trials while enforcing a rapid and precise elimination of errors are superior to those rules which limit the trials and let last the errors.

Institutional economics is moreover demanded to pay more attention to the differences between, and interrelations of, different levels or institutional rules–such as the corporate governance of specific firms and the corporate law of the entire economy. Most institutional economists appear to deal with only one of these levels, without being very clear on how the two levels interrelate. Clarity about their differences and interrelations is important for several issues of reform policies. Turning to evolutionary economics, the first implication is that not all the topics that economists who call themselves evolutionary study are really evolutionary. In particular, in the changes of technologies, firms, and industries within capitalist market economies, which, following the classical works of Schumpeter (1934) and Nelson and Winter (1982), are perhaps the most studied topics, the only evolution may be the one of the firms' institutional rules. Otherwise all of that is industrial development, implicitly assumed to take place under constant institutional rules of market capitalism. The main new question here is complementary to the one raised for institutional economics: How does industrial development depend on the prevailing institutional rules? In what ways and at what speed this development would unfold under different variants of institutional rules? The variants that now appear most important to examine are those of the rules for market economies with different degrees and forms of government regulation. This means that to be really evolutionary at the level of national economies, evolutionary economists would have to join the institutional ones who study the evolution of national and supranational institutional rules. Note that this is a promising research strategy for both: the former could learn from the latter what they ignore about institutional rules, and the latter could learn from the former what they ignore about industrial development. Such a cooperation of evolutionary and institutional economists also appears to be the only way to a clear understanding of this evolution.

SOME ELEMENTARY ADVICE FOR POLICY ANALYSIS AND DEVELOPMENT ECONOMICS

If all the above questions were given the right answers, these could help solve many problems of economic policy and economic development. The two categories largely overlap, as the most urgent problems of development are just policy problems, especially those concerning institutional reforms. But without waiting for the answers, the framework can provide some general advice already now. This advice is mostly limited to the framing and structuring of these problems, and getting an effective handle on them. It can be summarized in the following points: (1) identify all the relevant institutional rules; (2) distinguish their evolution from the development of the organizations they instruct; (3) map the effects that different institutional rules may exert on the performance and the development of different organizations; (4) consider how different institutional rules may evolve.

Three more points concern policy problems: (5) ask what government could do, and what it cannot do, to help, and not harm, the development of the economy and/or the evolution of its institutional rules; (5) keep in mind that the government itself, with its motivations and abilities, is the product of certain development under certain institutional rules; (6) when estimating the effects of any policy, do not forget to consider its secondary effects on all important developmental and evolutionary processes. This last point is particularly important, as it was because of these effects that many policies which appeared successful in the short turned out to cause a deep crisis, while many of those which at first appeared hopeless later proved successful.

4

Biological Adaptation in Human Societies

Accordingly, biological adaptation and its antipode, maladaptation are "variables" for humankind just as they are for any other species. Adaptation involves much more than simply "filling our bellies," as one critic of an adaptationist paradigm charged, and even in affluent Western societies the provision of adequate food and shelter are problematical for a significant number of people (Riches 1997). But more to the point, the problem of meeting basic survival and reproductive needs is an imperative for every one of us, whether we are aware of it, or care about, it or not. In fact, our biological needs routinely impose themselves on the daily rhythms of our lives. And if our basic needs are not met, there will be significant biological adaptive consequences, not to mention psychological disturbances. What the value-relativists overlook is the fact that survival and reproduction are inescapable daily problems for all of us; we must actively pursue the meeting of our survival and reproductive needs or we will fail to do so. In this light, an economic science that is focussed exclusively on the psychology of human preferences/ satisfactions and is studiously indifferent to the bio-logic of adaptation excludes by fiat a bedrock source of psychological motivation and causation in economic life.

THE PROBLEM OF MEASURING ADAPTATION

The core analytical challenge, then, is how do we measure adaptation? The ultimate biological criterion of adaptation is Darwinian "fitness". Traditionally, this has been defined as the ability of an individual to produce viable progeny, or of an interbreeding population to reproduce itself. However, in recent years the concept of inclusive fitness the summed proportion of one's own genes shared by close relatives as well as progeny has been increasingly favored as a more satisfactory measure. In population biology, which dominated evolutionary theorizing during the middle years of this century, the primary tool used to measure adaptation is the "selection coefficient," a quantitative measure of the relative reproductive efficacy of different genotypes in discrete breeding populations. This rigorously analytical approach has been widely used in laboratory and field studies of micro evolutionary change. However, the problems involved in applying this approach to the larger evolutionary process, including sociocultural evolution in humankind, are manifold. Only recently have biologists come to appreciate the complex relationship between adaptation at the micro level viz individuals and at higher levels of organization viz trait groups, social organizations, demes, species, ecological communities. Yet in dealing with complexly organized species such as humankind, nothing less than a multi-leveled approach will do. The most important unit of adaptation in humankind must often be defined in relation to units of economic and political organization – that is, units of functional interdependency – that go beyond anything in the rest of nature. By the same token, there has been a growing appreciation in recent years of the complex relationship in humankind between economic, social, psychological and biological measures of "well-being."

BASIC NEEDS AND ADAPTATION

The concept of basic needs can be grounded in the biological problem of survival and reproduction. To our knowledge, the first social scientist to espouse in significant detail a basic needs approach to adaptation was the anthropologist Bronislaw Malinowski (1944). For Malinowski a society is preeminently an organized system of cooperatively pursued activities. It is purposive in nature, and its purposes relate to the satisfaction of basic needs – i.e., "the system of conditions in the human organism, in the cultural setting, and in the relation of both to the natural environment, which are sufficient and necessary for the survival of the group and organism".In contrast with the hyphenated structural-functionalism so-called of Comte, Durkheim, and their descendants, Malinowski's "pure functionalism," like Herbert Spencer's before him, was concerned with relating the complexities of cultural behavior to "organic processes in the human body and to those concomitant phases of behavior which we call desire or drive, emotion or physiological disturbance, and which, for one reason or another, have to be regulated and coordinated by the apparatus of culture". The structure that Malinowski developed for his essentially biological functionalism is reproduced here in synoptic form:

Table I
Malinowski's Framework

Basic Needs	*Cultural Responses*
Metabolism	Commissariat
Reproduction	Kinship
Bodily comforts	Shelter
Safety	Protection
Movement	Activities
Growth	Training
Health	Hygiene

Malinowski drafted this listing only for the sake of simplicity; his textual discussion provides more detailed and more sophisticated treatment. For example, his "health" need has a dual significance. In a narrow sense it refers to the absence of physical impairment or sickness, but in a broader sense it is a condition that is affected by all the other categories. Malinowski also went on to show that these primary needs give rise to a set of "derived" societal needs. Malinowski used the fork as an example. Can anyone doubt that the function performed by a fork a "capability" in Sen's terminology is a significant part of the explanation for the existence and the design of this commonplace cultural artifact? Yet the fork is not a cultural universal. So more information is needed to account for how the fork was invented and diffused and why it is used in some cultures and not in others.

In light of contemporary anthropological theory one finds many shortcomings in Malinowski's formulations. One might take exception, for instance, to Malinowski's claim that his basic needs approach was the only valid set of external, or "etic," criteria for cross-cultural classification and comparisons. Nevertheless we believe that his basic approach was sound, indeed essential to a view of human societies that is in touch with the biological fundamentals. Another major progenitor of the basic needs approach is the humanistic psychologist Abraham Maslow. Maslow's famous hierarchy of human needs involved nothing less than a theory of human nature and motivation. According to Maslow, the human being is neither a behavioral sponge as the Behaviorists implied nor a tormented neurotic as some Freudians hold but a natural innocent endowed with an array of biologically based needs that ascend hierarchically through five categories from "deficiency motivations" which derive from such physiological needs as food, water, shelter, sleep, sex to "being motivations," at the apex of which is "self-actualization," a kind of beatific state in which one achieves the full use of one's talents and potentialities. Maslow's five categories are: (1) physiological needs, (2) safety needs, (3) "belongingness" and love needs, (4) esteem needs, and (5) self-actualization or "growth" needs.

Despite its popularity among various psychologically oriented social scientists, Maslow's hierarchy gained only marginal status among experimental psychologists because it did not have empirical support. Although it has been frequently invoked to justify a particular moral position or to anchor a model of social behavior, such uses are pseudoscientific. Fitzgerald concludes: "Most psychologists regard the purely empirical study and validation of a hierarchy of needs in Maslow's sense as presenting immense and perhaps insurmountable problems. It is clear that insofar as a potentially verifiable aspect can be abstracted from this ambiguous amalgam, Maslow's theory of human needs has not been empirically established to any significant extent" Another attempt to create a theoretical foundation for the concept of basic needs, and a major contribution to the debate, is Doyal and Gough's book, A Theory of Human Need (1991). As stated in their introduction, their goal was a "coherent, rigorous theory of human need. We argue that basic needs can be shown to exist, that individuals have a right to the optimal satisfaction of these needs and that all human liberation should be measured by assessing the degree to which such satisfaction has occurred"

Doyal and Gough also address the problem of defining basic needs. To be sure, the term is used in many different ways, from psychological motivations or "drives" to strictly physiological requisites viz food, water, sleep, waste elimination to any conceivable want or preference whatsoever. Following the lead of philosopher Garrett Thomson (1987) in his thoughtful monograph on the concept of "needs," Doyal and Gough argue that the bedrock implication of the term should be that some specific "harm" will occur if the posited need is unfulfilled, whether we are aware of it or not. Furthermore, some needs are universal. To quote Thomson (1987) "Fundamental needs are inescapable; we cannot escape the fact that we must all ail and eventually die without among other things food, water, and air." Accordingly, Doyal and Gough focus on "goals which are instrumentally and universally linked to the avoidance of serious harm"

Doyal and Gough claim that their theory provides clarification because it dictates which intermediate needs are important in any culture for the satisfaction of their two overarching basic needs. "The only claim for inclusion...is whether or not any set of satisfier characteristics universally and positively contributes to physical health and autonomy". Their list of eleven intermediate needs includes:

Table 2

Nutritional Food and Clean Water	*Protective Housing*
A Non-hazardous Work Environment	A Non-hazardous Physical Environment
Appropriate Health Care	Security in Childhood
Significant Primary Relationships	Physical Security
Economic Security	Appropriate Education
Safe Birth Control and Child-bearing	

SURVIVAL INDICATORS

The Survival Indicators approach is not grounded in any normative concern or public policy objective. It is grounded in the empirical problem of biological survival and reproduction adaptation for the human species. It attempts to measure the current status of an individual, or a group, or a population as objectively as possible with respect to this transcendent human concern. It is not about what ought to be — about well-being or happiness. It is about basic needs, sensu stricto. It is addressed to the widespread criticism that the concept of social indicators, particularly in relation to basic needs, lacks a theoretical foundation. It does not seek to promote any desirable political objective but rather to specify and measure human adaptation as precisely as possible. It does not contradict various ad hoc, pragmatic or normative approaches, nor is it antagonistic to the concept of well-being. But it does have a distinctive analytical focus that seeks to rationalize and give logical coherence to the effort to measure relevant aspects of the human condition in a systematic way. Finally, it is designed for use not only with the many millions of people who daily experience the deprivation of their basic needs, or who have a genuine anxiety about the problem, but also for those fewer among us whose basic needs are so well provided for that we may be complacent, or even oblivious to the problem. To repeat, biological adaptation is a problem that exists for all of us, whether we are aware of it, or care about it, or not.

A anunced point is that the Survival Indicators paradigm involves a highly nuanced conceptualization of basic needs. In particular, we attempt to distinguish between (1) primary needs, (2) instrumental needs, (3) perceived needs, (4) dependencies, and (5) wants or tastes and preferences. Basic needs refer only to the first two of these categories primary and instrumental needs. Primary needs are irreducible and no substitutable. One cannot substitute food for water, or sleep for sex (well, not as a rule). Primary needs coincide with the broad functional requisites for adaptation. They include a number of what Doyal and Gough define as "intermediate needs." Instrumental needs, on the other hand, are the derived adaptive means capabilities or satisfiers. Instrumental needs may be reducible to primary needs may be subsumed, may be substitutable for various functional equivalents e.g., beef, versus chicken or eggs and may vary widely, depending on the precise adaptive context internal, external and cultural.

Thermoregulation, for example, is a primary human need, but the instrumental needs for clothing, heating fuel, electric power and/or thermally insulated shelter will vary from one climatic environment and culture to another. Similarly, mobility is an irreducible primary need, but within that category there may be instrumental needs for horses, bicycles, snow shoes, automobiles or wheelchairs, depending upon the context. In fact, it could be argued that walking, though pancultural and biologically primordial in humankind, is not always essential—not a primary need. There are cultural contexts in which various substitutes for walking are available, among them prosthetic devices, the services of others caretakers and carriers, and transportation and communications technologies that provide functional equivalents. Walking can be viewed as a biologically evolved capability that is derived from a primary need, just as a compact body build or a thick layering of subcutaneous fat may represent physiological adaptations for cold climates that have evolved in relation to our primary need for thermoregulation. By the same token, cultures may significantly alter the adaptive value of various physiological adaptations like walking—or, for that matter, running. Human technologies may also compensate for various physiological deficiencies, say myopia, or diabetes, or even a defective organ.

It is also important to distinguish between needs and so-called "drives", or internal sources of motivation. Needs are functional requisites; drives are psychobiological mechanisms and various correlates that we may perceive as needs. Human sexuality involves a drive that we sometimes colloquially call a need, but in reality it is an evolved instrumentality for serving our primary reproductive need. The empirical distinction between the two concepts need versus drive is evident both in the practice of birth control and in artificial insemination. By the same token, a person may eat either more or less than is nutritionally-necessary in response to the promptings of hunger. Accordingly, in our paradigm the various motivational states, as distinct from basic needs, are catagorized under (1) perceived needs, (2) dependencies, and (3) wants.

The litmus test for a primary need, according to this formulation, has nothing to do with whether or not the need is reflected in correlative psychobiological motivations. Nor does it matter that these primary needs vary—as they do in systematic ways that are more or less well understood. Rather, it matters how much they vary, why they do so, and with what consequences. Primary needs vary within a relatively narrow range, are pancultural, cannot be substituted for one another or replaced by functional equivalents, are largely independent of our "higher" motivations and the specific environmental and cultural context, and may vary significantly as a result of biologically-based individual differences notably including age and somewhat less so in relation to the environmental and cultural context. But most important, they are tightly linked to the potential for doing "harm" in the biological survival sense. Instrumental needs serve the primary needs. Some instrumental needs are so pervasive as to be close to primary needs in their importance: e.g., exogenous energy, protective shelter, basic utensils and tools, clothing, language skills, and walking. Such instrumental needs are in fact the focal concern of many recent efforts to develop basic needs indicators. It could be noted that many of the items in these paradigms are not primary needs at all but actually refer to instrumental needs.

It should also be emphasized that instrumental needs can vary widely, depending upon the context. For instance, the instrumental need for a means of waste removal can range from dug latrines to open sewers to the latest high-technology waste treatment plants. Likewise, telephones and automobiles may be of little use in a simple folk society but may constitute a "need" in the strict sense of the term for people who live in a complex developed society. Also, some instrumental needs take the form of economic goods and services, while others relate to features of the cultural environment.

It is important to recognize that, over the long sweep of our cultural and technological evolution, our various primary needs have generated complex hierarchies of instrumental needs. Our need for mobility, for instance, has resulted not only in the invention of automobiles but in the creation of additional instrumental needs for auto mechanics, paved roads, stop signs, the oil industry, gas stations, highway patrols, traffic courts, and so on. In fact, many inventions have been catalysts for others; if necessity is the mother of invention, as the old saying goes, the reverse is also true; inventions are the mother of necessity. Moreover, many of our instrumental technologies involve complex networks of economic interdependency. Take away the tire industry, for example, and it would cripple the automobile and trucking industries and very likely devastate our economy.

Dependencies are induced, often non-survival-related needs, some of which may even be destructive such as an addiction to heroin, alcohol, or sugar; or compulsive gambling; or smoking. Perceived needs are those desired objects that the individual thinks he or she needs, regardless of the actual situation. And wants reflect the individual's less urgent motivations, goals, and aspirations, very possibly unrelated any biological requisite. Of course, these categories often overlap. For example, a person's primary nutritional need for protein, carbohydrates, vegetables and various vitamins and minerals may lead to the selection of a particular instrumental need, or "satisfier" Some of these primary needs domains may seem to be self-evident. Many of them can be found on other lists of basic needs. Others of our postulated needs may appear to be puzzling or vague and may call for some elaboration. In actuality, there are complications and ramifications associated with every one of these needs, some of which we view very differently from those in more conventional treatments.

Nutrition: It is a safe bet that nutrition is included on virtually every social indicators shopping list. Yet, as noted earlier, even an obvious primary need like nutrition has many components, many variables, and even perhaps some remaining unknowns. Appropriate quantities of calories are not enough to satisfy this need, no matter how many may be available to us—a point that was underscored recently when it was reported that the Chinese diet is seriously deficient in iodine, which has resulted in a very high incidence of mental retardation in that country. Indeed, malnutrition of one kind or another remains a serious problem in many parts of the world, despite our much better understanding today of what constitutes an adequate diet. Conversely, it is possible to consume too much of a good thing—sugars, fats and overdoses of certain vitamins being especially notable problems in some developed societies.

Not only does a simple term like "nutrition" mask the complexities involved in providing for this primary need but it does not even begin to account for the vast human enterprise, and the enormous range of absolutely essential instrumental needs, upon which our nutritional needs also depend. The list includes, among other things: fertile soil, a suitable climate, water, irrigation systems, fertilizers, seeds, tools in great profusion, farm machinery of great complexity, pesticides, animal husbandry, processing and packaging industries and personnel, transportation and distribution systems, plus exogenous energy inputs of various kinds in order to power farm equipment, move water, provide fuel for transportation systems, make fertilizers, process food stuffs and, not least, to cook the many foods that would be toxic or infectious if eaten raw. With the exception, perhaps, of the few remaining hunter-gatherer societies and even they depend on primitive technologies, all the rest of the world's economies depend, absolutely, on a formidable array of food production technologies, and this says nothing about the enormous quantity of information and human skill that is also involved. If there is food on our table tonight, it is only because a vast human "food-chain" performed its job with only minor glitches. In this light, it is a bit fatuous to claim, as some theorists do, that this basic need is not an important consideration in a developed economy. It is an adaptive modality in the strict sense in which literally billions of people participate worldwide, and it is a relentless daily challenge everywhere.

Mental Health: The inclusion of mental health as a primary need might seem questionable to some, except for the fact that biological adaptation also implies the capacity of an organism to engage in productive, life-sustaining activity. Mental health is not used here in relation to personal fulfillment, happiness or a carefree existence. Rather it refers to a "state of mind" that allows an individual to carry on "normal functioning" and self-care without significant impairment. There is a very large research literature on various cognitive, mental, even emotional dysfunctions in animals and humans alike. Furthermore, in the case of a complex social animal like Homo sapiens, the concept of mental dysfunction extends to more subtle aspects of individual psychology like self-esteem, emotional stability and social integration and status. The list of mental disorders for which biological causes are directly implicated includes, among others, schizophrenia and the schizoid spectrum, manic depressive psychosis, various depressive syndromes, Alzheimer's disease, Parkinson's disease, porphyria, Down syndrome, autism, aphasia i.e various speech disabilities, alexia i.e various reading disabilities, some forms of mental retardation, and possibly certain psychopathic behavioral disorders. Of course, many environmental and cultural influences can also greatly affect cognitive, emotional and behavioral functioning, from childhood experiences.

Reproduction: This is one of two primary needs domains in our framework that may seem to be problematic and debatable. They are not usually found on lists of basic needs, with the notable exception of Doyal and Gough's dubious treatment. Under the heading of reproduction, the focus is on conception and the status of the mother and fetus, along with attendant information, nutrition, health services and the like. The birthing process also involves a distinct set of health risks, services and skills. Indeed, these needs beg the question: In a world where excess population growth may in fact seem to be a threat to our survival—a part of the problem—how can we justify including reproduction and child nurturance among our primary needs? One reason is that it is absolutely essential from a theoretical perspective; it happens to be an inescapable part of the "struggle for existence." Nature has made reproduction an integral part of the adaptation problem for all living species, like it or not, and a significant portion of our collective activity as a species is devoted to reproduction and its "aftermath". Indeed, the world population problem is not a result of reproduction per se but of too much reproduction—an excess over what is needed to sustain ourselves, at least at the population and species levels.

Indicators of Biological Adaptation

We believe that these fourteen primary needs, and the instrumental means that are required to satisfy them in a given context, provide a solid foundation for evaluating adaptation in human societies in a manner that accords with Darwinian criteria. Equally important, we believe this framework provides a logical and solidly-grounded definition of "basic needs" for the purpose of social monitoring and welfare economics. We postulate that the denial, or serious deprivation, of any one of these needs will cause significant "harm" in relation to an individual's chances of continued survival and successful reproduction. While this perspective is to varying degrees compatible with other paradigms, it has the advantage of providing a rigorous external criterion for defining and measuring basic needs in any given society. So, how does one go about measuring basic needs-satisfaction? Where are the so-called Survival Indicators? If the problem of defining our basic needs is anything but simple and straightforward, measuring them is even less so. In fact, it is not possible to develop an allpurpose set of Survival Indicators. There are a number of different ways of measuring needs satisfaction, depending upon the analytical focus, the analyst's objectives, and various practical data-gathering considerations. In addition, there are many complex measurement and validation issues, especially where instrumental needs are involved.

Personal Fitness Profile: This involves direct assessments of an individual's status in relation to the fulfillment of each of his or her primary needs in a given context. The term Personal Fitness Profile does not refer to "physical fitness," of course, but to fitness in the Darwinian sense. It is not equivalent to health, or well-being, or the absence of relative deprivation but focuses pointedly on a person's functional capacities and the resources of various kinds that are needed to support them. Personal fitness defines the capacity to function effectively in relation to the activities that are instrumental to survival, reproduction and the nurturance of offspring in a given environment; it involves the ability to carry on normal functioning and to engage in productive activity. Several points are in order here regarding the concepts of "normal functioning" and the ability to engage in "productive activities." We are not here referring to self-actualization, or optimum human development, or the like. We are referring to the more limited capacity to provide for one's own basic needs—self-care and the ability to engage in whatever daily activities are required for adaptation in a given environment. Personal fitness is not unrelated to a broad definition of personal "health" but it is not as expansive as the WHO definition. Also, it should be stressed that the term "normally" is not as vague and imprecise as it may seem. "Normally" means in accordance with performance norms that can be specified in various ways that are not mutually exclusive: societal work and productivity standards, medical assessment standards, specific physiological and mental tests, and self-evaluations.

Personal Fitness Index: It utilizes a "negative" approach. That is, it is designed to measure degrees of "harm", or decrements to normal functioning by a given individual in a given context as a result of deficits in satisfying one or more of the fourteen primary needs—that is, in obtaining the relevant instrumental means.

Population Fitness Profile: This concept provides a framework for the use of aggregate indicators of adaptation, ranging from public health statistics to economic measures relating to the per capita provision of various instrumental resources. Measures of distributive equity would also be highly relevant. Among the obvious candidate measures at the primary needs level are life expectancy, infant and child mortality, accidental deaths and injuries, suicides, violent crimes, diseases, substance abuse data and pollution levels. Relevant instrumental needs would include such indicators as employment and income data, access to health services, immunizations, shelter, transportation, schooling, public health measures, and much more.

Given the fact that individual reproductive output varies widely in any given population, even when the population as a whole may be growing, we believe that this aspect of human adaptation is most appropriately measured at the population level. For a very small population with abundant resources, overall population growth is obviously adaptive. But for large human populations, especially those that are pressing the limits of their resources, population stability over time is arguably a more adaptive strategy in strict Darwinian terms. This criterion, in turn, implies a bipolar measuring rod; reproduction at the "replacement" level would be viewed as optimal, and anything either above or below that rate would be less adaptive.

Population Fitness Index: It may be that the most inclusive and practicable measure of "fitness" for any given human population will be found at the aggregate level, where statistical sampling techniques and routine bureaucratic reporting procedures provide a more economical means of acquiring the necessary data base. Very briefly, our Population Fitness Index is based upon the degree to which a given population falls short of its collective capacity to function normally and engage in productive activity during a given unit of time. Thus, over the period of one year, the maximum number of "Darwins" available to an entire population would be equal to the size of the population multiplied by 365. Births during the year would add units to the total "stock," just as deaths would deplete it. Of course, no population ever realizes its maximum potential productivity. Decrements or losses occur through mortality, morbidity, and a plethora of other restrictions to normal daily activity. The Population Fitness Index, then, represents a population-wide summary measure of the actual degree of "harm" to a given population - the decrement to its aggregate functional capabilities.

Compared to a sophisticated economic measure like GNP, Population Fitness Index is admittedly a very crude indicator. Some obvious shortcomings include the following: Much loss of productivity goes unreported, while some reported losses are bureaucratic artifacts and are not empirically-valid. Estimates of functional decrements based on various categories of disability can be very misleading, especially where compensatory prostheses are available. Some productivity losses are also implicit in the statistics on unemployment, but they were not included because the exact relationship is very uncertain. The functional losses suffered by our homeless population are also difficult to gauge. Conversely, the losses associated with the prison population may be overstated, since many prisoners do engage in various personal and/or prison related activities. Likewise, visits to doctors' offices may or may not be associated with a loss of functional capacities. Some of these visits involve routine medical examinations. Others may involve a variety of conditions that cause pain or discomfort but do not materially affect a person's functioning. Still others may involve conditions that are already reflected in our other categories of statistics. On the other side of the ledger, many patients endure much more than a single day of lost productivity in connection with a visit to the doctor, while those who visit nonphysicians or various unorthodox healers are not even included in the statistics.

SOME IMPLICATIONS

From a biological perspective, our primary needs provide the inner logic i.e the bio-logic of economic life. They represent the skeletal structure upon which economies are built, and it is possible to view all of economic, social and political life in terms of its relationship (if any) to the survival imperatives. It could be noted that much of our economic activity is in fact "instrumental" to our survival; it is either directly or indirectly related to the satisfaction of our biological needs. To be sure, some economic activity is very tangential or not at all related.

In fact, some activities are destructive to our adaptive needs. Smoking and hard drugs are obvious examples, but so is almost any other activity that is carried to extremes—for the simple reason that our survival and reproductive needs are manifold; if we satisfy any one of these needs to excess, we may well jeopardize other needs. In other words, there is an empirical, biological basis for Aristotle's venerable concept of the "golden mean."

Many insights about economic, social and political life may be gained by viewing them from an adaptation perspective. For instance, it might shed further light on such traditional economic concepts as "discretionary income," "demand elasticity," and the logic of "substitutability". But more important, our biological needs create economic imperatives which allow us to formulate many "if-then" predictions about our economic choices and behaviors. Many of these predictions already make intuitive sense to us. For instance, we can predict in general but not in every detail what would happen if the water supply for a major metropolitan area were to be suddenly, irreversibly contaminated. Likewise, we can make predictions at the individual level about how a person's priorities will change as a consequences of the prolonged deprivation of any one of their primary needs excepting possibly reproduction and child nurturance.

One of the major challenges for bioeconomics, then, is to utilize the biological/adaptation perspective as an analytical paradigm. This, in turn, implies a revisioning of our basic assumptions about the human condition and the underlying purpose of human societies. An organized society may be viewed as, quintessentially, a "collective survival enterprise." The bulk of our economic activities and processes are related to meeting our basic survival needs. Moreover, the functional interdependencies that exist within any complex economy are both profound and inescapable — and contingent. Such a revisioning presents an important theoretical opportunity. But more important, at this critical juncture in our evolution as a species it is also an increasingly urgent moral imperative.

BIOECONOMIC ANALYSIS OF DARWIN THEORY

In the Origin of Species, Darwin presents his well known theory of biological evolution. Inspired by Thomas Malthus, as Darwin himself acknowledges it in his notebooks, this theory exposes the concepts and mechanisms that guide biological evolution. These concepts - "natural selection" and "struggle for life" - have also been used by Herbert Spencer and other scholars to explain politics, economics, social and morals, giving birth to what is called social Darwinism. Social Darwinism can thus be described as a specific version of, a transference to human societies of Darwin's theory of biological evolution. Thus, a Darwinian or a biological theory of social evolution, this doctrine argues that the functioning and evolution of human societies follows the same mechanisms as nature or non human societies. However, to refer to "natural selection" only is too broad a way to characterise social Darwinism. In fact, a precise definition of this doctrine cannot be separated from the meaning it received in the second half of the 19th century. Now, within the context of triumphant capitalism, natural selection was closely associated with the survival of the fittest: "To the Anglo-Saxon imperialist, or to the rising capitalist produced by the industrial revolution, natural selection meant the survival of the fittest competitor". Then, social Darwinists used "survival of the fittest" to transform Darwinism into a "quasi-ontological racial discourse" based on "a redefinition of 'fitness' as 'intelligence' and an identification of 'intelligence' with the 'white' races". This is the reason why social is associated with unregulated and uncontrolled capitalism and unrestricted laissez-faire and some of its consequences such as racism, nationalism and imperalism.

Darwin's biology can certainly not be interpreted as social Darwinism defined so specifically. In particular, one of the most significant aspect of social Darwinism–the role given to "survival of the fittest" - plays a different and even minor role in Darwin's theory of social evolution. The distance with Spencer and social Darwinism that Darwin seems cautious to put forward illustrates the difference that exists between his theory of biological evolution and his theory of social evolution, which we found in particular exposed in the Descent of Man. In effect, although he was convinced that "man was part of the evolutionary process" and therefore that his theory was likely to apply to animals and to man also, Darwin nonetheless proposed a theory of social evolution that does not consist in a biological theory of social evolution. There are important differences between what happens in animal and human societies. Thus, the principle and target of selection in human societies is different as in natural selection. In effect, in Darwin's theory of social selection the group – rather than the individual– is the target of the selection process. Thus, Darwin notes that "with strictly social animals, natural selection sometimes acts on the individual, through the preservation of variations which are beneficial to the community With the higher social animals, I am not aware that any structure has been modified solely for the good of the community In regard to certain mental powers the case is wholly different; for these faculties have been chiefly, or even exclusively, gained for the benefit of the community, and the individuals thereof have at the same time gained an advantage indirectly"

That the group is the target of social evolution does not mean that social evolution does not rest on "natural selection"; however, the role of this principle is complemented by other factors such as moral sentiments and, more precisely, on sympathy:

"When two tribes of primeval man, living in the same country, came into competition, if other circumstances being equal the one tribe included a great number of courageous, sympathetic and faithful members, who were always ready to warn each other of danger, to aid and defend each other, this tribe would succeed better and conquer the other".

Thus, the theory of social evolution that Darwin indeed proposed departs at least slightly not only from any including his own or Spencer's or the ones proposed by social Darwinists biological theory of evolution. As such, Darwin's theory of social evolution differs from the Darwinian or biological theories of social evolution proposed by social Darwinists, as it has been stressed by many scholars. How do economists treat these differences between Darwin's theories of biological and social evolution, and the complex links with Spencer and social Darwinism? Do they take into account the different aspects of Darwin's works? Do they mention the many connections with classical political economists?

We then identify three ways to answer this question; that is three different modes of references to Darwin and thus three ways to depict Darwin. First, from the perspective of the origins of Darwin's theoretical framework and, in particular, with regard to the influence of economists on his works and writings, Darwin is considered as a biologist exclusively and quoted to evidence that his biological theory has its roots in economic theories; economists mention Darwin, refer to his writings and even quote him to remind the reader that his theory of biological evolution consists in a transposition of a theory developed in social sciences; no mention is never made to a possible theory of social evolution proposed by Darwin. Second, from the viewpoint of the possible use of biological concepts to model social evolution; then, Darwin is quoted as a biologist who inspired Spencer and social Darwinism; Spencer is mentioned as having developed a Darwinian theory of social evolution but Darwin's theory of social evolution remains ignored. Third, Darwin's general theory of evolution, and its twofold aspects - biological and social; from this perspective, Darwin is quoted as the first scholar who tried to bridge the gap between two scientific domains - economics and biology.

DARWIN'S THEORY OF HUMAN BEHAVIOUR

A third image can be put forward and discussed from the way economists cite Darwin within the frame set by the debates around the reciprocal transfers of concepts or tools between economics and biology that is proposed in bioeconomics or sociobiology–two approaches respectively based upon Michael T. Ghiselin' The Economy of Nature and the Evolution of Sex (1974) and Edward O. Wilson's Sociobiology: The New Synthesis (1975). The perspective then adopted goes beyond that of the use of analogies in either sciences. This rather corresponds to the argument that the use of economic tools to understand what happens in natural and animal societies or, conversely, of biological tools in the context of human societies is possible, legitimate and fruitful because nature and culture share the same features and that their functioning obey to the same mechanisms. Now, because of the similarities that are observed or assumed between nature and culture, economics or social sciences and biology should no longer be envisaged as separate and even antagonistic disciplines. To the contrary, "there is such a striking similarity between the basic problems attacked by economics and by social biology, we can expect to find parallels in the corresponding logical structures of thought". Economics and biology have thus to be considered from the perspective of a unified theoretical framework, that is of a single discipline in which "*natural economy* i.e biology and "*political economy* i.e economics ... constitute a single branch of knowledge ... which we may call general economy". Now, this approach has its roots in Darwin's theory. Thus, Hirshleifer considers that sociobiology proceeds to the "recent revival of Darwinian evolutionary theory" and on his side, Ghiselin argues that his 1974 book is "an up-dated version of the Descent of Man". In other words, the way economists perceive Darwin is associated with the conviction that his theory anticipated sociobiology and bioeconomics. He is considered as the first scholar having attempted both to use economic concepts in biology and, reciprocally, biological concepts in the social context. He is thus viewed, on the one hand, as a biologist who borrowed concepts from economists; his theory of biological evolution illustrates the possible transfers from economics to biology. On the other hand, it is also considered that Darwin extended his own framework to develop a theory of social evolution; his theory of social evolution evidences the transfers from biology to social sciences. As a consequence, it is no longer sufficient to mention Darwin's name only. It becomes important to refer precisely to his writings to demonstrate the twofold connection between bioeconomics and Darwin. Within this context, references to Darwin are first aimed at reminding that he inherited his biology from the theories developed by past economists. Thus, economists still quote Darwin to remind us of the economic foundations of Darwin's theory of biological evolution and to insist that economists invented the concepts used in biology.

However important it is, such a transfer is only partial; it only acknowledges that, although he was a biologist, Darwin had understood and accepted economic concepts. Now, bioeconomics or sociobiology are synthetic analyses which also require a transfer of ideas from biology to economics. To put it in other words, Darwin can be considered as a bioeconomist if and only if it can be shown that he has developed a theory of social evolution based on biological concepts. Therefore, other Darwin's writings are important to mention because they evidence that Darwin indeed was a bioeconomist or a sociobiologist. Hence, it is important to refer, in particular to the Descent of Man. From this perspective, Hirshleifer is thus probably the first economist making an explicit reference to Darwin's theory of social evolution, even mentioning.

Darwin's theories can then be considered as illustrations of the twofold connection between economics and biology – a connection that Darwin has then been the first to propose and put in an explicit shape. The first aspect of the connection is methodological while the second is much more substantive: not only Darwinism put forward the possibility to use economic concepts such as scarcity and competition and optimization to understand how nature works but, on the other hand, it also implies that human capacities and preferences are themselves the outcome of mankind's biological heritage. As a consequence, rather than considering that Darwin's theory of social evolution is an aside to his theory of biological evolution, bioeconomists considered it as a part of it. Therefore, besides the Origin of Species, the Descent of Man and the Expression of Emotions are put together to be considered as great Darwin's books. This perspective has led many economists interested in social evolution to include references to Darwin's theory of social evolution. A more complete and precise image of Darwin has emerged among economists. All organisms have to work, and they better work carefully as they search for nutrients, sexual partners, suitable habitats, and safety. All organisms must deliberate and choose among alternatives. The environment they face is neither uniform nor static. All organisms must make decisions, and make the best decisions possible, given the environmental incentives. If the making of the best decisions possible allows us to call human agents "Homo economicus," it should equally allow us to call other living agents "Organism economicus" or, in the above case, "Amoeba economicus."

But how could brainless organisms, from Amoeba economicus to plants, ever be rational? Rodolfo Llinás [2001] argues that plants do not need brains because they do not move. Brains, as the argument goes, are needed for animals that move in order for the animals to make predictions as they move. But there are a host of organisms, such as our Amoeba economicus, which move without the need for a brain. So, the brain might not be essential for rationality. But, first, what is rationality? As defined here, it amounts to two characteristics: Decisions must be consistent i.e., avoid intransitive preferences and decisive i.e., avoid incompleteness.

With this minimal definition, plants make rational decisions with respect to the economic use of water, nutrients, and exposure to the sun. They make choices that are neither inconsistent nor indecisive. And they do not need a brain to make such choices. So, brains might be needed in complex organisms that have to coordinate many functions. They may not be simply the product of mobility as suggested by Llinás. In simple organisms, there is no single specialized organ to take care of coordination. Instead, in brainless organisms, coordination of functions must be undertaken by less specialized tissues. If this is the case, we should thus not conflate rationality with the brain, as much as we should not conflate mobility with limbs or digestion with stomachs. Rationality, mobility, and digestion can be the prerogative of other, generalpurpose parts of the body. Can Darwin's theory of natural selection explain rationality, which seems to be the characteristic of organisms as primitive as Amoeba economicus? It could be noted that natural selection cannot explain rationality. Natural selection, by definition, is limited to the explanation of how a superior trait/technology becomes optimally spread in population. Given that rationality is not at par with traits/technology, it cannot explain rationality.

The Redundancy Thesis: We sometimes state that an agent makes a decision to maximize the objective function i.e fitness or utility only as a shorthand to stating that the agent is programmed to make such a particular decision in reaction to particular circumstances—otherwise, the agent would decrease his or her optimal fitness and, on average, would be deleted from the population by the forces of natural selection. There are many similarities between optimization in natural selection and optimization rationality. At least formally and mathematically, both involve the maximization of an objective function under constraints. Brian Skyrms draws on the formal similarity between the two kinds of optimization. He starts with the similarity, and only qualifies it under special circumstances:

The theory of rational deliberation and the theory of evolution both deal with processes which tend to move in the direction of a provisional optimum. In both areas, strategic interaction leads to complex game theoretic situations where the provisional optimum may be a moving target, and where equilibrium considerations must be introduced. In both disciplines, theories initially developed under simplifying independence assumptions need to be extended to deal with correlation.

Skyrms shows that the two theories are extended differently in the case of correlation, i.e., when agents interact non-randomly with other agents in the population. So, as long as one assumes non-correlation, the two kinds of optimization are identical, at least formally.

THE RATIONALITY ANOMALY

The most important feature of neo-Darwinian theory is that agents do not undergo change as a result of selectionist optimization. It is the population that undergoes improvement through "editing," i.e., the deletion of relatively less fit members. In contrast, the most important feature of rationality theory is that agents undergo change as a result of rationality optimization. What exactly is the difference in the conceptual apparatus of the two kinds of optimization? To answer the question, we need to distinguish two major criteria, the unit and the objective function as shown in Figure 1 with regard to each kind of optimization.

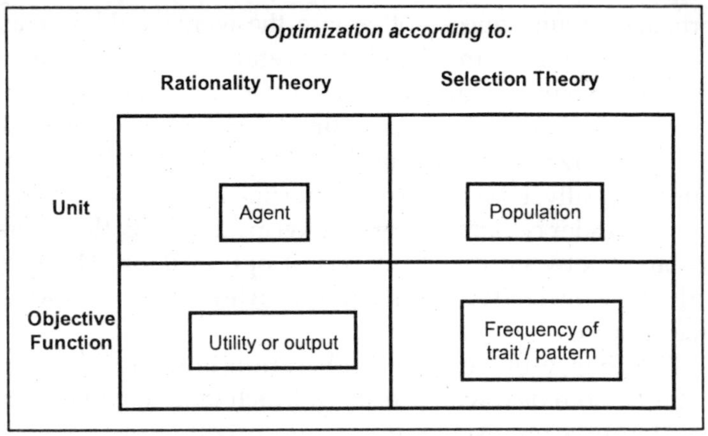

Figure 1: Optimization: Rationality vs. Selection

The unit criterion is the form that the objective function characterizes. For rationality optimization, the unit is the agent such as the cell, organism, colony of organisms, and human organization such as the firm. The agent makes decisions to satisfy its needs given its type and environmental constraints. For selection optimization, the unit is the population that is not organized as a colony or a group of cooperating agents. Thus, the population cannot be considered a decision-making unit or, in Richard Dawkins's [1976] lexicon, a vehicle even when the members of the population share the same taxonomic framework, or share, as what Dawkins calls, the same "replicator". A population in the neo-Darwinian sense is a unit consisting of members that interact for reproduction. An evolutionary change occurs when the members, for some exogenous shock, can be ranked according to differential levels of reproduction success—a ranking which the selecting mechanism nature or market can distinguish. A change that a population can experience is merely an unintentional product of the deletion of the less fit trait/pattern types as measured by the infrequency of their offspring. Such a change is not occasioned by an active decision as in the case with the change which one experiences when one acts rationally. Concerning the objective function criterion, it is not identical for both kinds of optimization. For rationality optimization, the function is either the agent's utility or the agent's output or offspring. For selection optimization, the function is the frequency of the adapted trait/pattern type in a population. In selection, the selector nature or the market "makes" the population of organisms or firms dominated by the best trait/pattern type possible via-à-vis the environment. Thus, rationality optimization differs from selection optimization. The redundancy Thesis cannot be allowed to enter from the back window. Nonetheless, the Rationality-qua-Trait Thesis faces another problem.

THE INCOHERENCE PROBLEM

The Rationality-qua-Trait Thesis faces a problem of incoherence, which is multilayered. The three sub-sections below discuss three such layers. The first layer shows the incoherence problem while assuming that traits undergo progress, i.e., ranking of traits without reference to environmental conditions or incentives, what is called here "constraints." The idea of progress is antithetical to either selection optimization or rationality optimization. If one subscribes to selection optimization, one cannot identify progress or what is the best trait in the abstract, without reference to the constraints. Selection optimization simultaneously determines, in light of the constraints, what is the best type and, consequently, what must proliferate throughout the population if there were no exogenous obstacles. Likewise, if one subscribes to rationality optimization, one cannot identify progress or what is the best technology in the abstract. That is, one cannot rank different production possibility frontiers, based on technological progress, without reference to the constraints. Rationality optimization simultaneously determines, in light of the constraints, what is the best type and, consequently, what is the efficient use of the resources if there were no imperfect information and other exogenous obstacles.

The second layer discusses the incoherence problem while assuming that traits can be ranked only in reference to environmental conditions—i.e., as conceived by selection optimization. The third layer discusses the incoherence problem while assuming that traits can be ranked only in reference to choices in light of incentives—i.e., as conceived by rationality optimization. Sober [1998] disputes this observation. He argues that even if rationality-as-trait is the product of the mechanism of selection optimization, it generates outcomes that are identical to the outcomes generated by the selection optimization. If this is the case, the Redundancy Thesis can assert itself from the back window, and hence it hence Sober's argument needs a close scrutiny.

For Sober, the two kinds of optimization are, in the final analysis, identical because they generate the same outcome. This is what he calls the "heuristic of personification": if the organism is given the chance to choose a trait present in the population, it would choose the best trait, i.e., the most productive. For instance, if a zebra were given a choice, holding everything else constant, it would choose the trait of fast speed over slow speed given environmental conditions. For Sober, given that both kinds of optimization engender the same outcome, there is no substantial difference between the two mechanisms in the final analysis.

Sober's thought experiment about the rational choice of zebras correctly entails that the agent adopts and uses efficiently the best technology in light of the decision maker's environmental constraints. Selection optimization, on the other hand, ensures the identification and the proliferation of the best trait in light of environmental constraints. Even if the environmental constraints facing both optimization mechanisms are identical, rationality optimization and selection optimization do not necessarily engender the same outcome, contrary to Sober's argument. Agents could select diverse technologies in accordance with their diverse tastes. And all these different kinds of technologies would meet the condition of rationality optimization. In contrast, selection optimization would set the different agents against each other, and measure whose type would be better than the other, according to a common criterion, such as the number of offspring or the size of monetary profit. Such a common criterion ignores differences in individual tastes.

Put succinctly, while the unit is a decision-making one in rationality optimization, it is not so in the case in selection optimization. Furthermore, while selection theory is concerned with explaining the frequency of types, this is not the concern of rationality optimization theory. Thus, the two kinds of optimization have different conceptual apparatuses. Biologists somewhat sense the difference between the two kinds of optimization when they label the function which the organism optimizes as the "fitness function," and the function which nature optimizes as the "adaptive or superior fitness function." Elliot Sober discussed seriously the difference between rationality optimization and selectionist optimization. In selection optimization, there is no actor to start with: Deliberation involves a change that occurs in an individual; evolution effects a change in the composition of a population, the individual members of which need never change their traits at all. So, given the fact that rationality involves an agent with a different kind of function when compared to selection, the Redundancy Thesis is fallacious.

PROGRESS VIEW

What does it mean to state that traits undergo evolution? Given that we are ignoring here optimization, the term "evolution" here means progress. Progress entails that we can measure the improvement of the trait without regard to environmental conditions or incentives. Such conditions or incentives, called here constraints, are relevant only with regard to optimization— whether of the rationality or selection kind. The criterion of progress may vary, depending on the trait under question. For instance, one can postulate that eyesight progresses according to the improvement of sharpness of image. For a vehicle, the criterion of progress is the speed of the vehicle. In either example, the trait becomes better as it approaches some ideal character defined in the abstract. The trait becomes better through mutation or invention. The invention/mutation allows the agent to increase its productivity in amassing greater surplus or offspring. The source of the invention/ mutation can be random shocks or intention. Whatever the source, it is irrelevant to the main issue. Namely, according to the progress view, we can rank the increase of productivity without regard to constraints.

There is no upper limit to the improvement of rationality—similar to the fact that there is no upper limit to the improvement of traits such as speed or sharpness of image. Even when particular tools, such as vehicle design or eye design, sets some limits, the limits can be surpassed by restructuring the technology or the trait itself. However, rationality, by definition, has an upper limit in the abstract sense. Even if we change the design of traits/technology, full rationality (100% rationality) does not change. So, there is an upper limit to the improvement of rationality, which undermines the idea that rationality is a trait. Even if evolution has not produced 100% rationality yet, there is no evolutionary change after reaching the telos.

SELECTION OPTIMIZATION VIEW

For neo-Darwinism, evolution is not about progress. It is rather about fitness or what is called here selection optimization. Fitness is the adaptation of a population to its particular environment. When fitness increases, it means that the most appropriate trait, as measured in relation to environmental conditions, has proliferated throughout the population. The judgment of what is the appropriate trait and the judgment of what is the dominant trait in the population are the same judgment: both are determined by comparing the varied traits in the population according to their relative effectiveness in a particular set of constraints. For instance, if a long beak is the fittest given other available alleles and environmental conditions, a short beak can become the fittest under different conditions. It is impossible to state that the long beak, or the short beak, is the fittest in the abstract sense. Likewise, within the temple of neo-Darwinism, we cannot state that 100% rationality is better than irrationality in the abstract sense. Both are simply different alleles of rationality and, hence, cannot be ranked without reference to particular constraints. So, it is possible that, under some conditions, for irrationality to be better than 100% rationality. We can, at best, call the different shapes of rationality by different names—similar to how we call the different shapes of beaks. All shapes of rationality are equivalent in the sense that they cannot be ranked innately, i.e., they can only be ranked with regard to particular constraints.

ASSUMING THE RATIONALITY SELECTION VIEW

Let us assume that agents can select their own traits—as actually the case of humans acquiring skills to become carpenters or neurosurgeons. If rationality is a trait, such agents are also capable of choosing rationality. To state that agents can choose a trait entails two assumptions. First, the chosen trait must be substitutable or fungible with other traits. If agents can only be carpenters, they have no choice. The fact that agents can make choices, the resources used to attain one product such as tables can be used to attain another product such as logged timber. Second, the trait must be scarce. If it is free, such as air, there is no need to make a choice in the first place.

Rationality must be costly and fungible. Concerning fungibility, the agent decides between investment in resources to nurture rationality or investment in same resources to nurture, e.g., the skill of carpentry. Let us assume that the agent chooses greater skill in carpentry at the expense of rationality. Let us assume that after investing in carpentry, there was a totally unexpected shock. The expected return from rationality suddenly rises, while the expected return from carpentry remains the same. If the difference of returns is high enough, and the transaction cost of switching of switching is low enough, the agent should forget the sunk cost of the earlier decision and start anew investment in more rationality at the expense of carpentry.

More broadly, can an agent, starting with any degree of rationality (X), trade it with another trait (Y)? For such substitution to take place, he must use the very skill (X). This leads to self-contradiction. As an analogy, let us examine an agent who uses a tool such as a saw (X) to make a product such as a table (Y). Can he give up X in order to gain more Y? If he gives up X, he would be forced to make less Y, ceteris paribus, for the very fact that he needs X to produce Y. That is, the making of tables or making choices requires a tool rationality. And as such, one cannot substitute between the tool and the product. One can only substitute between one product tables and another product logged timber produced by the same tool.

RATIONALITY-QUA-METHOD THESIS

The Rationality-qua-Trait Thesis leads to the incoherent world of self-reference of Escher. To avoid incoherence, we have to reject the Thesis. The alternative has been already suggested in the diagnosis of the incoherence problem. Namely, rationality can only be a tool or a method to make decisions because it cannot be an element (trait) about which decisions are made. In fact, rationality does not meet the first condition mentioned above concerning choice making. Namely, rationality is not fungible with traits. Also, rationality does not meet the second condition. Namely, rationality is not scarce.

While it has been shown that rationality is non-fungible with traits, we need to show why rationality is not scarce. To be scarce, rationality must be costly. The fact is that rationality is costless (which is, again, separate from the issue of heuristics in light of bounded rationality). The decision, e.g., to stop searching for information and to take action is costless. A prime example is the multitude of cases of moral hazard. When the government started to impose seat belt laws, for instance, economists predicted that agents would drive less cautiously, resulting in more accidents but less thanks to the seat belt fatalities per accident. The tradeoff between safety and time gained by greater speed was never conscious. Also, agents who have insurance tend to adjust to the insurance, and adopt new, less-careful habits with regards to the locking of doors.

To go back to Robinson Crusoe, he has to make a decision on whether to continue fishing or switch to hunting. So, he adopts a heuristic that states that, if he catches zero fish in the first two hours, then it is better to switch to hunting for the rest of the day. The establishment of this rule, like the search for resources, is costly. But the method used to determine the rule itself, i.e., rationality, is not costly. While the agent can economize on calculation, searching, and the use of other traits, he cannot economize on being economical. To make a choice implies that one is economical. Therefore, it is incoherent to assert that one can make a choice, or nature can make it on one's behalf, on how much rationality to use. As a method of making decisions, rationality is an endemic aspect of decisions. This "Rationality-qua-Method Thesis" entails that rationality is the way agents reconcile the objective function in light of the constraint function. And for the organism to do so, the method or the bridge between the two functions cannot be an element in either function. The method is rather about the use of non-method elements, such as eyesight, muscles, beak, and other tools needed for survival.

CONCLUSION

It could be seen clearly from the above discussion. First, it refuted the Redundancy Thesis by showing that rationality optimization differs from selection optimization. Irrespective of the origin of rationality, the objective function that rationality optimizes differs from the function that selection optimizes. Thus, rationality optimization and selection should not be assumed to be identical simply because they employ the optimization technique. Otherwise, one should also identify rationality with the physical principle of least action on the ground that both use the optimization technique. If rationality is not the child of rational selection, this opens vistas to understand evolution beyond the paradigm of natural selection. This does not need to entail the invitation of medieval scholastics and the idea of "uncaused cause" as Darwinists have warned. It is true that Darwin undermined the metaphysics of divine intervention, but by postulating the importance of rationality, which is uncaused by natural selection, does not mean that it is beyond scientific study. It only means that such a study has not begun, and in fact extinguished by the dominance of the natural selection paradigm.

5

Biophysical Economics

Biophysical economics is characterized by a wide range of analysts from diverse fields who use ecology and thermodynamics to analyze the economic process. The history of biophysical thought is traced from the 18th-century Physiocrats to current empirical research, with emphasis on those individuals who contributed to the development of biophysical economic theory. Attention is also given to a critique of the neoclassical theory of natural resources from a biophysical perspective, and how recent empirical biophysical research highlights areas of neoclassical theory which could be improved by a more realistic and systematic treatment of natural resources.

THE PHYSIOCRATS

In the 1750s there developed in France a school of economic thought which had as its first principle that natural resources and fertile agricultural land in particular, were the source of material wealth. Physiocracy, meaning literally 'rule of nature,'. The Physiocrats argued that the economic process was subject to certain objective laws which operated independent of human free will. They called such forces Natural Law,' which had two components, physical and moral laws. Quesnay defined physical law as "the regular course of all physical events in the natural order which is self-evidently the most advantageous to the human race." Moral law was "the rule of human action in the moral order conforming to the physical law which is self-evidently the most advantageous to the human race."

Physical laws determined important economic parameters such as rainfall and soil fertility, and embodied the Newtonian view of the physical world which dominated scientific thought at that time. The Physiocrats argued that Natural Law operated independent of human free will, and that if humans accurately deduced the 'proper' economic behavior implied by Natural Law, social welfare would be maximized. At the heart of the Physiocrats' model was the physical productivity of the extractive sectors, and especially the surplus produced by agriculture which was called 'produit net,' net product. The Physiocrats postulated that the course of the economy rose and fell with changes in the net product. Agriculture was the supreme occupation because it alone yielded a disposable surplus over cost. In the physiocratic model, economic rent was derived from unrecompensed work done by Nature since in setting food prices, cultivators take in account their labor and expenses as well as the surplus value contributed by the fertility of the soil. Quesnay measured and traced the dollar value of the flow of net product between the three classes in his *Tableau Economique*, a model which represented for the first time, albeit in crude from, economic concepts such as general equilibrium and Wassily Leontief's input-output system, both of which became widely used economic models.

LAWS OF THERMODYNAMICS

In the early 19th century, the physical and ecological basis economic production intuitively grasped by the Physiocrats was formalized by the discovery of the laws of thermodynamics. Soon after Carnot, Clausius and others formalized the laws of thermodynamics, many physical and life scientists realized that those laws had enormous implications for their respective disciplines. Thermodynamics and the study of energy flows became a universal index by which many disparant biological and physical processes were quantified and compared. Carnot's steam engine experiments demonstrated the relevance of the second law of thermodynamics of economics, namely, how much useful work could be obtained from an energy conversion. Carnot's experiments also showed that thermodynamic laws are essentially economic formulations of physical relations, for the terms 'useful' and 'unavailable' energy refer to the economy's ability to use energy to upgrade the organizational state of natural resources into useful goods and services.

Physical scientists and biologists were the first individuals to use energy flows to explain social and economic development. Joseph Henry, an American physicist and first secretary of the Smithsonian Institution, remarked that the "fundamental principle of political economy is that the physical labor of man can only be ameliorated by ...the transformation of matter from a crude state to a artificial condition...by expending what is called power or energy." The biologist-philosopher Herbert Spencer observed that human systems have the unique ability to temporarily halt and even reverse the spontaneous increase of entropy by tapping energy flows in nature. Spencer likened the evolutionary process, both biological and social, to the entropy law because the struggle for existence was a struggle for available energy and resources. Spencer stated that "evolution is a change from a less coherent form to a more coherent form, consequent on the dissipation of energy and the integration of matter."

The German chemist Wilhelm Ostwald incorporated thermodynamics into a general theory of economic development. Ostwald stated that energy was the "sole universal generalization" because energy possesses the principle of conservation under all circumstances. For this reason, and also because for any event in the universe it is always possible to state an equation every time between the "energies that have disappeared and those newly arrived," Ostwald believed that energy laws should be the "foundation of all sciences." Based on this principle, Ostwald sketched the beginnings of civilization in energy terms. If culture is a means by which humans control their natural environment, and if all events are at root energy conversions, then civilization becomes a history of ever-increasing control of energy for human purposes. Civilization advanced as new and better ways were devised to empower human labor with inanimate energies.

Ostwald stated that "...the progress of science is characterized by the fact that more and more energy is utilized for human purposes, and that the transformation of the raw energies...is attended by ever-increased efficiency."

Podolinsky, a Ukrainian socialist, was the first to explicitly scrutinize the economic process from a thermodynamic perspective. Podolinsky was keenly aware that he was in line of succession to the Physiocrats and Carnot and Clausius, citing the former group's emphasis on nature as the source of wealth, and the economic implications of the latter pair's discoveries. Podolinsky tried to reconcile the labor theory of value with a thermodynamic analysis of the economic process. In his conclusions, which he communicated to Frederick Engels on several occasions, Podolinsky stated the socialist model was flawed because it assumed that "scientific socialism" would overcome all natural resource scarcities and enable unlimited material expansion. Podolinsky's biophysical analysis led him to conclude that ultimate limits to economic growth law not in the shackles of the relations of production, but in physical and ecological laws.

Podolinsky's work foreshadowed by nearly a century three concepts now widely used by some biophysical analysts: the use of energy flow analysis to characterize the efficiency of food production systems; modeling labor productivity as a function of the quantity of energy used to subsidize the efforts of labor; and the importance of the energy surplus or net energy yielded by an energy supply process. Podolinsky calculated the energy surplus delivered by the food production system of his day by comparing the caloric value of food produced to the energy used to produce it, including the energy content of the seeds and the caloric expenditure of human and draft animals used in the process. Podolinsky calculated that yields per area and energy surpluses were greater in ecosystems that were subsidized by human-controlled energy inputs relative to unsubsidized natural ecosystems.

EARLY TWENTIETH CENTURY

The early 20th century was characterized by a growing body of literature devoted to the analysis of the role of natural resources in human affairs, and particularly in economic production. The most notable author was Frederick Soddy, a Nobel laureate in chemistry, who applied the laws of thermodynamics to economic systems and devoted a significant part of his professional career to a critique of standard economic theory. Like the Physiocrats, Soddy maintained that a comprehensive theory of economic wealth has biophysical laws as first principles because "life derives the whole of its physical energy or power not from anything self-contained in living matter, and still less from an external deity, but solely from the inanimate world. It is dependent for all the necessities of its physical continuance upon the principles of the steam engine. The principles and ethics of all human conventions must not run counter to those of thermodynamics."

Soddy emphasized that solar energy empowers all life processes. Human life is sustained by replenishing itself with solar energy captured and transformed by plants, which Soddy called the "original capitalists." Like Ostwald, Soddy believed economic progress was made possible by the transition from direct solar energy to successive masteries of nonrenewable stores of fossil fuels. When humans first tapped energy capital in terms of fossil fuels rather than energy revenue in terms of solar energy, unprecedented accounts of economic work became possible. The 'flamboyant era' society now enjoys stems not only from human ingenuity but also from our inheritance of solar energy from the Carboniferous era embodied in fossil fuels.

Soddy argued that the fatal flaw of economics was a confusion of wealth, which has a distinct physical dimension, with debt, a purely imaginary mathematical quantity with no physical dimension. Unlike wealth, debts can be created by a 'wave of the hand' or 'a will of the mind' because "debts are subject to the laws of mathematics rather than physics. Unlike wealth, which is subject to the laws of thermodynamics, debts do not rot with old age. On the contrary, they grow at so much per annum, by the well known mathematical laws of simple and compound interest."

Soddy believed this confusion led to the development of financial institutions that were divorced from the physical principles underlying the production of wealth. Banks create money arbitrarily through the fractional reserve requirement system, and then loan the 'fictitious' money at interest. Wealth, the physical quantity represented by money, cannot grow forever at a compound interest rate as the laws of thermodynamics clearly imply. Soddy postulated that at some point debts would outstrip wealth, causing the banking system to collapse. Citing the economic malaise of the Depression as evidence, Soddy proposed as remedies a 100 percent reserve requirement and a statue requiring a constant price level.

Writing at about the same time as Soddy was Alfred Lotka, a mathematical biologist who argued that the mechanisms of natural selection could be explained in energy terms. Lotka did not specifically apply his biophysical principles to economics, but his theories were subsequently used by other analysts to emphasize the relation between energy quality and living systems. Lotka proposed that the evolutionary process, combined with the laws of thermodynamics, formed a natural 'law' that underlay all human behavior. Lotka proposed that the battle of organic evolution was a "general scrimmage for available energy" in which all players were energy transformers-plants as energy accumulators animals as engines which burned the solar energy in plants. For Lotka, survival was game governed by the laws of thermodynamics: "in the struggle for existence, the advantage must go to those organisms whose energy-capturing devices are most efficient in directing available energies into channels favorable to the preservation of the species."

The use of energy as a unifying concept for social, political and economic analysis reached a zenith with the technocratic movement in the USA and Canada during the 1930s. Led by the flamboyant and energetic Howard Scott, the Technocracy movement began in 1918 as a group called the Technical Alliance. The Alliance conducted an industrial survey of North America in which economic parameters were measured in energy units rather than dollars. Although the Alliance lasted only a few years, the Depression provided fertile ground for the re-emergence of the technocratic movement which used depressed economic conditions as a rallying point for their call for a complete overhaul of existing economic and political institutions. Technocrats believed that politicians and businessmen could not manage a complex, rapidly advancing industrial society. The technocrats proposed replacing politicians with scientists and engineers who had the technical expertise to manage the economy. This would allow social and economic institutions to reap the full benefits technological progress had made possible. With technical trained people making decisions, the Technocrats saw no physical limitations on expanding industrial output. They favored the continual replacement of labor with capital and energy, realizing as did Podolinsky and Soddy that empowering labor with greater quantities of fuel increased the productivity of labor.

The technocratic philosophy assumed that energy was the critical factor determining economic and social development. The Technocrats measured social change in physical terms: the average number of kilocalories used per capita per day. Money would be replaced by energy certificates, the total supply of which would be determined by the total amount of energy used in the production of goods and services. Every adult above the age of 25 would receive an equal portion of the total net energy used. People under 25 would receive a special 'maintenance allowance.' Like Soddy, the Technocrats viewed with contempt the interest-bearing ability of regular money, so the energy certificate was to be non-transferable, non-negotiable, non-interest bearing, and had to be used within a specified period of time.

THE 1950s

This was an exceptional period for research on the role of energy and natural resources in social and economic development. The most comprehensive assessment of the role of energy in human societies was by W. Fred Cottrell, a sociologist at Miami (Ohio) University for many years after an earlier career as a railroad man. Cottrell's *Energy and Society* is an extremely perceptive and readable analysis of the role of energy in human affairs. Cottrell emphasized two aspects of the relation between energy quality and economic and social development. The first was a quantity he termed "surplus energy," the difference between the energy delivered by a process and the energy invested in the delivery process. The second point Cottrell emphasized was the connection between the amount of energy used to subsidize the efforts of labor and the productivity of labor. Cottrell was impressed by the way much of what was called 'technological change' operated: using increasing amounts of higher quality energy especially fossil fuels per laborer to perform a specific economic task. According to Cottrell, the Industrial Revolution was revolutionary in economic terms because human labor was supplemented by enormous quantities of inanimate energy in the form of fossil fuels. Such subsidies powered an unprecedented increase in the amount of work done per worker-hour.

Cottrell also examined the influence of energy quality and energy surpluses on the development of social and cultural patterns. For example, the unidirectional character of energy in flowing water dictated certain economic and social arrangements between those who lived at river mouths and those upstream from them. Bulky raw materials much as grains, ores and timber were often produced in the hinterland and sent downstream to river mouth cities where those raw materials were combined to produce more valuable goods. Great accumulations of wealth and populations occurred in downstream cities, but very often such wealth did not find its way back upstream.

Despite his emphasis on energy, Cottrell did not argue that physical laws determined all social arrangements. Rather, he argued that resource availability set the general direction of social change. According to Cottrell, nature says to humans, "if you want this, here are the conditions under which you may have it." The two most important conditions are: (1) the investment of a minimum amount of already extracted energy to find and develop additional amounts of energy from the environment, and (2) the use of some available energy to protect one's energy flow from others seeking to use it for their own preservation. In regards to the first condition, Cottrell believed that the most important quality of an energy source was the surplus energy it delivered. Cottrell observed that, in general, societies adopted a new energy technology only if it delivered a greater energy surplus, and hence a greater potential to produce goods and services. The Industrial Revolution produced unprecedented economic and social expansion in large part because the energy surplus delivered by fossil fuels dwarfed that produced by the renewable energy sources used prior to the Revolution. Cottrell also observed that economies are sensitive to change over time in the magnitude of the surplus delivered by an energy source. Such changes were a function of the physical properties of the resource and the technologies used to extract it, with the former factor being the most important in the amount of surplus energy delivered to society may be the ultimate limit to economic expansion: "it will only be when we get a response from nature, in the form of greatly diminished return in the form of surplus energy, that we can expect the present Industrial Revolution to slow down.

Cottrell also explored the differences between a biophysical and so-called humanist approach to biological and cultural evolution. Like Lotka, Cottrell emphasized the most fundamental relation in nature: organisms capture the radiant energy of the sun as a means to perpetuate the patterns that differentiate them from one another. On Lotka's hypothesis that natural selection favors those who maximize the energy flux through their systems, Cottrell stated that: "the evidence for Lotka's position is not yet sufficient to make it clear that it should be formulated into a law. But the tendency it expresses...fits other evidence that ability to control energy conversation is one factor involved in the persistence of patterns that require energy for their replication. Certainly the patterns of observable human behavior fall into that category. Man cannot escape thermodynamics...his effectiveness in controlling energy conversion so that is serves his needs and satisfies his values is one measure of his probable survival in a habitat." Energy technology may in some cases impose only limited restrictions on the society using it, while in others (e.g., controlled fusion and breeder reactors) the conditions necessary to utilize an energy source may be extremely narrow and the technical and social organizations required to operate them may be extremely precise.

Writing about the same time as Cottrell was M. King Hubbert who, like Cottrell and others before him, was impressed by the remarkable correlation between the burst of human civilization and the transition to a fossil fuel economy. Hubbert, a geophysicist by trade, used his extensive knowledge of physics, mathematics and geology to revolutionize the way in which the supply of nonrenewable resources were analyzed. Hubbert was one of the first to gather empirical data on rates of energy production, discoveries and consumption in order to make predictions on future energy availability. In 1949 Hubbert made the startling prediction that the fossil fuel era would be short-lived, at least relative to the time frame commonly assumed, and in 1956 estimated that United States domestic oil production would peak in the late 1960s. This work was based on a curve-fitting technique that became known as the Hubbert curve. Hubbert stated that "the epoch of the fossil fuels as a major source of industrial energy can only be a transitory and ephemeral event - an event, nonetheless, which has exercised the most drastic influence very experienced by the human species during its entire biological history."

It was the 'drastic influence' that energy quality and availability had on economic development that led Hubbert to criticize standard economics for its lack of a biophysical basis. Echoing the words of Soddy written almost a half-century earlier, Hubbert stated: "...when one speaks of the state of growth of GNP, I haven't the faintest idea what this means when I try to translate it onto coal, oil, iron, and the other physical quantities which are required to run an industry...the quantity GNP is a monetary bookkeeping entity. It obeys the laws of money. It can be expanded or diminished, created or destroyed, but it does not obey the laws of physics." History has proven Hubbert's petroleum supply models to be remarkably accurate. However, subsequent research suggests that Hubbert may have been lucky because his models do not explicitly account for short run economic and political forces that affect drilling, discovery, and production. It is ironic that the timing of what may prove to be one of the most important economic events in U.S. history, the peaking of domestic oil production, was predicted most accurately by a physical scientist.

THE 1970s

The environmental movement and the petroleum supply and price shocks of the 1970s made energy, and natural resources in general, and important social, economic and political issue. Virtually overnight, the amount of research devoted to energy-environment-economic interactions increased substantially. In *Environment, Power, and Society*, Howard T. Odum developed a systematic methodology using energy flows to analyze the combined system of humans and nature. Odum combined Darwin's theory of natural selection and Lotka's hypothesis of natural selection as an energy-maximizing process into a 'general energy law': maximization of useful work obtained from energy conversion is the criteria for natural selection. Odum coined this 'law' 'the maximum power principle'. The maximum power principle, while yet to be subjected to rigorous empirical testing, rests on the principles of natural selection set forth by Darwin and Lotka. Odum observed that ecological and other systems that survive and prosper used energy at some 'optimum' rate 'better' than competing energy utilization strategies. Since human systems are subjected to the same energy constraints as any other system, Odum suggests that any ethic for the survival of humans must meet this same logical and cultural, operated on differential rates and efficiencies of energy use by ecosystems and economies.

Two of Odum's most important contributions to biophysical economics are energy quality and the countercurrent flow of energy and money in the economy. Energy quality refers to the relative ability of the economy to use different fuels to produce economic output per heat equivalent burned. Odum argued that because fuels differ in quality, societies with access to higher-quality fuels have an economic advantage over those with access to lower quality fuels. Odum also stressed the importance of matching economic tasks with fuels of appropriate quality. High-quality fuels such as electricity are best used to control the flow of larger, lower-quality flows in the economy. Electricity is well-suited to operating a computer which can perform tremendous amounts of work per kcal of electricity. Electricity used for space heating is a poor use of high-quality energy because space heat could also be provided by lower-quality fuels such as petroleum, coal or wood.

Odum argued that energy was the source of economic value. He pointed out that wherever a dollar flow existed in the economy, there was a requirement for an energy flow in the opposite direction. Money is used to buy goods and services, of necessity derived from energy. Each purchase operates through the economy as a feedback, stimulating more energy to be drawn from the ground and into the economy to produce additional goods and services. Money circulates in a closed loop, whereas low-entropy energy moves in from the outside, is used for economic tasks, and then leaves the economic system as degraded heat. Odum also observed that the large natural energy flows—solar radiation, water, wind, etc.—that are essential for life, have no associated dollar flows. The costs of using these energy flows do not, therefore, enter into economic transactions directly, often leading to their misuse or the mismanagement of life-sustaining environmental services.

Empirical support for some of Odum's ideas was given by Robert Costanza who analyzed the relationship between the direct and indirect energy used to produce a good or service in the U.S. economy and the dollar value attached to that good or service in market transactions. Costanza used the term 'embodied energy' to describe the total energy cost of a good or service. He showed that there was a strong statistical relation between the embodied energy content of a good and its dollar value if energy calculations included an estimate of the energy costs of labor and government services as well as direct fuel use. Costanza used this empirical evidence to argue for an embodied energy theory of economic value which maintains that the value of any good or service to humans is ultimately related to the quantity of energy directly and indirectly used in its production.

Like Odum's, Costanza's embodied energy theory of value was roundly criticized by many economists, but he defended it with a theoretical argument based on two assumptions. First, solar energy is the only net input into our closed biosphere. Second, like Lotka and Odum argued, the struggle to sequester free energy to sustain life and maintain existing cultural arrangements was the most fundamental human activity. Based on these assumptions, Costanza hypothesized that a perfectly functioning free market would, through a complex evolutionary process, arrive at prices proportional to embodied energy content. Because the market is not perfect, however, embodied energy calculations can pinpoint problems and value nonmarketed goods and services i.e., externalities.

The late Earl Cook, a geologist and former Dean of Geosciences at Texas A & M University, was interested not only in empirical modeling of resource supply systems, but also in broader social issues associated with energy use, resource depletion, and environmental degradation. Cook's *Man, Energy, and Society* stands as one of the most complete books on the subject. Cook was concerned with the dangers associated with the apparent incompatibility of our society's fervent, almost religious devotion to economic growth, and the fact that such growth was dependent upon a finite, nonrenewable stock of fossil fuel. Cook observed that: The greatest danger in our bemused drift towards the energy waterfall is that the resulting shock will find us stripped of democratic government by an opportunistic group that comes out on top in the wreckage, a group that controls us through their control of the energy systems.

The empirical methodology of biophysical economics was greatly enhanced by Bruce Hannon used this information to argue that the U.S. should adopt a strong energy conservation ethic to offset diminishing supplies of domestic fossil fuels and increased reliance on foreign sources of fuel. Hannon stressed that consumers had to become more aware of the impacts their decisions had on energy demand, because different goods and services had different energy costs. For example, even if a household reduced its direct fuel use by lowering thermostats or driving less, the money saved by doing so could be respent on goods that required an equivalent amount of energy for their production, thereby negating the original act of conservation. Regarding consumer awareness of energy issues, Hannon stated:

An awareness of the stock of available energy resources, analogous to the perception of a savings account or a woodpile stacked by the fireplace, it also needed. The absence of this awareness is the root of the problem...The ignorance of the fact that there is a finite quantity of energy available is perhaps the greatest tragedy of this age. Hannon proposed several methods which could encourage energy conservation, the most interesting of which was an energy rationing scheme which would provide direct consumer control or energy use. Under this scheme, people would work for energy coupons, each representing a specified number of energy units. These coupons would be traded for the direct and indirect energy embodied in goods and services. The national government would own the energy sources and issue new coupons to meet targeted energy use rates. While not likely to be adopted in a dollar-oriented society, Hannon's proposal is consistent with the biophysical philosophy of Soddy and the Technocrats, who believed standard economic and financial institutions were inadequate allocaters of energy and other natural resources.

Robert Ayres was another physical scientist who used biophysical methods to gain insights into the economic process. Using a material-energy balance model, Ayres described the inconsistency of the closed, cyclic model of standard economics with the First Law of Thermodynamics, which states that what low-entropy matter and energy enters the economic process as useful raw materials must ultimately leave the process and return to nature as high-entropy wastes. One immediate implication is that so-called 'externalities' are necessarily pervasive rather than exceptional characteristics of the economic process as some economic theorists had generally assumed.

Ayres used the principles of entropy and the Second Law of Thermodynamics to describe natural resources quality in physical terms. High-quality negentropy stocks i.e., highly ordered deposits of natural resources are those which require low amounts of fuel and other natural resources to discover, extract and process. Ayres described a thermodynamic related to resource depletion. The faster we deplete mineral resource negentropy stocks, the more we accelerate the demand for a depletion of fossil energy resources, since lower-quality resources require more energy for their extraction. This ratchet effect is amplified as high-quality fuels such as coal must be used, which themselves require a greater energy investment per unit energy extracted. Ayres emphasized that the standard economic model of natural resource scarcity does not account for the positive feedback between decreasing resource quality and the rate of extraction of those resources. The standard model has until recently ignored the increased environmental costs due to the build-up of high-entropy wastes from increased use of energy matter.

Ayres and his colleagues propose a system of aggregating energy and materials based on energy. Energy measures the useful work obtainable from an energy or material, and is based on the chemical energy embodied in the material or energy based on its physical organization relative to a reference state. The physical units for energy are the same as for energy or heat, namely kilocalories, joules, BTUs, etc. For fossil fuels, energy is nearly equivalent to the standard heat of combustion; for other forms of energy, specific calculations are needed that depend on the details of the assumed conversion process. For materials, energy is defined jointly for a material and the reference state with which it must ultimately reach thermodynamic equilibrium. Thus, energy measures the degree to which a material is organized relative a random assemblage of material found at an average crustal abundance, an average concentration of sea water or of gases in the atmosphere. The higher the degree of concentration, the higher the energy content

Ayres argues that energy has a number of useful attributes for aggregating heterogeneous energy and materials. Energy is a property of all energy and materials and in principle can be calculated from information in handbooks of chemistry and physics and secondary studies. Thus, energy can be used to measure and aggregate natural resource inputs as well as wastes. For these reasons Ayres argues that energy forms the basis for a comprehensive resource accounting framework that could "provide policy-makers with a valuable set of indicators." One such indicator is a general measure of "technical efficiency," the efficiency with which "raw" energy from animals or inanimate source is converted into final services. A low energy efficiency implies room for the improvement in the efficiency of converting energy and materials into goods and services. Similarly, the ratio of energy embodied in material wastes to energy embodied in resource inputs is the "most general measure of pollution." Ayres also argues that the energy of waste streams is a proxy for their potential ecotoxicity or harm to the environment, at least in general terms.

In *Steady-State Economics,* Herman E. Daly points out the logical inconsistencies between the emphasis placed on economic growth and the energy and environmental realities confronting us. Like Soddy, Daly argued that our preoccupation with monetary flows at the expense of thermodynamics principles misleads us into believing that technological advance is limitless, and that perpetual economic growth is not only physically possible, but morally and ethically desirable as well.

One of Daly's most insightful contributions to biophysical theory was his critique of the conceptual model of the economic process found in most introductory textbooks. In this model, exchange value embodied in goods and services flows from firms to households and is called national product. A counter flow of equal value, in the form of factors of production, product. A counter flow of equal value, in the form of factors of production, flows back to firms from households and is called national income. This flow is depicted as circular, self-feeding, and self-renewing.

Like Ayres, Daly argues that the circular flow model is seriously incomplete because it focuses on the circular flow of exchange value i.e., money rather than the throughput of low-entropy natural resources from which all goods and services are ultimately derived (Figure 1). Daly emphasizes that the circular flow of exchange value is coupled with a physical flow of matter-energy which is not circular. The matter-energy flow is linear and unidirectional, beginning with the depletion of low-entropy resource stocks from nature and ending with the pollution of the environment with high-entropy wastes. In this view, nature is the ultimate source of the raw materials necessary to produce economic value, as well as the ultimate sink for the unavoidable by-products of the production process. Daly states: It is, of course, the linear throughout matter-energy, not the circular flow of value, that impinges on the environment in the forms of depletion and pollution. It is impossible to study the relation of economy to the ecosystem in terms of the circular flow model, because the circular flow is an isolated, self renewing system with no inlets or outlets, no possible points of contact with anything outside itself. Yet in economic theory the circular flow has the spotlight, while the concept of throughput is only dimly visible in the shadows. Consequently, the relation of the economy to its environment is a topic which economic theory has only occasionally illuminated and often obscured.

Daly argued the benefits of a steady-state economy in which the stocks of physical wealth (capital) and people (population) are held constant. The accumulation of physical wealth is controlled by controlling the rate of energy and matter use. Population is held constant by some form of birth control practice. Daly acknowledged that such controls are not palatable to most of us because we lie in a growth-oriented society. Daly believes, however, that such a transition is inevitable due to rising world population, resource depletion, and environmental degradation, and that the social costs associated with a voluntary transition to a steady-state will be far less than those that would occur if environmental conditions force people into such changes.

THE CONTRIBUTION OF NICHOLAS GEORGESCU-ROEGEN

Due to his enormous influence and to the theme of this volume, the work of Nicholas Georgescu-Roegen deserves more detailed discussion. Much of what follows is based on a review of his work published in a special issue of *Ecological Economics* devoted to Georgescu-Roegen. Georgescu-Roegen had a deep and thorough understanding of economic theory, economic history, and mathematics, as well as considerable knowledge of physics and the history and philosophy of science. His genius was rooted in his instincts about the relevance of biophysical principles for human economic aspirations. Georgescu had a vision of economics rooted in the physics, chemistry, and biology of human existence, and the analytical and intellectual capabilities to weave those pieces together with the humanistic tradition of economics. Traditional economic analysis concentrates on the exchange of commodities among the members of an economy, focusing on the role of consumer preferences, technologies, and capital endowments for the existence and stability of market equilibria. Georgescu sought to ground economic analysis in the biophysical realities of the economic process.

For Georgescu, a great sin of conventional economic analysis is the confusion of funds and flows, leading to a fundamental misrepresentation of the relation between manufactured and natural capital. A glaring example of this is the standard representation of funds and flows in models such as the Cobb-Douglas production functions, namely:

$$Q = K^{\alpha 1} L^{\alpha 2} R^{\alpha 3} \qquad (1)$$

where Q is output per time period, K is the stock of capital, R is the flow of natural resources, L is labor supply per time period, and a_1, a_2, a_3 are fixed parameters. As Georgescu observes, this implies that with a constant labor force L_0, one could obtain any given Q_0 if the flow of natural resources satisfies the condition

$$R^{\alpha 3} = \frac{Q_0}{K^{\alpha 1} L_0^{\alpha 2}} \tag{2}$$

Consequently, we could maintain a constant output indefinitely with an ever-diminishing amount of *R* if the quantity of *K* can be increased sufficiently. But Georgescu exposes this "conjuring trick," charging that excessive preoccupation with "paper and pencil exercises has led to accepting these exercises without any concern for their relation to facts." Of course, on an economy-wide level the increase in *K* implies an increase in the use of *R*, so that if *K*approaches infinity, *R* rapidly will be exhausted by the production of capital. Other analysts have echoed Georgescu's point that in certain applications or interpretations, widely used models such as the Cobb-Douglas or constant elasticity of substitution production functions embody the physically impossible assumption that a given output can be maintained as energy or material inputs vanish if manufactured capital can be increased sufficiently. The laws of conservation of mass and energy clearly dictate that no agent can create the stuff on which it operates, i.e., manufactured capital cannot create the resources it transforms and the materials it is made from.

One of Georgescu's most renowned arguments is that "matter matter's too." Georgescu reacted strongly against energy theories of value. He argued that the principle of entropy applied to materials as well as energy. Energy and materials always are used together; we can never handle energy without a material receptor, material lever, or material transmitter. Thus, Georgescu argued that there is a "dual" of the first law of thermodynamics, namely that no mechanical work can be performed without the use of some matter. He further asserted that the second law of thermodynamics, which precludes the possibility of a machine converting energy to work with 100 percent efficiency, is due to "imperfections in matter." That is, there are no frictionless materials, no perfect insulators, no perfect conductors, no perfectly elastic materials, etc. These imperfections preclude the perfect conversion of energy into mechanical work. Consequently, a full understanding of material and energy transformations requires explicit attention to matter.

The hand-in-glove relation between energy and material use produces a continuous conversion of matter from high quality to low quality state, in a manner directly analogous to the dissipation of energy. Georgescu states: All over the material world there is rubbing by friction, cracking and splitting by changes in temperature or evaporation, there is clogging of pipes and membranes, there is metal fatigue and spontaneous combustion. Matter is thus continuously displaced, altered, and scattered to the four corners of the world. It thus becomes less and less available for our purposes.

Georgescu emphasized that "the Entropy Law in its present form states that *matter, too, is subject to an irrevocable dissipation.*" This statement is, without doubt, correct for isolated systems. All changes in the thermodynamic state of materials must be accompanied by a degradation of the quality of energy. If the system is isolated, i.e., no mass or energy flows cross its boundaries, the system will ultimately reach a state at which no gradients in temperature, pressure or material composition exist that enable the system to change its state. Such a state of the system is referred to as heat death.

In subsequent arguments Georgescu asserted that "isolated systems present only a small interest to us. If we set aside the case of the whole universe, isolated systems are set up with some degree of tolerance only in laboratories." In much of his work on the role of matter in economic processes he then focused on closed, rather than isolated systems, i.e., systems that *do* have energy flows crossing their boundaries but *do not* have material flows across their boundaries:

Having in mind the statistical interpretation of thermodynamics, one may argue that we can certainly reassemble the pearls of a broken necklace scattered over the floor. Is not recycling such a type of operation? To see the error in extrapolating from the molar to the molecular level, let us suppose that the same pearls are first dissolved in some acid and the solution is spread over the oceans – an experiment which depicts what actually happens to one material substance after the other. Even if we had as much energy as we pleased, it will take us a fantastically long, practically infinite time, to reassemble the pearls. Inspired by this and similar examples, Georgescu went on to elevate his observations to a Fourth Law of Thermodynamics – or Law of Matter Entropy – describing the degradation of the organizational state of matter a system that can exchange only energy with its outside and performs work indefinitely at a constant rate is another thermodynamic impossibility. Sooner or later, some elements will become totally dissipated.

The bottom line for Georgescu is that due to material dissipation and the generally declining quality of resource utilization, materials in the end may become more crucial than energy. This leads him to criticize Boulding's claim of no law of increasing material entropy. He rejects Daly's version of a steady-state economy on the grounds that materials dissipate in a closed system such as the Earth just as energy does. Georgescu states: Complete recycling being impossible, even in the steady state the "transactions" between the economic process and the environment must necessarily consist of some available matter as well in order to compensate for the matter dissipated continuously and irrevocably. Georgescu also rejects the "infinite resources" arguments because they ignore the importance of changes in the quality of matter. For example, some optimists state that the literal notion of running out of materials is ridiculous because the entire planet is composed of minerals. Georgescu exposed the fallacy of this argument by observing that, by the same token, we could argue that we will never run out of energy because the entire planet is full of energy. Indeed, the ocean contains enough energy to support undreamed of economic activity for millennia to come. However, the temperature gradient in the ocean is so small that for all practical purposes the enormous store of energy is unavailable. Similarly, Georgescu argues that many of the materials are in low quality deposits that for all practical purposes render them unavailable.

Georgescu's emphasis of material quality shares a common theme with the biophysical perspective of resource scarcity held by some ecological economists and a number of physical scientists. The biophysical manifestation of scarcity is the use of, and often times the depletion of, increasing amounts of natural and human-made capital to deliver a unit of resource to society. A decline in the quality of the natural resource base due to cumulative depletion, an increase in the instantaneous rate of exploitation, or an increase in the scale of extraction, increases the amount of natural capital used to extract a unit of natural resource. The biophysical perspective of scarcity measures the cost of obtaining natural resources in physical terms, and thereby emphasizes the throughput of energy and materials required to extract resources, and the resultant impact of that throughput on a broad array of ecosystem services in different quantities and spatial scales.

Natural resources in a highly organized state are more economically useful because they have lower energy costs. The inverse relation between resource quality and the energy cost has been demonstrated for a wide range of minerals and fossil fuels. The increased effort required to develop lower grade resources also increases their environmental cost. In metal mining, for example, deterioration of ore quality in underground mines spurs the expansion of surface mining where the volume of waste material produced per ton of ore is twelve times greater. The stripping ratio (tons of waste per ton of ore extracted) in metal, nonmetal, and coal surface mines in the U.S. has increased sharply in the last half-century. That decline in resource quality increases the land required to produce a ton of coal which, in turn, increases the amount of degraded land that must be reclaimed and the quantity of water used in reclamation. Cutler J. Cleveland found that the increase in the energy cost of petroleum extraction in the U.S. also is associated with an increase in the quantities of water used and CO_2 released in the extraction process.

Georgescu's Fourth Law has been criticized by a number of analysts in economics and the physical sciences. Ayres and Miller argue that Georgescu's assertion that intrinsically scarce materials cannot be recovered regardless of energy expenditure from average rocks and the ocean is just plain wrong. They observe that physical dissipation of materials can never result in a distribution worse from the standpoint of recovery than a hypothetical homogenous regolith in which every element is present exactly in its average crustal abundance. They argue that all elements can be extracted from such a regolith provided there is enough available energy. Ayres and Miller conclude that, in theory, energy is the only resource that could ultimately limit economic growth. It recently has been pointed out, that on a fundamental physical level, there is no such *law* as the Fourth Law of Thermodynamics stated by Georgescu. Whether at the molar or molecular level, in principle it is always possible to use the incoming high-quality energy to trace, collect and reassemble the dissipated elements. Well-documented counter examples to Georgescu's Fourth Law include the biogeochemical cycles—driven by the influx of solar radiation—that constantly funnel dissipated materials through a closed, global ecosystem and temporarily generate high material concentrations. It is those processes that lead to the formation of pearls from ocean water in the first place, the agglomeration of metals in ores and the formation of fossil fuels.

The theoretical flaws of Georgescu's Fourth law have led some to dismiss Georgescu's ideas or deny their significance. What should be at issue, however, is not a "categorical impossibility" of perfect recycling asserted by Georgescu. More important are the relationships among the processes that lead to a dissipation of high-quality energy and degradation of material resources on the one hand and the processes that capture high-quality energy and change materials from less desired to more desired thermodynamic states on the other hand. With thermodynamics, central for an assessment of these relationships are the concepts of information and time. To be able to trace and collect dispersed materials requires not only the availability of energy but also information and time. The fundamental physical relationships among those three inputs into processes that upgrade the state of materials have been described by Szilard (1929) and applied to industrial systems by Spreng, Chen, Ruth and Bullard and Ruth. The role of information relative to the other inputs into production processes prompted Boulding to claim that energy itself is unimportant. What is important is the knowledge to make use of material endowments that are present in less desired forms and change their state to more desired ones. In the case of biological systems, that knowledge is embodied in their genetic make-up. In the case of economies, it is present in the capital goods, human capital, institutions and other repositories of knowledge such as computers and libraries.

Biological systems, however, differ markedly from economic systems with regard to the time available to trace, collect and upgrade materials. Ore deposits and fossil fuels have been formed over time periods that are far too long to be of relevance for economic decision making. The formation of ore deposits and fossil fuels is powered by the inflow of solar radiation, utilized at low efficiencies, and heat from the Earth's core. In contrast, economic systems use significant amounts of nonrenewable resources to speed up the production of goods and services. Thus, from an economic perspective, an increasing dispersal of materials is constraining as long as tracing, collecting and upgrading those materials requires expenditures of finite, costly sources of low-entropy energy.

These perspectives highlight human participation in biogeochemical cycles and the importance of thermodynamics for understanding the environmental significance of that role. For example, the price of a material produced from virgin sources or from waste is a direct function of its degree of concentration in the parent source material or its dilution in the waste stream, respectively. Hence, the recycling potential for materials in hazardous waste streams is determined by their dilution, because highly dilute materials require more work, and hence higher cost, to upgrade to a desired raw material state.

The increase in entropy from energy use can be compared to the decrease in entropy that results from upgrading the state of materials either from virgin ores or waste residuals to arrive at a physical measure of the efficiency of economic processes. Comparisons of this measure over time provide insight into the ability of technical change—that itself requires materials and energy to take place—to counteract depletion and pollution. An advantage of these measures over traditional economic measures of efficiency is their ability to make judgments that are irrespective of changes in consumer preferences, market forms or other institutional settings that mask the physical reality of production and consumption processes.

Despite the flaws in Georgescu's definition of a Fourth Law, his insistence on the importance of materials for production and consumption processes highlighted the differences between economic processes and "natural" processes. The wide-ranging impact of his work is evident in a number of ways. Economists and ecological economists continue to discuss and debate important details of Georgescu's work, and they debate conventional economists about the usefulness of thermodynamics in economic analysis. Numerous studies of material and energy flows across the economy-environment boundary applied mass and energy balances to account for those flows and their contribution to economic production. Others have expanded on the use of mass and energy balances to account for changes in the quality of the material and energy flows as production and consumption occur. Georgescu's focus on the dispersal of materials and limits on recycling foreshadowed the development of the fields of industrial metabolism and industrial ecology in which the analysis of material cycles is used to understand how production and consumption impact the environment, and how to design new technologies that reduce such impacts. Finally, the importance of the entropic perspective advanced by Georgescu and the other pioneers is evidenced by the prominent attention devoted to it in histories of thought, surveys of ecological economics, and this volume in his honor.

ECOLOGICAL ECONOMICS AND INDUSTRIAL ECOLOGY

Concepts and methods in biophysical economics have become cornerstones of the new fields of ecological economics and industrial ecology. The International Society of Ecological Economics was formed in 1989 with the goal of integrating ecology and economics and other fields into a transdiscipline aimed at developing a sustainable world. Specific research areas include ecological modeling, ecological limits to growth, integrated assessment of climate change, biodiversity, valuation of natural capital, and ecological tax reform.

The basic points of consensus in the ecological economics vision are:

1. The vision of the Earth as a thermodynamically closed and nonmaterially growing system, with the human economy as a subsystem of the global ecosystem. This implies that there are limits to biophysical throughput of resources from the ecosystem, through the economic subsystem, and back to the ecosystem as wastes;
2. The future vision of a sustainable planet with a high quality of life for all of its citizens both humans and other species within the material constraints imposed by

The recognition that in the analysis of complex systems like the Earth at all space and time scales, fundamental uncertainty is large and irreducible and certain processes are irreversible, requiring a fundamentally precautionary stance; and

That institutions and management should be proactive rather than reactive and should result in simple, adaptive, and implementable policies based on a sophisticated understanding on the underlying systems which fully acknowledges the unerlying uncertainties. This forms the basis for policy implementation which is itself sustainable.

CONCLUSIONS

Biophysical economics is based on a conceptual model of the economy connected to, and sustained by, a flow of energy, materials, and ecosystem services. That simple but fundamental principle has formed the basis for wide-ranging research on the economy-environment relationship by an analysts from a variety of disciplines. The power of the biophysical perspective is evidenced not only by the long history it has enjoyed, but also by the fact that the analysis of energy and material flows is central to current issues about sustainability, environmental quality, and economic development.

6

Economics of Biodiversity

WHAT IS BIODIVERSITY?

Biodiversity can be defined in a variety of ways. A very narrow definition is to focus on genetic diversity which occurs within species, e.g. subspecies/forms or species diversity, perhaps taking into account the functional role different species play. A broader definition is to focus not just on species but also habitat and ecosystem diversity. Here varied landscapes, uplands, lowlands, wetlands and coastal areas all contribute to the diversity of the natural environment. The growing use of the concept of ecosystem services generally leads to the observation that the costs and benefits of these services are not sufficiently taken into account by public and private actors. To remedy this situation, many experts-well beyond the circle of economists-recommend not only developing payment for ecosystem services mechanisms, but also putting prices, or monetary values, on ecosystems.

There have been a number of economic arguments advanced regarding evaluation of the benefits of biodiversity. Most are anthropocentric but economists have also debated whether biodiversity is inherently valuable, independent of benefits to human. Diverse ecosystems are typically more productive than non-diverse ones, because any set of species can never fully exploit all potential niches. Since human economic productivity is largely reliant on Earth's ecosystems, adequate bioproductivity needs to be maintained.

The wealth of natural innovation found in biological organisms rivals all known technologies derived through synthetic means. A single human genome has some three billion bits of information but the human species also has many variations. There are many millions of species of life on the planet each with valuable information. Many chemical formulae and forty-five percent of all drugs have bio-origin. In the long run keeping genetic records of all species could, however, be just as useful in this regard. Some of the important economic commodities that biodiversity supplies to humankind are:

FOOD

Biodiversity provides high variety of food: crops, livestock, forestry, and fish are important food source of human species. However, the number of species have been domesticated and cultivated are small if comparing with the number of species existing. Wild species and varieties can supply genes for improving domesticated species by improving their yield, disease resistance, tolerance and vigor; this can increase the profit of farming. Using control species is often considered as more enivronmentally friendly method with compared with using pesticides. The control species can be used to protect the crops against pests and weeds. The economic loss due to the loss of crops/food can be reduced with the use of the control species. Also, the population of disease vectors (for example, mosquitoes) and the invasive species can be controlled; thus, the economic loss led by the invasive species and vectors can be reduced. However, it should be noted that even with extensive research into the control species, their use is a risky business, as in the importation of the Cane Toad to control beetles in Queensland.

WHY IS BIODIVERSITY IMPORTANT?

Humanity receives countless benefits from the natural environment in the form of goods and services such as food, wood, clean water, energy, protection from floods and soil erosion. Natural ecosystems are also the source of many life-saving drugs as well as providing sinks for our wastes, including carbon. Human development has also been shaped by the environment, and this interlinkage has strong social, cultural and aesthetic importance. The well-being of every human population in the world is fundamentally and directly dependent on ecosystem services.

EUROPEAN FOOTPRINT

Most biodiversity and ecosystem benefits are public goods which have no price: no single world citizen can be excluded from most of its services. Citizens profit to a large extent of unvalued biodiversity services from ecological recourses world wide. Although Europe is the second smallest continent, its population density and high per person consumption make it a significant contributor to the global ecological footprint.

THEORY OF ECONOMIC INSTRUMENTS

Economic instruments can be broadly defined as those measures that make use of the price system and market forces to achieve their objectives. The essential element of a market is that prices are determined by the collective supply of and demand for a particular good or service of individual actors. However, markets not always work perfectly well. There are several causes for market failure, one of them being the existence of public goods. The free rider problem arises here.

FREE-RIDER PROBLEM: TRAGEDY OF THE COMMONS

Free-rider behaviour means that an individual may decline to share in the costs of a certain good or service knowing that he or she cannot be precluded from sharing the benefits. Since it is assumed that each individual acts out of self-interest, every individual will consume as long as the benefits outweigh the costs. This might eventually lead to serious over-use of the particular public good, a situation which is often referred to as the 'tragedy of the commons'.

In a famous essay, Hardin (1968) illustrated the mechanism by showing how the sharing of a pasture by local herders may lead to overgrazing. Adding an additional animal to the land will provide the individual herd extra income (= an individual benefit), while it degrades the pasture (= a commonly born cost). Since all herds are interested in their own utility, they continue to add animal to the field, so that in the end the pasture is totally degraded. Other examples are fishing behaviour causing over fishing and human population growth that may outweigh the Earths carrying capacity. Biodiversity is a public good, meaning that most of its benefits are available to society in general. They do not exhibit complete rivalry and excludability in the market place. Subsequently, a wedge is driven between the value of biodiversity to individuals and to society as a whole. While there are ways of using market mechanisms to pay for the conservation of biodiversity, most aspects of biodiversity will always be difficult to 'market'.

Working through the price system, the various economic instruments that governments have at their disposal can improve private decision-making on biological resources by reducing the gap between the private and social value of biodiversity. They increase returns to activities that conserve or restore valuable biological ecosystems and increase the cost or lower the return to activities that damage ecosystems. They work to level the playing field between the observable returns to destructive activities and the non-observable returns to conservation. For example, farmers who receive a return in the form of a government payment for maintaining biological diversity on their land will be more willing to use farm practices that sustain biodiversity values than they otherwise would.

DESIGN OF ECONOMIC INSTRUMENT

It could be observed that many of ecological and forest functions are not marketed. They do not generate financial flows since their prices are zero. For example, in the absence of markets in carbon dioxide sequestration carbon stored in forest has a zero price. This creates the illusion that their value is zero, which is not the case. The timber production has a clear price causing commercial timber at a non-sustainable level. Increasingly CO2 capture in forests gets a price by carbon deals and the flexible Kyoto mechanism. However, most services as water protection and regulation, prevention of soil erosion are not paid in the absence of relevant markets

The design of appropriate markets for capturing these economic values implies two steps:

1. Estimation of the economic value of forest functions in a non-market context.
2. Internalise the resulting values in market systems so that they affect land use decisions.

The use of economic instruments for biodiversity protection is based on the idea that the social costs of biodiversity loss can be imputed into the price of the activities that cause this loss. This requires the monetary measurement of the preferences for the public good aspects of biodiversity. Once the correct value has been derived, economic instruments can achieve ecological and economic efficiency. However, whereas the determination of exact monetary values for biodiversity is feasible in principal on the bases of techniques developed by economic theory, the intrinsic complexity of biodiversity makes this difficult to accomplish in practice.

VALUATION OF BIODIVERSITY

Not all values of biodiversity can be measured in economic terms. To many people nature has an intrinsic value that is unrelated to its usefulness to humans. Besides, only part of the full range of benefits provided by biodiversity and ecosystems can be assessed due to current limitations in the understanding of ecological functions. Value estimates from case studies usually take into account only some of the benefits. Also data and valuation studies are not yet available for all types of ecosystems - for example marine ecosystems are less well covered than terrestrial ecosystems. Therefore, it should be kept in mind that estimates of the economic value of biodiversity and ecosystem services are surrounded by many uncertainties. The economic value of biodiversity is measured in a number of ways. A useful abstraction for policy purposes is to view biological resources as assets that provide a series of flows that benefit people. Even intangible values such as the existence value of species or ecosystems can be thought of as a flow of services. A concept that is often used in this regard is the concept of Total Economic Value (TEV) of a biological asset. The preference for a particular biological asset over another provides the indicator of its economic value.

There are two approaches to assess the economic value of nature:

1. Revealed and stated preferences: the valuation of ecosystems relies on welfare measures in terms of consumer and producer surpluses. Methods to asses these values are stated and revealed preference techniques.
2. Compensation/prevention costs: deduct shadow prices on the base of environmental pricing techniques. This set of pricing techniques relies on data from actual or potential maintaining or preventing environmental degradation as a proxy for the environmental value.

The Ecobalance concept is in line with the second type of assigning values to biodiversity assets, namely the compensational cost to provide a alternative hectare of natural area with minimal an equal ecological value in terms of species. This approach should not be seen as a way to fully value the services of ecosystems. It is more a practical useful and implementable concept for internalizing a part of the costs of loss of species with the above mentioned limitations.

In order to give land owner effective incentives to protect biodiversity values of their land the price should reflect two components:

1. Cost of conservation measures.
2. Opportunity costs.

Cost of Conservation

The annual costs of effective field-based conservation vary enormously. A study of Balmford (2002), using data for 139 terrestrial programs worldwide, found a variation across seven orders of magnitude, from < $ 0.1 to > $ 1,000,000 per km2 per year, with a typical cost estimate of 1,000 $/km2/year. This variation can be closely predicted from positive associations between costs per unit area and an array of indices of local development. Corresponding measures of conservation benefit are limited but show opposing global trends, being higher in less developed parts of the world. The benefit-to-cost ratio of conservation is thus far greater in less developed regions, yet these are where the shortfall in current conservation spending is most marked. Substantially increased investment in tropical conservation is therefore urgently required if opportunities for costeffective action are not to be missed. The gross mismatch between the costs of effective nature conservation and current global spending means that prioritization of conservation effort is essential and should be based on economic as well as biological information.

Opportunity Costs

The second part of total costs of conservation consists of opportunity costs. Conservation has costs for local people in terms of the opportunity costs such as the loss in potential agriculture returns of not converting such habitats. Transferring some of the rich world benefits back to local people could be one approach to improving incentives to conserve those natural habitats and species locally that clearly have wider benefits globally. Possible alternative land uses might be timber harvesting, conversion to agriculture or conversion to urban development, etc. A measure of the opportunity costs are the agricultural returns of a regions. Depending on location and alternative land use opportunity cost vary $ 2 to $ 6,000/hectare/year. For developing countries opportunity costs amount to maximum of $ 100/hectare/year, with typical values of < $ 5 /hectare/year. Opportunity cost can be zero for those areas that are not economically productive. However it can be questioned whether conserving these areas will be additional compared to business as usual. If developers do not gain from converting forests opp. cost zero, they would have restrained from land conversion anyway. The value of protected area thus depend on the biodiversity values of the area and the degree of threat from economic productive land use.

TOTAL COSTS

Incorporating both price components cost of protection measures and alternative land use is essential in developing an effective incentive framework for protecting biodiversity. Rewarding conservation activities through incentive-based instruments increase the profitability of conservation as a land use activity. Thus, land management for conservation can be brought in closer competition with more destructive management activities such as mining and agriculture. This competition will most likely engender the beneficial side effect of increased land prices in those areas where conservation is an economically viable alternative. Facing higher land prices, developers will opt for more area-intensive production that minimises harm to biodiversity. Total costs are summarised in Table 1.

Table 1
Conservation and Opportunity Costs in Euros/Hectare/year

	Lower Limit	*Upper Limit*	*Typical Costs*
Conservation Costs	0,0	7,300	7
Opportunity Costs	0,1	73	4
Total Costs	0	7,373	11

TARGETING LAND USE

Targeting land use change in order to slow biodiversity loss, however, is extremely difficult. Habitats are altered by international, national and local actors for a number of diverse motivations. In order to effectively address biodiversity loss, we need to examine the 'broader context' in which these processes function. Kiss (2002) elaborates on this argument insightfully. Acknowledging that attributing biodiversity loss to only or even primarily over-population and poverty is 'overly simplistic', maintains that 'the fundamental cause of biodiversity loss worldwide is that those in a position to preserve it lack sufficient incentives to do so'. Thus, according to Kiss and a number of other conservationists, an effective approach to halting biodiversity loss requires an incentive-based approach that operates at the global level in order to address the multiple factors driving this phenomenon.

WHO PAYS?

A difficult aspect in the development of biodiversity policy is how to decide when to make payments direct to people, when to pay them indirectly and when to require resource users to pay the full costs of biodiversity conservation (OECD, 1996). It is important to understand the distribution of costs and benefits among three target groups.

Those whose behaviour actually enhances biodiversity-related goods, since these people tend to bear conservation costs.

1. Those who actually benefit from biodiversity-related goods and services, as they attach value to biodiversity.
2. Those whose behaviour actually diminish or harms biodiversity-related goods and services, as this groups affect both 1) and 2).

A properly designed economic incentive can encourage behaviour that promotes conservation i.e. compensate landowners for forgone revenues/opportunity costs and discourages behaviour that does not, thus transferring the amount of currency among these target groups in question. Those who use or damage biodiversity should pay at least a part of the cost of resource use, in line with the generally accepted polluter pays principle. In contrast, it is often the case that those who benefit from biodiversity use pay nothing. Young (1992) has suggested that this concept could be called the beneficiary compensates principle, meaning the reimbursement of incremental cost above normal costs of conservation measures. Offsetting and habitat banking can provide the international financial flow from damager to provider of biodiversity. Offsetting and habitat banking thus cover the above two blocks, but exclude the block below. They can be considered as a form of International Payment for Environmental Services.

THE NEED FOR GLOBAL SCALE

There is a large gap between the development of the global carbon market and other markets for ecosystem services. Despite the existence of many schemes around the world, there is still insufficient institutional support for these efforts at an international level. Biodiversity-related ecosystem services are in particular need of attention, as their global importance implies the need for international cooperation.

HABITAT BANKING AND OFFSETTING

Biodiversity offsets are unique among other incentive based instruments in that they have the potential to simultaneously address some drivers of biodiversity loss. They have the potential to create incentives for conservation at two levels. First, offset requirements discourage activities that reduce biodiversity by increasing the cost of development. Developers must pay an additional fee for their activities in the form of compensation for residual biodiversity loss. Second, offsets create a demand for conservation land. By increasing the demand for conservation, offsets provide an additional incentive to 'manage' land for conservation as opposed to more biodiversity-destructive economic activities. Initiatives for biodiversity offsetting have been developed in a number of regions around the world.

ON-SITE OFFSETTING (FIRST ROW)

It is the most rudimentary form of biodiversity offsetting. Compensation takes place on a project by project basis and requires on-site mitigation of development impacts to biodiversity.

OFF-SITE OFFSETTING (MIDDLE ROW)

This type of offsetting creates the opportunity to compensate at a lower cost by allowing biodiversity conservation on another site with a lower opportunity cost, but equal or greater biodiversity value. Biodiversity loss within the project area is offset by the protection of an equivalent or greater amount of biodiversity at another off-site location. No trading is allowed under this regime, offsets are non-transferrable.

HABITAT BANKING (LAST ROW)

Trading in off-site compensation is introduced. Offsets can be traded through a standardized market. A third party - the habitat bank - will implement and maintain the offsets on behalf of the developer in exchange for financial compensation. Habitat banking is the relevant form of offsetting here as a market for offsetting is formed. It has some important advantages as compared to traditional (on-site) offsetting.

- Through habitat banking an implicit price is set for the quality of biodiversity that could raise the supply of biodiversity enhancing projects at a much larger scale than under traditional offsetting. In principle, through the establishment of habitat banking, any land owner is being faced with opportunity costs of not improving the biodiversity on their lands.
- Through habitat banking the establishment of larger conservation areas is possible. From a biological perspective, larger areas enhance biodiversity. Habitat banking can be seen as an effective mechanism for linking existing habitat patches into more coherent ecological networks.
- Through habitat banking compensation can - in principle-be achieved at lower costs than with on-site compensation. Static efficiency can be increased through economies of scale and dynamic efficiency can be enhanced by increasing competition of suppliers of biodiversity. In addition one should mention that for developers risks are being reduced as habitat banking allows them to use pre-defined prices for compensating measures.

Nevertheless, we also realize that there are some major controversies connected to the concept of offsetting:

- *Environmental Quality of Offsetting.* Guaranteeing equivalent biodiversity values requires measuring and quantifying biodiversity, determining an appropriate geological scale over which offsets can be located, and determining an appropriate time scale over which the offsetting conservation activity can be completed. Of these obstacles, the quantification of biodiversity appears to be the greatest. Complexities on measurement make biodiversity markets distinct from constructed markets for pollution e.g. CO2, NOx, fish quota, etc. This implies either considerable administrative costs for handling or over simplifying the scheme which could possibly harm the environmental effectiveness.

- *Additionality.* Other issues relate to the 'additionality problem'. One of the main challenges of habitat offsetting is to make sure that compensation only relates to the additional efforts undertaken and not ecological developments that would have taken place anyway. Some forest certification schemes have, for instance, been blamed for certificating 'business as usual' activities rather than additional efforts of sustainable forestry and similar complaints are being heard for the market of carbon offsetting or the Clean Development Mechanism.

Given these problems, offsetting should be seen the last step on the 'mitigation hierarchy' - avoid, minimise, mitigate, offset here, offset there-employed by many land developers. In this light, economic instruments should not only generate funds for protecting unique and biodiversity-rich areas worldwide, but also have a significant contribution to a sustainable use of biodiversity from.

THE TRADING ENTITY

One of the fundamental questions in the design of an offset market is who will be obliged to offset. Do consumers need to buy biodiversity offsets debits or should producers acquire them? In the case of imported products, should importers be charged? The trading entity refers to the party that is required to hand in biodiversity offsets debits. In systems of habitat banking the project developer, causer of land change decisions, is obliged to hand in the offsets. However, in theory many different parties can be eligible to do so, depending on their position in the product chain upstream, middle stream, downstream. We can distinguish under a system of offsets:

- *Upstream:* 'high impact' international developers (such as mining, agro forestry and agricultural companies) that are responsible for the land use changes.
- *Midstream:* the importers and the national industry that manufactures these primary products from agricultural sources to products that are to be sold on western markets.
- *Downstream:* consumers of 'high impact' products. Several criteria can be used to determine the optimal point of trading in the product cycle. These criteria are:

EFFECTIVENESS

- Market coverage. The trading system would be most effective in internalizing the external costs of biodiversity use if it covers most of the products whose manufacturing harmed biodiversity. In some cases, not all products reach the consumer so that this would not be the best choice of application. An example of such a case is wood usage in the Netherlands. A large share of wood is used by companies and will never arrive at the consumer such pallets, and paper use, while it has the same environmental pressure as wood that does reach consumer markets. It is, therefore, preferable to oblige Dutch importers rather than Dutch consumers to buy biodiversity debits.
- Steering intensity. By steering effect, we mean the extent to which the instrument may be effective in ensuring reduction and compensation for biodiversity pressures. The impact on land use changes might partly depend on the choice of application point. In principle, it is argued that economic instruments have a larger impact when they are implemented closer to the source of the external effect,

the land change decision. The effectiveness will be optimal when international developers will be obliged to compensate their biodiversity loss. Effectively, compensation can be achieved by the impacting company financing the protection of a commensurate amount of threatened land. At the level of consumers, a relatively small price increase might not have the desired effect on buying behaviour. For communication and awareness purposes, however, it is better to focus on consumers. At the import level, the biodiversity trading system may have more impact on the buying behaviour of importers.

Implementation

- Transaction costs. Transaction costs can vary considerably among the types of emission schemes as well as compared to a general tax. Schemes with expected high transaction costs are, generally speaking, not preferable from both the viewpoint of economic efficiency as well as political acceptability. The transaction costs of implementing an economic instrument are linked with the amount of actors that is liable to pay. If end consumers are the trading entity, transaction costs may be very high. From this point of view, the focus would lie on the group which relatively limited and easy to identify, presumably importers.
- Synergy with other policy instruments. When other measures are present, it is worth noticing which system design attunes best to these existing measures. For instance, an argument for using importers as application point is that the system would fit with the existing import tariffs.

Schemes directed at end users in terms of buyers of high impact products lead to high transaction costs and may be difficult to implement, compared to schemes aimed at the project developer directly responsible for land use change. On the contrary, in upstream developers or midstream trade schemes the number of trading entity can be relatively limited. Especially, when offsetting is the main principle, the environmental effectiveness is best guaranteed when the international project developers form the trading entity. A firstbest option would thus be the inclusion of the international developers into an international scheme. The trading system is directed to actors engaging in extensive land use change activities in order to sell products with significant biodiversity impacts (e.g. wood, beef, oil, minerals, etc.) on international markets. The price effect of an upstream system would spread out throughout the economy, raising the price of high impact goods produced in proportion to their impacts. Upstream solutions will benefit from greater coverage and simpler implementation than downstream solutions.

However, upstream solution may be less politically acceptable given their wide coverage of sectors for which price increases may be particularly unpopular. This would require a broad international consensus on a global system that includes the large international developers to offset residual impacts to biodiversity. The effort to establish a multilateral institutionalized trading scheme can be comparable with the implementation of EU carbon trading. The process of negotiations will be time consuming and complex, and the outcome is even then highly unsure as the vested economic interest of certain countries are considerable. This can be an important argument to fall back on a midstream European scheme targeting the importers and producers of 'high impact' products, as a second-best solution. Compared to end users offsetting a midstream offset scheme would mean a considerable reduction of transaction costs, whilst still guaranteeing a part of the steering intensity of a down stream model.

REVENUES

Based on the typical costs of 11 Euro/hectare/year for offsetting the biodiversity impact, the total amount in 2010 is expected to be 130 million Euros, covering an additional protection area of 12 million hectares. As can be expected from the land use perspective wood and meat are the largest financial contributors to offsetting biodiversity. European coverage of an offset scheme will generate approximately two to three billion dollar.

ECONOMIC VALUES OF ANIMAL GENETIC RESOURCES

Human preferences regarding genetic traits of livestock differ across regions, countries, communities and production systems. For example, in marginal areas, the most valuable livestock attributes are often those that successfully guarantee multifunctionality and flexibility or resilience in order to deal with variable environmental conditions. In contrast, in zones with high production potential, livestock attributes maximising productivity of specific products under controlled conditions are more valuable. Thus, there is no single answer to such question. However, if breeders could better estimate the value assigned to developing livestock species for particular production systems, they could make better decisions on which

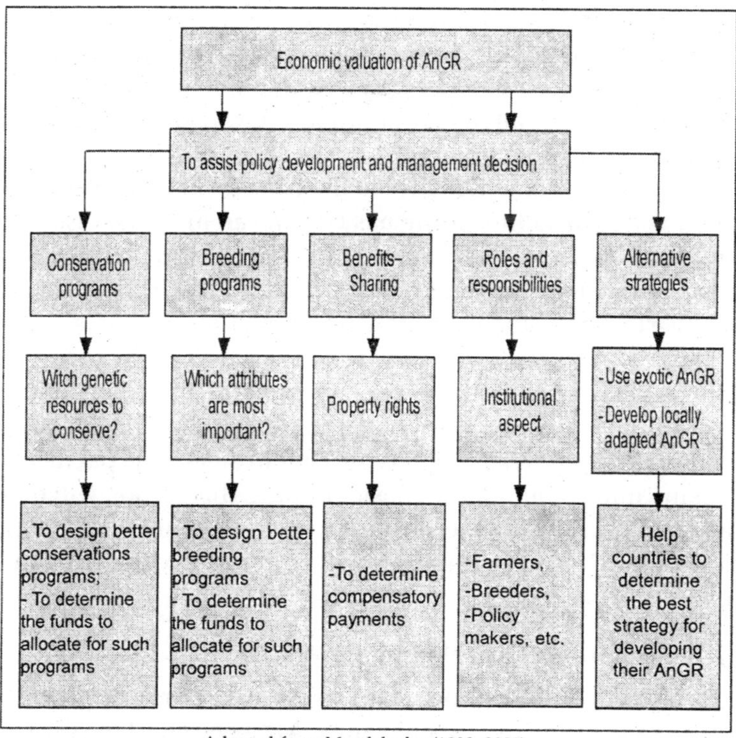

Adapted from Mendelsohn (1999, 2003)

Figure 1: Schematic Summary of Arguments to Economic Valuation of AnGR

breeds to utilise for intervention. This would also help geneticists design better programmes of sustainable intensification, and it would help decision-makers in determining the effort allocated to such programmes

As for the second argument, society might want to protect the genetic stock. The economic valuation of conservation and sustainable use of anima genetic resource can be an effective means of garnering the necessary public and political support, including the development of appropriate policies. This requires an evaluation of benefits generated by anima genetic resource conservation programmes. There are two reasons to carefully state the benefits of these programmes. First, identified benefits could be quantified so that society has some sense of how much the conservation is worth. Society can then determine how much it wants to spend on a conservation effort. Second, by identifying the benefits, conservation managers will have a better idea of what they are trying to accomplish. The benefits of alternative conservation strategies can guide the design of the programme.

The last argument relates to the concept of benefit sharing cited above. Benefit-sharing has become an important issue in international biodiversity negotiation in search for a just mechanism to remunerate local people for their contribution to livestock development. Benefit-sharing mechanisms evoke property-rights issues and demand alternative forms of payments to compensate for the transfer of these genetic resources. However, without an understanding of the value of anima genetic resource, it is difficult to determine payments. Taking into account these considerations, this section will treat aspects relating to the various types of values of genetic resources. Particular emphasis will be devoted to the economic bases of these values.

THE PUBLIC GOOD NATURE OF ANGR

For conventional goods and services, markets provide important information about values. Markets reflect the relative scarcity of traded goods and the preference for these goods. For public goods and externalities, markets are not available to provide such information. Animal genetic resources fall into this category of public goods. According to table we can distinguish public goods from private goods along their degree of non-rivalness and non-excludability.

Table 2
Rivalness and Excludability in Consumption

	Rival in Consumption	*Non-rival in Consumption*
Excludable	E Private good	Club good
Non-excludable	Open access resource	Public good

Private goods are excludable and rival in consumption. These properties make markets for these goods work well. An owner can exclude others from the consumption of a resource. Furthermore, the consumption by one person reduces the availability of the good, so that no welfare gain can be achieved by making the good at the same time available to another person. Public goods are characterised by non-excludability and non-rivalness. On the one hand, a public good is non-rival. The pure notion of non-rivalness signifies that the consumption of a good by one person does not reduce the availability of the good to other individuals. The good hence can be provided "in common". On the other hand, a public good is not excludable. This often leads to a free-rider problem.

While farm animals can be considered as private goods, animal genetic resources embedded in these animals should be considered as quasi-public goods. Their degree of excludability is low, as animals of a breed carrying the desired genetic resources can often be bought at low cost. Breeds are a natural resource that, if properly managed above a critical population number, retains its property of a renewable resource. Using animals from this breed to one breeding purpose does thus not rival other purposes. Measuring the value of public goods is difficult because they are not evaluated in markets. Evaluation may also fall foul to the free-rider problem, leading individuals to a systematic understatement of value. As for public goods, values typically are not exclusively derived from private use of the resource, and it appears useful to first provide a classification of different resource values, before reviewing the methods measuring these values.

VALUES UNDER CERTAINTY

Use and Non-Use Values

We distinguish between use values and non-use values. Use values are those that result from direct use of the resource. They include value created by productive activities. In the case of sheep and goat anima genetic resource, production values are primarily those of wool, milk, and meat. Another category of use values includes amenity values that individuals associate, e.g. to the viewing of a species or to the knowing about a species existence. Having a preference for a breed results thus in value. Hence defined use values can be distinguished into active-use values and passive-use values. Sticking to our example, the act of tourists viewing a traditional breed results in an active-use value. Active-use values are always complementary to observable consumption and production choices and can for instance be observed when tourists choose to spend their vacation in a particular area for the sake of viewing a particular breed, given all other things equal. Non-market good evaluation techniques try to exploit this complementarity in consumption.

Passive-use values are a second category of use values. In the previous example, citizens might value the conservation efforts for a traditional breed, even if they never visit the region where these are breed. If the region is located in a very remote area and the cost of travelling to the park exceeds the willingness-to-pay for some citizens, they may not visit the park but still value the possibility. In this case it is not possible to exploit the complementarity between the breed of value and the recreational activity.

Passive-use values of woodland caribou preservation the measurement of passive-use values has become an important issue in environmental economics. Passiveuse value is the economic value that arises when changes in environmental quality are not reflected in any observable behavioural change. Since passive-use value is not reflected in observed behaviour, stated preference approaches are used for the elicitation of these values. Adamowicz et al. (1998) estimate the passive-use value of a habitat enhancement programme in a study of Mountain-dwelling woodland caribou habitat. Woodland caribou are listed as "threatened" by the Wildlife Act of Alberta. Lands managed under forest management agreements contain superior woodland caribou habitat. To protect this habitat, restrictions need to be imposed on the industrial and recreational uses of this land.

Adamowicz et al. (1998) employ the contingent valuation method to estimate the value of an old-growth forest programme. Under this programme, lands are removed from forestry activity and a wilderness area is created. It requires that recreational activities be restricted in the area no fishing, no hunting, or off-road vehicles. Biologists predict that under these conditions the caribou population to increase from the current level of 400 individuals to a viable population of 600 individuals. The proposed programme thus contained attractive features building a viable caribou population and unattractive features employment effects and restrictions on recreation. A referendum-type question was employed to measure respondents' willingness to pay (WTP). WTP was measured using a proposed tax increase ranging from Ca-$ 1 to 150. Respondents could bid for or against the programme given the tax amount indicated or respond "I don't know". The survey was conducted on a random sample of residents in Edmonton, Canada. A total of 402 valid responses was obtained. The data were analysed in the random utility framework using a conditional logit model. Under a linear specification, welfare measures result in an average WTP of Ca-$ 142.82 per individual. Because the increase in value is not complementary to observed actions, empirical evaluation methods relying on complementarity cannot be used. It has been argued that, to capture this passive-use value, only contingent evaluation methods can be employed.

Non-use values are compounded by existence values and bequest values. Existence values are those that are not related to direct, neither present nor future, use of a species but to the simple fact that people value the existence of a species without ever directly using it. Existence value can partly be motivated as bequest value by altruism towards future generations. Said in another way, existence values may be interpreted as sympathy to nature, and cultural or regional values. Feelings of responsibility for nature, the desire to leave a cultural legacy to future generations, may lead to positive values for the preservation of farm animal genetic resources. A strict definition of existence values, which is adopted in this discussion, approaches the existence value from a non-anthropocentric view. The value is attributed to the existence of the breed and not to the valuation by people. The existence is of value in itself and does not depend on active or passive use by humans. In this respect, existence value is not commensurate with the concept of economic value that is based on the notion of human preferences. Consequently, we will not consider it in this discussion without denying the importance of existence value outside the realm of economics.

VALUE OF DIVERSITY

In all that has been said before, value is attributed to specific traits of breeds because of their intrinsic use or non-use value. As explained above, traits have to be interpreted in a large sense to include phenotypic expressions typical for traditional breeds as related to cultural and historical passive-use values. In addition, diversity in itself can be of value. It is not only important to preserve one species or another because of their specific values, but when choosing the right mix of species to preserve, the diversity of the mix will also be of importance. Diversity is of importance in production and consumption. In the following, we can discuss the two contexts as a source of diversity value.

DIVERSITY IN PRODUCTION

Production environments can be diverse. Sheep and goat are raised in different conditions. Sheep used in pasture management. Because of varying conditions, the productive use value of a breed depends to a large extent on the environment in which they are evaluated. Indeed, the development of distinctive breeds is in part due to the diverse production environments in which the breeds have been developed. Current agricultural practices lead to a loss of diversity because nowadays breeds have to be less adapted to regional environmental conditions. The increase in capital use in agricultural production increases the potential of high-yielding uniform breeds. Capital intensive production technologies have been adopted by farmers in many regions in Europe. These technologies reduce the need for adapted breeds even in adverse environmental condition.

DIVERSITY IN CONSUMPTION

It is common in economics to attribute value to diversity. The standard axiom of preference convexity leads automatically to this property. The convexity axiom can be presented as in Figure 2.

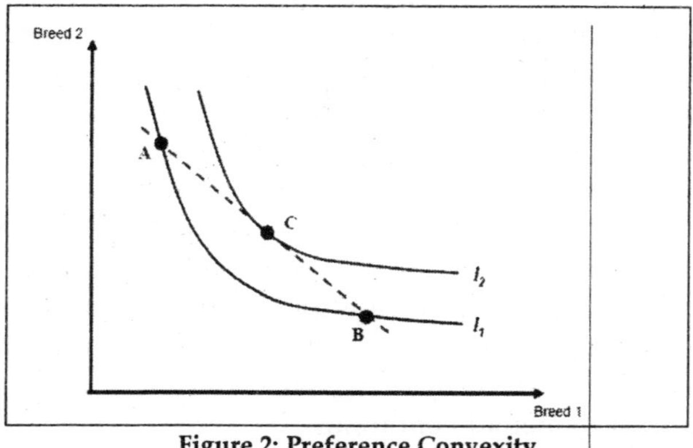

Figure 2: Preference Convexity

In this figure the two axes measure the population sizes of breeds 1 and 2. The indifference curve I1 indicates the combinations of (breed 1, breed 2) to which the consumer is indifferent, e.g., points A and B. A more balanced mix of breeds, as in point C, where populations of breed 1 and breed 2 are about equal in size, would lead to a higher degree of utility for the consumer. He could then achieve indifference I2 which indicates a higher level of utility.

VALUES UNDER UNCERTAINTY

According to Swanson (1998) two types of value best describe the role of genetic resources in agriculture: information and insurance. These values are of particular importance when considering decision making under uncertainty and when considering the search for new breeding strategies adapting breeds to an ever-evolving environment.

OPTION VALUE

Many conservation efforts for genetic resources are motivated by the desire to preserve a diverse gene pool that can serve as a source for future breeding. In the past much of agricultural breeding and development 'aid' has concentrated on the propagation of few 'improved livestock breeds'. This has led to a loss in genetic diversity. Genetic erosion has resulted from this concentration on few 'improved' breeds. An estimated 16 % of uniquely adapted breeds have been lost since the beginning of the last century and another 30 % are at risk of becoming extinct (FAO, 1999). A species, once extinct, would be lost forever. The genotype-environment interaction can limit to an important extent the productivity of improved livestock breeds in unfavourable environments. In addition, intensive livestock breeds concentrate often on single-use breeds, i.e., either milk, wool, or meat. Multiple-use breeds are left at a disadvantage. Multiple uses and adaptive traits are of particular importance in marginal rural areas and under difficult environmental conditions.

Conservation of genetic diversity gives an option to use alternative traits and to develop new ones in the future. Because decision making on breed development is characterized by inherent uncertainty about future developments of market and natural environments, this option can be highly valuable. A resource of no interest in one situation can be particularly useful under alternative conditions. Moreover, uncertainty about market and policy conditions can also enhance the desire for diversity conservation in order to insure against adverse scenarios. In such uncertain environments, many decision-makers behave risk averse. They add a risk premium to the value of a resource such that the total value attributed to the resource exceeds its expected use value.

Suppose a farmer considers two alternative scenarios, one where the demand for goat-milk products increases and another where market conditions remain constant. Thus the expected value of keeping a specialized trait will be the sum of the probability-weighted respective profits under each scenario. But because the farmer is risk averse, he adds an additional value to the conservation of the trait. The total value, the option price, results as the sum of expected surplus plus the option value:

OPTION PRICE = EXPECTED SURPLUS + OPTION VALUE

With regard to the preservation of animal genetic resources, farmers may not fully consider the uncertainty over future developments in their decision. Indeed, even if they do not preserve a specific trait, others may. Thus they rely on others to preserve the desired degree of diversity. This free-rider problem relates to the public good character of animal genetic resources and is likely of considerable importance in explaining the erosion of animal genetic diversity. In contrast to the diversity value valid in situations without uncertainty, this option value is defined in a context of uncertainty. Decisions about conservation are made before uncertainty about future environmental and market conditions is resolved. This type of value has been discussed by Swanson (1998) as portfolio value. The value is derived from the retention of a relatively wide range of assets within the agricultural production system. A portfolio of different breeds allows spreading the risks posed by an inherently uncertain production environment that is subject to random environmental conditions and disease pressures. Variability of returns is smoothed out by having (i) a broader portfolio of assets breeds within a species, (ii) a wider portfolio of assets agricultural commodities within a country, and (iii) a wider portfolio of assets available methods of production across the globe. Society has a preference to conserve a larger portfolio of breeds than under risk neutrality. Diversity is conserved for the sake of future adaptation of breeds to changing environmental conditions and in a desire to improve their economic performance.

QUASI-OPTION VALUE

A second value associated to decision making under uncertainty is the quasi-option value. In contrast to the option value that is motivated by risk aversion and the resulting risk premium, the quasi-option value arises even under risk neutrality (table 2). It results from the irreversible nature of breed loss. It measures the benefits that accrue, because learning about the value of preservation leads to more informed and better decisions. A more informed decision reduces the risk of taking the wrong decision that can be very costly, or even impossible, to reverse. A positive quasi-option value encourages the conservation of resources until uncertainty about future scenarios has been resolved and more information about the true value has been obtained. The learning potential embedded in genetic resources has been analysed with respect to the possibility to develop new plant varieties and in the search for new pharmaceutical products via bioprospecting. The latter study is also of interest for the in-situ conservation of agricultural genetic resources. Simpson, Sedjo, and Reid have found that the value of a single species lost, its scarcity value, will be small because biodiversity is abundant. However, Rausser and Small (2000) claim that biotechnology companies do not search randomly but use research leads and prior information to guide their search for new production. They show that promising research leads can induce significantly higher biodiversity value.

In-situ conservation of agricultural genetic resources allows gaining important information about the value of a breed. Landraces have formed on the basis of human selection processes over long time horizons. They have accumulated a stock of previously successful strategies and 'traditional' farmers have survived by observing their performance in their specific production environment. Subsequent selection and use of desirable traits and characteristics have aided in creating these landraces adapted to the particular environment. Animal breeders can make use of this knowledge when searching new strategies to improve the genetic resource base of a breed. As a consequence, knowledge about the merit of traditional breeds is available from local breeders that have developed this breed over long time horizons. The knowledge of useful breed characteristics, e.g. environmental adaptability or disease resistance, increases the information value of this resource, even if its scarcity value derived under complete ignorance is small.

Table 2
Biodiversity Values

Value	*Description/Origin*	*Main Characteristics*
Values under Certainty		
Use values		
Active -use values	• Production • Consumption • Amenity	• Static • Ex-post
Passive-use values	• Amenity	• Static • Ex-post
Non-use values	• Existence value • Bequest value	• Sympathy toward animal • Intergenerational altruism
Diversity values	• Variety in space • Variety in production and consumption	• Maintain variability • Preference for diversity
Values under Uncertainty		
Option value	• Option to use alternative • traits and to develop new ones in the future	• Static • Risk aversion • Soft uncertainty
Quasi-option value	• Preference for flexibility • Hysteresis, learning about breed values	• Ex-ante • Dynamic • Hard uncertainty (irreversibility)

THE CONCEPT OF VALUE ON THE CONSUMER AND ON THE PRODUCER SIDE

To measure economic value, a multitude of empirical methods is available. These methods make use of economic concepts in demand and supply analysis. Before explaining the methods, it will be useful to review the underlying theory that allows evaluating resources from data collected in surveys and markets.

VALUE TO CONSUMERS

A common measure evaluating welfare impacts of a price change on the consumer is the consumer surplus. Consumer surplus is defined as the area under the demand curve and above the price. As an example we will consider the impact of technical change in meat production (figure 3). An increase in productivity reduces the marginal cost of meat production. The supply curve shifts downwards. At the market level, the price for meat decreases from P0 to P1. The change in consumer surplus resulting from the increase in production hence is measured by the shaded area, CS, in Figure 3

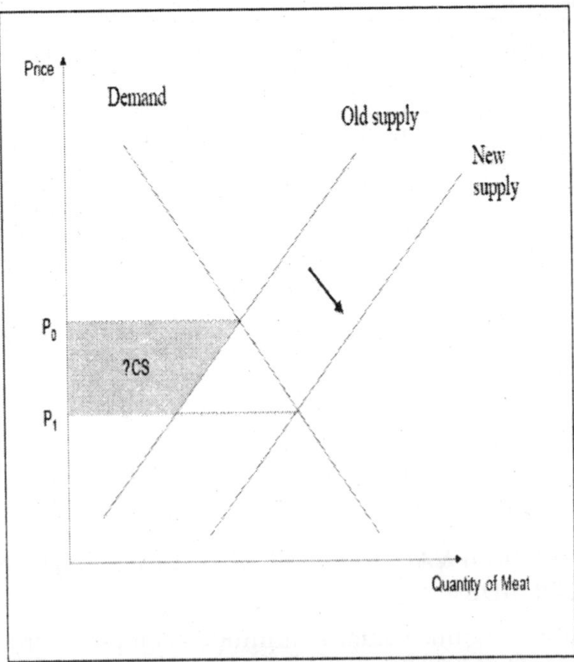

Figure 3: Change in Consumer Surplus

Consumer surplus is an exact welfare measure only under particular hypotheses on consumers' preferences. If these conditions are not met consumer surplus can only serve as an approximation to consumer welfare. There are alternative, exact, measures of welfare on the consumer side: compensating and equivalent variation. The former is based on the level of utility before a proposed price change, the latter is based on the level of utility after the proposed price change.

COMPENSATING VARIATION

After a price change, the compensating variation (CV) measures the necessary change in income, R, that maintains the initial level of utility at new prices. Consider an economic agent consuming two goods: meat and other consumption goods. The price of the other consumption goods is normalized to one. In figure 4 the preferences of the consumer are mapped using the indifference curve, U. The budget constraint is presented by the straight line. Before the price change, the optimal level of consumption results in point A.

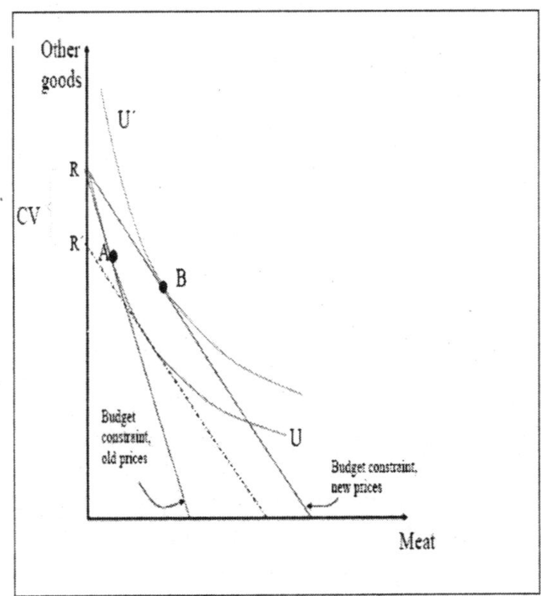

Figure 4: Compensating Variation

Following a reduction in the price for meat, the budget constraint rotates outwards. The consumer can reach a higher indifference curve, U′, representing a higher level of utility. The compensating variation, CV, is the change in income that would leave the consumer indifferent between the situations with and without the price change. Since the price of meat decreases, the amount of goods that can be bought at a given income increases. The economic agent is thus willing to pay and amount equal to the difference between R to R′, without being worth off.

EQUIVALENT VARIATION

Given a price change, the equivalent variation (EV) measures the change in income that at old prices would be necessary to obtain the same, equivalent change in welfare. Figure 5 demonstrates the idea. Since a price change makes the consumer better off, it would be necessary to increase the income of the consumer if he were to forego the price change and increase his utility by as much as done by the price change.

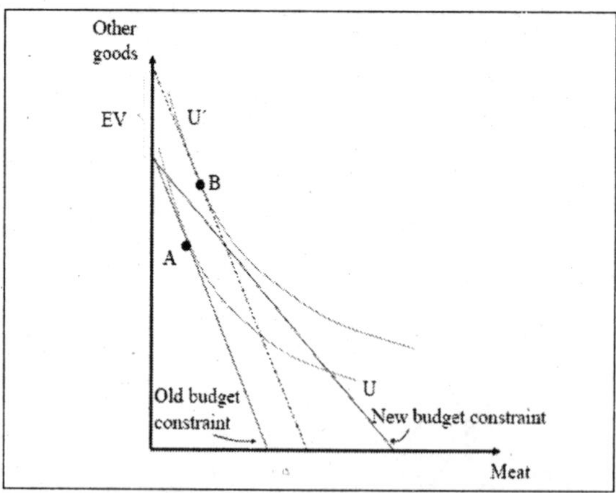

Figure 5: Equivalent Variation

In general, CV and EV will not be equal. The variations measure the distance between indifference curves and this distance depends on the point of evaluation. For normal goods we obtain: CV CS EV.

WILLINGNESS TO PAY AND WILLINGNESS TO ACCEPT

Empirically, compensating and equivalent variation are evaluated using the concepts of willingness-to-pay (WTP) and willingness-to-accept (WTA). Table 3 shows the relationship between willingness to pay and willingness to accept and EV and CV.

Table 3
CV, EV, WTP and WTA

	Compensation Variation	*Equivalent Variation*
Price fall	WTP Amount of income the consumer is willing to pay to obtain the price fall	WTA Amount of income the consumer is willing to accept foregoing the price fall.
Price rise Evaluation on the producer side	WTA Amount of income compensating the increase in price	WTP Amount of income the consumer is willing to pay to avoid the increase in price.

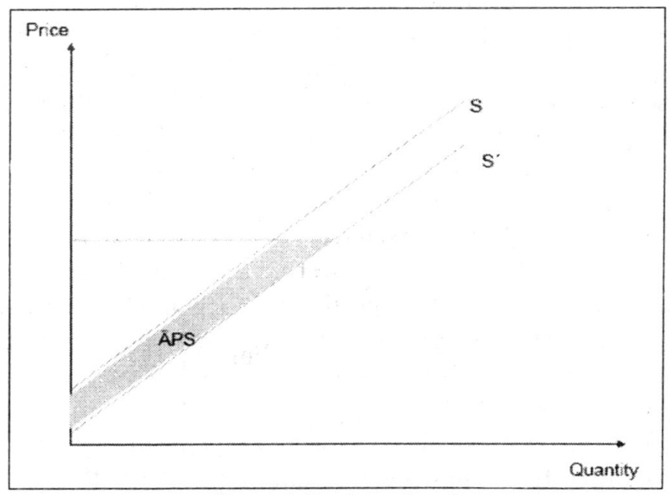

Figure 6: Producer Surplus

Two approaches to measure producers' valuation of breeding traits exist in the literature. One focuses on a pure profit-maximization objective. According to Hotelling's lemma the first derivative of the profit function with respect to output prices gives the product supply curve, the derivative with respect to input prices yields the derived demand curve for inputs. We illustrate at the example of a change in technology, such as a change in genetic traits. An increase in productivity shifts the supply curve downwards as in figure 7. Using either the supply curve or the derived demand curve, measures of producer surplus can be obtained.

Producer surplus is measured as the area above the supply curve and below the price. The change in producer surplus of the productivity gain, assuming constant market prices, is measured by the shaded area, PS, in figure 6. Similarly, producer surplus can be evaluated using the derived demand curves. Farmers' choices might directly influence the status of endangerment of a breed. Norton, Phipps, and Fletcher (1994) have shown that if farmers personally value conservation activities, then compensatory payments can be lower than profit loss incurred from conservation. Because their utility is increased by satisfaction about conservation, the impact of income loss on utility is partially compensated. A number of empirical studies have confirmed that farmers actually value conservation. Dupraz et al. (2000) employ the willingness to accept approach in a contingent valuation study and show that farmers are willing to implement environmental practices even if the compensation payment is less than the revenue lost. Hubbell and Carlson (1998) have analysed pesticide use of US apple growers. They have shown that the choice of a pesticide is not only determined by pesticide productivity but also by its environmental and user safety. This research shows that farmers do not exclusively base their choices on profit-maximizing motives.

A second approach to measuring the value of conservation to farmers thus focuses not exclusively on the profit maximization motive but is based on the utility function of the farmer. Assuming that different breed characteristics influence not only farmers' profits but also their utility directly, surveys often proceed using Lancaster's approach. According to Lancaster (1966) a good is not valued because of itself, but because of the characteristics it carries. Farmers' utility is a function of different breed characteristics. Denoting these characteristics by a vector $(t_1, t_2, \ldots, t_n)$, the utility function of the farmer then depends on these characteristics:

$$U(t_1, t_2, \ldots, t_n)$$

Under these assumptions, the theory of choice under utility maximization applies and the same surplus measures as in the consumer case can be used.

EVALUATION METHODS FOR ANIMAL GENETIC RESOURCES

Much of the literature on the economics of biodiversity has dealt either with wildlife preservation, in particular in the context of the US endangered species act and in relation to bio-pharmaceutical research, or the value of plant genetic resources. Recently Rege (1999) and Drucker, Gomez, and Anderson (2001) have provided a review of methods that can serve the economic evaluation of farm Animal Genetic Resources. They mostly draw on methods that have been employed in the study of plant genetic resources. We can distinguish two different types of approaches to the evaluation of animal genetic diversity: approaches based on profit maximisation and approaches based on utility considerations. Within the first set of approaches, the partial budgeting approach is a pure accounting approach not taking into account subsequent adjustment in production techniques and markets. While very restrictive from an economic point of view, it is widely used in agricultural administrations to determine the subsidies paid for the in-situ conservation of rare breeds.

Rural development plans subsidising rare animal breeds the European Union co-finances rural development plans in its member countries. Agri-environmental programmes aiming to improve environmental practices and conservation measures are part of these plans. In many countries, the programmes offer subsidies to farmers for raising traditional animal breeds. The Belgian Rural Development Plan, passed into law in 2001, pays subsidies for the following breeds:

Table 4

Species	*Breed*	*Subsidy/Animal/Year*
Cattle	Rouge de Belgique	120 €
Sheep	Mouton laitier belge	20 €
	Mouton entre Sambre et Meuse	
	Mouton ardennais tacheté ou mouton des collines	
	Mouton ardennais roux ou Voskop	
	Mouton Mergelland	

The subsidy rate has been fixed on the argument that the traditional breeds do not respond to the demand of the meat processing sector that demands very uniform animals of the type Blanc-Bleu Belge for beef or Texel for sheep. As traditional breeds cannot respond to this demand, breeders face losses in the order of 370 € per cattle or 37 € per sheep. Other approaches go further, in that they introduce a full framework of farm-level decision making. They may either be based on a profit maximizing framework, or on a utility function approach. The latter use either revealed preference or stated preference data.

APPROACHES BASED ON THE PROFIT FUNCTION

One way to create a cost effective biodiversity preservation programme is to compare the contribution of species preservation with the cost of doing so. Evaluating the cost to farmers of in-situ preservation is often done using a partial budgeting approach.

PARTIAL BUDGETING

Subsid ies are paid for the continued usage of breeds typical for the region or in status of endangerment. The subsidies paid are calculated on the basis of a partial budgeting approach estimating lost revenue and/or additional cost of undertaking the conservation activity in comparison to the best available alternative.

SHEEP FATTENING IN BURKINA FASO: BIOLOGICAL PERFORMANCES AND PROFITABILITY

Sheep fattening is an activity increasingly practiced by agricultural producers in Burkina Faso. Complementing traditional practices of fattening, research has developed improved techniques which currently interest producers. These techniques combine traditional agricultural inputs and agro-industrial products. Indeed, the zootechnical and veterinary inputs were divided into exchangeable cotton cake and cubed bran, parasite treatment, vaccine, salt and non exchangeable inputs labour, crop waste products and depreciation. In order to evaluate the biological performances and the financial profitability of these new techniques, Somba (2001) adopted a partial budgeting approach. The advantage of this method is that it is easily implemented and that the necessary data is available via accounting sheets etc. The disadvantage is that it models farmers' choices as artificially inflexible. The partial budgeting approach assumes that inputs are used in constant proportions. Furthermore, all other farm activities are considered to not be affected by the husbandry of the endangered breed.

FARM SIMULATION MODELS

Farm simulation models can overcome the inflexibility of the partial budgeting approach. Depending on the depth of the model, all farm activities may be included. Precise technical relationships have to be established between production processes, inputs and outputs. animal genetic resources are modelled as part of the input set determining the available production technology. We follow Groen (1988) to explain the principal components of a farm simulation model evaluating AnGR. Groen developed a simulation model to estimate the economic value of black and white dairy cows in the Netherlands.

The principal structure of a farm simulation model is shown in Figure 7. Inputs flow into and outputs exit the herd enterprise. Inputs and outputs can be modelled as market goods or goods internally produced and processed. Also labour and capital may be freely bought on the market or restricted using suitable constraints. At the farm level, inputs are constraint by roughage production, and available capital and family labour. Concentrates, additional roughage and labour can be bought in the market place.

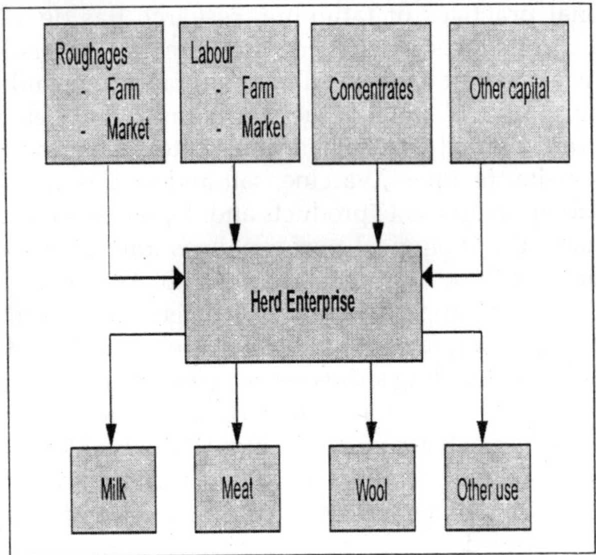

Figure 7: Structure of a Farm Simulation Model

If a detailed link between genetic traits and farmers decision-making is desired in the modelling exercise, then simulation models can use mathematical animal growth and yield models whose parameters are determined by the genetic traits of the herd. The model is then divided into two parts: (1) an objective function, usually based in the maximization of profits or the minimization of costs, and (2) a set of constraints linking inputs and outputs according to technical relationships. Often the model is built on what is considered a representative farm that describes the typical circumstances under which the breed is kept. The simulation model can be extended to other types of farms that differ in the technological and institutional constraints that the farms are subjected to.

The model can be used to estimate the economic value of genetic traits using farm level simulations. A change in animal genetic resources can change the relationships between inputs and outputs represented by the animal growth model or the yield parameters. Using alternative types of model farms, the economic value of genetic traits can also be estimated for differing production environments. Production environments can differ according to weather and soil conditions influencing roughage production or climate and disease pressures influencing the animal growth model. Ladd and Gibson (1978), for example, designed a methodology to generate economic values of genetic traits for different types of farms in the US state of Iowa.

To adapt the simulation model to farms producing multiple outputs for multiple markets, data are needed on stylized technical relationships between input and outputs in all farm activities and across all farm typologies. These should account for possible input and output substitution across farm activities.

Models for a number of individual farms can be aggregated and subsequently integrated into a market model. As the production technology changes, market price changes will results. These can be simulated using the appropriate demand elasticities. The resulting price changes in turn will change the parameters to producers, who will adapt to the changing market environment. The advantage of simulation models is that the modelling of the production relationship is more realistic than in budgeting approaches. Substitution effects in input and output choices are taken into account. However, this method requires detailed data on technical coefficients and prices and technical knowledge to relate production functions to genetic traits.

MICROECONOMICS OF TECHNICAL CHANGE

Breeding and animal selection cause technical change that may lead to modifications in the economic environment and to changing prices. The genetic traits selected are those desired by individual farm operators, product processors or consumers. For an animal breeder, the relative importance of a trait, or the relative value of a genetic type, does not only depend on the average value of a trait as measured in experimental studies. It varies with the production system under consideration, prices, and constraints governing the production processes of an individual farm. In this framework,

Ladd and Gibson (1978) designed a methodology to generate economic values of genetic traits for different types of farms in the US state of Iowa. The authors define economic value as the amount by which maximum profit may be expected to increase for each unit of improvement in the genetic traits. To develop a measure, they formulate a linear programming model of the farm's profit-maximizing problem. This approach makes it possible to generate the maximum level of profit when some parameters of the linear programme change in response to a change in the genetic composition of livestock.

7

Economics of Biopesticide

A number of plant-based commercial products have come into the market in recent years manufactured by medium-sized laboratories. However, so far, there has been no attempt to acquire ownership of formula since under Indian law, agricultural and medicinal products are not patentable. In the last few years, a sudden enthusiasm has erupted from the West to study the pesticidal properties of neem and other plants. Several US patents have been issued for neem-based solutions. P. J. Margo has set up a plant in India which will process neem seed for export to the US, which has a pesticides market worth an estimated US$2 billion. At the moment, biopesticides such as pyrethrum, together with their synthetic mimics, constitute about US$450 million but this figure is expected to rise over US$800 million by 1998. making money out of the neem ought to be relatively easy.

Various companies claim that their respective projects benefit the Indian economy by providing employment opportunities at the local level and higher remunerations to the farmers. This is due to the increase in prices of neem seeds and other plant products as a result of the value added during the production process. The increase in the price of plant products is now turning a hitherto often free resource into an exorbitantly priced one, with local users now competing for the products with an industry supplying consumers in the North. As the local farmer cannot afford to pay the high price, the diversion of seed as raw material from the community to industry will ultimately establish a regime in which a handful of companies holding patents will control access to the raw material and the production process.

The current technology and practices described are aimed at protecting people's right to these plants and ensuring that common people continue to derive benefits from these plants centuries into the future as they have done in the past. Providing and experimenting with authentic information to rejuvenate self-help techniques based on plant products in the context of agriculture, especially plant protection, is an immediate need. The current practice and innovation fulfils this need. The use of non-chemical methods for pest control and crop protection is already gaining importance in several countries, including India. The integrated pest-management programmes developed and promoted by the government departments have the use of botanicals such as neem extracts as one of their major components. The governments are also promoting the manufacture of plant-based pesticides today. If an effort is made towards production of neem products on a cottage scale, this can be economically viable option for unemployed youth in the village. Rejuvenating the local low-cost use of neem can also defend people's rights in an age of biopriacy-a strategy of rejuvenation of local traditions.

BENEFITS COST OF BIOPESTICIDES

One of the strongest benefits of biopesticides are that they offer a more sustainable solution than synthetic alternatives, or more specifically that they allow chemical pesticides to be deployed where and when they are most needed and most appropriate so that a precious resource is not squandered. In this connection, it is important to bear in mind the thinking of the Bruntland Commission that 'Sustainable development is conceived as a process, in which society is becoming less unsustainable, rather than an end state which we could describe as a blueprint'. Hence as chemical pesticides are commercially viable, a space is created for biological solutions to occupy. Indeed, it is often not commercially viable to develop chemicals for niche markets, posing a challenge for minor crops which include the salad crops and other vegetables that make a substantial contribution to health policy objectives.

One of the clear benefits of biopesticides is that they can be combined with other solutions. They can complement other forms of biological control, e.g., conservation measures such as beetle banks. They can allow the use of other forms of control with low efficacy, e.g., where there is partial resistance to existing products. They are also relatively cheap to develop and need to be redeveloped less frequently, saving expenditure on research and development. Herbicides remove bird food but because biopesticides are less efficacious, more bird food is available and bird populations (a key indicator of environmental stress) should increase. Biopesticides do not have residue problems which are a matter of significant concern for consumers and may deter them from purchasing fresh fruit and vegetables. For retailers' biopesticides offer the possibility of brand security, e.g., they could be applied late on top fruit and would leave no residues.

COSTS

Many of the issues relating to costs are grouped around the question of efficacy. In general terms, biopesticides are not as effective as chemicals. With a chemical product, provided one knows its composition it is easy to predict what it will do, whereas with a biological product one has less confidence about how it fits into the ecosystem. Biopesticides may not work immediately as he ecological background must change. Compatibility with synthetic pesticides varies. Shelf life is often shorter. Speed of kill may not be as fast, although in part this is a consequence of thinking within a chemical paradigm and can be got round by appropriate labelling which is one of the functions of the regulatory system.

There are differences in efficacy between performance in protected and field crops, although it should be remembered that biopesticides have been used successfully with broad acre crops. However, it is easier to monitor a crop in a greenhouse and to demonstrate to crop consultants that it works.

Farmers have to decide to take more risks with biopesticides, but the incentives may be absent as most of the benefits are external to farmers. They have to be used in relatively complex knowledge intensive management systems which act as a disincentive. More knowledge is required for their use, but there is a shortage of relevant technical skills in horticulture, reflecting low wages.

Ownership structures do not help. A long term commitment may be n needed, but there may be less interest because of landlord / tenancy laws. Growers often use rented land which provides no incentive for longer term investment. This means that biopesticides often become a short term solution. As soon as no chemical control is available, interest goes up, but then disappears when a chemical solution returns. Te regulatory system has tended to ask the wrong questions with those appropriate for chemicals not relevant to biopesticides. Regulators tend to be risk averse for understandable reasons. The regulator faces a complicated environment in which the precautionary principle mitigates against reduction in regulatory oversight.

This is often interpreted in a way that is not consistent with its original definition in an attempt to prohibit use of any substance that might speculatively be though to be potentially a problem, i.e., the demand is made to prove a negative. What the 1992 Rio Declaration required was that 'Where there are threats of serious or irreversible damage, lack of full scientific certainty shall not be used as a reason for postponing cost-effective measures to prevent environmental degradation'. In its interpretation of the precautionary principle, the EU emphasises, inter alia, that measures should be proportional to the chosen level of protection and based on an examination of the potential costs and benefits.

The regulatory system is changing, but work still often has to be undertaken on a case by case basis, making it hard to generalise. Problems of consistency of effect make them harder to regulate. Obtaining efficacy data to meet the needs of the regulatory system can be expensive. Market failures are serious challenge, particularly in terms of the fragmentation of the market. In particular it is hard to launch on the European market, although regulatory agencies are increasingly talking to each other and improving the information flow. As a consequence of market and regulatory factors, there are no biopesticides available to solve at least 50 per cent of pest problems. The availability problems with chemicals are still ones of relative availability, there are still a lot more available than biologicals. Good chemical pesticides are available with good characteristics to provide solutions. Some chemical are very cheap as they are out of patent and biopesticides have to compete on cost. The available products do not always meet the specification of retailers. There is a 'yuk' failure in terms of dead organisms in the product for which there is zero tolerance. The name 'biopesticides' is not helpful as it has negative connotations.

AREAS OF POTENTIAL CONFLICT

Although not numerous, these areas of potential conflict are significant in terms of the acceptability of biopesticides in relation to a number of audiences. Biopesticides have long-term effects, particularly as ecology adjust o them, but there may not be an immediate pay off. This is a cost within the food chain itself for users, retailers and consumers, but may be perceived as a benefit by developers, regulators and opinion formers. The level of knowledge in primary production about how best to use biopesticides is likely to increase over time, but this is of little immediate benefit to the grower and retailer. Their persistence is good for pest control, but raises questions about environmental risk. Products are unlikely to reduce the natural carrying capacity of the ecosystem, but risk assessment is important. If the product is too persistent, the company producing it will not achieve repeat sales and will go out of business.

As biopesticides are regulated by he same regulator as for synthetics, the public may put them in the same group as chemicals. This reflects the general ambiguity of the product, not organic, but not chemical, somewhere in the middle. This may be in part a marketing issue, but there is a disincentive for the retailer to label environmentally positive goods as it detracts from the rest. From the developer's perspective, biopesticides need an artificially created level playing field for the first few years in terms of tax subsidies and reduced fees. However, the regulator has to think about balancing the books given the requirement for cost recovery and the issue of cross-subsidisation. Agro-chemical companies may be concerned about anything that is seen from their perspective as giving an unfair advantage to biological control agents. Any assistance provided is to the fixed cost of getting the product to market, not the marginal cost of producing it and using it. Hence, such measures will ensure that the product gets to market but not that it is used.

POSSIBLE SOLUTIONS IN THE CONTEXT OF SUSTAINABILITY

It could be noted that costs and challenges of biopesticides outweigh identified benefits. Are biopesticides a policy cul-de-sac and might the way forward lie with new synthetics that are more environmentally friendly? It is suggested here that there are some ways forward which may increase use of biopesticides and their contribution to sustainability. One challenge made in the discussion is that the aspiration that biopesticides are durable and sustainable is an assumption which needs justification. Are biopesticides a second best solution?

As noted, he name itself is unfortunate. One alternative, biological control agents, lacks simplicity and consumer appeal. 'Natural Enemies' could be better, although the word 'enemy' is negative in tone. What is clear is that the products need a generic marketing ploy which overcomes the perception that they are neither organic nor chemical but somewhere in the middle. This reflects a more general problem in terms of a polarisation between organic and conventional products in the framing of the debate and insufficient public attention to Integrated Crop and Pest Management. It might be possible to provide an ethical marque for products on the lines of 'Freedom Foods'. Feel good brands can be differentiated, although in part public attitudes, and the willingness of the consumer to pay a premium depends on the commodity, e.g., food for small children and baby food. To achieve this, NGO involvement would be necessary and better links between different parts of a fragmented policy network. Public procurement could be used for demonstration purposes.

New chemical formulations could be used to solve biopesticide storage and efficacy issues and might lead to greater interest from large companies. Biopesticides need to be fitted into current stewardship schemes to provide incentives for their use. This would also integrate crop and environmental management in a way that promoted sustainability. A pesticide tax would make chemical products as special as they claim they are, although this is a controversial policy instrument. Of fundamental importance is the distinction between private and public benefits and costs and how these are shared out among the various actors in he production and food chain. In terms of liability the regulatory process is about sharing that out between the manufacturer, regulator, government and society. The externality impacts confirm that regulation is important. Food is not just a private individual good, although it may be perceived as such and does not have all the characteristics of a public good. It is, however, easier in principle to charge the consumer for food safety as part of a 'bundled' good, but a free rider problem arises in charging for the collective good of environmental protection.

One then encounters problems of the structure of power in the food chain with value concentrated at the retail end and the question of how much money goes back to the farmer. In retailing one has a private system of governance not determined by public goods, but could private and public benefits go hand in hand?

ECONOMICS OF BIOFERTILISERS

Most biofertilisers are nitrogen-fixing in nature; they fix atmospheric nitrogen to ammonia by a complex metabolic process. Broadly speaking, these are of two types: symbiotic and free living. The former, which require symbiotic association with plants, are represented by Rhizobium. The latter, which can fix nitrogen independently, include Azatobacter, Azospirillium, blue green algae (BGA) and Azolla. Rhizobium is the most researchedand well known biofertiliser, and its role in nitrogen fixation in legumes is well established. It infects the lateral roots of these crops to form nodules, where nitrogen fixation is carried out. Although Rhizobium forms symbiotic association with legume crops naturally, in many cases its numbers are too small to fix sufficient nitrogen. Furthermore, not all strains of Rhizobium are efficient fixers of nitrogen. For example, in a survey of 87 groundnut rhizobial strains isolated from different parts of India, only five were found to be effective. Artificial inoculation of soil with suitable Rhizobium strains to augment their nitrogen-fixing capability of soil with suitable Rhizobium strains to augment their nitrogen-fixing capability can contribute to crop yield in such situations. It is reported that, in favourable conditions, Rhizobium can fix 40-60 kilograms of nitrogen / hectare, and that 200 grams of Rhizobium is enough to meet one third of nitrogen crop requirements.

Azotobacter and Azospirillum, which are commonly found in the rhizosphere of cereals, grasses and vegetables, are also bacteria. In addition to fixing nitrogen, they are known to produce growth-promoting substances and antibiotics. As in the case of Rhizobium, they can either be applied as seed inoculants, or the roots can be dipped in a suspension before planting. Reports suggest that in favourable conditions their use can reduce the nitrogen requirement by 25 to 50 per cent. The other important, free-living, nitrogen-fixing agents are blue green algae (BGA) and Azolla. While, as he name suggests, BGA is an algae, Azolla is a water fern. Both prefer standing water for growth and are suitable for use as a source of nitrogen for rice.

In addition to the nitrogen fixing micro-organisms, there are biofertilisers which can improve the availability and uptake of other nutrients. Two of these are considered to be most important. The first group consists of certain fungi mycelium which form a symbiotic relationship with plant roots. The symbiotic relationship, called vesicular-arbuscular Mycorrhiza

(VAM), is considered to be associated with increased plant growth and enhanced accumulation of plant nutrients such as phosphate, zinc and copper. The second group of non-nitrogen-fixing biofertilisers are phosphate solubilising microorganisms. These micro-organisms, which include bacteria, fungi and yeast, excrete organic acids which solubilise rock phosphate and tricalcium phosphate by decreasing the size of particles to near amorphous forms. Indian soils are characterized by poor to medium phosphorus availability; only about 25-30 per cent of the phosphorus applied to the soils is available for the crops. The presence of these microorganisms is reported to increase he availability of phosphorus considerably.

PRODUCTION

More than 60 units are engaged in the production of biofertilisers; the total output in 1992-93 was 2211.8 tons. Most of the producers are small and only a handful of them produce more than 100 tons of biofertilisers per year. These include the production facilities set up under the National Biofertiliser Project, which produced about 350 tons o biofertilisers in 1992-93. In addition to these and various state agricultural departments, some industries in the public and private sectors and cooperatives are also engaged in the production.

Rhizobium is the most commonly produced biofertiliser in India. About 1000 tons of Rhizobium is being produced currently. A very large proportion of this is produced by government departments and public-sector firms. The private-sector firms account for only 16 per cent of Rhizobium production. Government agencies dominate the production of other biopesticides also.

DEMAND CONSTRAINTS

In spite of the government's policy of encouraging their use, the demand for biofertilisers continues to be very small. Even the comparatively small amount of biofertiliser produced can not be sold on commercial basis and, in most cases, is procured by the government for free distribution among farmers. Efforts to sell them on a commercial basis have, by and large, failed and, according to one of the producers, the production cannot be continued without substantial government support. The situation is unlikely to improve in the near future. According to official projections, the production of various biofertilisers at the end of this decade will be sufficient to meet less than 2 per cent of the perceived requirement.

PERFORMANCE

Most of the field trails highlight the fact that the contribution of biofertilisers to crop yield varies greatly, and that the farmers are justified in being sceptical of their contribution. The results of some these trails are listed in the following paragraphs.

- Rhizobium: An increase of only 3 to 12 per cent in yield has been achieved in chickpea. Similar results, showing poor and inconsistent effects on crop yield have been reported by other researchers.
- Azospirillum: An increase in yield was achieved in only 6 out of 9 tests on pearl millet. The change in yield varied between -10 to 17 per cent. In case of sorghum, an increase in yield was achieved in only 4 out of 9 tests. In case of rice, the application of Azospirillum was found to make an important difference in only 48 out of 108 trials.
- Mycorrhiza: Only in 50 per cent of the cases was a significant improvement in yield achieved. The plant response to VAM varied with soil type, soil fertility and VAM cultures.
- Azotobacter: significant response to inoculation was observed in 342 out of 411 trials in wheat.

Phosphate- solublising micro organisms: Out of 37 field trails conducted, only 10 showed significant increase in yield in the case of rice, wheat, chickpea, pigeonpea, soybean and groundnut.

The crop response to biofertilisers depends on a number of factors. The most important of these are:

1. Number of living cells in the inoculum;
2. Suitability of the strain to soil and crop;

3. Competitiveness of the inoculant against microorganism already present in the soil;
4. Tolerance of inoculants to abiotic (salinity, pH, moisture and heat shock) stresses;
5. Application techniques.

BIOPESTICIDES

The high intensity of chemical pesticide application has become a serious cause of concern in recent years. Although the use of pesticides is comparatively small in India, the damage caused by them to the environment and health is already evident. Furthermore, the current trends suggest that the use of chemical pesticides is likely to continue to increase in the near future. In the circumstances, there is a growing need to promote the use of alternative methods of crop protection. It is particularly important that efforts are made to substitute chemical pesticides with biopesticides, which are environmentally friendly.

MODE OF ACTION

The mode of action of microbial biopesticides creates difficulties. Most chemical insecticides introduced since World Ware II are nerve poisons and can enter the insect in a number of ways. Also, most of them affect all stages of insect development. As a result, chemical insecticides are effective even when the spray coverage is not through. On the other hand, all microbial insecticides excepts fungi, enter the insect primarily by ingestion. Also, in most cases only one stage usually larva/ nymph of the pest is susceptible. Therefore, in order to be effective, biopesticides must be paced exactly where the susceptible target stage of the pest will consume it.

EFFECTIVE LIFE

The other important difference is in the effective residual life on the plant surface. Most chemical insecticides have an effective life ranging between several days and 4 weeks. The effective life of most microbial pesticides, on the other hand, is much smaller; commercial preparations of Heliothis NPV, for example, are reported to have a half life of only 12 hours. These, and other, advantages as perceived by the farmers put the chemicals in a preferred position. In most cases farmers are interested in using biopesticides only when the use of chemical pesticides is not feasible as with the use of Trichogramma on sugar cane or when the pest has developed resistance to chemicals as in the case of Heliothis. In other instances, farmers are reluctant to try biopesticides. In fact, a recent study based on an international survey of researchers shows that there is little likelihood of biopesticides making a major breakthrough in the near future. According to experts, unless the effectiveness of biopesticides improves drastically, the growth in their popularity is likely to be only gradual. Research acti·'ies on various biopesticides are described in the following paragraphs.

TRICHOGRAMMA

Trichograma belongs to a group of minute wasps, which parasitise eggs of more than 200 insects species, many of which are common pests of important crops such as sugarcane and cotton. The use of Trichogramma is particularly beneficial as they destroy pests before they have a chance to do any damage to crops. Trichogramma is one of the most popular biocontrol agents and is widely used against Lepidopteran insects in a number of countries. For example, in the former Soviet Union more than 10 biological factories were reported to produce about 50 billion Trichogramma and other parasites per season. Similarly, more than 50 commercial insectaries are reported to be producing Trichogramma and other parasites in the United States and Canada. A number of communes in China are also known to produce Trichogramma on a large scale.

TRICHODERMA

The use of Trichoderma, which is a fungus, to control plant pests has been common for a number of years. Trichoderma is effective against root pathogens and is used for seed treatment. First used in 1930, it is one of the oldest and most widely used fungi-based pesticides in the world. Trichoderma (and other fungi-based biopesticides) is particularly effective as it does not have to be ingested by pests but acts through physical contact. It is particularly effective in the case of groundnut, sunflower, sesamum, blackgram, green gram and chickpea crops, which are particularly susceptible to root rot. It can also be used for greenhouse crops and commercial nurseries, where environmental factors can be controlled.

BACULOVIRUSES

Baculoviruss are target specific viruses which can infect and destroy a number of important plant pests. A number of these viruses have been registered in the United States, Europe and the former USSR. At least seven baculoviruses are registered in the United States and Canada, four in Europe and eight in the former USSR. They have also been developed in China. The most commonly used baculoviruses are the NPV of Heliothis and Spodopetra. As the process requires a very large number of larvae, the mass production of baculoviruses has faced serious problems. The maintaining of these larvae on a large scale poses serous technical problems due to the possibility of contamination. The difficulty in maintaining optimum conditions on a large scale and the cost of automation have limited the popularity of baculoviruses in the past.

The acceptance of baculoviruses has also suffered from competition from chemical and other biopesticides (mainly B.t). In fact, even large multinationals have faced serious difficulties in setting up commercial production facilites. An example is the case of "Elcar", a NPV of Heliothis introduced in the United Stated by Sandoz. The production facilities, set up in 1974, had a production target of 50, 000 larvae / day. Even though, in order to reduce production costs and achieve high and consistent quality, the production process was partially automated, the level of contamination was found to be very high (40 per cent). After initial success (160,000 acres of cotton were covered during 1976-1977) the production was found to be commercially unattractive, and the facility was closed down.

Recent increased concern for the environment has, however, led to a renewal in research interest in baculoviruses, and new approaches to production and application are being tried. The most promising of these is the possibility of using insect cell lines for the mass production of baculoviruses, without the use of host larvae.

BACILLUS THURINGIENSIS

With a world market of about $140 million a year, Bacillus thuringiensis is the world's largest selling biopesticide. In fact, 80-90 per cent of biopesticides produced in the world are Bt based. It is primarily a pathogen of lepidopteran pests. When ingested by pest larvae, it releases toxins (commonly known as B.t toxin) which damage the mid gut, eventually killing the pest. The use of B.t in India was delayed as there were fears about its possible damaging effect on silk worm. It is only in the last few years that government permission to use B.t. has been given. Estimates of the total market are not available, but a large demand, especially in cotton cultivation areas is said to exist. A number of firms-Sandoz, Lupin, Rallis and the Gujrat State Fertilisers Corporation (GSFC)- are importing B.t to sell in the Indian market. The GSFC has entered into an arrangement with Ecogen, according to which it will be the exclusive distributor of Ecogen's bio-rational agricultural products in India and neighbouring areas. It will first introduce Cutlass for vegetable crops and then Condor for cotton. Both are based on B.t. Later, NoMate PBW Spiral, a pheromone based insect attractant to control pink bollworm on cotton, will also be introduced.

Research aimed at reducing the possibility of accidental damage from B.t toxin to silk worms is also being carried out. Researchers at the IARI are working on the transfer of B.t gene to non pathogenic bacteria (such as Pseudomonas) which are found naturally on plants. Unlike B.t, these bacteria do not form spores and can not be transported by wind to neighbouring fields where silk worms are cultivated.

DESCRIPTION OF THE PRACTICE / INNOVATIVE EXPERIENCE AND ITS MAIN FEATURES

Neem has attracted worldwide attention in recent decades mainly due to its bioactive ingredients that find increasing use in modern crop and grain protection. Research has shown that neem extracts have an effect on nearly 200 species of insects. It is significant that some of these pests are resistant to pesticides, or are inherently difficult to control with conventional pesticides (floral thrips, diamondback moth an several leaf miners). Most neem products belong to the category of medium-to broad-spectrum pesticides, i.e., they are effective over a wide range of pests.

The practice describes a range of neem products such as the neem leaf extract, the neem seed kernel extract, the neem cake extract, the neem oil emulsion and also neem in combination with other plan t extracts for the control of a variety of pests. The technologies using neem are extremely simple and these products can be made by the farmer in his own backyard. They have been tested in the farmers' fields and satisfactorily proven to be effective in controlling a wide range of pests. They have also been used in controlling stored grain pests.

PROBLEMS OR OBSTACLES ENCOUNTERED AND HOW THEY WERE OVERCOME

Farmers have gotten used to purchasing pesticides / fertilisers as a prepared product from a shop rather than preparing them themselves. They have been conditioned to use these prepared products which they can pick up from the shelves. They are also used to the knockdown effect of the chemical pesticides. They are currently in a situation where they have lost confidence in their own technologies. Initially, farmers were sceptical about the efficacy of the extracts which were prepared in their backyards. They were used to buying pesticides from shops rather than preparing them themselves. Some of them initially felt that preparing these extracts would be quite laborious and would increases their workload. They also felt that only a product that is available commercially would work well. Farmers are also used to the knock-out effect of chemical pesticides while plant-based pesticides such as neem do not work in the same way. These extracts may cause disturbances in the physiology of the insect, rendering in inactive. Although the insect might still be present in the plant, it would not cause any harm. But the farmer may not be convinced about this, hence the need for education. After several demonstrations over a period of time, however, the farmers were quite convinced of the efficacy of these products. They were also attracted by the economics of the technology.

8

Bio-Economic Analysis of Aquaculture

Anderson's Theory that in Competitive Conditions Aquaculture Favours Conservation of Wild Stocks of a Species

Anderson (1985) contends, on the basis of his theory, that market entry of competitive aquaculturists of a fish species subject previously only to capture "increases natural fish stocks, reduces price and increases total supply. If initially the natural fish stock is at a level below maximum sustainable yield, entry of the aquaculturalist[s] results in an increase in supply from the commercial fishery". However, this positive result for conservation of wild fish stocks is only true under favourable conditions. The results are not general ones. They rely on the assumption that the supply and demand for captured fish is independent of the supply of aquacultured fish and that aquacultured fish are perfect or close substitutes for captured fish of the same species. Furthermore, even given Anderson's (1985) assumptions, there is one circumstance in which economically viable aquaculture fails to increase natural fish stocks and to save a species that is both captured and aquacultured from extinction in the wild.

Let us consider the simplest illustration of Anderson's proposition using a modified form of his Figures 1. In this case, the capture fishery has a single equilibrium and it occurs at E_1in Figure 1 implying that the stock of the fishery is below the level that yields maximum sustainable yield. The supply curve marked *SASÍ* represents the supply curve of captured fish of a particular species and line *DDÍ* represents the market demand curve for these fish. The residual demand curve for aquacultured fish of the same species is marked *RGRÍ*. In the absence of aquaculture, the equilibrium at E_1 is stable and the price of the fish is P_3 per unit with supply being. Now if aquaculture becomes profitable, total fish supplies can be expected to increase and the surplus from the capture industry may also rise as fish stocks increase with reduced harvesting pressure.

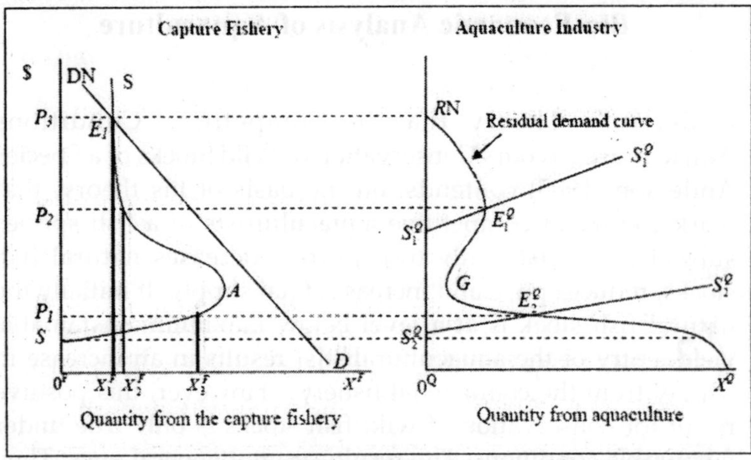

Figure 1: A Case in which Aquaculture is Favourable to biological Conservation of Wild fish Stocks

If, for example, in Figure 1, $S_1^Q S_1^Q$ represents the aquaculture supply curve, the aquaculture industry comes into equilibrium at E_1^Q. The price of the fish species concerned falls from and the capture fisheries supplies rise from X_1^F to X_2^F. Total fish supplies are up. This is also true if the aquaculture supply curve is $S_2^Q S_2^Q$. But now supplies from the capture fishing are below maximum sustainable yield. In fact, if is sufficiently low, supplies from the capture fishers may fall below and in the extreme case, exploitation of wild stocks could become completely unprofitable. This, therefore, calls for qualification to Anderson's statement mentioned earlier that if initially the natural resource stock is overexploited, aquaculture results in increased supply from the commercial fishery. Anderson (1985) also illustrates his theory for a triple equilibrium case for the capture fishery. But in none of the cases that he illustrates does he allow for the possibility that open-access capture fishing could lead to the extinction of wild stocks. In all the cases considered by him aquaculture increases the size of the wild stock.

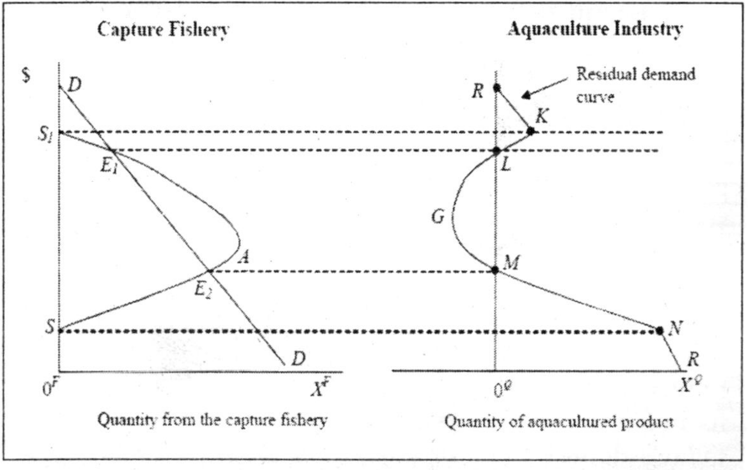

Figure 2: A Case in which Aquaculture may Fail to Prevent Extinction of Wild Fish Stocks

From Figure 2, it can be observed that if the supply curve from aquaculture cuts the residual demand curve (the demand for the aquacultured product between *RÍ and K* aquaculture fails to prevent extinction of natural stocks given that E_1 is an unstable equilibrium. So even under the type of conditions envisaged by Anderson (1985), aquaculture may fail to have a positive effect in saving wild stocks from extinction. However, it is true that if the supply curve of aquaculture intersects the supply curve of aquaculture in the segment between *K* and *L*, its development will be a positive force for conserving wild stocks. This is given the implicit assumption that harvesting of wild stocks will cease at population levels that are so low as to result in elimination of these stocks. At stock levels above this where harvesting continues, survival of the wild population is assumed to occur. In further extension of the argument, this assumption could be varied. Note that if the aquaculture supply curve does not intersect sections *LKRÍ* or *RNM* of the residual demand curve, the aquaculture industry is not competitive with the capture fishery and cannot survive if the equilibrium price of capture fish falls in the range *LM*.

Observe that given the assumptions involved in Figure 2, a species continues to survive only in aquaculture if the supply curve for aquaculture intersects the residual demand curve in its segment *RÍK*. In the long-term, the farmed species may show little or no resemblance to its wild ancestors. Many of the genetic characteristics of its wild ancestor may be eliminated by selective breeding. Thus the genetic pool will change, and genetic loss could occur even though the domestication of the species ensures its survival. But there could also be a possibility of some genetic gains as well as losses because human selection of farmed animals or species ensures the survival of genetic variants that may have failed to be selected in the wild. While it is probably true that human influenced selection on the whole reduces genetic diversity, it may not always do so even though its likely to alter the pool of genetic resources. The pool of today's domesticated or farmed livestock may show greater genetic variation than the pool of their distant ancestors, despite some genetic loss, even though the degree of this genetic variation has begun to decline in the last 200 years or so.

In any case, the genetic stock present in farmed animals is likely to become a different set to that of the original wild genetic stock. Therefore, if the species becomes extinct in the wild but is farmed, a part of its original genetic stock is liable to be lost. Thus, in Figure 3, if set A represents the original genetic stock of a species prior to its farming and if set B represents that after farming has occurred for some time, set B intersects with set A. If the wild species becomes extinct, genetic material represented by the set A~B is lost and only $B \cap A$ if the original genetic material is conserved. However, B~A represents new genetic material. Nevertheless, it should also be recognized that over a long period of time the genetic material in the natural stock might change so that rather than say set A of genetic material being present in the wild stock, another set C might apply after a period of time. Once again, set B might only partially overlap with this set. In this context, it might be noted that farming may result in irretrievable loss of some valuable genetic material present in the original wild stock or expected to evolve in that stock but it may also supplement the gene pool, although it need not. In other words, in some cases B could be a subset of A or of C.

However, even under the types of conditions envisaged by Anderson (1985), successful aquaculture may fail to save wild stocks from extinction. While it may save wild stocks from commercial extinction, it need not do so. This can be illustrated by Figure 2.

From Figure 2, it can be observed that if the supply curve from aquaculture cuts the residual demand curve (the demand for the aquacultured product between *RÍ and K* aquaculture fails to prevent extinction of natural stocks given that E_1 is an unstable equilibrium. So even under the type of conditions envisaged by Anderson (1985), aquaculture may fail to have a positive effect in saving wild stocks from extinction. However, it is true that if the supply curve of aquaculture intersects the supply curve of aquaculture in the segment between *K* and *L*, its development will be a positive force for conserving wild stocks. This is given the implicit assumption that harvesting of wild stocks will cease at population levels that are so low as to result in elimination of these stocks. At stock levels above this where harvesting continues, survival of the wild population is assumed to occur. In further extension of the argument, this assumption could be varied. Note that if the aquaculture supply curve does not intersect sections *LKRÍ* or *RNM* of the residual demand curve, the aquaculture industry is not competitive with the capture fishery and cannot survive if the equilibrium price of capture fish falls in the range *LM*.

Observe that given the assumptions involved in Figure 2, a species continues to survive only in aquaculture if the supply curve for aquaculture intersects the residual demand curve in its segment *RIK*. In the long-term, the farmed species may show little or no resemblance to its wild ancestors. Many of the genetic characteristics of its wild ancestor may be eliminated by selective breeding. Thus the genetic pool will change, and genetic loss could occur even though the domestication of the species ensures its survival. But there could also be a possibility of some genetic gains as well as losses because human selection of farmed animals or species ensures the survival of genetic variants that may have failed to be selected in the wild. While it is probably true that human influenced selection on the whole reduces genetic diversity, it may not always do so even though its likely to alter the pool of genetic resources. The pool of today's domesticated or farmed livestock may show greater genetic variation than the pool of their distant ancestors, despite some genetic loss, even though the degree of this genetic variation has begun to decline in the last 200 years or so.

In any case, the genetic stock present in farmed animals is likely to become a different set to that of the original wild genetic stock. Therefore, if the species becomes extinct in the wild but is farmed, a part of its original genetic stock is liable to be lost. Thus, in Figure 3, if set A represents the original genetic stock of a species prior to its farming and if set B represents that after farming has occurred for some time, set B intersects with set A. If the wild species becomes extinct, genetic material represented by the set A~B is lost and only *B)"A* if the original genetic material is conserved. However, B~A represents new genetic material. Nevertheless, it should also be recognized that over a long period of time the genetic material in the natural stock might change so that rather than say set A of genetic material being present in the wild stock, another set C might apply after a period of time. Once again, set B might only partially overlap with this set. In this context, it might be noted that farming may result in irretrievable loss of some valuable genetic material present in the original wild stock or expected to evolve in that stock but it may also supplement the gene pool, although it need not. In other words, in some cases B could be a subset of A or of C.

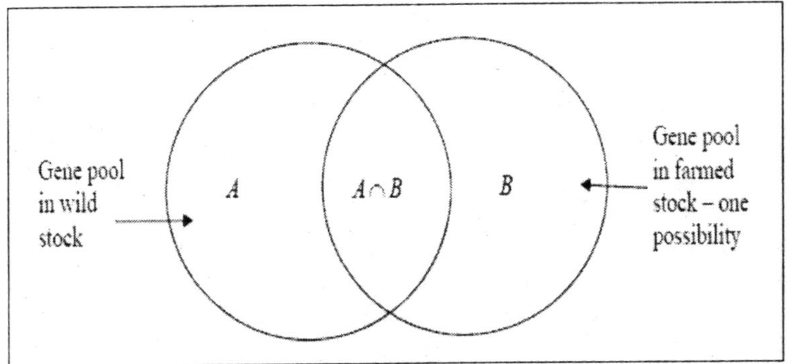

Figure 3: Gene Pools of Farmed Stock and Wild Stock Rarely Coincide

Clearly this matter is quite complicated. It is especially so because under natural conditions, genetic stock is not stationary but changing and evolving. According to Lutz (2001) Around the globe, concern is growing over genetic conservation of wild populations of aquatic species - not only in terms of genetic variation within isolated populations, but also among populations of any given species. The later issue is more concerned with future evolutionary potential than current efforts to maintain species survival, but it has begun to play an important role in shaping conservation genetics policy for many aquatic species.

NEED TO MODIFY ANDERSON'S CONCLUSION TO ALLOW FOR IMPACTS OF AQUACULTURE ON SUPPLY AND DEMAND FUNCTIONS FOR CAPTURED FISH

Let us, however, return to Anderson's theory. Possibly the most serious limitation of Anderson's competitive model is failure to allow for possible impacts of aquaculture on supply and demand functions applicable to the capture fishery. Tisdell raises this issue in connection with farming generally. While the development of aquaculture need not always affect supply conditions in the capture fishery, in many cases such development shifts the supply curve of the capture fishery to the left. A leftward shift may come about because the aquaculture industry appropriates habitat used by wild stock competes with wild stocks for food resources, creates health or genetic risks for wild stock and relies on wild stock for seed/ fingerlings, broodstock or "recruits" for aquaculture. While there might be some cases in which aquaculture has beneficial effects on the wild stock e.g. due to nutrient-enrichment of the environment as result of aquaculture, these cases are likely to be very rare indeed, if they occur at all.

Furthermore, there is also a possibility that aquaculture will raise the overall demand schedule for a fish species. This could occur because aquaculture should permit greater regularity of market supply of a species subject both to capture and aquaculture and add to its market promotion. Nevertheless, there is also a small chance that aquaculture might on occasions reduce overall demand for a species e.g. if the aquacultured product is not identified and is subject to off-flavours. This problem is akin to the famous lemon versus plum problem. It is observed that some factors that may cause the supply curve of a capture fishery to move left as a result of aquaculture development, and some that may cause the demand curve for a species that its both captured and aquacultured to move to the right. Some Circumstances in which Aquaculture has Negative Impacts on the Supply Curve of the Capture Fishery and Positive Impacts on Demand for the Fish Species Involved

NEGATIVE IMPACTS ON QUANTITY OF WILD STOCKS

- Aquaculture appropriates habitat used by wild stock for breeding, feeding, protection and so on.
- Ranching involving collection of broodstock, seed or fingerlings or capture of more mature stock for aquaculture
- Competition for shared food resources e.g. capture of prey of wild stock to feed aquacultured stock
- Pollution or loss of resources used by wild stock because of spillover or environmental impacts of aquaculture
- Disease and genetic risk to wild stocks from aquacultured stocks

Positive Impacts on Demand for Species as a Whole

- Regular and widespread availability of product as a result of aquaculture may stimulate demand for the fish species involved
- Aquaculturalists may add to the market promotion of the fish species as a whole
- The development of aquaculture may enable greater standardisation of the fish product. This is usually a plus as far as supermarkets are concerned and could have positive effects on demand both for the aquacultured and the captured product

If the development of aquaculture causes a leftward shift in the supply curve of the capture fishery or an upward shift in market demand for the species both captured and aquacultured, the development of aquaculture may have negative effects on wild stocks and Anderson's conclusions need not hold. For example, when aquaculture development shifts the supply curve for the capture fishery to the left, a lower price brought about by aquaculture suppliers may be associated with reduced supply of captured fish if the capture

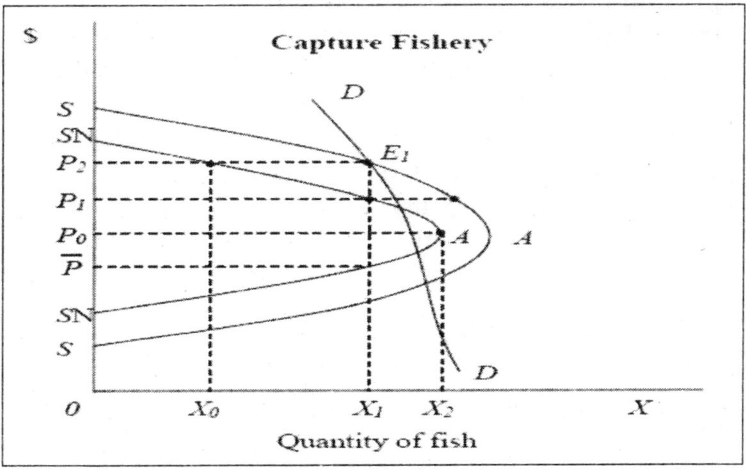

Figure 4: A Case in which Aquaculture has Negative Supply Effects on the Capture Fishery

fishery is expending so much effort that it is operating at a level resulting in less than maximum yield, that is on the backward-bending portion of its demand curve. This case is illustrated in Figure 4

In Figure 4, only the position of the capture industry is shown. Curve SAS represents the supply curve of this industry and DD the demand for its fish before the development of a competing aquaculture industry. Once the aquaculture industry develops, then because of negative supply spillovers, the supply curve of the capture industry shifts leftwards to *SNASN*. However, assume that the market demand curve for the species involved remains constant. Furthermore, suppose that initially the capture fishery is in equilibrium at E_1. If aquaculture develops and causes the price of product cultured or captured to be in the range $P_1 < P < P_2$ supplies form the capture fishery fall. This contrasts with Anderson's case in which they rise in such circumstances. Supplies for the capture industry only increase in this case if $\overline{P} < P < P_1$.

Note that even if the capture fishery should attain maximum sustainable yield in the post-aquaculture situation, this yield and the maximum sustainable stock will be lower than in the absence of aquaculture. However, the impact of aquaculture on the yields of the capture fishery and its stock is liable to depend on the scale of aquaculture and the techniques used in aquaculture. Below some threshold of operation, for example, it is possible that aquaculture has little or no effect on the capture fishery. If on the other hand, aquaculture is on a considerable scale, it is liable to have negative supply consequences for the parallel capture fishery and can increase the likelihood of elimination of wild stocks. Because of the externalities involved, this may occur irrespective of whether replacement of wild stock by cultivated stock is the economically most efficient solution, and irrespective of whether aquaculture results in sustainable production and survival of the cultivated species in the long run.

The demand-side effects on the capture fishery from aquacultural development can be similar to the supply-side effects. An example is given in Figure 5. In this figure, the curve SAE_0S represents the supply curve for the capture industry. For simplicity, this supply curve is assumed to be independent of aquaculture development. *DD* is assumed to represent the demand for the fish concerned in the absence of aquaculture and D_1D_1 this demand after the development of aquaculture. Initially the industry is in equilibrium at E_0 with fish selling for P_0 per unit and X_0 being supplied by the capture fishery. But imagine that after aquaculture develops the price of the fish concerned rises to P_1. This price results in wild stock being fished to extinction in the case illustrated. In other cases, the price of fish after the development of aquaculture may be higher than P_0 but still intersect the supply curve for the capture fishery. In such cases, supplies from the capture fishery continue but are reduced compared to the pre-aquaculture situation. Once again this is a consequence not predicted by Anderson's (1985) model.

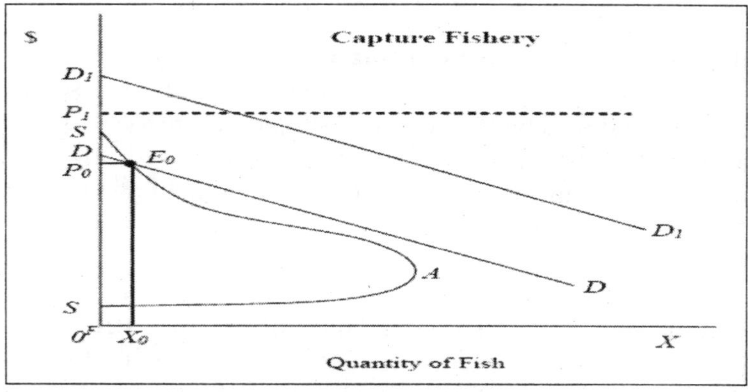

Figure 5 Demand-side effects from the development of aquaculture are liable to put pressure on wild fish stocks and in some cases may result in their elimination and results different to those predicted by Anderson's (1985) model. Thus, it is clear that both demand-side and supply-side spillovers from the development of aquaculture can have negative impacts on the biological conservation of wild stocks, even

though in some circumstances neutral or positive consequences are possible. While the above modelling, assumes, as does Anderson (1985), that captured and cultured fish of the same species are perfect substitutes, this assumption can be relaxed. It is even possible for these products to be complements to some extent and for the type of conservation consequences outlined above to occur.

AQUACULTURE AND LONG-TERM PATTERNS OF CHANGE IN THE STOCK OF AQUATIC GENETIC DIVERSITY

The timing and pattern of development of aquaculture has implications for its effects on biodiversity. Meryl Williams (1997) observes: "Despite great technical advances, modern aquaculture is still a new technology and requires further progress to meet the supply challenges ahead. Enhanced development of aquaculture is only recent. Even though the aquaculture of carp began at least 2500 years ago in China, carps were only successfully bred in hatcheries as recently as the early 1960s. Most current aquaculture is still quite rudimentary, relying on natural supplies of seed stock, unimproved wild types of fish, and simple culture technologies and inputs. Feeds are also largely unimproved, and the nutritional requirements of most species are not known at all except in general terms from studies of diet and feeding preference."

Therefore, aquaculture has not developed globally as widely and as intensively as agriculture. It is still much involved in the process of selection of species for culture and developing different strains of cultured species. This is occurring at a time when the world is already highly globalised and humans have intensive techniques that tend to isolate husbanded species from their surrounding natural environment. By contrast, livestock husbandry developed widely at a time when livestock were more dependent on their surrounding natural environment than now and when there was much less globalisation, economic and otherwise. The early circumstances involved in animal husbandry resulted in the development of diverse breeds globally. It seems probable that the extent of diversity of domesticated livestock increased until a few centuries ago. It has, however, declined in the last two centuries or thereabouts for reasons outlined in Tisdell (2002). These reasons include market extension as reflected, for example, in economic globalisation and scientific advances that have enabled animal husbandry to be undertaken most profitably in relatively uniform artificial environments. Wild ancestors of many domestic livestock have disappeared in this development process due to factors such as the conversion of their habitat to agricultural use and due to hunting. For example, the Auroch *Bos primigenius*, the ancestor of cattle, disappeared in the 1600s.

Given its later development, it is possible that aquaculture will not develop genetic diversity to the extent that it existed in domestic livestock. Nevertheless, it is likely that the number of species and variation of species aquacultured will continue to increase for some time to come. This may occur for several reasons. (1) Aquatic farming environments on the whole and not as closely regulated and uniform as those for livestock and a greater range of environments for aquaculture may exist globally. To take full advantage of the diversity of these aquatic environments, further human selection of breeds and species and development of strains is needed. (2) Much learning is still occurring and search is required to discover new species and varieties suited to aquaculture and techniques for aquaculture are still being developed. Aquaculture is probably still on the lower branch of the learning curve. In the earlier stages of learning about production possibilities, the number of techniques and products tried in a developing industry tends to rise and then decline as 'superior' techniques and products are identified. One might expect a similar pattern to emerge in the development and selection of species and varieties of species for aquaculture. Eventually, however, aquaculture husbandry might become more standardised and greater control might be achieved over environments for such husbandry. As with livestock, this growing uniformity is likely to result in fewer species or varieties of aquacultured species in the very long run.

Hence, the time-path of evolution of the diversity of genetic stock used in aquaculture might accord with the pattern illustrated by curve *ABC* in Figure 6. Furthermore, as aquaculture first develops, it may have little impact on the diversity of wild aquatic genetic stock, but subsequently may cause this to decline at a rapid rate before its further negative effect on the stock is moderated, as is indicated by curve *DEF*. We are probably still far from reaching the peak of curve *ABC* because as yet only a small proportion of food fish are used in aquaculture.

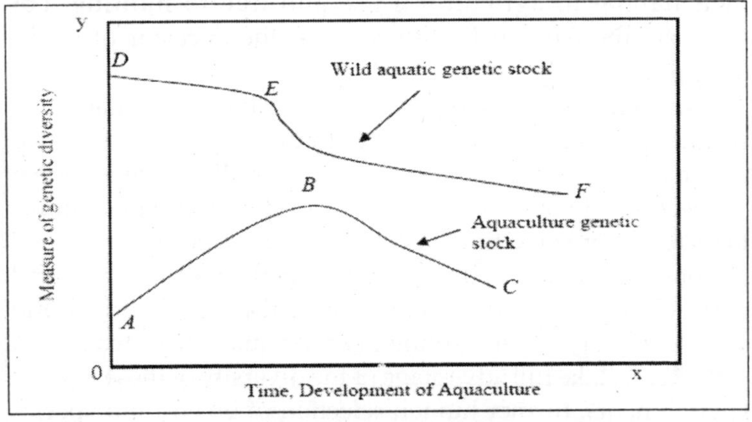

Figure 6: Possible Relationships of Biodiversity to the Development of Aquaculture. Relationships are not to the Same Scale

Given our experience with the long-term genetic consequences of agriculture, it seems highly likely that as aquaculture develops and expands, this will tend to reduce wild genetic stock. In addition, although genetic diversity within aquaculture may initially rise, in the very long-term, it might be expected to decline after peaking. However, the later development of aquaculture compared to agriculture, especially compared to livestock husbandry, may result in some differences in the evolving extent of animal diversity in aquaculture. The institutional arrangements affecting aquaculture's development today, particularly globalisation factors, are quite different to those surrounding the earlier development of livestock husbandry. So some differences in patterns of global genetic development in aquaculture and in livestock production might be anticipated.

BIO-ECONOMIC ANALYSIS OF SHELLFISH-CULTURE

Bio-economic models are not in common use in the field of shellfish culture and may prove to be an important analysis and evaluation tool. Here we discuss only with the potential contribution of these models to furthering knowledge of the dynamics of production and marketing systems. Such models should enable one to determine interactions between the strategies used by the various participants in this field, as well as between the shellfish industry and other areas of economic activity, whether it be at the level of the individual operation, the shellfish basin or the industry. In particular, it can be shown that external factors have an influence on the shellfish industry for example by determining the relationship between tank load and quantity and value of production, and an evaluation may be made of the economic repercussions of various space allocation and environmental utilization scenarios.

Culture of shellfish is basically being done in small-scale facilities, often as family operations. There are a number of similarities between shellfish-culture and certain forms of agriculture: work is mainly performed by family members, supplemented where necessary by a small number of permanent employees and a larger number of seasonal Employees, and the future of the operation is normally dependent on the manager of the facility. Above all, shellfish-culture activities, like agriculture, require the permanent use of a given space, and production levels are partially dependent on the area under culture. Shellfish-culture activities nevertheless differ from agriculture in several ways, and we shall discuss two of these: production levels in a shellfish-culture operation do not only depend on the surface farrned and the means of production used. They are also dependent both on total basin load and on water quality that is, in both cases, on decisions made by other operators or users of the space. These interdependencies, which affect the production of each operator, make up what economists call "external factors". These external factors in the shellfish-producing industry are related to those that exist in the fishing industry: the production of a fishing vessel depends in part on the total fishing effort applied to a fish stock. They differ by the fact that, in the fishing inélustry, sorne operators may increase their fishing capacity and make a profit, to the detriment of other operators, while in the shellfish industry, all operators in a given basin share the consequences of pollution or epizootic disease: there are only losers.

- allocation of operating space is not done, in France, on the basis of acquisitions or the location of private property. These areas are part of state-owned maritime lands. They are not allocated bY, a free market process; rather, allocation is governed by regulations. Granting of concessions on state-owned maritime lands is the responsibillity of a state official,

ECONOMIC ANALYSIS

Economic analysis may play a three-fold role:

(i) contribute to better knowledge of the structure and dynamics of production and marketing systems, since economic analysis is aimed at producing explanatory outlines that are meant to represent causal interdependencies,

(ii) clar if y future actions, that is, to forecast the economic consequences of sorne decision that is currently being envisaged,

(iii) contribute to defining the process of allocating resources in fields where the free market does not come into play.

Only the potential contribution of bio-economic models to knowledge of the dynamics of production and marketing systems be discussed here. The causal interdependencies to be studied in analysing the shellfish industry have to do with:

(i) the shellfish industry itself, actions by individuals and enterprises (individual strategies), relations between production zones and within a given basin (collective strategies),

(ii) relations between this sector and other competitive or complementary economic activities.

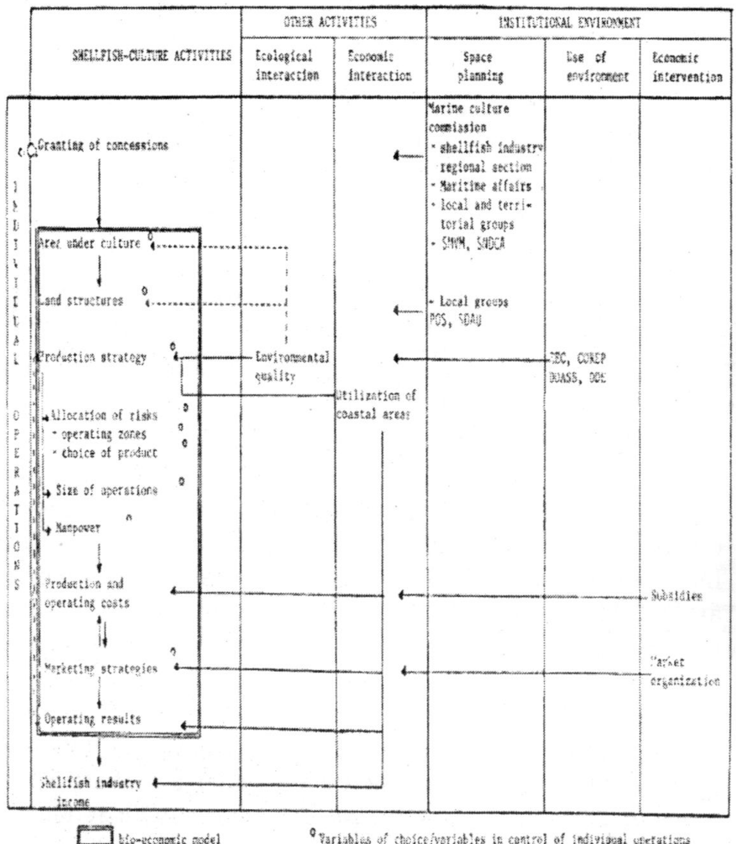

Table 1: Interactions and Environment: Individual Off Rations

It is possible to break these interactions down into three aggregate levels: individual operations individuals or enterprises, shellfishculture basins, and the sector as a whole. At each of these levels, interdependencies cannot be understood outside the social and institutional context in which they occur (Table 1).

INDIVIDUAL OPERATIONS

The results of a shellfish-culture operation depend on its choice of operating strategy. These choices will have an effect on its income and on the make-up of its production and/or operating costs, for example:

- choice of product, collection of spat and/or nursery culture and/or maturation,
- allocation of risk, distribution of concessions over several producing basins. This distribution may lead to specialization of production, which is a function of costs,
- choice of marketing strategy: among oyster-farmers, for example, there are both producers and shippers,
- choice of size of operation: use of family labour alone or hiring of permanent or seasonal employees.

Each shellfish-culture operation develops its own strategy on the basis of the limited information it has in order to attain its own objectives. Each producer does not necessarily react on the basis of all the interdependencies listed above, since most of the time the information he has deals only with prices and working time. Entering the field and leaving it, as well as individual development strategies, involves land-tenure problems. The way in which shellfish concessions are managed reduces the degree of freedom enterprises have in developing their own strategies: marine culture commissions often feel it is best to take back a concession that is not used at least 50% of its capacity. In the same way, the lack of systematic renewal of expiring concessions may be a disruptive factor. The influence of other economic activities being carried on in the same area as the shellfish operation may be felt in various ways:

1. existence of activities that complement shellfish-culture, such as agriculture, fishing or tourism, may make it possible:
2. for the operator to exercise another activity, and thus to have other sources of income fisherman/shellfish-farmer, for example

3. to have seasonal labour available to the shellfish industry.

on the other hand, the existence of permanent activities that are less demanding or more profitable may deprive shellfish farmers of the manpower reserves they require.

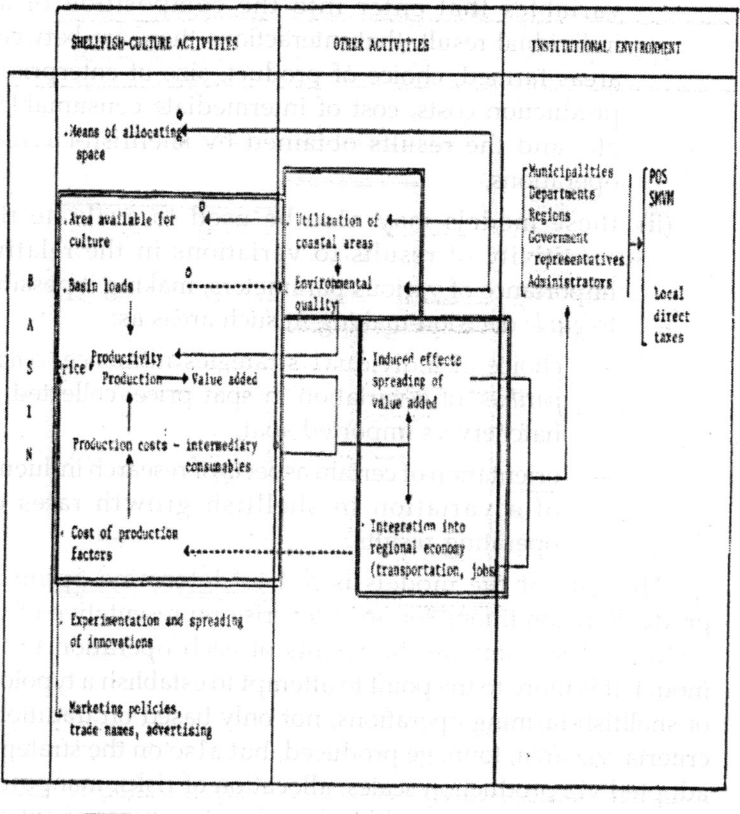

Table 2: Interactions and Environment: Shellfish Basins

Economic analysis of shellfish-farming operations is a new field, and while bio-economic models have been developed in sorne countries in particular in the U.S.A., they are non-existent in France. Bio-economic models, at this level of aggregation, are built without explaining external factors; variations in the various parameters are considered to be exogenous, no matter what their origin. The purpose of these models is to establish relations between the various inputs and their costs and the value of production. The bio-economic models thus constructed have two main functions:

(i) pedagogical function, by showing the parameters and variables that enter into the composition of an individual result: that interactions there are between areas farmed, choice of product, size of enterprises, production costs, cost of intermediate consumables, etc. and the results obtained by shellfish-culture operations,

(ii) these models may also be used to evaluate the sensitivity of results to variations in the relative importance of various parameters, making it possible to *guide* decision-making in such areas as:

- choice of individual strategies influence, *ceteris paribus,* of a variation in spat price, collected vs hatchery vs imported spat,
- orientation of certain aspects of research influence of a variation in shellfish growth rates on operating results.

The role of the models is not to determine optimum production conditions for an enterprise representative of the sector and to compare the results of each operation to the model. It is more to the point to attempt to establish a typology of shellfish-farming operations, not only based on traditional criteria viz area, tonnage produced, but also on the strategies adopted viz production scales, allocation of risks, manpower, growth. This typology could be based on two types of criteria:

- total or partial completion of a culture cycle. This may result from a natural constraint or from a deliberate choice pinpointing the existence of markets at various stages in the culture process. Based on strategical choices such as spat producer and/or culturer and/or finisher-shipper, Dumont (1) was able to distinguish 19 categories of operations.

- production structures. These are many and varied: capital invested, manpower employed, number of activities exercised by operator, etc., and at the present time are difficult to quantify.

The models thus developed would make it possible to test, for each type of operation, their sensitivity to the results of variations in parameters and then to compare these sensitivities for the various types of operations in a given environment.

BASIN

Total production and value added in a shellfish basin, as well as operator income, are related to the area under culture and production per unit of area. The *area available for shellfish culture,* as well as the possibilities for land installations is the result of decisions taken at the institutional level with respect to use of coastal areas. To a great extent, these decisions are an exogenous variable for shellfish operators. They may influence the decision-making process through pressure from their professional association and the economic arguments this organization may present. The stakes are quite large: development of the shellfish industry is partly through the creation of concessions outside areas already being used, and the development of other, competitive activities, in terms of space or use of the environment, may be nearly irreversible.

The strategies of various shellfish-industry groups may act directly through *the criteria chosen for the use of available space.* Shellfish-industry organizations may propose a local policy for operating structures. Officials will thus be led to adopt regulations, after consultation with marine culture commissions, on the minimum and maximum dimensions of new concessions granted. The means for applying for vacant concessions and allocation of these concessions play an important role, due to the possibility for encouraging or preventing certain types of activity. Biological production models make it possible to take into consideration external factors due to the effect of basin loading on carrying capacity or the impact of other ecological variables in the environment. Bio-economic models may enable the results obtained by biological shellfish production models to be translated into terms of costs and income. These bio-economic models may be confined to interactions between the production factors used, basin loading and production, with unit costs and prices being considered exogenous. They may be integrated into larger models that trace the integration of the shellfish industry into the regional economy as well as induced effects through spreading of value added through the economy. These models make it possible to consider the following aspects:

- potential for seasonal employment or supplementary income; costs, such as transportation, which depend on the regional economic climate,
- an overall increase in shellfish-culture activity would bring with it an increase in consumption of intermediate goods and in purchases of equipment; suppliers of goods and services would see an increase in their activities, which would lead to a rise in their purchases.
- an increase in value added in the shellfish industry causes a rise in total wages and salaries to employees and operations; the effects of this increase may cause a chain reaction through expenditures by employees and operations in other sectors of activity.

These studies of the effects of variations in final demand on regional economies have been used, for example, to calculate the economic consequences of pollution

THE SHELLFISH SECTOR

Interrelations between the various shellfish operations may occur on a national level, through the existence of a professional organization and training structure, and through processes for determining prices markets and costs. Professional organization: Based on a system close to that of fisheries; the shellfish industry is characterized by the weakness of its union representation and the absence of a local structure, like that of the local maritime fisheries committees, in individual basins. There are six regional sections, which together form an interprofessional shellfish industry committee, which is in term represented in the CePM.

Training is provided by maritime trades schools and by specialized vocational high schools. Overall influence of the national and international economic climate on the shellfish industry as a whole depends on several factors (Table 3).

- Production costs: The cost of a number of consumables is beyond the control of producers, e.g. cost of hatchery or imported spat, cost of equipment such as sorters which partly depend on the existence of industries using similar techniques, manpower costs.

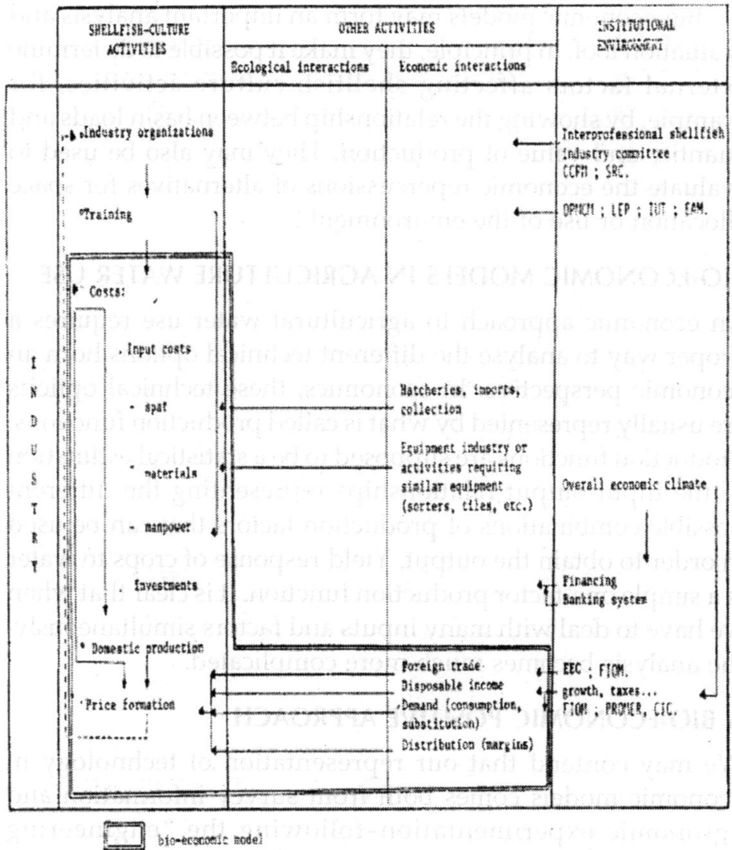

Table 3: Interactions and Environment: Shellfish Industry

- Investment: Financing mechanisms such as subsidies, banking system, interest rates, etc are crucial factors in investment decisions.
- Industry turnover: the industry has very poor control over demand factors. Producers can only act on consumption through collective advertising and cooperative financing by the State and producers. Other parameters that are just as important are not controlled: available income, foreign trade, constitution of reserves, etc.

Bio-economic models may form an important analysis and evaluation tool. In principle, they make it possible to de termine external factors affecting shellfish-culture activities, for example, by showing the relationship between basin loads and quantity and value of production. They may also be used to evaluate the economic repercussions of alternatives for space allocation or use of the environment.'

BIO-ECONOMIC MODELS IN AGRICULTURE WATER USE

An economic approach to agricultural water use requires a proper way to analyse the different technical options horn an economic perspective. In economics, these technical options are usually represented by what is called production functions. Production functions are supposed to be a statistical estimation of the input-output relationships representing the different possible combinations of production factors that can be used in order to obtain the output. Yield response of crops to water is a simple one-factor production function. It is clear that when we have to deal with many inputs and factors simultaneously, the analysis becomes much more complicated.

A BIO-ECONOMIC POSITIVE APPROACH

We may contend that our representation of technology in economic models comes both from survey information and agronomic experimentation–following the "engineering production function approach". It is complemented with simulated data, for the techniques that are not actually used or experimented and for the estimation of erosion and pollution levels.

The essential specificities of bio-economic positive models may be synthesised as follows:

- High level of technical specification. Characteristics of weather, soil, crops, technical schedules are very detailed.
- Part of the data used in the model are obtained from simulation results of bio-physical models.
- It is possible to calculate negative externalities associated to each solution of the l", both temporal and spatial. An example of temporal externalities is the level of soil erosion. This means that it is possible to analyse, for example, the interrelationships between different irrigation practices, tillage systems and long term consequences on soil erosion. The same is applied to nitrate or pesticide pollution, that can be considered spatial negative externalities.
- The high detail of technical Specification characterising these models determines the aggregation level. In principle they can be applied at farm or small regional level. It is more difficult to use them dealing with big regions or national levels. Of course this is just a matter of acceptable error and complexity in data manipulation.
- Bio-economic models need an interdisciplinary approach. This is perhaps the most difficult problem to overcome. What we usually call "data" we introduce in a model, is already a complex product that has its origin in another discipline. This means that interdisciplinary work requires a minimum understanding of the basic approaches followed by the different disciplines taking part in the research. We met this problem when we wanted to define intensity levels of agricultural techniques: the implicit criteria used by agronomists are different from those employed by economists. If an economist just take

information provided by agronomists without understanding thoroughly how these data had been generated, the errors may be important. We present a simplified scheme of a bio-economic model, in order to clarify the essential relationships present in this approach.

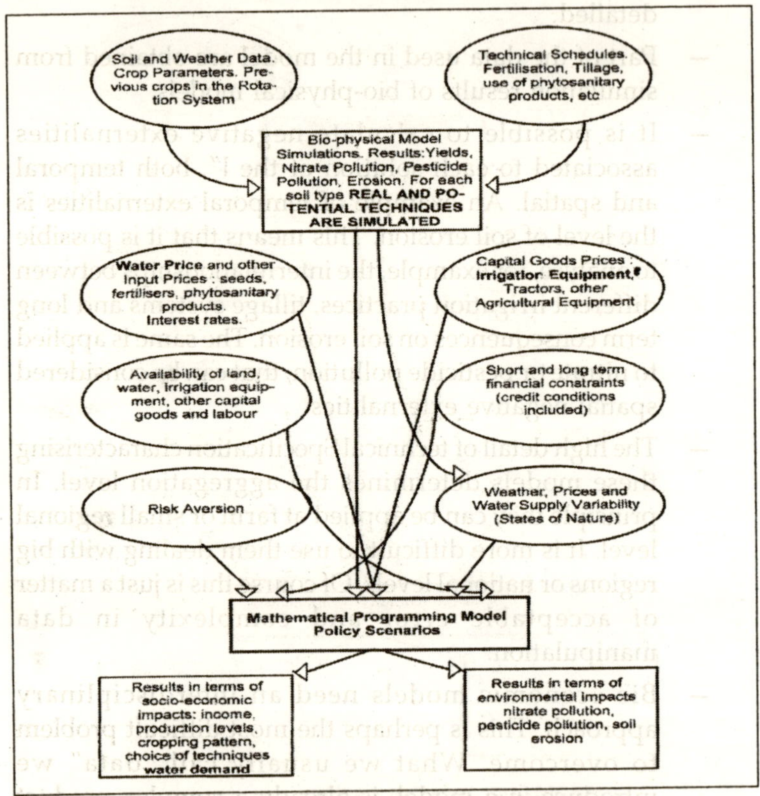

Scheme of a Positive Bio-Economic Model

BIO-ECONOMIC MODELS ON WEED MANAGEMENT

The Bio-Economic Framework

An important motivation for a bio-economic modelling approach is the expectation to achieve economic and environmental gains by using flexible weed management plans in which weed control is varied each year based on observed conditions instead of fixed plans. Typically, weed scientists and modellers use mathematical bio-economic models to link observed conditions such as weed seedling densities to annual weed management recommendations. The decision framework uses experimental results, field data, and expert opinion to define biological relationships between weeds and crops, which are then incorporated into an optimizing economic model.

The weed management can be studied in the following ways.

- Spatially explicit weed growth and spread model in a large cropping area at risk of infestation.
- The probability of detection of a new weed and its control effort.
- Damage functions associated with weed functional types.
- Efficacy/performance of policy and management options.
- Dynamic programming model to determine the economically optimal weed management strategies over time.

THE SPATIALLY EXPLICIT WEED GROWTH AND SPREAD MODEL

A spatially explicit framework can be developed for regional-level modelling of alien plant spread in arable fields. A raster-based approach to be used to represent a large region as a grid of neighbouring cells. The model uses an annual time step and a two-dimensional grid of sites representing space. The mathematical model incorporates both population growth and dispersal processes to represent the spread of a weed from a point source. The space the region at risk of invasion is divided into an $n \times m$ array (grid) of rectangular cells of equal size. The grid size can be readily changed to suit the representation of a particular case study region. The starting point is with an initial population at a point source, such as might arise with the arrival of a newly invading species, a re-emerging sleeper weed or the first herbicide resistant plants in the arable field. The location of this point source is set in the centre of the hypothetical grid field.

POPULATION GROWTH

The first part of the model comprises a population growth sub-model which describes the weeds population growth based on the logistic equation:

$$\frac{dX}{dt} = rX\left(1 - \frac{X}{K}\right) \qquad (1)$$

where r is the intrinsic growth rate, $X = X(t)$ denotes the size of the weed population at time t, and K is the environmental carrying capacity or saturation level. Such models have had wide application in a variety of biological resource stock problems (Clark, 1990). This equation is modified to obtain the following discrete version of the logistic growth relationship:

$$X(t+1) = X(t) + rX(t)\left(1 - \frac{X(t)}{100}\right) \qquad (2)$$

where $X(t)$ and $X(t+1)$ are the weed populations expressed in percentage infestations corresponds to the percentage of a grid cell occupied by the weed at time t and $t+1$ respectively and $K=100$ denotes the maximum carrying capacity i.e. 100% infestation. Here, and in the following determinations of weed populations within a cell $X(t)$ at time t is restricted to the range [0, 100]. That is, $X(t)$ is set equal to be min[100, max(0, $X(t)$)]. Using Equation (2), weed population size $X(t)$ can be computed for different values of intrinsic growth rate parameter r and $X(0)$. Conversely, this equation can be used to determine a r value for a particular case study weed spread scenario in the field. Depending on the initial size of the invasion and number of years a weed may take to reach a 95% spread level in one grid cell, the model is set to compute the corresponding r parameter value. It is expected that the required information "how many years it takes to reach 95% infestation level in one grid cell" can be obtained for a particular case study weed spread scenario.

To denote the infestation level post growth but prior to dispersal, for each cell across the $n \times m$ array Equation (2) can be written as:

$$X_{ij}^{pd}(t+1) = X_{i'j'}(t) + r_{i'j'}(t)X_{i'j'}(t)\left(1 - \frac{X_{i'j'}(t)}{100}\right) \quad (3)$$

where *ij* denotes the cell at *i*th row and *j*th column of the hypothetical grid field with the constraint that $X_{ij}^{pd}(t)$ Î [0, 100]. Here *rij*(*t*) is set up to allow dependence on both cell and time. Replacing *rij*(*t*) with *r* would have the growth parameter independent of both space and time. The superscript *pd* denotes "prior to dispersal". When modelling $Xij^{pd}(t)$ above we restrict percentage intensity to the nearest decimal place. Hence the unit of infestation is 0.1% and each cell can be considered to have an integer number of infestation units between 0 and 1000 inclusive.

DISPERSAL

The second part of the model comprises a dispersal process sub-model. In addition to growth within each time interval, weed dispersal takes place with a proportion $P_{ij}^{i'j'}$ of the weed intensity in the (*i*, *j*)th cell dispersed to the (*i*′, *j*′)th cell. Hence, after growth and dispersal the weed intensity in the (*i*, *j*)th cell is given by:

$$X_{ij}^{pc}(t+1) = \sum_{i'j'} P_{i'j'}^{ij} X_{i'j'}^{pd}(t+1) \quad (4)$$

where superscript *pc* denotes "prior to control". As already noted, the *Xijpc*(*t*) values are restricted to [0, 100]. Incorporating Equation (3) we get:

$$X_{ij}^{pc}(t+1) = \sum_{i'j'} P_{i'j'}^{ij} \left\{ X_{i'j'}(t) + r_{i'j'}(t)X_{i'j'}(t)\left(1 - \frac{X_{i'j'}(t)}{100}\right)\right\} \quad (5)$$

Here we see that the model for weed intensity at time $t+1$ relates to the growth since time t and then dispersal. When modelling dispersal, focus is given to the term $P_{i'j'}^{ij} X_{i'j'}^{pd}(t)$, which is the infestation in the (i', j')th cell dispersed to the (i, j)th cell. It is essential that the model captures the possibility of long distance dispersal in this modelling process. This represents rare events in the dispersal process, often less than 0.1% of the total infestation, whereby units are moved unusually long distances, e.g. by vehicle. One approach to modelling such dispersal is to use a radial Cauchy distribution. A related approach has been used in Diggle et al. (2002) to model dispersal of Anthracnose spores. The problem with this approach is the high computational effort required when undertaking simulations. We use an alternative dispersal mechanism which retains the possibility of rare long distance dispersal. We first assume that each infestation unit is independently distributed of each other, and decompose dispersal from each cell into two components, being short and long distance dispersal components. The probability a unit is dispersed short and long distance is denoted by *psd* and *pld* = (1 - *psd*) respectively.

For modelling short distance dispersal we use the approach of Auld and Coote (1990). They define distribution of new plants as determined by the proportion of these that can move into predetermined grid units away from the spreading source on a rectangular grid. In line with this approach, we set-up the short distance conditional probability distribution, letting each unit dispersed locally to have a probability equal to *p*0, *p*1, ... *p*w, of being dispersed to a "ring" 0, 1, ..., *w* cells away respectively from the dispersing cell. Within a ring each cell is equally likely to be selected. For this purpose a matrix (*DM*) of short distance dispersal probabilities is established. Based on this matrix we simulate the contribution from the dispersing cell to infestation in the neighbouring cells, that is, the sub-grid of cells receiving short distance dispersed units. Here the simulation is based on the multinomial distribution with parameters *nij* the number of infestation units in the cell dispersed short distance and probabilities as given in *DM*. The variable *nij* itself is a binomial variate, (*Binomial* $\left(10X_{ij}^{pd}(t).p_{sd}\right)$. It is assumed that units dispersed short distance and falling outside the full $n \times m$ grid are lost to the system. The remaining units, $\left(10X_{ij}^{pd}(t).n_{ij}\right)$ are distributed long distance. Each long distance dispersed unit is then assigned at random to one of the "long distance" cells of the grid, these being those cells of the grid that are the complement to the short distance cells. The probability of a unit being assigned to any particular long distance cell is set inversely proportional to the squared distance the cell is from the dispersing cell. These probabilities approximate the probabilities for a Cauchy distribution in the tails and hence the long distance dispersal approximates a radial Cauchy distribution.

Currently *DM*, the matrix of short distance conditional probabilities, is established with a maximum number of rings equal to four so that a maximum of 81 cells (9 × 9 sub grid) receive short distance dispersal. It is also assumed that, on average, of the units dispersed short distance;

- 95% of infestation units remain within the dispersing cell itself,
- 2% move to the 8 neighbouring cells,
- 1.5% move to the next 16 neighbouring cells,
- 1% move to the next 24 neighbouring cells, and
- 0.5% move to the last 32 neighbouring cells away from the dispersing middle cell.

These parameters can be readily changed to suit the need of a particular case study weed problem. It should be noted here that dispersal of weeds in arable fields has been studied in relatively few cases. A rule of thumb developed in a summary of dispersal data by Cousens and Mortimer (1995) and later adopted by Woolcock and Cousens (2000) is that in species without clear dispersal adaptations, half the seeds are distributed within a distance of half the height of the parent plant. While most seeds are likely to be dispersed short distances by passive means, it is possible for a small proportion of seeds to disperse considerable distances due to rare events such as gale force winds, birds, farm machinery etc. Some evidence of these rare events is presented in field experiments by Auld (1988) in which he found a single *Avena fatua* plant established at 14m from the nearest source in the second year.

Rare long-distance dispersal events are critically important in invasions and plant migration. The conclusions drawn by Higgins and Richardson (1999) are that data on rare long-distance dispersal will remain (by definition) hard to come by, and that the rare long-distance dispersal component of the model can, if sufficiently rare, be estimated independently of the local dispersal components. In their analysis, they suggest that relatively large errors in estimating the long distance dispersal component are unlikely to strongly influence the predicted spread rate. Hence, it may be that accurate characterization of the long distance dispersal component is not as important as its identification. The spread modelling incorporated both short and long distance weed spread. As shown in Figure 7, the new weed infestation starts in the middle of the grid field and spreads along the two dimensional fields both length and breadth. Much of the spread takes place from

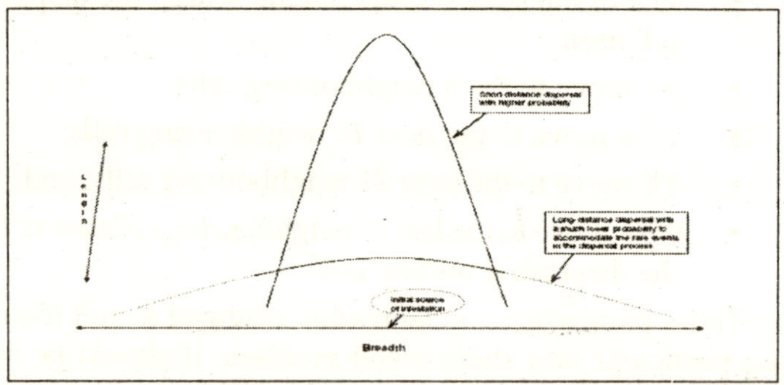

Figure 7: Mixed Distribution of Weeds Dispersal Adopted in the Model

Note: Bivariate Distribution takes a Two Dimensional Plane Both Along the Length and the Breadth of the Field

the short distance dispersal while a much lower level of spread occurs from the rare long distance dispersal of this mixed distribution spread model. The movement of the spreading weed populations on the grid space for a possible set of parameters is illustrated in Figure 8. The spreading population moves along two dimensional fields as a 'wave' of population density. The weeds 'search and control effort' is incorporated into this model as described in the next section.

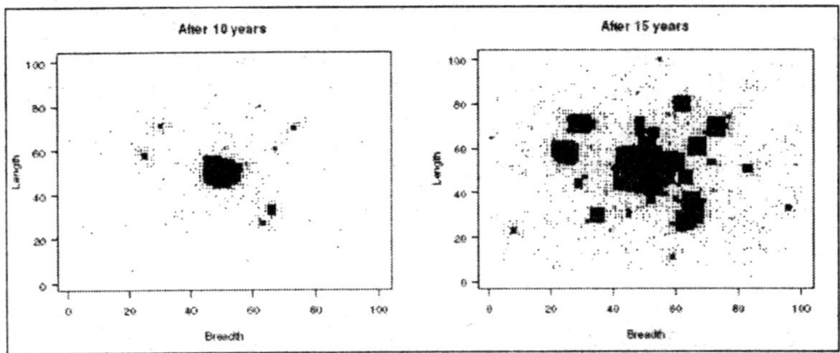

Figure 8: Spreading Weed Populations on the Grid Space

Note: On 100 × 100 grid under parameterization given in Table 1 with $r = 1.35$ and $pld = 0.1$

THE PROBABILITY OF DETECTION OF A NEW WEED AND ITS CONTROL EFFORT

Cacho et al. (2006) modelled detection curves representing the proportion of targets detected (*p*detect), or the probability of detecting a single target, as a function of coverage (*c*) defined as the ratio of the area actually searched over the total area of the invasion:

$$c = \frac{sp \times sh \times sw}{A} \tag{6}$$

where *A* is the total area (km2) at risk of invasion, *sp* is the speed of search (km hr-1), *sh* is time spent searching (hours) and *sw* is the effective sweep width (km). Time spent searching *sh* is the product of two components namely; the number of man days employed on search and the number of hours of search time spent per man day. Effective sweep width *sw* is a measure of the detection capability of the searcher taking into account target characteristics and environmental conditions, and is referred to as the detectability of the weed. The numerator of Equation (6) represents the area searched as the product of search effort in terms of distance traversed ($sp \times sh$) times the detectability of the weed (sw).

Under random searching there is no pattern to the search process, some areas will be searched repeatedly while others may not be searched at all. This provides a conservative estimate of search effectiveness. As commented by Cacho et al. (2006), random searching would be expected to produce the fewest detections unless there were systematic biases in the search process. The proportion of targets detected (*p*detect) for random sweeping is given by:

$$P \text{ detect } = 1 - e^{-c} \quad (7)$$

Cacho et al. (2006) reported a *p*detect value of approximately 0.63 under the random detection function at c=1.0 coverage. Once detection is made, it is assumed that an attempt is made to kill all the weeds found, subject to the effectiveness of the control method used. The mortality caused by the search and control effort (D) is:

$$D = \text{detect } P \text{ kill} \quad (8)$$

where *p*kill is the probability that a target organism will die each time a control is applied.

SEARCH EFFORT

When a large area cropping system is considered, localised search for a new invader would begin when a certain level of threshold is reached in terms of visible detection of weed densities in those locations. While it is not rational to equally distribute the search and control effort across the large region, the modelling becomes complex when smaller sized sub grids have to be defined to focus this control effort. Previously Jayasuriya et al. (2008) adopted a method to allocate search and control effort proportionately into each grid cell based on the weed density in those cells each year. This approach implicitly assumed that individual farmers in the large region are accurate in observing the weed densities and thus focus their search and control effort on those locations. The size of this sub grid is defined in terms of its diameter which is also equivalent to the number of cells along both the length and breadth axis (Figure 1). This approach is more appropriate given the extremely large size of the cropping area considered in this analysis assuming a new invasion is discovered in a particular locality. Therefore *shij* for each (*i, j*)th cell across the $n \times m$ array ($n = m$) in this newly defined sub grid at time *t*, is set proportional to $X_{ij}^{pc}(t)$ so that $\sum_{ij} sh_{ij}(t) = sh$.

RE-INFESTATION FROM THE SOIL SEED BANK

Though a visible infestation can be killed after applying 'search and control effort' as shown in Equation 8, there is always the possibility of re-infestation occurring from the soil seed bank. Process-based demographic modelling such as Woolcock and Cousens (2000) has incorporated effective germination rates separately for new and old seeds in the seed bank. Literature citations on the seed germination rates vary for different weeds ranging from 25 to 50% for new and old seeds respectively in the case of *Raphanus raphanistrum* wild radish, while it may be just 2% for *Orobanche ramosa* branched broomrape in field conditions. Due to the existing complexity of the spatial modelling framework, weed demography was not included as it would add considerably to the computational burden. Therefore, a more simplistic approach on incorporating weed re-infestation from the seed bank is required. We have re-adjusted the mortality caused by the search and control effort (*D*) to accommodate the re-infestation of weeds from the soil seed bank:

$$M = D(1 - q) \qquad (9)$$

where *M* is mortality caused by the search and control effort after adjusting for the seed bank reinfestation rate (q) where q Î [0, 1]. To include dependence of *M* on cell (*i, j*) across the $n \times m$ array and on time *t*, Equation (9) can be written as:

$$M_{ij}(t) = D_{ij}(t)\left[1 - \theta_{ij}(t)\right] \qquad (10)$$

Hereq $\theta_{ij}(t)$ is set up to allow dependence on both cell and time. Replacing q*ij* (*t*) with q(*t*) would have the re-infestation parameter independent of space. In resembling the overall weed control effort in the defined sub grid field, this $Mij(t)$ is then applied to Equation (5) to obtain:

$$X_{ij}(t+1) = X_{ij}^{pc}(t+1)\left[1 - M_{ij}(t)\right] \tag{11}$$

DAMAGE FUNCTIONS ASSOCIATED WITH WEED FUNCTIONAL TYPES

The presence of weeds results in damage to the grains cropping system. Damage in terms of crop yield loss (Z) is considered a proportional variable and is a function of the initial weed population in adult stages $Xij(t)$ and the number of weeds killed expressed as the final mortality $Mij(t)$, which is dependent upon the search and control parameters and the soil seed bank re-infestation rate as discussed above. Therefore,

$$Z_{ij}(t) = f\left[X_{ij}^{pc}(t), M_{ij}(t)\right] \tag{12}$$

There are various functional forms that have been used to modelling damage functions in annual crops. Cousens (1985) has assumed that yield loss is best represented by a rectangular hyperbola. The biological grounds for this argument are that at a low weed density, weeds are most competitive to crops and hence cause a maximum marginal reduction in crop yield. The effect of an increase in weed numbers at low densities is additive. However, when the density is high, increased intra-specific weed competition tends to reduce the marginal yield loss. This relationship dealing with intra-specific weed competition is appropriate for small scale paddock level modelling. A simple crop damage function is considered to be more applicable. For this purpose, a simple crop damage parameter is introduced and the crop yield is adjusted by this parameter whenever there is a weed invasion. This assumption of a simple linear crop damage function is said to be reasonable in the case of agriculture, where damage can be conveniently calculated as the difference in gross margins per hectare before and after the weed invades. Hence, assuming a fixed crop damage function the damage in terms of crop yield loss for each (i, j)th cell at time t, $[Zij\ (t)]$ is considered a fixed value.

Yield (*Y*) is a function of the weed-free crop yield (*Ywf*) and crop damage (*Z*):

$$Y = Y_{wf}\,(1 - Z) \tag{13}$$

Including dependence of Y on cell (i, j) across the $n \times m$ array and on time t, Equation (13) can be written as:

EFFICACY/PERFORMANCE OF POLICY AND MANAGEMENT OPTIONS

Once the problem is well defined, the final stage is to make the decision on which management strategy or combination of strategies to use. A wide variety of both qualitative and quantitative processes are available for making such decisions. In some simple cases the choice of control and how to implement it may seem obvious. In more complicated scenarios, subjective or qualitative procedures such as multicriteria assessment may be useful, and optimization techniques also extend to more mathematically formal methods.

$$Y_{ij}(t) = Y_{wf\,ij}(t)\left[1 - Z_{ij}(t)\right] \tag{14}$$

Cacho (2004) expressed the cost of weed control in terms of the target rate of spread as shown in Figure 3. The invasion is assumed to spread in a circular pattern and the size of the invasion is measured by its radius. The rate of spread can be slowed or reversed by targeting the invasion front. The decision as to attempt to eradicate the invasion is based on evaluating net benefits i.e benefits minus costs. The cost of slowing the weeds spread i.e control cost is zero when the invasion is allowed to spread uncontrolled (*vmax*). As the target rate of spread decreases with increased control intensity by moving left in Figure 9 the control cost increases. The cost function is expected to be convex to the origin as cheaper and easier control methods are used first, and more expensive options may be required for more intensive control. When the cost curve crosses the vertical axis, weed spread is stopped total containment is achieved. When the rate of spread is negative, implying depletion in the weed seed bank, the invasion decreases with time and will eventually result in eradication. Partial control can slow the spread and although the entire area at risk will be eventually invaded, this option could have a value. Delaying the transition to a fully invaded environment means that benefits from the uninvited area are obtained for a longer period and the costs of treatment are delayed. Slowing the spread also enhances the possibility of making eradication feasible if new technologies become available in the future.

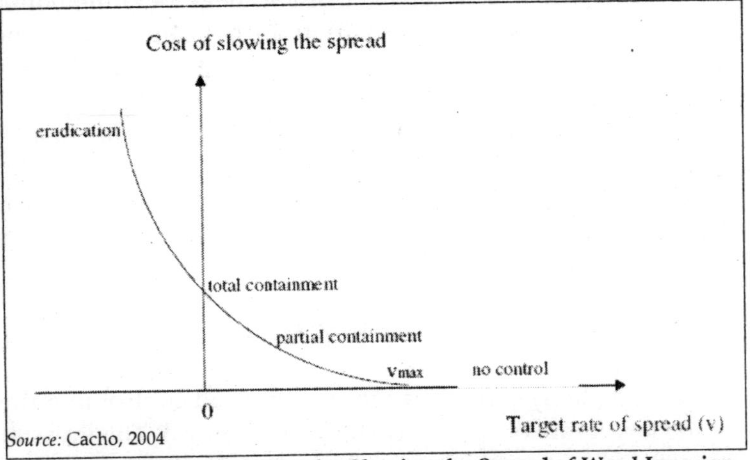

Source: Cacho, 2004

Figure 9: The Cost Function for Slowing the Spread of Weed Invasion

The weed management policy is evaluated in a benefit-cost framework to evaluate the difference between the with-control and without-control options. The benefit cost ratio (BCR) is given by:

$$BCR = \frac{\sum_{t=1}^{T} \left(I_{wc_t} - I_{nc_t}\right)/(1+\beta)^t}{\sum_{t=1}^{T} C_t/(1+\beta)^t}$$

where *I*wc and *I*nc are the incomes from the cropping enterprise under with-control and withoutcontrol respectively, C is the annual weed control cost and _ is the discount rate.

STATE VARIABLES

There are two state variables defined for the weed incursion management problem. The first is the size of the invasion (*I*) and the second is the budget available (*B*) for search and control. The invasion state is defined as the proportion of the total area invaded, and is comprised of 200 discrete values ranging from 0 to 100% infestation. An exponential equation is used to define the state values so as to give greater discrimination power at the critical lower invasion state levels. The set of invasion states was calculated as follows.

$$I_{j+1} = 1.0725 \, . \, I_j \qquad for\, j = I, \ldots .200 \qquad (16)$$

$$I = \{0.0000, 0.00005, 0.000107, 0.00011, \ldots ,90.5, 97.1, 100.0\}$$

In the dynamic programming model solution process, the proportional state variable is transformed into an area based variable as follows.

$$IA = \frac{I}{100} \, . A \qquad (17)$$

Where *IA* is the area invaded by new weed incursion (ha), and *A* is the area at risk of invasion (ha). This allows the computation of the non-invaded area (*NA*) in any year *t*.

$$NAi = A - IAt \qquad (18)$$

The change in the invasion area state is a function of the intrinsic growth of weed spread (_*IA*), and the area controlled (*CA*) due to the impact of search and control decisions.

$$IA_{t+1} = IA_t + \Delta IA_t - CA_t \qquad (19)$$

The annual increase in weed spread is obtained from a logistic growth equation, with the intrinsic growth parameter (_) being obtained from solution of the weed spread model described in section 2.1.

$$\Delta IA_t = \sigma . IA_t \left(1 - \frac{IA_t}{A}\right) \quad (20)$$

The concept of a harvest function of a natural resource stock is used to represent the reduction in weed invasion area due to search and control efforts and is described in the decision variable section below. The budget state is included to account for any limits on public funds available for a weed eradication program. It is unlikely that funding for such a program would be unconstrained, either annually or in total. Consequently, two constraints are included in the model – the total budget and an annual funding limit. For this analysis there are 101 discrete budget states ranging from \$0 to \$50m.

$$B = \{0.0, 0.50, 1.0, K, 50.0\}$$

The transition in the budget state is as follows.

$$B_{t+1} = B_t - WC_t \quad (21)$$

$$WC_t = F_{COST} + (L_{COST} . E_t) + [(p_{detect} . IA_t)(MC_{COST} + L_{COST})] \quad (22)$$

Where *WC* is the annual weed control costs (\$), *F*COST is fixed administration costs (\$), *L*COST is labour costs (\$/day), *E* is the labour effort decision variable in terms of man days, *MC*COST is the cost of materials for control (\$/ha) and *LC*COST is the cost of labour for control (\$/ha). The annual budget limit (*BA*) is defined by the following constraint.

$$WC_t \leq BA \quad (23)$$

DECISION VARIABLE

There is a single control variable – the annual search and control effort (*E*) defined by the number of man days. The set of control decisions is defined as:

$$E = \{0, 2500, 5000, K, 50000\}$$

As the effort devoted to searching for weed infestations increases there is a corresponding increase in the probability of detection. This is directly derived within the dynamic programming model by amending the coverage variable in Equation (6) as follows. The derivation of *p*detect, and *M* remain as given in Equations (7) and (10).

$$c_t = \frac{sp.(E_t .s_h).sw}{S_{area}} \tag{24}$$

The search area (ha), *S*area, is a user defined variable. Increasing the area to be searched for a given level of *E* reduces coverage and consequently the probability of detection. However, setting too small a search area means that some infestations may lie outside the search area and miss detection entirely.

STAGE

The stages modelled are production years. The planning horizon (*T*) consists of 50 years.

PROFIT FUNCTION

The stage return is measured as the profit (_) from the grains enterprise from both the noninvaded and the invaded areas within the total cropping region.

$$\pi_t = IAt.max\left[\left(P_c .Y_{wf}(1-Z)-VC\right),LR\right]+$$

$$NA_t\left[P_c .Y_{wf} - VC\right]-WC_t \tag{25}$$

Where *Pc* is crop price ($/t), *Ywf* is weed-free yield (t/ha), *Z* is the crop damage factor, *VC* is crop variable costs ($/ha), and *LR* is livestock returns ($/ha). The opportunity cost of a new weed incursion is explicitly taken into account by including the variable *LR* which represents the returns from a livestock alternative. Consequently, if the post invasion return per hectare is less than *LR*, this alternative land use option is used in the profit function calculation. This condition is included so as to reduce the potential for overestimating the benefits of a weed control program.

The objective of the dynamic programming model is to maximise the net present value (NPV) of returns from the area (*A*) over the 50 year planning horizon. The recursive equation is given as follows.

$$V_t(IA_t . B_t) = \max_{u_t}\left[\pi\left(IA_t, B_t\right) + \delta V_{t+1}\left(IA_{t+1}, B_{t+1}\right)\right] \quad (26)$$

Where *Vt* (·) is the maximum present value of returns from both invaded and non-invaded areas from year *t* to the end of the planning horizon, *ut* is the decision variable (ie. *Et*), _(*IAt* ,*Bt*) is the immediate return associated with *ut* decision alternative, and _ is the discount factor (1/(1+_)) where _ is the discount rate. It is assumed that the terminal value equals zero, i.e. at *t* = 50, *Vt*+1(·) = 0. The solution of the recursive equation provides the optimal policy which indicates the level of control (*ut*) and NPV of returns for all combinations states and stages for any given size of invasion (*IAt*). Associated with the optimal control is the optimal state transition *IAt* _ *IAt+1* which indicates whether the invasion area increases (*IAt* < *IAt*+1), decreases (*IAt* > *IAt*+1) or remains stable (*IAt* = *IAt*+1) when subject to the optimal control.

9

Marine Bioeconomics

Marine fishes exhibit a great diversity of sizes, shapes, and behaviors, ranging in size from an inch long goby to a 25 foot long great white shark. Shapes can be unique, such as the spiny box fish, or typically fish-like, such as the red snapper. Fishes can be categorized by their habitats, which are as diverse as the fish species themselves. Pelagic fish are those species that spend their time in the open ocean. Pelagic species include sardines and jack fish, which are known to associate in large schools. Some pelagic species get very large and are solitary hunters, such as the adult bluefin tuna and swordfish. As juveniles and small adults, these species exhibit schooling behavior, becoming solitary as they mature. Coral reef fish are, obviously, fish species that are typically associated with coral reef habitats. Many of these fish have evolved especially to associate with coral, such as the parrot fish, that crunches hard coral in order to eat the soft-bodied coral animal inside its calcium carbonate home. Butterfly fish have very small, pointed mouths that allow them to pick small particles from the coral, including the soft coral animals. The coral reefs of the world exhibit an incredible diversity of fish species that are typically brightly colored and make up the majority of marine fish found in the aquarium trade.

Estuarine fish are species of fish that are typically found in estuaries, which are coastal areas where fresh and salt water come together. Species of fish found in estuaries must be able to tolerate wide shifts in salinity and temperature, since their habitat is known to be extremely variable. Estuarine species in the southeastern U.S. include flounder, seatrout, mullet, and drum. Reef fish are typically associated with areas where the bottom topography is uneven, often with deposits of limestone or other rock forms. While these areas are significantly different from coral reefs, the species associated with them are known as reef fish, and include a variety of snapper and grouper species, triggerfish, porgies, among a variety of others.

Some species of fish require both nearshore and offshore habitats to satisfy their life history requirements. The red drum is one of the most popular, sought-after species in the recreational fishery of the Southeastern U.S. Large adult red drum inhabit marine waters offshore and mate, and spawn their eggs there. The eggs are moved by currents to nearshore areas where they hatch. The young red drum stay in estuaries until their second or third year, before moving offshore to join the adult spawning stock. Another important species that utilizes nearshore and offshore habitats is the gag grouper. Such multiple habitat requirements of fish species complicate their life cycle and can make management difficult.

MARINE PLANTS AND ANIMALS

There are 300 to 500 million species of organisms in the ocean. Most of this life occurs along a relatively narrow strip formed by the continental shelves. These areas contain the world's most productive habitats: mangroves, salt marshes, mudflats, sea grass and seaweed beds, and coral reefs. Marine organisms display a staggering variety of shapes and sizes, including the smallest of planktonic plants and animals to the largest animal on earth, the blue whale. Many people believe that the health of the world's oceans is directly tied to the quality of human life on earth. Certainly, from an economic perspective, the sea supports a world market that exceeds $20 billion, just from our natural resources. That figure is multiplied many times when we include shipping, mining, oil and gas extraction, and water recreation. Coastal communities are unique areas typically defined by businesses and activities that are associated with our oceans and natural resources. Fishing and SCUBA diving are two significant activities that often include harvesting marine life, either for commercial sale or for recreational and personal use. Businesses that support these activities range from dive shops, fishing tackle shops, net shops, fish dealers, seafood restaurants, and eco-tourism. The overall value of these businesses and activities exceed the economic value by influencing the flavor of communities and defining cultures that are unique across the U.S.

MARINE INVERTEBRATES

Invertebrates, animals without backbones, occur on land and in the water, making up over 95% of the animal species on earth. Marine invertebrates are a diverse group of over 50,000 species including crustaceans, such as crabs, shrimp, and lobsters; cephalopods, including octopus, squid, and cuttlefish; mollusks, including oysters, clams, and snails; jellyfishes; corals; sea stars; sponges; just to name a few. With so many different kinds of marine invertebrates, it is easy to see that they occupy a broad diversity of habitats around the world, ranging from intertidal zones, to estuaries, to deep seas. Marine invertebrates are some of the most sought after foods for human consumption, providing a healthy source of protein and much enjoyment. Included in this group are the shrimp, crabs, and lobsters, which make up much of the fare at popular seafood restaurants. Also included are squid, octopus, clams, and mussels.

Marine invertebrates range in size from the giant squid, featured in 20,000 Leagues Under the Sea, to tiny organisms less than a single millimeter long. As an animal without a backbone, many marine invertebrates protect themselves with a hard exoskeleton, or outer shell, such as those found on sea snails, oysters, and clams. However, quite a number of marine invertebrates do not have a hard exoskeleton. How, then, do they protect themselves? Many of them have developed defense mechanisms, such as the stinging cells (nematocysts) of jellyfish. Sea slugs are often brightly colored, but when a fish or other organism attempts to eat this attractive food item, they find the taste to be unpalatable. Cone shells, a marine snail, are notorious for their poisonous sting.

MARINE BIRDS

Birds that live in association with marine habitats fall into three main groups: shorebirds (such as plovers, sandpipers, etc.), water birds (such as ducks, cormorants, and loons) and seabirds (such as albatrosses, petrels, puffins, penguins, frigate birds and boobies). Seabirds, particularly albatrosses, are becoming increasingly threatened at a faster rate globally than all other species-groups of birds. Seabirds face a variety of threats, both on land and at sea. Currently the most critical conservation problem facing seabirds is thought to be bycatch caused by mortality in longline fisheres.

MARINE MAMMALS

Of all the animals in the oceans, marine mammals evoke the emotion of the public more intensely than any other group. They are often called "charismatic megafauna," because they are so large and spend time at the surface where people can view them. Marine mammals are distributed throughout the world's oceans and exhibit great diversity, with more than 75 species of whales and dolphins, 35 species of pinnipeds, including seals, sea lions, and walruses, and several species of manatees, dugongs, and otters. Because of their appeal to people and their wide global distribution, interactions between marine mammals and people occur frequently. This has led marine mammals to be considered by regulatory agencies and conservation groups as species of special concern.

THE ECONOMIC VALUATION OF MARINE RESOURCES

Natural marine ecosystems require our attention for two reasons. Firstly, they provide a wide range of benefits to humans, ranging from the provision of food to climate regulation, from coastal recreation to habitat conservation. Secondly, human activities have contributed, and still contribute, to an unprecedented strain on marine ecosystems, and the biodiversity they host. Our experience in the field of environmental economics teaches us that many marine ecosystem values cannot be incorporated in conventional market transactions. The question then is how to translate such values into monetary terms. This is a challenging question to be posed to economists. In order to provide an answer to such a question, economists first need to work with scientists from other disciplines so as to understand the complexity of the relationships between the functioning of marine ecosystems and their capacity to provide ecosystem goods and services. Economists, at a second stage, proceed with the valuation of these ecosystem goods and services, bearing in mind their impact on human welfare. This valuation is expressed in monetary terms, exploring a wide range of methodologies.

MARINE ECOSYSTEM AS A SOURCE OF ECONOMIC VALUE

Motivation for Economic Valuation: Why are Economists in this Picture?

The economic valuation of environmental assets, in general, and marine ecosystems and biodiversity, in particular, is among the most pressing and challenging issues environmental economics is confronted with. One of the main reasons for pursuing economic valuation arises from its potential for benefit-cost-analysis, which is a corner stone in the evaluation of any policy design. The basic rule of benefit-cost-analysis in decision-making is to approve any potentially worthwhile policy if the benefits of the policy exceed the costs. Therefore, there is the urgency to identify and estimate the economic values of the full range of benefits provided by the marine ecosystems. Major organisations across the world such as the World Bank, Conservation International, the Environmental Protection Agency, the European Commission and others promote the application of an economic value assessments and its use in the policy agenda. Environmental accounting is also recognised as an important steering factor in carrying out an economic valuation of marine ecosystems and biodiversity services. In this context, various efforts have been made to adjust national accounting systems and associated gross national product statistics to take into account the depreciation of environmental assets and the loss of biodiversity. Green accounting is one possible strategy. The underlying idea is to add information on physical flows and stocks of environmental goods and services to the traditional national accounting system–the so-called physical satellite accounts.

GENERAL FEATURES OF THE ECONOMIC VALUATION PERSPECTIVE

The economic valuation of marine ecosystem and biodiversity services (MEBs) is based on an instrumental perspective of the value. This means that the value of MEBs is anchored in a human perspective and therefore interpreted as the result of an interaction between who attaches value (humans) and the object of valuation (flows of ecosystem goods and services). In other words, the economic valuation perspective subscribes an anthropocentric value orientation, thus rejecting the notion of intrinsic values. Secondly, humans elicit MEBs in terms of their impact on human welfare, including human knowledge, use, experience, and consumption of MEBs. Thirdly, the economic valuation of MEBs has a reductionist approach since it is based on the idea that one is capable of subdividing the total economic value into use value and passive use value, reflecting the different human motivations with respect to the (non)use of biodiversity values - see Table 1. In a conceptual framework, one can define the total value (TV) of the marine ecosystem and biodiversity benefits in terms of the use value (UV) and non-use value (NU). The former can be further divided into direct and indirect use values (DUV and IUV). Direct use values include: (a) marine and coastal recreation benefits; (b) natural and cultured marine species with commercial value; and (c) insurance with respect to potential risks to human health. Indirect use values refer to benefits that relate to the good functioning of the marine ecosystem and the survival of marine living resources, even if these have no direct commercial value. Finally, nonuse values of marine quality can be divided into a bequest value (BV) and an existence value (EV). Bequest value refers to the benefit accruing to any individual from the knowledge that future generations might benefit from a sustainable marine ecosystem. Existence value refers to the benefit derived simply from the knowledge that the marine ecosystem is protected without even being used. Fourthly, economic valuation of MEBs is pursued through explicit changes in the current state of the world. On average, these are described by the use of scenarios and economists focus on the welfare changes involved. In other words, an economic valuation of the system in its current state is not pursued but rather of the changes of the system. For example, in the field of climate change, one may be willing to assess the total economic value provided by MEBs when moving from an A1 to a B2 storyline scenario. Fifthly, economic valuation of MEBs is a monetary indicator. The reason is that from a theoretical perspective, economists assume that consumers are willing to trade changes in the level of provision of MEBs with variations in their income (e.g. compensation

Table 1
Classification of Economic Values Provided by the Marine Ecosystems

Value Components		*Examples of Benefits*
Use value (UV)	Direct use value (DUV)	Tourism and recreational benefits, e.g. visits to the beach, swimming and sailing
		Marine resource with commercial value, e.g. fish, shellfish and molluscs
		Human health, e.g. prevention of skin allergies and gastrointestinal disorders
	Indirect use value (DUV)	Marine ecosystem and ecological functioning, e.g. climate regulation, protection of local marine living resources diversity
Non-use value (NUV)	Bequest Value (BV)	Legacy benefits, e.g. heritage of marine living resources for future generations
	Existence value (EV)	Existence benefits, e.g. knowledge guarantee that some marine living resources are not extinct

Source: van den Bergh et al. (2002)

measures or payments for ecosystem services). This means that the economic valuation results can be easily fitted to benefit-cost-analysis, a crucial tool for the design of effective and broadly accepted management policy. Finally, a European review on the economic valuation of ecosystems and biodiversity points out that most of the economic valuation studies lack a uniform, clear perspective on MEBs as a distinct, univocal resource. Therefore, an integration of the economic valuation exercise within a fully integrated approach such as the one recently proposed by the United Nations, the Millennium Ecosystem Approach, is solicited. However, the different economic valuation methods that an economist can refer to are discussed before this.

ECONOMIC VALUATION TOOL BOX

Various valuation methods are available to give an economic value to environmental benefits. We can distinguish two groups of valuation methods: the direct and indirect or dose response valuation methods–see Table 2.

Table 2
A Classification of Economic Valuation Methods

Revealed Preference	*Stated Preference*	*Dose Response*
Travel cost	Contingent valuation	Production cost
Hedonic pricing	Stated choice	Production factor
Averting behaviour		

Source: World Bank (2004) pag. 11

The dose response methods are similar in that they put a price on environmental commodities without establishing people's preferences for these commodities. The production cost techniques such as the dose response methods rely on the presence of physical input-output relationships. For example, if one intends to estimate the monetary value of the benefits of clean air on human health, one can take into account the relationship between air pollution and the number of visits to physicians and the purchase of drugs. This valuation method results in underestimates as it omits preferences for health, the value of which cannot be easily estimated. Conversely, the direct methods rely on individual preferences. These methods are further divided into revealed preference methods and stated preference methods depending on the process by which the individuals' preferences are obtained. The group of revealed preference valuation methods consists of three methods: travel cost, hedonic pricing and averting behaviour. The common underlying feature is the dependency on a relationship between a market good and the environmental benefit. For example, when using the travel cost method, researchers estimate the economic value of recreational sites by looking at the costs of the trips made by the visitors to these sites. When using the hedonic price method to estimate the economic value of clean air, researchers examine the analysis of house market prices and surrounding air characteristics. Researchers who use the averting behaviour method try to estimate the economic value of clean air on the basis of expenditures on technological equipments made to avert or mitigate the adverse effects of air pollution.

Whereas economists who use revealed preference valuation methods have to carry out estimation exercises bearing in mind the existent market price data, economists who use stated preference valuation methods have to collect their own data by means of questionnaires, based on constructed markets. The underlying feature is the use of the questionnaire to ask the individuals directly to state their economic values for environmental commodities. The use of questionnaires require economists to work closely with experts from market and survey research, sociology and psychology in order to guarantee the authority of the stated choice methods as a valid instrument to assess economic value of an environmental benefit. In contrast, revealed preference methods have remained an exclusive valuation tool for economists. Stated preference valuation methods are contingent valuation, contingent ranking, pairwise comparison and allocation games. The respective differences relate to the way in which the economic values are elicited. For example, whereas the contingent valuation method asks respondents to express their preferences for some defined environmental benefit in monetary terms, the contingent ranking method asks the respondent to rank a number of described environmental quality alternatives.

It is important to note that an alternative valuation method, benefit transfer, is currently popularized and applicable for any of the ecosystem goods and services in question. The development of benefit transfer technology provides a low cost and less time consuming opportunity for the economic valuation of most of the environmental goods and services. The idea underlying this method is to transfer the biodiversity benefit estimates from original CV studies to the policy site, where no original studies have been done but policy decisions need to be made. However, the validity and accuracy of the estimate results need to be improved. In Table 3, we display all the valuation methods mentioned so far, and list detailed information regarding the respective application fields, data requirements as well as main limitations of each individual method.

AN ECOSYSTEM SERVICE BASED APPROACH

The Conceptual Integrated Ecological-Economic Framework

The Millennium Ecosystem Assessment (MEA, 2005) has fundamentally changed the approach that has characterised natural and social scientists, and has mapped the complex relationships between biodiversity, ecosystem functioning, and human welfare. The MEA distinguishes four broad categories of benefit: provisioning services, cultural services, regulating services and supporting services – see Figure 1.

Following the MA approach, Beaumont et al. (2007) and Balmford (2008), identified a range of marine ecosystem goods and services for each category – see Table 4. An accurate, complete and reliable monetary assessment of marine ecosystem benefits also requires the application of specific monetary valuation tools. Bearing in mind both the classification of the economic value component and the respective marine benefits, Table 4 shows the most suitable valuation methodology to be used.

Table 3
Main Economic Valuation Techniques : A Summary

Methodology	*Approach*	*Applications*	*Data Requirements*	*Limitations*
		Revealed Preference Methods		
Production function	Trace impact of change in ecosystem services on produced goods	Any impact that affects produced goods	Change in service: impact on production; net value of produced goods	Data on change in service and consequent impact on production often lacking
Replacement/ Avoidance Cost	Use cost of replacing the lost good or service them	Any loss of goods or services	Extent of loss of goods or services, cost of replacing	Tends to over-estimate actual value; should be used with extreme caution
Travel cost method (TCM)	Derive demand curve from data on actual travel costs travelled	Recreation	Survey to collect monetary and time costs of travel to destination, distance	Limited to recreational benefits; hard to use when trips are to multiple destinations
Hedonic pricing(HP)	Extract effect of environmental factors on price of goods that include those factors	Air quality, scenic beauty, cultural benefits	Prices and characteristics of goods	Requires vast quantities of data; very sensitive to specification
		Stated Preference Methods		
Contingent valuation (CV)	Ask respondentsdirectly their WTP for a specified service	Cultural values, Passive use values	Survey that presents scenario and elicits WTP for specified Service	Many potential sources of bias in responses;guidelines exist for reliable application
		Other Methods		
Benefit transfer	Use results obtained in one contest in adifferent context	Any for which suitable comparison studies are available	Valuation exercises at another, similar site	Can be very inaccurate, as many factors vary even when contexts seem 'similar' should be used with extreme caution

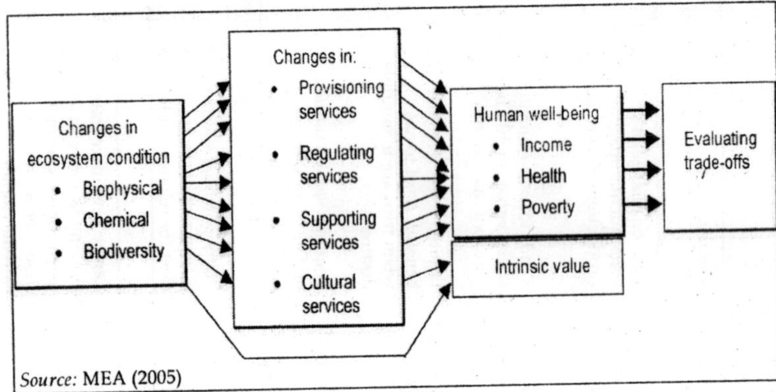

Source: MEA (2005)

Figure 1: Mapping the Links between Biodiversity, Ecosystem Services and Human Wellbeing

Table 4
Goods and Services Provided by Marine Biodiversity: A MEA Approach

MEA Category	*Goods or Services*	*Most suitable valuation method*
Provisioning services	Food provision Raw materials	Aggregate price analysis(1)Aggregate price analysis(1)
Regulating services	Gas and climate regulation Disturbance prevention (food and storm protection)	Avoidance costAggregate price analysis(1),Avoidance
Cultural services	Cultural heritage and identity Cognitive, educational values Leisure and recreation Bequest and existence values of habitats and species	Stated preference methodsAggregate price analysis(1) Travel cost methodStated preference methods Production function,Stated preference methods (2)
Supporting services	Resilience and resistance (life support) Biologically mediated habitatNutrient cycling	Production function, Stated preference methods (2) Replacement/ Avoidance cost,Stated preference methods (2)

Source: adapted from Beaumont et al. (2007), p.p. 256, van den Bergh et al. (2002), Sudhkev et al. 2008, Markandya et al 2008 (1) market price method, (2) no clear understanding of the potential of these economic valuation methodologies to fully capture the magnitude of the benefits due to high degree of uncertainty.

As one can see, the travel cost method is the most suitable valuation method for a monetary value assessment of marine quality benefits that relate to the provision of tourism and recreational opportunities. Moreover, stated preference methods can fulfill an important role in the overall assessment of marine quality benefits. Indeed, stated preference methods can be applied to assess the monetary value of most of the types of benefits provided by the protection of marine quality, including both bequest and existence values. Furthermore, these methods have the advantage that marine policies may be valued even if they have not yet been adopted ex ante valuation or lie outside the current institutional arrangements. Thus, it offers much scope and flexibility for specifying different marine protection, restoration and amelioration programmes. For these reasons particular attention will be paid to the analysis and discussion of stated preference methods, including the stated choice method (SC) and contingent valuation method (CV). In addition, we will also focus on the use of the travel cost (TC) method to assess marine recreational values.

SC and CV are survey based valuation techniques that are widely used in the context of environmental valuation. CV is a surveybased approach that directly estimates the preferences for risk reductions in the overall marine ecosystem quality. Therefore, CV gives an immediate monetary estimate of the willingness to pay (WTP) welfare measure associated with an increase in the marine quality. In short, CV and SC make use of a questionnaire that describes a survey market in which non-market goods can be traded. It is assumed that the values elicited with CV will correspond to those that would emerge on real markets. The contingent market defines the good itself, the institutional context in which it would be provided, and the way it would be financed. Respondents are then asked to express their maximum WTP for a survey-described change in the level of the environmental good. Alternatively, in the SC approach respondents are presented with a set of two or more survey-described alternatives that differ in terms of the respective attributes and attribute levels. The respondents are asked to select the alternative they prefer. Both a CV and a SC questionnaire contain two important elements. The first is a clear description of the environmental good to be valued. The second element is a mechanism for eliciting the WTP of the respondents. CV describes the elicitation process directly with a WTP question, while in SC, individual WTP is inferred from the choice of the described alternatives or choice sets. Finally, the travel cost method (TC) can be used when the valuation exercise, and underlying policy proposals, refers exclusively to the recreational use values provided by protection of marine quality. In short, the travel-cost method is a demand-based model used for a recreation site – see Nunes and van den Bergh (2004).

VALUATION STUDIES

From the theoretical view point, climate change is expected to have inter alia an impact on the Arctic sea-ice cover and its thickness and on the Atlantic meridional overturning circulation. This may be translated inter alia into higher surface/water temperatures that, in turn, will strengthen near-surface stratification and decrease the ability of the winter winds to mix the water column – see Figure 2. Several coupled ocean-atmosphere models have shown global warming to be accompanied by an increase in vertical stratification (IPCC 2001). These physical and biological impacts need to be clearly identified and measured – for example by exploring the use of

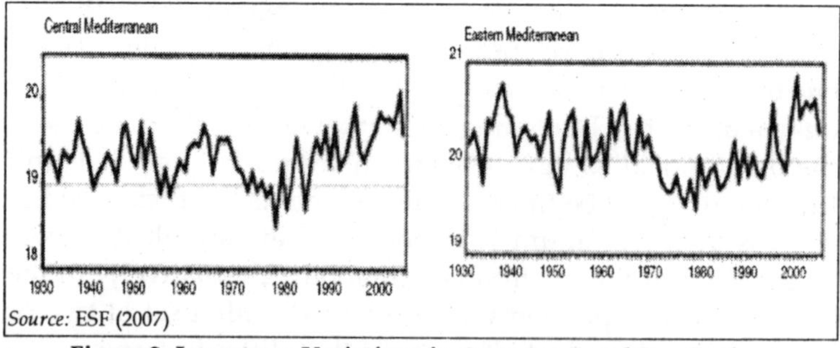

Source: ESF (2007)

Figure 2: Long-term Variations in Area-Averaged Sea-Surface Temperatures (°C)

climate scenarios such as the Arctic Climate Impact Assessment: ACIA 2005, which uses the B2 intermediate scenario describing a world with moderate population growth, economic development and technology change. This scenario predicts a doubling of atmospheric CO2 after approximately 80 years. Once the physical and biological impacts are mapped and quantified, an economist would then proceed with the economic valuation of these impacts, expressed in terms of their significance with regard to changes in human welfare.

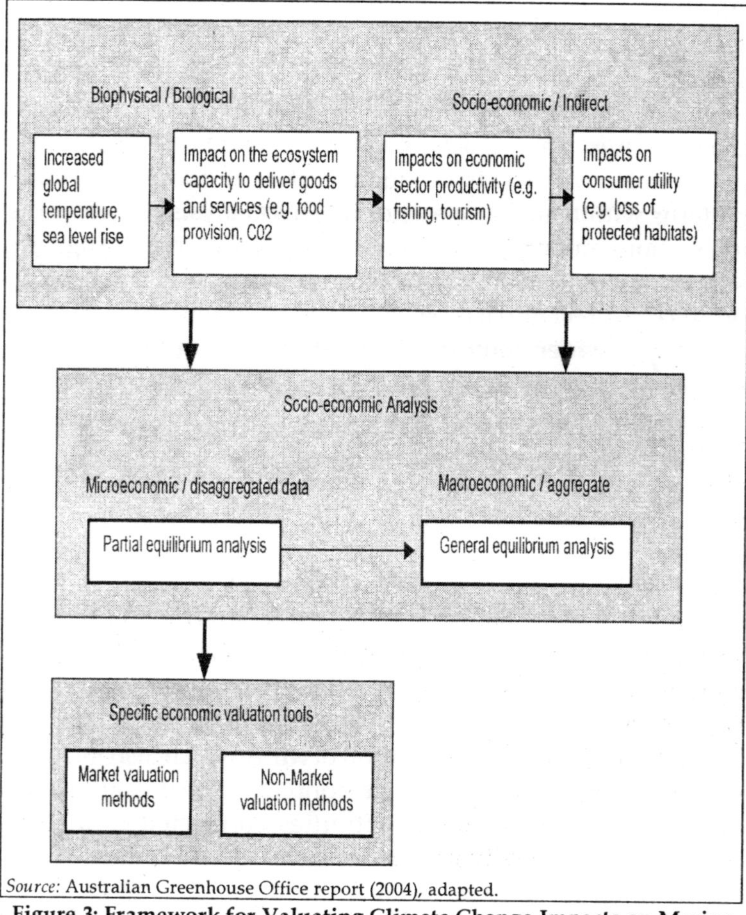

Source: Australian Greenhouse Office report (2004), adapted.

Figure 3: Framework for Valuating Climate Change Impacts on Marine Ecosystems and Services

In Figure 3, one can see that there are two basic levels of analysis that can be used to assess the net cost of impacts of climate change and marine biodiversity effects, namely partial equilibrium analysis and general equilibrium analysis.

Partial equilibrium analysis: According to this economic analysis the impacts of climate change, and its implications in terms of the ecosystem provision of EGS, can be examined in terms of its direct effects on a specific, single market, an industrial sector or economic activity e.g. the local or regional effect of a reduction of the supply EGS on forest recreation activity. General equilibrium analysis: This kind of economic assessment method is widely used for studying the indirect economic impacts or economy-wide impacts caused by climate change. Thus, the impacts of climate change can be assessed for a number of markets, economic sectors and respective trade patterns within an entire economy. This analysis considers the interactions among the different economic sectors and suggests that any climate change impact on one specific market will produce indirect impacts on many other markets, thus affecting prices in a wider context. Alternatively, from the empirical valuation perspective, today we find neither a partial equilibrium nor a general equilibrium application that focuses on the monetary value measurement of the wide range of impacts of climate change on marine ecosystems. A recent review of the economic valuation literature of ecosystems and biodiversity services showed that among the 291 valuation studies submitted to the international call for evidence issued by the European Commission, only 4 referred to marine and coastal valuation studies. A further set of recent European market-based studies of marine biodiversity value and the value of marine ecosystem services not submitted to the call, but of relevance to the application of MEA which also includes valuation based on stated value approaches that estimate the value of various economic activities connected to marine ecosystem biodiversity and, more generally, to conservation– for more information.

AN OVERVIEW OF GOODS AND SERVICES PROVIDED BY MARINE ECOSYSTEMS

Raw Materials

Raw materials refer to the marine organisms extracted for all purposes except human consumption, e.g. pharmaceutical and ornamental uses. Even though this category of MEBs is highly underestimated due to a lack of market value data, it represents considerable market value. For example, figures show that the total value of fishmeal in the UK market in 2004 was £81 million (European Parliament Report 2004), whereas the estimated total gross income from seaweed was between £349,819 and £583,032. Therefore, any alteration of marine biodiversity will influence the provision of raw materials as well as the respective human welfare.

Gas and Climate Regulation

Gas and climate regulation is a consequence of the natural functioning of marine living organisms that balance and maintain the chemical composition of the atmosphere and oceans. However, the monetary magnitude of this value component is rather difficult to obtain by using market valuation methods; instead an avoidance cost method can be employed so as to estimate the savings from damage avoidance due to marine conservation policies. For instance, Beaumont et al. (2006) obtained a value estimate ranging between £420 million and £8.7 billion for the UK territorial waters area.

Disturbance Alleviation and Prevention

The damage caused by flooding and storm events can be alleviated and prevented by biogenic structures. For instance, the salt marshes attenuate and dissipate wave and tidal energy and thereby substantially reduce the cost of flood defence measures. By using the avoidance cost method, King and Lester (1995) and Beaumont et al. (2006) have calculated cost savings from sea defence for the UK waters and obtained an estimated value between £17 billion and £32 billion. The authors acknowledge that this value estimate is underestimated as only salt marshes were considered.

Cultural Heritage and Identity

This service of marine ecosystems reflects the cultural value associated with marine biodiversity e.g. for religion, folklore, painting, cultural and spiritual traditions. However, little information is currently available on the cultural benefits of marine biodiversity, although this is believed to be indicative of a lack of documented research, as opposed to a lack of value.

Cognitive Values

This value component refers to the economic values of cognitive development in marine science, including education and research. For example, in the UK, marine research and application areas involved total funding of about £292 million in 2002, in addition to £24.8 million generated in education and training in marine science (Pugh and Skinner, 2002).

Leisure and Recreation

The leisure and recreation service provided by coastal marine biodiversity has significant economic value, including support to the related employment and small businesses. More specific valuation studies are undertaken for open marine waters, e.g. whale-tourism and seal watching. Statistical figures show that the whale-tourism in West Scotland generated total income at £7.8 million in 1994, whereas the seal watching provided at least £36 million to the UK economy in 1996.

Bequest and Existence Values

This value component captures the non-use value of marine ecosystems. Therefore, the stated preference method is considered the most appropriate valuation method, e.g. the contingent valuation method. Studies by Hageman (1985) and Loomis and White (1996) estimated an annual average household's willingness to pay for surviving species of sea mammals in the £19 - £46 range per species, depending on the mammal species. By multiplying the unit estimate by the total number of households, the non-use value of marine mammals was estimated to vary between £469 million and £1,136 million in the UK in 2004.

Nutrient Cycling Value

Nutrient cycling has an essential role in terms of alleviating excessive nutrient loading and sustaining the productivity rates of marine species. The economic valuation of this service is rather difficult due to the high degrees of uncertainty about anthropogenic effects. Costanza et al. (1997) employed a replacement cost method and estimated the value of marine nutrient cycling in the £0.10 - £0.29 per m3 range, which corresponds to a total replacement cost between £800 billion and £2320 billion derived from the sea waters. However, this value estimate should be used with caution.

Biologically Mediated Habitat

A biologically mediated habitat is provided by living marine organisms supporting a large number of species. It has an essential role in the marine ecosystem functioning. The loss of these habitats will result in a decline of biodiversity due to a loss of nursery and refuge areas. However, the valuation of marine biologically mediated habitats is currently missing due to lack of information. A number of points should be noted about these estimation results: (1) Estimates of market values are partial and generally not comparable. Sometimes the figures are given as net income, sometimes as gross income. Gains in terms of employment or increased local economic activity found in some reports are not necessarily economic benefits or they might be only partially that depends on what alternative employment opportunities exist and what alternative economic activities are possible. With the current state-of-the-art, however, it is possible to carry out proper valuations based on economy-wide impacts of biodiversity loss or conservation and some studies have done this; In some cases estimates are based on the costs of restoring lost services. Albeit useful, such estimates could be higher or lower than the market value that is lost. Indeed one of the purposes of valuing loss of biodiversity is to see if replacement or restoration is justified. Using the former as a measure of value does not allow one to answer that question; (3) Underlying the market-based approach are scientific studies linking the estimated impacts on biodiversity to certain causes e.g. the effect of pests on forests, of forests on air pollution etc. We should recognise that there are still many uncertainties regarding these links, which should be reflected in the reported benefits; (4) The majority of the studies refer to marginal changes in local areas. At the same time there are a few that value the broad scale of services provided globally. The numbers from the latter studies are extremely high; (5) The purpose of many of the studies was to show that the services provided by nature are significant and either merit protection where biodiversity is threatened or merit expansion where there is potential for it. Estimates of the 'opportunity cost' of coastal habitat, wetlands – i.e. what it would be worth if it were not conserved - are often much lower than the value of the biodiversity services provided if it was conserved.

CRITICAL DISCUSSION OF THE VALUATION STUDIES

Biodiversity is a complex, abstract concept. It can be associated with multiple, widely ranging benefits to the human society, most of them still poorly understood. From the economic valuation studies under review it is clear that the few empirical assessments of marine biodiversity and ecosystem values do not provide an unequivocal, unambiguous monetary indicator. In any case, one should always keep in mind that economic valuation of biodiversity values does not pursue total value assessment of biodiversity, but rather of biodiversity changes. Therefore, it is nonsense to try to value extremely large changes in biodiversity, and certainly a waste of time to examine extreme changes like one resulting in a situation in which there is no natural living creature. Economists have assessed the economic value of biodiversity through tradeoffs between money and changes in biodiversity at different levels of life diversity, including genetic, species, ecosystem and functional diversity. Most of the time, there are no market valuation mechanisms that price biodiversity values. Therefore, valuing biodiversity requires the use of special valuation tools. The choice of the valuation tool will, in turn, depend upon the biodiversity value category under consideration. For example, it will be hard to set a contingent valuation survey to elicit the economic value related to changes in ecosystem functions and ecological services that are far removed from human perceptions, such as CO2 storage or groundwater purification processes. On the contrary, the contingent valuation method is the most appropriate method whenever one focuses on the monetary valuation of biodiversity non-use values. Having said this, we strongly believe that the neo-classical economic valuation of biodiversity does make sense. Nevertheless, it is important to mention that economic valuation studies have arrived at an important crossroad. On the one hand, one may opt for combining contingent and non-contingent valuation strategies so as to assess the complexity involved at multiple life organisation levels in more detail. This strategy signals the need for a multidisciplinary approach that seeks a clear perspective on the direct and indirect effects of changes in biodiversity on human welfare. This would contribute to more sturdy economic value estimates that could serve to guide biodiversity policies. On the other hand, researchers can continue to work on creating more sophisticated versions and applications of the non-market valuation methods.

SHORTFALLS IN KNOWLEDGE AND SUGGESTIONS FOR FUTURE RESEARCH

From the above, and from a review of the valuation literature, we conclude that while methods have been developed and used widely for some environmental values especially non-market values, there are still several gaps in the literature. Notable among these are the lack of valuation studies and of the assessment of economic value. In fact, we would argue that the following issues need to be addressed urgently:

- to promote the development of valuation studies that focus on the valuation of loss of marine species other than keystone species; marine cultural and spiritual values; and the dynamic aspect of all ecosystems and values–changes over time are at the core of all ecosystems.

- equally important, information on the impact of climate change on the marine and coastal environment is still patchy. Therefore, a greater effort has to be made to gather, store and analyse previously and currently collected marine environmental data (e.g. common open access database and annual pan-European reporting based on national contributions).

Given that there are thousands of ecosystems and sites of importance within the EU, let alone the whole world, it is impossible to conduct individual studies to obtain the relevant information in a timely way. Hence some kind of benefit transfer will be essential if the goal of obtaining national, regional and global estimates of the damages from biodiversity loss in the absence of any action is to be obtained. The same applies, a fortiori, to estimating the reductions in such damages when some actions to protect the ecosystems are implemented. The solution to this problem is that one needs to improve the application of benefit transfer for specific evaluations of ecosystem service benefits. In this context, we need to establish a clear set of guidelines about which kinds of benefit transfer are possible. Such guidelines need to stipulate not only the kind of ecosystem services but the areas and countries where the transfer can be carried out, given the available set of valuation studies. Secondly, further research should be carried out on how 'packages' of ecosystem services may be valued without undertaking whole new studies. Where there is an adding up problem, it may be possible to develop approximations for adding up benefits that can only be transferred individually. Thirdly, where transfer is not possible, we should develop toolkits that can be used to carry out location specific studies. Given the large database of existing studies, these can help simplify and demystify the process of valuation so it can be conducted in a more routine and cheap manner. Finally, an inventory of all major ecosystems should be drawn up and the loss of services expected under different scenarios should be prepared. Some of this is underway for some ecosystems but not for all the important ones.

In any case, one should always keep at the back of one's mind that any economic valuation exercise refers to an incremental value. To be useful, the valuation of the service has to be an incremental one. There is little advantage in knowing the total value of an ecosystem unless there is a threat to eliminate it or a policy or reconstruct it in its entirety, which is rarely the case. Yet many valuation studies provide estimates of the total cost of whole systems and there is even one regarding the value of the ecosystems of the whole world. Carrying out an incremental analysis which may entail estimating significant non-marginal changes in ecosystems, however, is not as easy as it might sound. If one is using revealed preference methods, a link has to be established between a change in the environmental attribute and the demand for a visit to a site or the value of a property. If one is carrying out a stated preference analysis the respondent has to understand the nature of the incremental change, which is more difficult than asking for the value of access to a site or use of a particular recreational facility. Finally, any economic valuation exercise needs to address the multiple services and the 'adding up' problem. Many ecosystem services that individuals receive are multidimensional and there is an adding up problem. The value attached to one forest area for recreational or other use is not independent of whether another forest nearby is conserved or not. The implication is that studies need to be undertaken allowing for substitution effects, which makes them more specific to a particular application and less capable of being transferred to other applications.

THE BIOECONOMICS OF MARINE RESERVES

A huge literature exists in terms of marine reserves, mostly written from a biological perspective. A key insight is that how many, and under what conditions, fish migrate or spillover from reserves to harvested areas is critical to maximising the direct benefits of 'no take' areas. These spillovers occur whenever individual fish are afforded a measure of protection in a reserve, but also provide a source of recruitment for exploited areas outside of the reserve. Roberts et al. (2001) and McClanahan and Mangi (2000), among others, provide empirical evidence that reserves can generate positive spillovers that may improve harvests in adjacent exploited areas. Pezzey et al. (2000) and Sanchirico and Wilen (2001) have shown in theoretical models, with density-dependent growth, that a reserve can increase the abundance of the population and, in some cases, may even raise the aggregate harvest in the exploited population. However, this 'double payoff' only arises when the chosen area for the reserve is at a low population level such that the marginal benefits of a closure—reduced mortality, but with spillovers—outweigh the loss of harvest in a previously exploited area.

DETERMINISTIC BIOECONOMIC MODELS

One of the earliest economic contributions to the reserve literature is by Holland and Brazee (1996) who use a deterministic model to show that the relative benefits of reserves depend on their effects on harvesting in exploited areas and also the discount rate. They find that with very high levels of fishing effort that a reserve provides insurance against a collapse in the population, but emphasise that reserves give little or no benefit if there exist effective controls on effort or catches. Hannesson (1998) obtains a similar result. He shows that a reserve is redundant if the total catch can be perfectly controlled, and that a reserve would need to be of a very large size to generate harvesting benefits associated with an optimally controlled fishery. By contrast, Neubert (2003) uses a spatially explicit model to show that reserves can increase yields, but this result critically depends on boundary conditions that assume fish live in patches of suitable habitat, beyond which they die.

Holland (2000) observes in a spatially explicit model that optimal controls on effort and catches make reserves superfluous, but stresses there can be a positive economic payoff to a reserve if fishing effort is excessive. Sanchirico (2004) also finds in a spatial model that a firstbest strategy is to optimally set fishing effort in every possible fishing location, but that establishing reserves in some patches can generate a higher resource rent in an open access fishery. He emphasises, as do Sanchirico and Wilen (1999), that the costs and returns of harvesting in different locations, as well as the spillovers, play an important role in determining where to establish reserves.

STOCHASTIC MODELS

Lauck et al. (1998) show that given management uncertainty over population size, marine reserves should increase with the size of the negative shocks to ensure population persistence. (Mangel, 2000) generates a similar result whereby reserve size should increase with the size of an uncertain harvest rate so as to ensure sustainability of the population. Li (2000) finds that if the probability of total stock collapse decreases with the size of a marine reserve, a reserve has an economic value. Sumaila (1998) also shows that reserves mitigate against biological losses that may arise due to recruitment failure. In a bioeconomic model, Conrad (1999) shows that reserves may generate economic benefits by reducing the variance of the population if net growth in the reserve and the fishery are uncorrelated, or if they are perfectly correlated.

Those who incorporate stochasticity into their models show that reserves have value because either they mitigate the effects of environmental surprises and help ensure population persistence given management error in terms of inability to control harvests or management uncertainty in terms of imprecise information on current population, or because they reduce the variance of populations and harvests. Many fishers and some fishery managers have used these findings to conclude that if harvesting is 'optimal', and the population is persistent, marine reserves generate no harvesting payoffs to fishers and are a redundant management tool. Using a stochastic bioeconomic model, we examine whether fishers can, in fact, benefit from a marine reserve under conditions where 'no take' areas are, at best, viewed as superfluous or even harmful to fisher incomes.

A STOCHASTIC BIOECONOMIC OF A MARINE RESERVE

To address the question of what is the economic payoff of a reserve to fishers we explicitly model environmental uncertainty. We assume that the population, without harvesting, is governed bydensity-dependent growth defined by

$$f(x) = rx\left(1 - \frac{x}{K}\right) \qquad (1)$$

where x is the population or biomass, f (x) is its growth, r is the intrinsic growth rate, and K is the carrying capacity. The model assumes the economic benefit from the population is simply the resource rents it generates, and thus ignores the value of reserves in terms of biodiversity. This assumption allows us to determine if a reserve is worthwhile only in terms of the economic payoffs it provides to fishers, separate from any benefits associated with population persistence, management error, management uncertainty over stock size, or the existence of ecological (Roberts et al., 2003) and non-market values.

Inter-temporal rents from harvesting the population are defined by

$$\Pi(h, x_{NR}) = p(h)h - c\left(h.\frac{x_{NR}}{K_{NR}}\right) \qquad (2)$$

where h is harvest, NR x is the size of the harvested population, is the carrying capacity of the harvested population, K_{NR} p(h) is the inverse demand function, and $(NR)\ c\left(h,\frac{x_{NR}}{K_{NR}}\right)$ is the aggregate cost function where costs rise with the harvest, but do not increase with population density of the harvested population. In the case of a permanent reserve that protects proportion s€ (0,1] of the population, the carrying capacity of the harvested population is defined by (1 – s)K. Thus for s > 0 the growth function of the reserve population, $f(\chi_R, s)$, and the harvested population, $f(\chi_{NR}, s)$, are

$$f(x_R, s) = r\, x_R \left(1 - \frac{x_R}{sK}\right) \tag{3}$$

$$f(x_{NR}, s) = r\, x_{NR} \left(1 - \frac{x_{NR}}{(1-s)K}\right) \tag{4}$$

where and NR x are the reserve and harvested populations. In this model we assume r and K are the same for both the reserve and harvested populations, but they may differ – especially in the case of a long-established reserve.

To analyse the effects of reserves on resource rents, we incorporate two stochastic shocks that may affect both the reserve and harvested populations. One shock may be either a positive or negative and represents a temporal variation in both populations, as defined by a Wiener diffusion process i.e Brownian motion that follows a normal distribution (W_1). The other stochastic process is a negative shock that occurs randomly over time and is defined as a jump process (q) that follows a Poisson distribution, governed by the parameter λ. Brownian motion in the reserve and harvested population is defined by $g(\chi_R)$ and (χ_{NR}) that represent the proportional effect on the two populations from the same realization, Sensitivity to negative shocks in the reserve and harvested population is defined by $\psi(\chi_R)$ and (χ_{NR}) that represent the proportional effects on the populations from the same realization, dq.

The functions ψ and γ differ to allow for the possibility that the sensitivity to the negative shocks may vary in the reserve and harvested populations. To solve for the optimal harvest trajectory and reserve size we must first determine the optimal harvest for a given reserve size, and then select the reserve size that maximises the overall value function defined over s € (0,1] . Thus the solution to the overall optimization problem is defined over all possible values of s and involves the selection of both a harvesting trajectory and a reserve size that maximise the discounted net returns from fishing. The initial harvest optimisation problem, incorporating the two stochastic processes and for an arbitrary s, is defined by equations (5) to (8),

$$V\left(x_R, x_{NR}\right) = max_k \int_0^x e^{-pt}\Pi\left(h, x_{NR}, s\right) \tag{5}$$

subject to :

$$dx_R = \left[f\left(x_R, s\right) - \phi\left(1-s\right)K\left(\frac{x_R}{sK} - \frac{x_{NR}}{\left(1-s\right)K}\right)\right]dt +$$

$$g\left(x_R\right)dW + \Psi\left(x_R\right)dq \tag{6}$$

where $V\ (x_R,\ x_{NR})$ is the value function, x_0 is the sum of the initial population in and outside of the reserve, ϕ is the discount rate and φ is the transfer coefficient. The transfer function,

$\phi\left(1-s\right)K\left(\frac{x_R}{s_K} - \frac{x_{NR}}{\left(1-s\right)K}\right)$ is compatible with diffusion models

in fisheries that suggest reserve size directly influences dispersal, and is also consistent with evidence that dispersion is strongly density dependent. Our specification ensures the transfer of fish is governed by both reserve size and the relative population density of the reserve and harvested populations, but also allows for the possibility of transfers into the reserve if the population density is greater outside of the reserve. Using Ito's Lemma, Bellman's fundamental equation of optimality can be used to solve for the harvest trajectory for any given reserve size, i.e.,

$$\rho V(x_R, x_{NR}) = \max_h \left\langle \begin{array}{l} \Pi(h, x_{NR}, s) + V_{x_{NR}}(x)[f(x_{NR}, s) + \phi(1-s)K(\frac{x_R}{sK} - \frac{x_{NR}}{(1-s)K}) - h] \\ + V_{x_R}(x)[f(x_R, s) - \phi(1-s)K(\frac{x_R}{sK} - \frac{x_{NR}}{(1-s)K})] + \\ \frac{1}{2}V_{x_R x_R} g(x_R)^2 + \frac{1}{2}V_{x_{NR} x_{NR}} g(x_{NR})^2 + V_{x_R x_{NR}} g(x_R) g(x_{NR}) + \\ \lambda[V(x_R + \psi(x_R), x_{NR} + \gamma(x_{NR})) - V(x)] \end{array} \right\rangle \tag{6}$$

Given the complexity of the stochastic jump-diffusion process, it is not possible to find a solution to (9) analytically, but it can be solved numerically with a modified form of the perturbation method introduced by Gaspar and Judd (1997). The method involves introducing two auxiliary variables one for a Brownian diffusion process and another for the jump process defined as η and ε to the Bellman equation, where if $\eta=\varepsilon=0$ the deterministic problem results. Following the substitution, for a given, the decision function and value function can be defined as $\Pi(h, x_{NR}, \eta, \varepsilon)$ and $V(x_{NR}, x_R, \eta, \varepsilon)$ and a nth order Taylor series expansion can be defined around the steady state in the deterministic case. In the first step to solving (9), we find the steady state in the deterministic case ($\eta=\varepsilon=0$) by using the maximum condition for the Bellman equation, applying the Envelope Theorem and the equations of motion for the reserve and non-reserve populations. In the second step, we differentiate the maximum condition and Envelope theorem equation with respect to the state variables x_R and x_{NR}. In step three, we differentiate the Bellman equation to find $V\eta$ and $V\varepsilon$ that are expressions of higher order derivatives with respect to the state variables found in step two. Successive differentiation of the Bellman equation with respect to the auxiliary variables, control variables and state variables allows us to solve with greater precision for required values in a grid-like pattern.

We automated the solution process for all possible values of s by using MAPLE to calculate the partial derivatives of the optimal value function and control variables with respect to the state and the auxiliary variables. This allows us to solve for the optimal harvest levels for any given reserve size. The optimal reserve size $V^*(x_R, x_{NR})$, is that which gives the highest economic value for all possible reserve sizes and maximises the overall value function, , that is an envelope of value functions for all possible values of s for the two stochastic realisations and.

$$\text{In } p = \alpha + \text{b } In \text{ h} \tag{10}$$

VALUING MARINE RESERVE

Capture fisheries face problems of both biological and economic overfishing and many stocks are in decline. For the period 1974-1999, the Food and Agricultural Organisation (FAO) calculates that the proportion of fisheries harvested beyond the estimated maximum yield tripled from around 10% to 30% of surveyed stocks while Myers and Worm (2003) estimate that the stocks of predatory fish in the world's oceans have declined by over 90% in the past 50 years. In Europe, several cod stocks have declined precipitously in the previous two decades and some important stocks are at their lowest levels ever. To overcome excess fishing both managers and scientists have argued for a more holistic approach to management and the greater use of marine reserves. Reserves are justified on theoretical grounds because they can increase yields when population levels are overexploited, reduce the variance of the population and harvest and provide a 'hedge' against management failure. Empirical studies of reserves also indicate that they can raise the spawning biomass and mean size of exploited populations, increase abundance and, relative to reference sites, raise population density, biomass, fish size and diversity. Reserves have also been shown to generate positive spillovers to fishers in adjacent areas subject to harvesting.

Despite the apparent benefits of marine reserves, they remain a controversial management tool and measures to establish or enlarge reserves are often met with protest by fishers. Indeed, many fishers are strongly opposed to all but the smallest 'no-take' areas. The concern is that reserves will reduce their harvests, increase costs and restrict when and where they can go fishing. The reluctance of harvesters to support reserves has also found some support in the economics literature which has used deterministic models to show that if effort and harvests can be perfectly controlled then reserves are of little or no value, reserves need to be in the order of 70-80% of a fishing area to generate yield and conservation benefits to fishers equivalent to optimal harvesting, and that reserves can increase sustainable yields and revenues only when the population is overexploited.

ECONOMICS VIEWS OF MARINE ENVIRONMENT

Economists are often charged with the difficult task of placing a value on environmental resources. The air we breathe and the water we drink are environmental resources that are required to sustain life on this planet. The environment also serves as a source of pleasure to humans in viewing the sun on the horizon, admiring the tranquil beauty of a forest-ringed lake, or driving along a scenic ocean road. Many people argue that environmental such as land, air, and water and natural resources such as coal, trees, and fish are, in fact, priceless. Thus, they say, it is not appropriate to consider them within the context of economic valuation. However, the world's population has proven unwilling to forgo all future economic

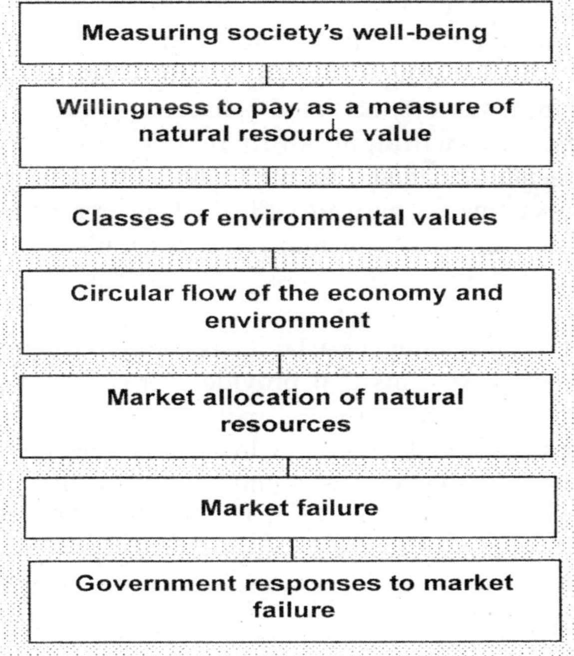

Figure 4: An Economic View of the Environment

activity to eliminate all factors that cause environmental damage. Human societies are willing to give up certain environmental assets to generate other kinds of economic gains. The value placed on environmental assets is illustrated in our choices against other competing economic needs. Figure 4 shows an economic view of the environment and outlines the topics discussed below. Economic principles suggest that the well-being of a society can be measured as the sum of all the individuals' level of well-being. This well-being, or what economists call "utility," is not derived solely from purchasing and consuming goods and services, but also from things like safety, and our physical, mental, and spiritual well-being.

The fact that all these things have utility is evident in that we are willing to trade our time, effort, money, and other resources to get them. The utility or degree of satisfaction experienced by individuals, and thus society, can be quantified in terms of the "willingness to pay" for goods and services, including environmental resources. In many cases, individuals do not pay for the environmental benefits they receive. However, their willingness to pay for these benefits can be derived from surveys, observed behavior, or through other methods. The willingness-to-pay concept is key in environmental valuation, granting analysts a framework upon which to examine and measure individual preferences. Positive preferences for environmental resources translate into an expressed or observed willingness to pay for them. Conversely, individuals are not willing to pay for environmental resources that they do not value. Coastal areas contain resource-rich environmental systems that provide a broad spectrum of services to humankind. From recreational opportunities, such as hiking and wildlife observation to the harvesting of fish and other seafood for human consumption, coastal habitats provide many direct benefits. Indirect benefits such as cal support and water and air purification and non-use benefits in terms of the satisfaction that we get from knowing that the environment has been preserved for future generations also affect the decision to exploit or conserve natural resources (Figure 2).

Figure 5: Direct Benefits of the Coastal Environment include (a) Whale Watching and (b) Shrimp Harvesting, while an Indirect Benefit is (c) the habitat provided. Non-use Benefits are derived from the Satisfaction of Knowing an area will be preserved for Future Generations (d)

Figure 5 Direct benefits of the coastal environment include (a) whale watching and (b) shrimp harvesting, while an indirect benefit is (c) the habitat provided. Non-use benefits are derived from the satisfaction of knowing an area will be preserved for future generations (d).

Natural resources are also valuable in the production of other goods. The output of any firm is a function of several important inputs, which economists call "factors of production." The factors of production include labor, capital such as buildings and machinery, and an array of environmental inputs. These environmental inputs include the land upon which production takes place, raw materials extracted from the environment, such as minerals and timber, and often, clean air and water. It is sometimes, but not always, possible to offset declines in the natural resources required in production processes by increasing labor and capital. However, environmental depletion and damage ultimately lead to declining input availability and reductions of output and utility. The decisions society makes about how to use its natural and other resources involve tradeoffs. All other things being equal, when we decide to increase the flow of one service of coastal resources e.g., fish nursery, we are also implicitly deciding to decrease the flow of another service e.g., disposal of wastewater. In other words, our decision to harvest fish is tied to a decision to damage the fisheries output by disposing of polluted wastewater.

The decisions we make regarding resource use are governed by scarcity. To economists, scarcity is a function of supply and demand. If resources are highly valued, it is because they are scarce and the demands placed upon those resources are large relative to their availability. Further, the decision of how to allocate these scarce resources has an impact on all sectors of the economy because of the complex relationship between natural resource inputs and economic output.

THE CIRCULAR FLOW OF THE ECONOMY AND THE ENVIRONMENT

The economy and the environment are inextricably linked. The environment supplies the raw materials and energy that are used to produce the goods that we consume. Waste generated by this production process is either recycled or dumped back into the environment. Figure 6, which represents a small part of

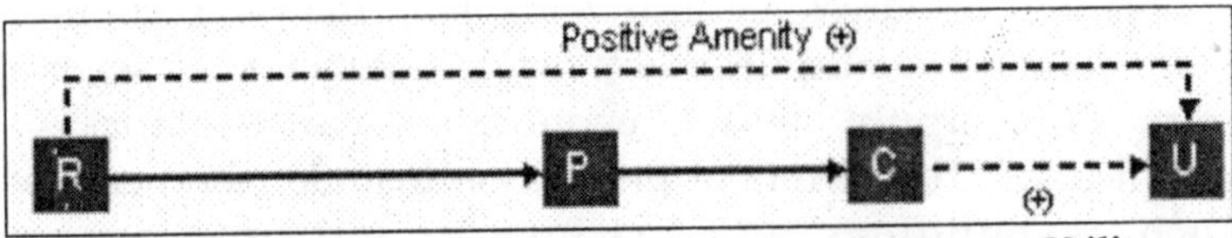

Figure 6: Resource Inputs and Positive Amenity Creates Utility

the overall picture, partially demonstrates the interconnectivity of the economy and environment (Pearce and Turner 1990).

Later we will demonstrate that the relationship between the economy and environment does not represent an open, linear process, but is rather illustrative of a closed, circular system. Within the environment and economic flow diagram, raw materials (**R**) are used as inputs into the production process (**P**) that creates the goods consumed by households (**C**). The end result of production and consumption is the creation of utility (**U**) or satisfaction. Thus, the function of the environment, as highlighted within the diagram, is to provide material inputs into the production process and positive amenity to humankind. In Figure 7, the resource box, R, is expanded to encompass two forms of natural resources: exhaustible and renewable resources. Exhaustible resources (ER), which are not renewable, include oil, coal, and minerals. Renewable resources (RR), such as water and trees, may be replenished. In the diagram, "h" refers to the harvest of the resource and "y" to the sustainable yield. With respect to exhaustible resources, the harvest always exceeds the sustainable yield because these resources have no regenerative capacity. For renewable

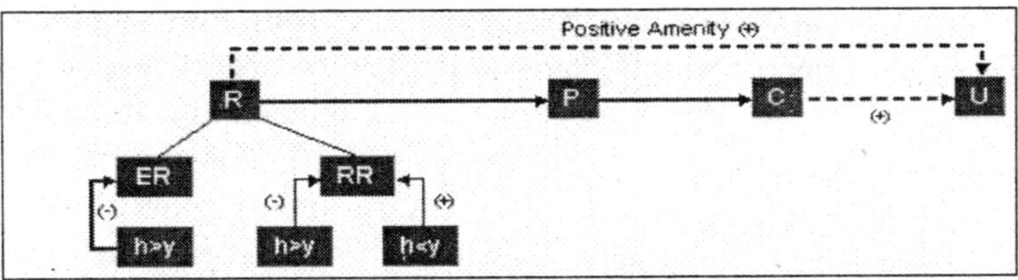

Figure 7: Exhaustible and Renewable Resources

resources, the resource stock will decline if the harvest exceeds the yield but may actually grow if the harvest is less than the environment's capacity for regeneration. Thus, to guarantee the continued use of a renewable resource, it must be harvested at a rate slower than the sustainable yield.

The diagram is expanded in Figure 8 to include the generation of waste products (**W**) new elements are highlighted in green. Waste products arise from processing or mining of resources. Waste products, such as the emissions and solid waste generated by industrial facilities, are also created by the production process. Final consumers also create waste by disposing of product packaging and, ultimately, the product itself.

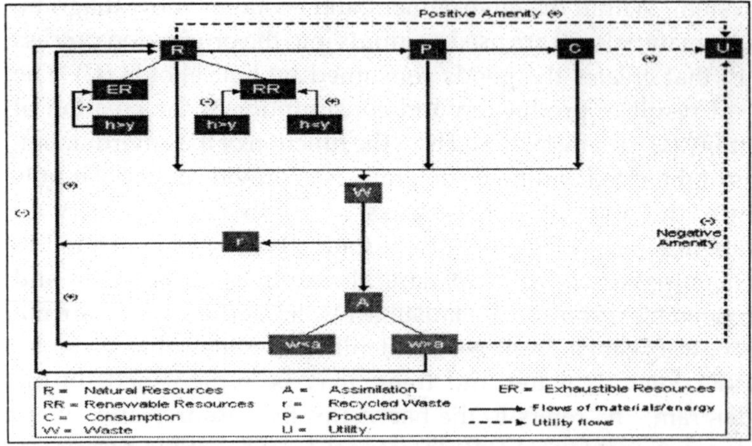

Figure 8: Interconnectivity of the Economy and Environment

The box labeled "**r**" represents the share of total waste that is recycled and thus put back into the production process. Bottles, paper products, cans and plastics are all products commonly recycled by households. Scrap metal and water used in industrial processing are often recycled. The practice of recycling has expanded significantly in most sectors during the past 20 years, during which time the number of curbside recycling programs expanded from a single program to more than 9,000 programs. What happens to the remainder of the waste that is not recycled? It is dumped back into the environment. From the industrial and municipal sewage that flows into the seas to the carbon dioxide emitted by motor vehicles, the environment serves as the ultimate repository of many waste products. Thus, the second function of the environment is to serve as a waste sink (**W**).

Natural systems also generate waste, from leaves that drop from the trees every fall to animals that perish every winter due to starvation or exposure. The important difference between natural and economic systems is that waste generated by natural systems is generally recycled. Leaves decompose and serve as organic fertilizer, and carrion serves as an important food source for scavenging hunters. Economic systems have no similar built-in system for recycling waste. Thus the environment has a limited capacity to absorb waste and convert it into biologically benign material. This absorption capacity is known as assimilation (**A**). Provided that the environment's assimilative capacity exceeds the volume of waste generated through economic activity, the environment remains unharmed. Unfortunately, however, the volume of waste often exceeds the assimilative capacity of the environment, and damage occurs. Environmental damage reduces the future productive capacity of the environment and adversely affects amenity values. Waste resulting in the decline of the environment has an adverse impact on individual and societal utility, which brings us to the third, and final, function of the environment highlighted in the diagram: the positive amenity value it provides to humankind. For example, wetland areas provide amenity values that include hiking and bird watching. Though difficult to quantify, such values matter to individuals. Thus, economists attempt to quantify those values.

MARKET ALLOCATION OF NATURAL RESOURCES

The goals of consumers and producers are in conflict. Rational consumers try to achieve the highest level of utility that is possible within the limits of their budget, and rational producers try to maximize their profits. Lower prices enable consumers to purchase more of a good, thus expanding their utility. However, lower prices reduce the revenues, and thus profits, that accrue to producers. In a market economy, these conflicting goals are reconciled at a competitive market equilibrium price that balances the forces of supply and demand. Demand is a schedule of how much of a good or service individuals will purchase during a specified period, depending on price and other factors. The law of demand states that as prices increase, the quantity demanded will fall, and as the price falls, more will be demanded, all other things being equal. Supply is a schedule of how much of a good or service firms supply during a specified period, depending on price and other factors. The law of supply states that as prices grow, the quantity supplied will increase, and as prices fall, firms supply less to the market.

Figure 9 demonstrates how demand and supply work together to determine the price of a commodity. Other factors being unchanged, the demand curve shows the relationship between price and quantity demanded, whereas the supply curve shows the relationship between price and the quantity supplied. Figure 6 demonstrates these concepts by examining the market for farmed oysters. In Figure 6, the competitive market equilibrium point b is reached at a price of $0.62 per pound of oysters, resulting in a supply of 500 thousand pounds. Note, however, that unlike oyster farms, most fisheries are characterized as common property resources with open access, and fisheries often become overfished economically and sometimes biologically as well. For example, the market supply curve for salmon does not represent the marginal cost of supplying salmon because of the common property aspect of the resource combined with open access to the fishers. These two institutional characteristics lead to application of

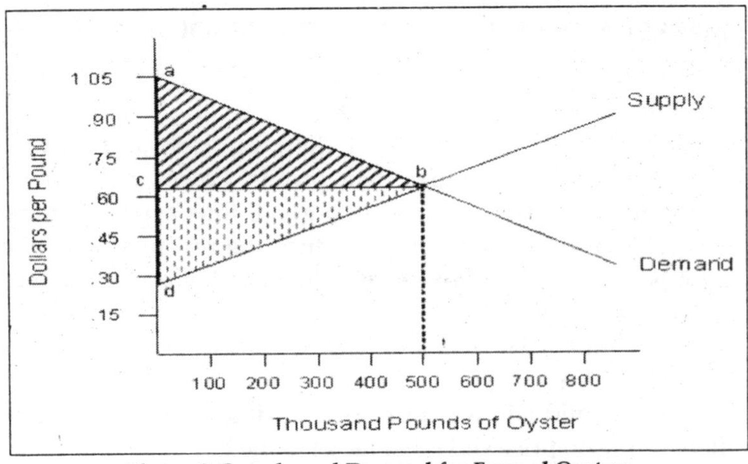

Figure 9: Supply and Demand for Farmed Oysters

additional capital and labor until economic returns are equal to average rather than marginal costs and the economic benefits of fishing are dissipated. When a fishery is being overfished from a biological standpoint, production will not be sustainable. Thus, any benefits associated with habitat restoration could be negated by overfishing. There are techniques, however, to resolve the problem of overfishing, including limited entry programs and individual transferable quotas (ITQs). These institutional solutions must also be considered when conducting habitat restoration.

The supply curve for farmed oysters mirrors the marginal cost to the oyster farming industry of harvesting oysters e.g., purchasing juvenile oysters, purchasing algae for feeding, growth monitoring, extraction, and transportation. Provided that the full costs to society associated with harvesting oysters including environmental are captured, the equilibrium point "b" highlighted in Figure 6 will result in an efficient resource allocation and a maximum level of economic benefit to society. At any quantity below 500 thousand pounds of oysters, the benefits associated with increasing the yield would exceed the costs of harvesting the oysters. Alternatively, any quantity that exceeds the market equilibrium would result in costs to industries that exceed the benefits supplied to the consumer.

The supply and demand for farmed oysters, however, are not static and can shift over time. A number of variables can lead to a shift in the entire demand curve for a product. These variables include tastes and preferences, the number of buyers, income, prices of substitute goods, prices of complement goods, and expectations. Figure 7 demonstrates how a change in one of these shift variables can lead to an increase in demand. Imagine that a medical report hailed the health benefits of oyster consumption. The demand for oysters would increase and a new equilibrium price of $0.76 and quantity in terms of 680 thousand pounds would be reached. A number of variables can cause a shift in supply as well, including resource prices, the number of sellers, technology changes, prices of alternative outputs, expectations, taxes, and subsidies.

Economists measure the net economic benefit in a market as the difference between what it costs to produce a good or service, on the one hand, and what consumers are willing to pay for it, on the other. In an efficiently functioning competitive market, the net economic benefit is divided between consumers and producers. The net economic benefit is, therefore, divided between what is known as consumer and producer surplus. Consumer surplus is the difference between what each customer is willing to pay at each point in time and the price of the good or service and is represented by the area falling above the price line and below the demand curve. Consumer surplus in Figure 9 is represented by area *abc* and is represented by area *gef* in Figure 10. Producer surplus is the difference

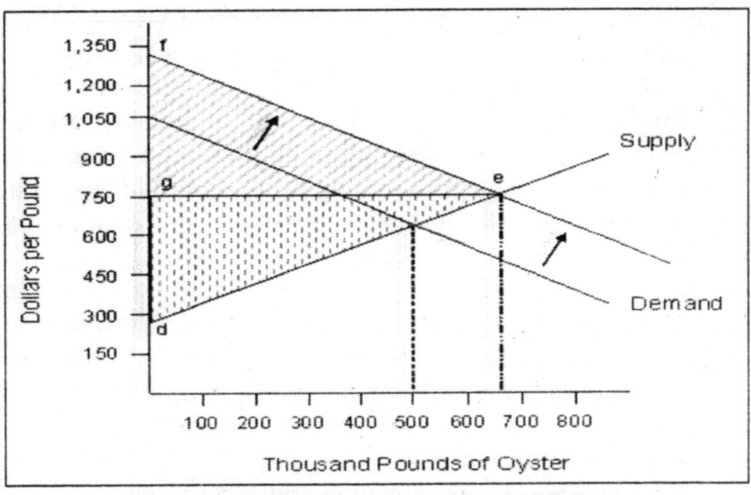

Figure 10: Shifting Demand for Farmed Oysters

between what a supplier is paid for a good or service and what it costs to supply, and is represented by area *bcd* in Figure 6 and area *deg* in Figure 10. The total economic benefit of a sale is the sum of the consumer and producer surplus. Consumer and producer surplus is a function of both supply and demand. Figure 10 demonstrates that as demand increases as represented in the outward shift in the demand curve, consumer and producer surplus is increased.

MARKET FAILURE

The market represents a decentralized exchange mechanism that enables society to allocate resources efficiently. Markets, however, efficiently can fail to allocate environmental assets through the price mechanism if they are unable to accurately capture the full social costs of exploiting the natural resource. Thus, there are a number of factors such imperfect information, uncompensated environmental damage that constrain the capacity of the market to achieve an accurate competitive market equilibrium. For example, the previous analysis would not measure net economic benefit if the oyster industry damaged the environment while harvesting. These are additional societal costs that are not necessarily reflected in the industry supply curve and market clearing price. When there are factors that prevent the market from achieving an efficient allocation of resources, market failure is evident. Externalities and nonprivate goods are two of the most recognized forms of market failure.

Many economic activities may provide secondary benefits or impose spillover costs to individuals and to society. These secondary effects, which are not recognized in the market transaction, are referred to as externalities. A negative externality occurs when the byproduct of an economic activity imposes a cost on society not captured in the market. For instance, motor vehicle emissions e.g., carbon dioxide, nitrogen oxide contribute to the warming of the troposphere through the greenhouse effect. In turn, atmospheric warming contributes to rising sea levels. Rising seas, in turn, lead to increased flooding and corresponding loss of coastal wetlands. These costs are not captured through registration fees or the price of a gallon of gasoline. Returning to our example, the full social cost of harvesting oysters is captured by the social supply curve in Figure 11, reflecting the marginal cost to society of consuming oysters. Because the firm does not pay the full economic or opportunity cost of providing the good, the private supply curve is too low and the good will be oversupplied i.e 500 thousand pounds of oysters rather than 380 thousand pounds and offered at a price below the social optimum it terms of \$0.62 rather than \$0.75. Thus, the benefits of consuming oysters are exceeded by the full social costs of harvesting the resource. The loss of benefits due to overharvesting is illustrated in area *abc*.

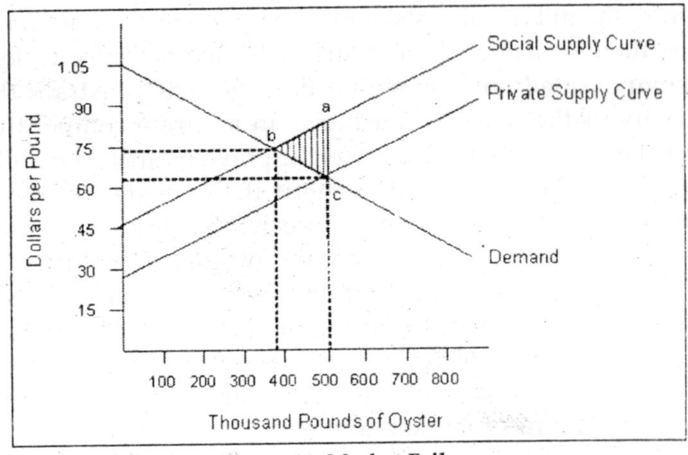

Figure 11: Market Failure

Nonprivate goods represent another form of market failure. Most goods in our economy are classified according to two criteria: excludability and rivalness. Excludability is present when ownership is clearly identified and benefits accrue only to the owner. Rivalness is present when the owner's capacity

Table 5
Typology of Goods

	Rival ?	
	Yes	*No*
	Private Goods	*Club Goods*
Excludable? Yes	-Clothing -Housing -Automobiles	-Fire Protection -Cable television -Electrical power
	Common Resources	*Public Goods*
Excludable? No	-Fish in the ocean -part of the environment -Congrested public roads	-Un-congested public roads -Air -Oceans

to derive utility by consuming the good or service diminishes the capacity of others to enjoy the same benefit. Table 1 presents a typology of goods. The four types of goods highlighted are a) private goods, b) common resources, c) club goods, and d) public goods. How do public goods vary from private goods? Private goods are exchanged in a market with buyers and sellers agreeing on a price and exchanging ownership rights. Private goods are, therefore, excludable, meaning that owners are clearly identified and the stream of benefits accrue only to the owner. Private goods also demonstrate rivalness.

Public goods on the other hand are nonexcludable and nonrival in competition. Oceans provide a good example. An ocean will not cease to exist, even if large numbers of individuals enjoy its benefits. Further, one consumer generally cannot prevent another from enjoying the recreational and amenity values an ocean provides, nor can they claim ownership of an ocean. Other examples of public goods include clean air and public roadways. In turn, externalities arise from public goods because there are no prices attached to a good that has value. Thus, individuals receive benefits without paying for them.

Public goods are at one end of the spectrum in terms of nonrival, nonexludable, completely private goods such as rival, excludable at the other end, and goods with varying degrees of excludability and rivalness are located in between. Common resources are not excludable but are rival goods because one person's use of the common resource reduces the benefits that accrue to other users. Thus these resources are available to any consumer at no cost, but consumption of the resources diminishes their availability to other consumers. Common resources tend to be overexploited or used excessively. The government can solve the problems associated with common resources by defining property rights and by regulating private behavior such as catch limits, taxes. Club goods are excludable but nonrival. Examples of club goods include toll roads, swimming pools, fire protection, satellite television transmission, and electrical power. Environmental regulators are using the concept of excludability to regulate and protect natural resources. The opportunity to regulate a club good occurs when the government exercises its power as a "gatekeeper" and restricts entry to companies that pay into an externality-remediation fund or adopt practices that limit externalities.

- Market failure is evident in the case of many environmental resources, including those associated with coastal habitat. For example, sport fishing and wildlife viewing provide an important source of recreation and amenity to the population. When private firms damage the quality of the habitat and reduce the recreational and amenity value it provides, governments often intervene to reduce the harmful impact of the environmental externality. For example, water quality permits are issued by states to individuals and businesses that discharge pollutants into surface and ground waters. Water quality permits are issued to protect surface and ground waters by regulating sewage and wastewater discharges and stormwater runoff from industrial and construction-related activities. Discharges can occur through a number of sources, including irrigation, on-site sewage systems, dry wells, and seepage ponds. The permit, which generally varies in price based on the type of operation and anticipated discharge levels, is designed to monetize and collect compensation for the impact of an environmental externality (i.e., decline in water quality) resulting from construction and industrial activities.
- Coastal areas provide a broad range of values to humankind. Environmental values are categorized as direct use such as hiking, wildlife observation, inputs into the production process, indirect in terms of biological support, water and air purification, and nonuse bequest and existence values. Each of these values affects the decision to exploit or conserve natural resources.

- The environment and economy are inextricably linked. The environment supplies the raw materials and energy that are used to produce the goods that we consume. Waste generated by the production process is either recycled or dumped back into the environment. Thus, the relationship between the environment and the economy does not represent an open, linear process, but is rather illustrative of a closed, circular system.
- The demand for products and the supply or availability of natural resources determine the market allocation of natural resources. A number of factors such as scarcity, tastes and preferences, the number of buyers, income, prices of substitute goods, prices of complement goods, expectations, resource prices, number of sellers, technology change, prices of alternative outputs, and taxes and subsidies collectively determine the supply and demand for products, thus dictating how best to allocate scarce natural resources efficiently.

INTERGENERATIONAL EQUITY

It is generally agreed that problems which are costly to solve in the short term but whose solution will yield benefits in the long term are difficult to fix because the short term costs loom large even if the long term benefits are much larger in absolute terms. The main reason for this is that in comparing the present values of policy alternatives, we discount net benefits that will accrue in the future and compare them to net benefits that can be achieved today. Because of the exponential growth of compounded interests, the difficulty becomes greater as the future benefits are more distant. In the case of the environmental and resource problems affecting humanity today, such as greenhouse gas emissions and climate change, or overpowering of the world's ocean resources, it becomes almost overpowering. The Stern review, for instance, states that the course of the next fifty years is already set, so that the effects of any policy will be felt in the range of 50 to 200 years from now. In the following table, we give the present value of $ 1; 000; 000 at 50; 100; and 200 years, discounted at 10%, 4:6% and 1:4%, which is the value that the Stern Review took:

	50 ys	100 ys	200 ys
10%	8; 519	73	< 0:00
4:6%	105; 540	11; 140	124
1; 4%	499; 000	249; 000	62; 000

This clearly illustrates the importance of discounting. But there exists no financial assets in that range, and therefore no market rates: the longest US Treasury bond matures in 30 years. So one has to take a normative approach. Consider the benchmark case when there is a single good x in the economy, and society consists of a single, infinitely-lived consumer, with utility function u (x), and with a constant rate of time preference δ> 0. The welfare function at time 0 then is:

$$\int_0^{\infty} e^{-\delta t} u\left(x(t)\right) dt$$

If the utility function is of the form $u(x) = \frac{1}{1-\theta} x^{1-\theta}$ (constant absolute risk aversion), the equilibrium interest rate then is

$$r = \delta + \eta g$$

where g is the growth rate of consumption. This has to be corrected to take into account uncertainty on the growth rate, as well as the existence of environmental goods beside industrial goods: we discuss intergenerational equity, in a framework where u (x) is a linear function of x, so that μ = 0 and r = ± The classical interpretation of the discount rate ± is the rate of time preference of the present generation: In other words, when evaluating environmental policies, one has to take into account the fact that the benefits will not accrue to the present generation, but to others, so that the discount rate no longer can be understood as a pure rate of time preference, but also has the character of a Pareto weight: as pointed out in, using the 'discounting clock' of the current generation in fates cost to the current generation and diminishes the benefits to future generations. To deal with this problem, Sumaila introduced the concept of intergenerational discounting, which was further developed by Sumaila and Walters, and which takes into account, not only the pure rate of time preference of the present generation, but also the Pareto weight which is attributed to future generations. Consider a public good, available in quantity x ¸ 0. Society is confronted with a scenario x (t), where t ranges from 0 today to infinity we are interested in the long term. Its members have to agree on a present value for this scenario. We make the simplifying assumption that all individuals are identical: they all, born or unborn, have the same utility function u (x). They also have the same rate of time preference ±. In other words, an individual born at time t attributes to the scenario x (t), or rather to the portion of that scenario which he/she experiences, the utility:

$$\int_t^{\infty} e^{-\delta(e-t)}\, u(x(s))\,ds = \int_0^{\infty} e^{-\delta e} u(x(t+s))\,ds \tag{1}$$

We will also assume that the birth rate is ® and the death rate w<a so that the growth rate is η = α - ω. In other words, if the population at time 0 is N, the population at time t is Ne^{nt}; in the interval between t and t+dt, there will be α Ne^{nt} dt births and ω Ne^{nt} dt deaths. More precisely, of the generation born at time s, only a proportion e¡! (t¡s) is still alive at time t > s; so the total population at time t consists of Ne $(\alpha\text{-}\omega)^t$ individuals, Ne wt of whom were alive at time 0, and $N\alpha e^{ns} e^{-\omega(t-s)}ds = N\alpha e^{-\omega t} e^{\alpha s} ds$ were born between s and s + ds, where 0 £ s £ t. We have to aggregate the utilities of all the generations: the present one, consisting of N individuals alive at time 0, and the future ones, who enter the fray at the rate ®. As usual in the theory of social choice, we will use a linear aggregator, ascribing the coecient e¡¾s to the s-generation: in other words, each individual born between s and s + ds carries the Pareto weight e¡¾s. At time t, the quantity of the public good is x (t), and it asects all individuals who are still alive at that time, Ne¡!t of whom were alive at time 0, and N®ense¡!(t¡s)ds = N®e®se¡!tds of whom were born between s and s + ds. Each of them discounts the future at the constant rate ±, so that the aggregate utility evaluated at time is:

$$\left(Ne^{-\omega t}e^{-\delta t}+\int_0^t e^{-\sigma s}N\alpha e^{-\omega t}e^{\alpha s}e^{-\delta(t-s)}ds\right)u(x(t))=NR(t)u(x(t))$$

with

$$R(t)=\lambda e^{-(\omega+\delta)t}+(1-\lambda)e^{-(\sigma-n)t},\ \text{with}\ \lambda=1-\frac{\alpha}{\alpha+\delta-\sigma}\ \text{and}\ n=\alpha-\omega \qquad (2)$$

The intertemporal welfare function $W(x)$ then is:

$$W(x)=\int_0^\infty R(t)u(x(t))dt \qquad (3)$$

From now on we assume that

$$\sigma > n$$

The discount factor given by formula (2) corresponds to a non-constant discount rate

$r(t)$. We have:

$$r(t):=-\frac{R'(t)}{R(t)}=\frac{(1-\lambda)(\sigma-n)+\lambda(\omega+\delta)e^{(\sigma-\alpha-\delta)t}}{(1-\lambda)+\lambda e^{(\sigma-\alpha-\delta)t}} \qquad (4)$$

$$r(t)\longrightarrow\delta-n\ \text{when}\ t\longrightarrow 0 \qquad (5)$$

$$r(t)\longmapsto\min(\sigma-n,\omega+\delta)\ \text{when}\ t\longrightarrow\infty \qquad (6)$$

Note that the short-term rate is independent of ¾: it is equal to d-n, where ± is the pure rate of time preference, and n =α is the growth rate of the population. Note also that it is negative if ± < n. When σ=α+δ so that ω+δ=σ-n, formula (2) breaks down. It has to be replaced by its limit when σ→n, namely:

$$R(t)=(1+\alpha t)e^{-\rho t},\ \ \text{with}\ \rho=\omega+\delta=\sigma-n \qquad (7)$$

leading to a non-constant discount rate:

$$r(t) = \rho - \frac{\alpha}{1+\alpha t} \tag{8}$$

$$r(t) \to \rho - \alpha = \delta - n \text{ when } t \to 0 \tag{9}$$

$$r(t) \to \rho \text{ when } t \to \infty \tag{10}$$

We will refer to (2) as a quasi-exponential discount of type I, and to (7) as a quasi- exponential discounts of type II. Note that in the first case, when ¾ > ±. In the second case, r (1) > r (0)

ECONOMICS FOR COASTAL MANAGERS

Managing coastal resources often means making hard decisions about the best way to use those resources—especially when there are competing demands. For example, do we Maintain the green space or build more homes? Develop a new marina or keep the existing oyster beds and Construct a mall that would draw in new industry or preserve the wetland? Although there is no simple way to answer these questions, economic methods can help coastal resource managers understand the trade-offs and make better-informed decisions about managing the resource.

THE POWER OF ECONOMIC METHODS AND CONCEPTS

Economic tools can be used to maximize the usefulness of coastal resources and make the community as well off as it can be—socially, economically, and environmentally. When considering the best way to manage a resource, managers can use economic tools to express the values of alternatives in common terms usually dollars so that an "apples to apples" comparison can be made and the alternative that maximizes the benefit to the community will be chosen.

APPLYING ECONOMICS TO COASTAL RESOURCES

To apply economics to the management of coastal resources, the cost, expertise, and type of economic information required to make resource decisions should be considered.

COST AND EXPERTISE

The cost of conducting economic research and analysis can be considerable, but knowing the economic value of coastal resources can help ensure that we don't trade off things that are worth more – for things that are worth less. Because of the difficulty in placing a dollar value on many of the benefits provided by coastal resources, these benefits are often assigned a value of zero, even though the resources provide considerable value to the community and the local ecosystem. For example, part of the value of a coastal resource comes from the ecosystem services it provides, such as those services supplied by a maritime forest and salt marsh: Habitat and feeding grounds for commercial, recreational, and other fisheries, Habitat for threatened species of birds, Filtration and purification of runoff water, Protection of buildings and other infrastructure from coastal storms, by absorbing energy and holding off floodwaters and Enhancement of aesthetics (and, consequently, market value) of adjacent homes

If these services are assigned a value of zero, cutting down the forest and filling in the wetland to build a new business district might look economically advantageous. However, the development may actually have hidden costs to the community because the true value of the resources was not considered. For example, property damage from floods may increase, causing higher insurance premiums and lower house values in the area. That being said, development may be the right choice in some cases. Only when the true value of a coastal resource is known can one make decisions that make the most long-term economic sense for the community – be it leaving the resource alone, developing it, or designing a partial development plan with fewer impacts.

The cost of economic research and analysis depends on many factors, including, Size of the area where the resources are located, Number of people who use the resources, Type of survey method and Type of economic value involved. However, if a full economic assessment is too costly to consider, economic methods to manage coastal resources can still be used. For example, information from an existing economic study conducted by someone else can be applied to other situations that are similar. This method is called benefits transfer. Expertise Required. Performing an economic assessment is a complex—and often controversial—process, so make sure someone who has a background in economics is involved. Even the methods that are seemingly straightforward require judgments based on economic theory. When trying to estimate the more complicated types of economic value, it is especially important that we work with someone with proven experience with that type of valuation. Otherwise, the results may not be acceptable in certain contexts such as damage assessments or regulations.

ECONOMIC OPTIONS

The term "economics" encompasses a broad spectrum of methods and concepts, so there are a lot of different ways to use economics to help manage coastal resources. No single method will be appropriate for all situations, so one of the first things to consider is what type of economic option will provide the necessary information to manage the coastal resource most effectively.

FOR EXAMPLE

- To show how the local economy would be impacted by resource management decisions, an economic profile, including information such as industries and the number of jobs, would be created. This profile would serve as an economic baseline to see whether a proposed management action, such as prohibiting fishing in some areas, would have positive or negative effects on the local economy.
- To understand the total economic value of a resource, one would estimate many different types of value and then add them together.
- To consider alternative management options, one might look at the economic benefits and costs associated with each option and choose the option that offers the best value—the greatest benefits at the least cost.

A complete economic analysis of water and related land resources can be accomplished by identifying problems and opportunities for the resource—and then assessing and selecting the best option.

Identify problems and opportunities. Consider potential problems such as coastal development resulting in the loss of ecosystem services and opportunities such as creating a marine protected area to increase fishery stocks. Ideally, one should move beyond the local perspective and consider the resource from a regional or national perspective.

- *Take Inventory.* Determine the current state of the resource, including ecosystem services provided, and future development pressures.
- *Decide on a Focus.* Consider the problems and opportunities identified in step 1, and decide which ones to investigate further.
- *Consider the Options.* Define the alternative options for the management of the resources—for example, development, no development at all, or a modified development plan with fewer negative impacts.
- *Assess the Options.* Use an assessment method to weigh the effects of various options, such as looking at the benefits and costs associated with each.
- *Rank the Options.* Compare the options, using the results of the assessment in the previous step, and rank plans based on net benefits. For example, the options rank might be based on the ratio of benefits to costs.
- *Select the Option.* Using all the collected information, select the management option that maximizes the benefit to the community.

The rest of this document provides additional information about how economics can be applied to coastal resource management by

– Describing different ways of assigning value to resources
– Discussing a few methods for comparing and assessing different management alternatives

- Providing several case studies that show how economic methods were applied to coastal resource management in real-life situations

ECONOMICS DEFINED: THE LONG AND SHORT OF IT

"Economics is the study of how men and society end up choosing, with or without the use of money, to employ scarce productive resources which could have alternative uses, to produce various commodities and distribute them for consumption, now or in the future, among various people and groups in society." Nobel laureate Paul A. Samuelson, Economics, 1970.

HOW MUCH ARE RESOURCES WORTH?

One of the most common ways of using economics to help manage coastal resources is to estimate how much resources are worth. Knowing the value of resources will help society make better decisions about the use, or non-use, of those resources and maximize the benefits.

However, assigning values to resources can be challenging:

- Value is often associated with what is important or what has meaning – which isn't always easy to put in terms of dollars.
- Value depends on a person's preferences and how those preferences contribute to that person's welfare. A community will contain many different ideas about how valuable a resource is, depending greatly on how the individual community members interact with the resource now.

The management of coastal resources can be complex, so a simpler example is better for illustrating the challenges of assigning value to a resource, in this case, a carton of eggs. What is the value of the eggs? To the person selling the eggs, the value might be the selling price. To the person buying the eggs, the value might be in their nutritional content, their flavor, or in the enjoyment of cooking them. All of these are valid ways of considering the worth of the eggs, but some of them are easier to measure than others. The different types of value can be grouped broadly into two categories: market and non-market values. Market values are the easiest to calculate, but non-market values are usually more important to estimate if we want to determine the true worth of a coastal resource. Non-market values are categorized according to use. The aggregation of use and non-use values is the "total economic value" of the resource. Unfortunately, non-market values can also be costly and difficult to estimate.

In many situations where economic values are necessary for coastal management, there may not be enough time or money to conduct original research to assign economic values to a resource. A potential solution to this challenge is to use the benefits transfer methodology, which uses values from previous economic studies as approximate values of resources in similar situations.

MARKET VALUES

The economic value of some resources can be estimated by considering the market value, which is the net value i.e benefits minus price of goods or services that are traded on the market. The most common measures of market value are the amount of money taken in by businesses revenue or the number of people with jobs in terms of employment. Also important is the amount that people are paid for their jobs i.e income.

Generating a snapshot of the economic makeup of an area is one of the basic ways of using market values. To create an economic profile of an area, information such as the types of industry, employment rates, and average incomes is gathered. Although this kind of economic assessment doesn't apply directly to coastal resources, the information can be used to

- Consider potential pressures on coastal resources. Knowing about the types of industry in the area can help when estimating the types of resources that are required by industry to produce goods and services i.e inputs to production and how much of the resources will be required. For example, the oil and gas industry requires coastal habitat for platforms and pipelines, uses water for extraction operations, and produces waste.

– Consider potential impacts that resource management actions may have on the local economy, using knowledge about the number and types of jobs as an indicator of how the local population earns its livelihood.

To estimate the market value of coastal resources, the first step would be to estimate direct impact: the sales, income, and jobs directly related to the resource. However, there are other market impacts indirect and induced impacts that occur only as a result of the direct impacts. A direct impact is like throwing a stone in a pond, which creates ripples on the water that can then cause additional changes. For example, people on vacation spend money on a variety of things such as food, lodging, and transportation. These are the direct impacts. To provide these goods and services to the tourists, local firms must purchase other goods and services. For instance, a hotel must purchase items such as telephone service, running water, mattresses, food, and beverages. These purchases are indirect impacts that occur as a result of the direct impact in this case, a tourist needing to rent a room. Additionally, the employees in the industries affected by tourism will use their salaries to purchase goods and services; these are induced impacts. If the tourism in the area declines, employees will be laid off, and that may result in a decline in local businesses where the employees spend their salaries. All of these impacts can be calculated in dollar values and used to estimate the market value of the resource.

For coastal management, market values are extremely important ideas. Any management action taken by coastal managers has the potential to affect the local or regional economy. Being familiar with market concepts will not only contribute toward informed decisions—it will also aid in making those decisions more acceptable to those whose livelihoods are potentially affected. For example, creating no-fishing areas along the coast may help restore fisheries stocks in the area—both in the number of fish and the variety. A decision like this will have some negative effects on the local economy in the near term: commercial fisherman may earn less money, and there may be a decrease in tourism from recreational fisherman. So how can this decision be made acceptable to the local community? Keeping the local fisheries healthy is important to the livelihood of the community, and if it can be shown that this decision will be economically advantageous in the long term as the number of fish increase, the fishing community may be more willing to accept some short-term negative impacts.

Market values are the easiest values to calculate, but often more knowledge is gained about a resource by estimating its total economic value.

TOTAL ECONOMIC VALUE

The total economic value of a resource can be calculated by determining the non-market use and non-use values and then adding them all together (as shown in the Figure 12 below).

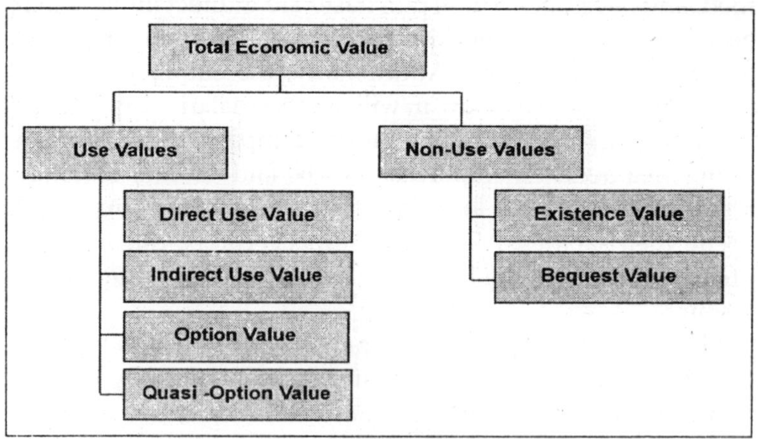

Figure 12

Because it is not always possible to calculate an estimate for all these values because of time or funding constraints, resource managers usually are not able to estimate total economic value. However, if only some of the values are included, the resource may be undervalued in the assessments.

NON-MARKET VALUES: USE VALUES

Any type of non-market economic value that is related to the usefulness or consumption of a resource is considered a use value. These types of value may also be called instrumental values. Typically use values make up most of the total economic value, because they are easier to assign dollar values to than non-use values. However, because use values aren't traded on the market, assigning a dollar value to them is still more difficult than it is for market values.

Four examples of use values are

- *Direct Use Value:* The current use value of a resource, based on using the resource itself. Direct use values are consumptive uses, such as cutting a tree for firewood or harvesting nuts to eat. Most people think of value in terms of direct use of a resource.
- *Indirect Use Value:* The current use value of a resource, based on using the resource indirectly. Indirect use values are non-consumptive uses, such as viewing scenery, hiking in the wilderness, or conserving wetlands that support fisheries.
- *Option Value:* The future use value of a resource. For example, keeping resources, such as a lake, available and pristine for future generations. Option values can include consumptive and non-consumptive uses.
- *Quasi-Option Value:* The potential future use value of a resource. For example, a wetland may be the home of a plant, which we will later discover has medicinal uses. Eliminating the wetland would prevent that medicine from being used, so this is another type of use value that can be estimated—although it is much harder to assign dollar values to quasi-option values.

Because use values aren't traded on the market, economists have developed techniques to assign dollar values to these types of non-market values by estimating people's willingness to pay for an environmental improvement or their willingness to accept compensation for an environmental degradation. There are a variety of methods to estimate the non-market value of coastal resources, two of which are briefly discussed below.

Travel Cost Method: This method assigns a value to recreational services provided by coastal resources, using the cost of travel as an approximate for price. A sample of the people who use the resource for recreation are surveyed about the number of trips that they've taken, the costs incurred in travel to the site such as hotel costs and park entrance fees, and other factors that may affect their demand for the resource such as income and demographic variables. The survey results are used to estimate the difference between what the consumer paid for the resource and what they would be willing to pay.

When this difference is to the consumer's benefit, it is called the consumer's surplus, and it can be used to approximate the dollar value the consumer places on the resource.

Hedonic Price Method: This method is based on the idea that there is a connection between a public good such as beaches and the demand for a private good such as real estate. Specifically, this method involves creating a model in which, for example, the price of a house relates to the attributes such as proximity to the beach, distance to a central business district, square footage, and neighborhood characteristics that might affect price. To use this method, you would look at how one attribute such as beach quality would change the price of the house. If a decline in beach quality would lead to a decline in housing prices near the beach, then that dollar value can be used to estimate the non-market indirect use value of the beach. The feasibility of the hedonic price method depends in large degree, in this case, on the availability of data both on house prices and on the attributes used. Specifically, the way in which the attribute to be valued such as beach quality is measured will be extremely important to the accuracy of the results. As challenging as non-market use valuation may be, the method at least produces concrete illustrations of the value people place on resources. Non-use values are much more obscure, and their estimation is therefore more difficult.

NON-MARKET VALUES: NON-USE VALUES

Any type of economic value that is unrelated to the usefulness or consumption of a resource is considered a non-use value.

Two examples of non-use values are

- *Bequest Value:* Value derived through preserving a resource for future generations. This value is based on the belief that people have a responsibility to provide for future generations by curtailing current consumption, including the use of natural resources. Thus, some resources may be conserved, not for the current or future benefit of the person choosing to conserve them, but for the benefit to future generations. Although this type of value is widely understood and acknowledged, it is difficult to incorporate it into a coastal management framework because of the complexity involved with assigning a specific dollar figure to it.
- *Existence Value:* Value derived from the appreciation of something for its own sake, which does not require contact or proximity. For example, some people care deeply about the health of coral reefs in the Northwest Hawaiian Islands—even though they may not ever plan to go there. Existence values are among the most difficult to identify and estimate. Some people believe that existence values are intrinsic values i.e values that are related to the resource itself, rather than its uses, because existence values are unrelated to human beings altogether. Intrinsic values are just as legitimate as instrumental values, but estimating intrinsic values can be more costly and contentious.

One of the most common methods of estimating non-use values is the contingent valuation method. This method uses a survey that describes the resource being valued and then asks the people taking the survey to indicate whether they would be willing to pay for specific environmental improvements or whether they would accept environmental degradation. The results from all the survey participants are added together and then divided by the number of participants to find the average value for willingness to pay and willingness to accept. These numbers are then used to estimate the value of the resource by assuming these are the typical responses for everyone who uses the resource—not just the survey participants.

EVALUATING ALTERNATIVES USING ECONOMIC METHODS

Economists have developed a number of tools that use measures of value to help choose the goods and services that make people as well off as they can be. Below are three common economic methods that coastal resource managers can use to help evaluate alternative options:

- Benefit-Cost Analysis
- Cost-Effectiveness Analysis
- Incremental Analysis

WEIGHING PERSONAL VALUES AGAINST PUBLIC VALUES

As discussed earlier, people will each value a resource differently according to how they feel about the resource and how they interact with it. One of the goals of a coastal resource manager is to consider all of those different ideas of value in order to determine a value for the resource that reflects the worth of the resource to the entire group. This is an already challenging task, but it is made harder by externalities.

An externality is a benefit received or a cost paid by someone who isn't directly involved in an economic transaction. When a resource is being purchased, the natural tendency of the purchaser is to place more importance on the benefits he or she will receive—than on the possible benefits to others. The ability to impose costs on others such as those associated with increased pollution or the inability to be compensated for the benefits provided to others such as the contributions natural habitat makes to local fisheries often puts the interests of landowners at odds with those of society at large. The benefits that accrue to society from conserved lands are externalities to the landowner, which tends to tip the balance in favor of development.

BENEFIT-COST ANALYSIS: APPLES TO APPLES COMPARISONS

Use benefit-cost analysis when

- There are two or more alternative options about how to manage a resource, and
- Dollar values can be assigned to all the benefits and costs.

Here's an example: A port city wants to decide if the benefits of a deeper harbor outweigh the costs associated with deepening and maintaining the harbor. To begin the analysis, the city would need to identify all the benefits and costs associated with the alternative options – in this case, to deepen the port or keep it as is. The benefits and costs should cover the entire scope of the project, including design, implementation, and maintenance. Some sample benefits and costs for one alternative are shown below.

Table 6
Alternative 1: Deepening the Port

Costs	*Benefits*
Administrative overhead (e.g., designing the plan, getting permits, overseeing the operation)	Larger, more efficient ships can use the port
Dredging equipment Contractors to run the equipment	Lower cost of imported goods Lower shipping costs for exported goods
Sediment disposal costs	Fewer tidal delays
Adjustments to port facilities to allow for larger ships and increased traffic flow (such as adding additional docks and port personnel)	Fewer accidental groundings
Maintenance costs to keep the sediment from building up again	Increased volume of cargo can be handled with existing port facilities

In this type of analysis, as many costs and benefits as possible should be considered, but there may still be some unintended results. For example, deepening the harbor might release toxic chemicals trapped in the sediment, impact marine life, increase noise and local pollution from increased ship traffic, or decrease global pollution from more efficient ships.

Sometimes these items can be foreseen, but they are often hard to measure. These externalities tend to be underrepresented in benefit-coast analyses. Once the benefits and costs have been identified, dollar values should be assigned to all of them. One way to conduct a benefit-cost analysis is to calculate a benefit-to-cost ratio based on dollar values for each alternative option, and then compare those ratios to determine the most effective alternative.

LONG-TERM DOLLAR VALUES MUST BE DISCOUNTED

The dollar values associated with long-term costs and benefits need to be adjusted, because a dollar received today is considered more valuable than one received in the future. Applying a discount rate helps to ensure that dollar values associated with long-term costs and benefits can be compared equally against the values of short-term cost and benefits. The discount rate is the rate at which society as a whole is willing to trade off present for future benefits, and it helps to account for inflation and other factors. However, determining the discount rate can be a source of controversy, so it should only be calculated by someone with an economics background.

COST-EFFECTIVENESS ANALYSIS: APPLES TO ORANGES COMPARISONS

Use cost-effectiveness analysis when

- There are two or more alternative ways to achieve the same goal or to produce the same type and level of results, and
- It isn't possible—or practical—to assign dollar values to all of the benefits.

Cost-effectiveness analysis allows people to compare different alternatives, even when dollar values can't be applied to the benefits. That is, it allows the comparison of items with a dollar value for apples to items without a dollar value oranges. To use this method, the dollar values for all the costs associated with each alternative would be estimated. If there are short-term and long-term values, the long-term values will need to be discounted so that all the costs can be added together to get the total cost for each alternative. Since all the alternatives yield similar outcomes, there is no need to estimate their dollar value; the most cost-effective means of achieving the desired outcome is chosen. If the alternatives are significantly different in scale, this method can't be used to identify the best alternative. However, it can still allow cost considerations to be incorporated into the decision-making.

Here's an example: A dam is blocking several types of salmon from travelling upriver to spawn, which has resulted in a decrease in the salmon population and decreased tourism in the area because of fishing restrictions. The resource manager in charge of the fisheries wants to determine the best method to ensure that specific types and numbers of salmon can get upriver. The manager can use a cost-effectiveness analysis to determine which method is the least-costly means of achieving this goal—without having to assign dollar values to the benefits associated with the improvements to the fisheries stock.

INCREMENTAL ANALYSIS

Use incremental analysis when

- Alternatives will produce similar benefits, and
- Alternatives differ primarily in the amount or size of the benefit.

Instead of assigning dollar values to the benefits as would be done in a benefit-cost analysis, this method only requires that the benefits be quantified in some manner, such as the amount that different alternatives would decrease phosphate in the water. Next, all the costs associated with the alternatives would be considered to determine which alternative was the most cost-effective for the benefits it produces. Like the other methods discussed, long-term costs need to be discounted. Here's an example: A plan has been proposed to restore the salinity of a wetland. This plan includes several different components, like replacing undersized culverts and reopening several of the original channels. The groups funding the project want to know how cost-effective each component is, so that they can determine if any should be eliminated from the plan. To make this determination, they perform a cost-effective analysis for each component that is being considered. Each component has the same benefit restoring the salinity of the wetland, so it is not necessary to estimate the monetary value of the expected salinity changes. Instead, they need only to estimate the salinity change benefit and monetary cost of each component and convert these to some meaningful ratio degree of change per dollar. If any component provides too little benefit to justify the cost, it can be eliminated from the plan or replaced with a better option.

CASE STUDIES

Three case studies are summarized on the following pages to illustrate how economic methods are applied to coastal resource management in practice:

1. Estimating Non-Market Values of Coastal Marshes (Whitehead and others 2006)
2. The Value of a Coastal Wetland (Barataria-Terrebonne NEP 1996)
3. Management of a Man-Made Lake (Washington State 2007)

Case Study 1: Estimating Non-Market Values of Coastal Marshes

Saginaw Bay is an extension of Lake Huron that separates Michigan's "thumb" from the rest of the Lower Peninsula. The watershed that drains into Saginaw Bay is Michigan's largest, encompassing nearly 9,000 square miles and including at least part of 22 counties. It is home to 1.4 million people.

The Saginaw Bay watershed is rich in resources that support agriculture, manufacturing, tourism, and outdoor recreation. Its resources also provide habitat for a wide variety of wildlife, including songbirds, waterfowl on the Mississippi Flyway, and 138 threatened or endangered species. People care about all these things, which places many—often competing—demands on the resources of the watershed. Making good choices about how to meet those demands requires a careful assessment of a wide range of trade-offs. In each decision, resource managers must assess what will be gained and what will be given up. Resource management decisions are further complicated by the fact that some of the goods and services supported by the watershed resources are commonly bought and sold, and some are not. For example,

- It is relatively easy to assess the value of the sugar beets and auto parts that are produced in the watershed. People's willingness to pay for these items, one of the best measures of value, is demonstrated in the marketplace every day. Data are collected by businesses, reported to the government, and continuously analyzed by researchers and industry experts.
- It is much harder, though, to assess the value of bird-watching or of preserving endangered species whose existence is not widely known and whose ecological significance is not widely appreciated. These non-market goods and services have real economic value, which may be significant. However, because no one pays for them or earns money on them, their value is often treated as zero in public decision-making.

Luckily, resource managers can use economic tools and methods to estimate the value of non-market goods and services to compare them alongside market values. This will allow managers to avoid trading things that are worth more to the community for things that are worth less. In 2005, a study was conducted to estimate the value of wetlands in Saginaw Bay. The study used two variations of the travel cost method to estimate the recreation values of Saginaw Bay coastal marshes by looking at the money spent by people who use a "free" resource as they travel to and from the site:

- The first variation looked at visits to a single site to determine the factors that influenced the number of visits to that site. This information was used to estimate the total value of Saginaw Bay marshes to recreational users using travel costs as an approximate.

- The second variation looked at the number of recreational sites available for use and assessed the cost and other factors that influenced which site was chosen. This information was used to estimate the value of adding to the existing acreage available for recreational use.

Each year Saginaw Bay wetlands provide $16 million of non-market benefits to recreational users, yielding a total value of $239 million. However, the study also found that the value that people place on these wetlands is not limited to their recreational use. For example, people place a value on the preservation of threatened and endangered species of wildlife. One of the survey questions asked people how much they would give in a one-time donation to a hypothetical "Saginaw Bay Coastal Marsh Trust Fund" to avoid the loss of specific non-market goods. Resource managers were able to use the contingent valuation method to use the responses to this question to estimate the value of preserving additional wetlands or the cost of losing them. They estimated an additional value of Saginaw Bay wetlands to be about $3,600 per acre—less than half of which accrues to recreational users. The remaining value of the wetlands represents the value to the public of the other non-market goods and services provided by the wetlands.

Case Study 2: The Value of a Coastal Wetland

Coastal wetlands are one of the nation's most valuable resources, providing direct values such as recreation and indirect values such as flood protection. Often, wetlands are also valued for their development potential. How do practitioners assign dollar values to these very different benefits? The Barataria-Terrebonne estuarine system offers an example. These extensive wetlands are a valuable source of oil and gas, and they are also valued for fishing, hunting, and wildlife viewing. State officials were interested in placing a dollar value on these wetlands for two reasons:

- To compare the estimated costs for conserving the system's resources to the benefits associated with the conservation effort

- To help people see that protecting these resources can be economically beneficial in the long term

Once the types of values to be investigated were defined, several methods were used to estimate dollar values:

- Benefits transfer can be used to estimate the value of recreational services. From a non-market value perspective, the economic benefits accruing from recreational activities ranged from $327 million to $1 billion.
- Impact Analysis for Planning, a regional economic model, was used to estimate the market value of estuary-dependent industries to the local economy. Examples of estuary-dependent industries include oil and gas production, aquaculture industries, and commercial fishing, hunting, and trapping. The estuary's role in the commercial economy was about $3.5 billion of which about $2.3 million was from oil and gas production.
- Avoided cost method was used to estimate the value of other wetland services on an annual, per-acre basis. Examples include protection from hurricane damage ($186), storm surges ($280 to $904), damage to the water supply ($84 to $157), and property losses from inundation ($6,599 to $7,116).

The results of this study all in 1994 dollars show an extremely valuable resource with a diverse set of services. These results have been used to evaluate management options and justify conservation efforts, which in some cases resulted in curtailing certain economic activity and completing other measures to ensure that the region's way of life could be sustained.

Case Study 3: Restoration of a Man-Made Lake to an Estuary

Capitol Lake provides a reflecting surface for the Washington State Capitol Building. This man-made lake was created in 1951 by building a dam on the Deschutes River, which prevents the water in the river from flowing into Budd Inlet and Puget

Sound. Maintaining the artificial lake has caused several problems, including sedimentation, invasive species, and compromised water quality. The state officials in charge of maintaining the lake wanted to evaluate the feasibility of restoring Capitol Lake to its original estuary state. To determine the best way to manage this resource, they wanted to know how much it would cost to keep maintaining the lake and how much it would cost to eliminate the lake. Some of the costs (such as removing the dam) were easy to estimate, while others (such as decreased aesthetic value and recreational services) were more complicated to estimate.

To better understand the restoration options, economists used the following process:

- Establish the geographic scale of the study (that is, the areas that are going to be impacted)
- Identify the existing conditions of the lake
- Assemble information about the physical or biological changes that estuary restoration would cause
- Determine general economic effects (both quantitatively and qualitatively) of those physical or biological changes

This process was used to determine the economic impacts of restoration on infrastructure (including ports), tourism, and the categories of ecosystem services denoted in the Millennium Ecosystem Assessment. Primarily, the benefits transfer and avoided cost methods were used to determine the costs of estuary restoration. In general, the results were a mixture of qualitative and quantitative results—and they weren't easy to compare. In the end, the investigation team decided to look at each category individually and determine whether the economic impact from estuary restoration was

- Positive
- Negative
- Unknown (not enough information about future conditions to make a determination of the economic impact)

- Divergent (there are strongly held perspectives in the community on whether the change is positive or negative, but there is insufficient information to determine the absolute direction of the net effect)

Several phases of the feasibility study are complete, but there is still more information to collect before a decision about the potential estuary restoration can be made. Having a better understanding of the economic benefits for a wide variety of ecosystem services will help the community make a better-informed decision.

FISHERIES ECONOMICS

An economy, much like an ecosystem, is composed of many economic actors, each with different abilities performing different, and many times, complementary roles. Each economic actor consumes certain goods while at the same time producing others. Furthermore, just as one can organize the organisms in marine ecosystems by phylum, class and lower taxa, we can decompose an economy into groups that allow us to investigate these parts so we can gain meaningful insights into the wider economy and how agents function within it. Once one divides the economy into several parts, we can begin to understand a little about how these sectors operate, the agents who contribute to t hat industry and its eventual outputs. Fishing is one such industry that we may try to understand in this manner and forms the focus of this paper. A great deal of the inputs for the fishing sector come from natural resources, however, the industry also relies upon products from manufacturing boats and netting, as well as many others eg. agriculture and management services. Clearly, changes to the fishing sector will affect many other sectors whose output is used as an input in the fishing sector, which should make many people outside of the fishing industry directly interested in the inputs to fishing.

A second item that may interest us when investigating the fishing sector is the final destination for the outputs of this industry. It is clear that the vast majority of outputs from the fishing sector will find their way to the dinner table, but the path taken by output of the fishing sector before it reaches this destination can be very important. Some fish are sold directly to the consumer while others may be sold to an intermediary who combines the fish with other inputs to produce something different that is then purchased by consumers as a different product. Since we are interested in both the inputs and outputs of the marine fishing sector, we can gain much more from considering these items simultaneously than separately. Input output analysis allows us the unique ability to do just this and, as is shown later, we use the results of this analysis to determine the role of marine capture fisheries in the global economy. Using the coefficient matrices, we express the economy of each nation as a system of linear equations summarized by the equation:

$$Ax + d = x \quad (1)$$

where A is the matrix of technical coefficients describing input requirements for each sector, x is a vector of sector inputs, and d is a vector of final demand. The above equation then simply states that the sum of intermediate demand (Ax) and final demand (d) is equal to supply (x). It is then a simple problem of linear algebra to solve for the vector of inputs (x) required to satisfy a given final demand vector (d) using I as the identity matrix. This solution is expressed as

$$x = [I - A]-1d \quad (2)$$

Type I Output Multipliers

Given the solution in equation (2) above, we calculate the change in output with respect to final demand. To do this, we take a partial derivative of equation (2) with respect to final demand (d):

$$\partial x \; \partial d = [I - A]^{-1} \quad (3)$$

Equation (3) describes a new relationship that proves to be very useful in macroeconomic analysis. The right hand side of this equation, [I – A]-1, is commonly called the Leontief inverse or multiplier matrix. This square matrix is of such interest because each entry (denoted $l_{i,j}$) describes the marginal inputs required from sector i when the output of sector j increases by one unit.

Specifying a row vector **L** as the column sum of the Leontief inverse matrix, we obtain a vector of Type I multipliers. Each entry in this row vector is an output multiplier that allows us to compute both the direct value of a given sector, as well as indirect activity required from the rest of the economy to satisfy an additional unit of demand for the sectors output. For example, for a sector with a Type I multiplier of 1.5, demand for an addional unit of its output will change total economic output by 1.5 units. We can also predict that $100 in output from this sector supports $150 of activity in the economy.

Type II Output Multipliers

Type I multipliers account for the downstream effects of changes in demand that may result when a change occurs to some other sector which is linked by sales or purchases. However, Type I multipliers fail to account for changes that may occur, for example, when additional demand for a given sector increases household incomes and in turn induces demand for additional output. An estimation of Type II output multipliers follows a similar procedure to that of Type I, however, we capture induced economic effects by including households as endogenous. With Type I multipliers, household consumption is part of the final demand sector, and therefore assumed to be exogenous, but with Type II multipliers we make household consumption endogenous by treating it as an additional intermediate sector in the technical coefficients matrix A.

There is a close relationship between Type I and II multipliers that will be used when presenting results. The Type I multiplier includes both direct and indirect effects while the Type II multiplier includes all Type I effects plus induced effects. Consequently, Type II multipliers are strictly greater than the Type I version.

Income Multipliers

A third item that can be obtained from the Leontief inverse matrix allows us to investigate the influence that output in the fisheries sector has on household income. These multipliers can be obtained for each sector using the equation:

$$Zj = yj\sum_{i=1}^{N}[1-A]_{j}^{-1} \tag{4}$$

where $\mathbf{y}_i = \mathbf{Y}_j / \mathbf{Q}_j$ represents income per unit of output for the jth sector. The vector of income multipliers **Z** summarizes the marginal change in income that will occur when output in a given sector changes by one unit and $\mathbf{Z}_j$ is the income multiplier for the jth sector.

USING ECONOMIC OUTPUT MULTIPLIERS

Once input-output multipliers, whether it be Type I, Type II, or income, are computed, we have a great deal of valuable information in need of context. We can make use of input-output multipliers by considering them alone as the marginal change in output of the fishing sector when final demand for it's output changes. However, one can use the current output of the fishing sector to determine total economic activity supported by fishing in the broader economy. This is done in a simple and concise manner, which can be expressed using matrix notation as:

$$V_{fish} = [1-A]_{fish}^{-1}\, d \tag{5}$$

where we substitute the vector of final demand d with a vector containing the current demand for marine capture fishing output – called landed value by – and zeros for all other sectors to isolate the economic impacts of ocean fish populations. This is done for each country for which landed value is available using national input-output multipliers where the data permits and regional multipliers when national tables are not available. When considering fisheries in the economic context of developing countries, government agencies generally rely on fisheries data reported by their fisheries agency. For many Pacific islands, these are dominated by large-scale, industrial Distant Water Fleets targeting tuna resources or local, small-scale commercial fisheries supplying local markets. In contrast, non-commercial small-scale fisheries e.g., subsistence fisheries, while recognized as fundamental for social, cultural and food security reasons, have catches which are seldom comprehensively accounted for in official statistics, either due to perceived difficulties of estimating a spatially dispersed fishery, or due to limited financial and human resources. Hence, the contributions of small-scale fisheries to Gross Domestic Product (GDP) of a country are often not taken into full consideration as part of national accounting. Thus, the importance of fisheries to a country's economy, if only based on officially reported commercial statistics, may be substantially undervalued in cases where small-scale and non-commercial fisheries are significant, yet under- or not reported. This situation may add further to the marginalization of small-scale fisheries, often already disadvantaged by their socio-economic, physical and political remoteness from urban centers. Fisheries in developing countries, and especially in small-island countries of the Pacific, can be difficult to categorize by size, level of commercialization, or subsistence activity, since any one fishing trip may include commercial, subsistence and recreational aspects. Nevertheless, divisions usually exist that can be used to differentiate, for the sake of catch estimation, different fisheries sectors.

ECONOMIC POTENTIAL FOR OFFSHORE AQUACULTURE: INSIGHTS FROM SUPPLY AND DEMAND ANALYSIS

Supply and demand analysis provides a useful starting point for thinking about factors affecting the economic potential for offshore aquaculture. Each existing or potential farming operation for a particular species has a cost of production per pound. This cost may be expressed as the sum of costs per pound for facilities, feed, juveniles, and other operating costs. These costs may vary between farms depending on their location, type of technology, scale of the operation, and the costs of various factor inputs in terms of labor, energy, etc. A farm is economically viable if and only if the price it receives per pound is greater than or equal to the total cost of production per pound including the risk adjusted cost of capital. As illustrated in Figure 13, we may plot the costs of all existing and potential fish farms for a particular species on a graph, with costs per pound on the vertical axis, and annual production on the horizontal axis arranged in ascending order of cost per pound. Plotted in this way, the total costs per pound form a supply curve for the species: the horizontal axis shows the volume of fish production that is economically viable at any given price per pound.

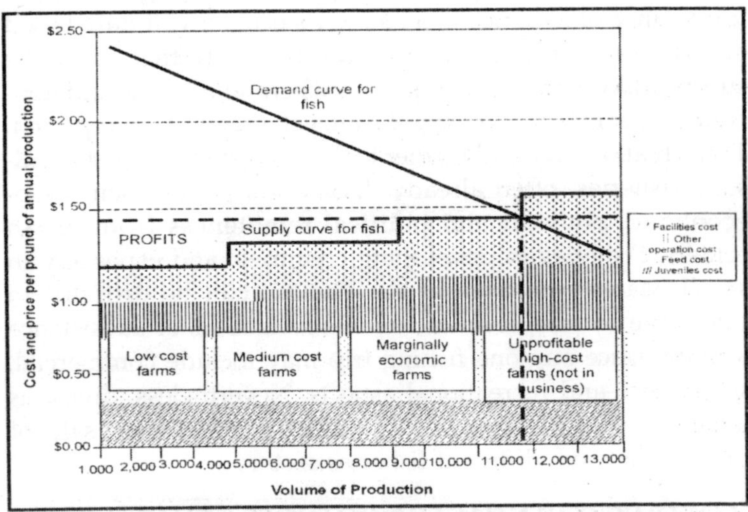

Figure 13: Hypothetical Short-run Fish Supply and Demand Curves

We may also plot a demand curve in the same figure, showing the volume of fish that is demanded at any given price. In the example shown in Figure 1, the demand curve and the supply curve determine the equilibrium price ($1.50/lb) and aggregate production (10,000 metric tons). Note that in this example, low-cost farms and medium-cost farms are earning profits. The marginally economic farms are earning zero profits and are just able to stay in business. Unprofitable high-cost farms are not in business. This simple figure illustrates a basic but important point in considering the economic potential for offshore aquaculture. It is possible for a fish farm to be economically viable even if other farms have lower costs, as long as the total supply from lower-cost farms remains limited. What matters for the economic viability of offshore aquaculture is not whether some competitors can produce fish at a lower cost, but whether they can produce enough fish at a lower cost to hold down the price below levels at which offshore aquaculture production is profitable. We may use this supply and demand framework to discuss factors affecting the ability of offshore aquaculture to compete with three potentially lower-cost competitors: 1) domestic inshore aquaculture; 2) foreign aquaculture; and 3) wild fisheries.

COMPETITIVENESS OF OFFSHORE AQUACULTURE WITH INSHORE AQUACULTURE

Considering first inshore aquaculture, for purposes of illustration we make two simple assumptions about the shape of the marine aquaculture supply curve:

- As aquaculture production moves offshore, from sites with relatively low exposure to sites of moderate and high exposure, costs of production increase.
- There are a limited number of potential farming sites with low exposure; there are more sites with moderate exposure; and there are a great number of sites with high exposure.

Given these assumptions, we might expect the supply curve for marine aquaculture to look something like that shown in Figure 2. Costs of production are relatively low for a limited number of inshore sites with low exposure to waves and wind. As farming expands to the limited number of sites with moderate exposure, costs of production increase. As farming expands to offshore areas with high exposure, costs increase further and the supply curve flattens out because of the very large offshore area potentially available for farming.

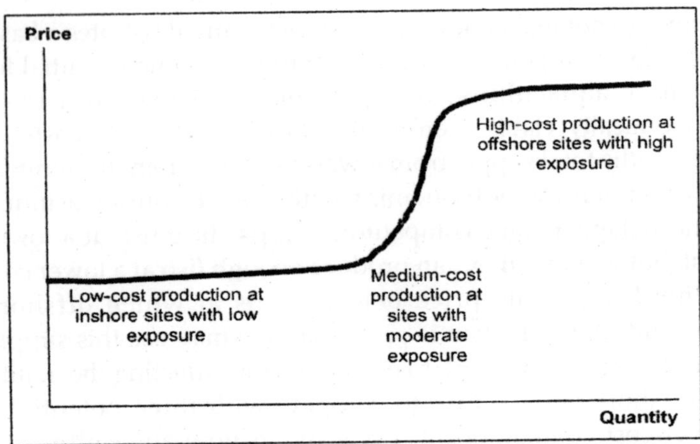

Figure 14: Hypothetical Marine Aquaculture Supply Curve

Figure 14 illustrates a domestic situation in which offshore aquaculture would not be economically viable because of competition from inshore aquaculture. The demand curve for fish intersects the supply curve at an equilibrium quantity, Q, which can be met by lower-cost inshore farms. The equilibrium price, P, is too low for offshore farms to be profitable. Thus, offshore farming will not be economically viable if lower-cost inshore farms can fully meet demand at prices below the cost of offshore farming.

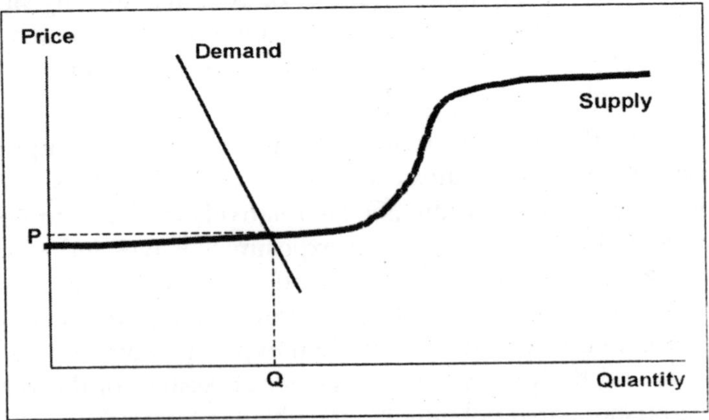

Figure 15: Demand and Supply Conditions in which Offshore Farming is not Economically viable because Lower-cost Inshore Sites can meet Demand

Figure 15 illustrates four ways in which demand or supply conditions could change from those in Figure 16 so that offshore aquaculture would become competitive with inshore aquaculture:

- Higher-cost offshore farms can compete with lower-cost inshore farms if demand exceeds the volume that can be produced from lower-cost, inshore sites (Figure 16A).
- Offshore farms can compete with inshore farms if costs for offshore farming decline sufficiently to become competitive with inshore farming (Figure 16B).

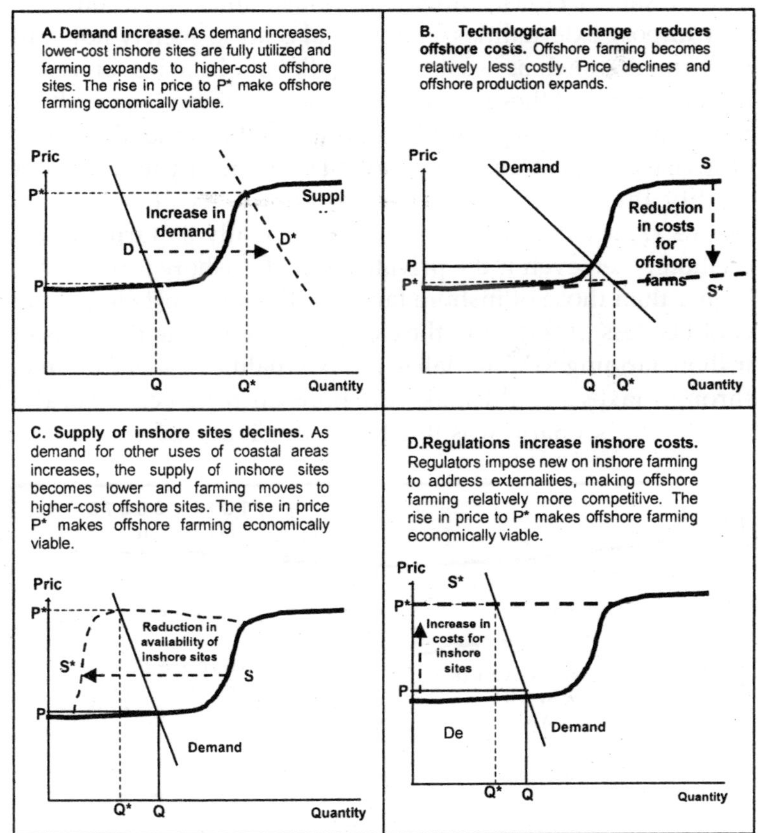

Figure 16: How Offshore Aquaculture could become Competitive with Inshore Aquaculture

- Offshore farms can compete with inshore farms if the availability of inshore sites declines so that inshore farms are no longer able to meet demand (Figure 16C).
- Offshore farms can compete with inshore farms if the cost of inshore farms increases so that offshore farms are competitive with inshore farming (Figure 16D).

Note that two of the situations illustrated by Figure 4 have nothing to do with the relative costs of inshore and offshore fish farming. Even if inshore farming incurs lower costs, offshore farming can successfully compete with inshore farming if demand increases sufficiently or if the number of inshore sites declines sufficiently. Some kinds of fish farming may impose externalities—additional costs to society not paid by farmers—such as wastes, navigational obstacles, or visual impacts. Some of these externalities may decline as aquaculture moves offshore. For example, an offshore farm may have less of a visual impact and may have less of an impact on water quality than an inshore farm. In theory, as illustrated in Figure 17, if externalities decline sufficiently as farms move offshore, then even if the private costs of offshore farming are higher than those of inshore farming, the total costs to society could be less. If this were the case, then increasing the costs of inshore farming to "internalize the externalities"—for example, through taxes—could make offshore farming economically viable. This scenario was illustrated by Figure 4D

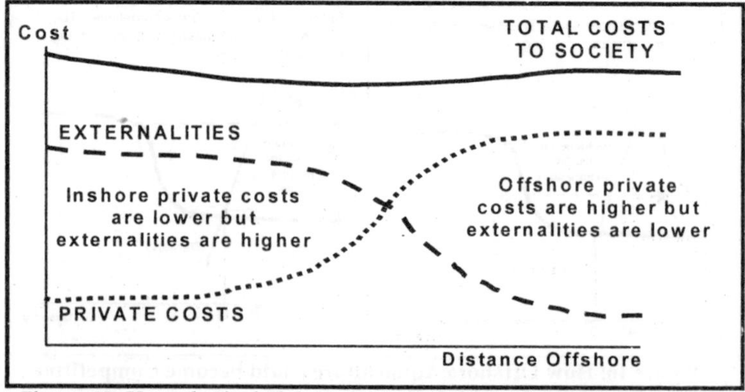

Figure 17: Hypothetical Fish Farming Private Costs and Externalities

BASIC ECONOMICS OF AQUACULTURE

We next discuss basic economics of aquaculture. We focus on factors important for considering the potential economic viability of a farm and the relative competitiveness of offshore farming. For purposes of this discussion, we simplify the analysis by expressing all costs and revenues on a per-pound basis. This requires converting all costs and revenues—including one-time investment costs—into costs and prices per pound.

A CONCEPTUAL FRAMEWORK

Figure 6 provides a conceptual framework for thinking about factors affecting the economic viability of a fish farm in a given location growing a particular species of fish. This is a useful conceptual framework to think about how the economic viability of farming in a particular type of location—offshore waters—compares with the economic viability of farming in other locations, such as inshore waters and foreign waters. A fish farm is economically viable if the average price per pound received for the fish exceeds the average cost per pound of producing the fish. The cost per pound may be divided into four major cost components: facilities costs, feed costs, juvenile costs, and other operating costs. Each of these cost components is determined by cost parameters, which are driven in part by the farm design. A wide variety of external factors—shown on the left side of the diagram— drive both farm design and cost parameters. Some of the same and other external factors drive supply and demand conditions, which determine the price for which the farm can sell its fish. Below, we first discuss major farm cost components and cost parameters. We then discuss how these are affected by different external factors, both directly and indirectly through farm design. We then discuss major factors affecting supply, demand and prices.

FACILITIES COST

A marine fish farm requires a variety of capital investments. The most significant investments are typically for cages, boats,

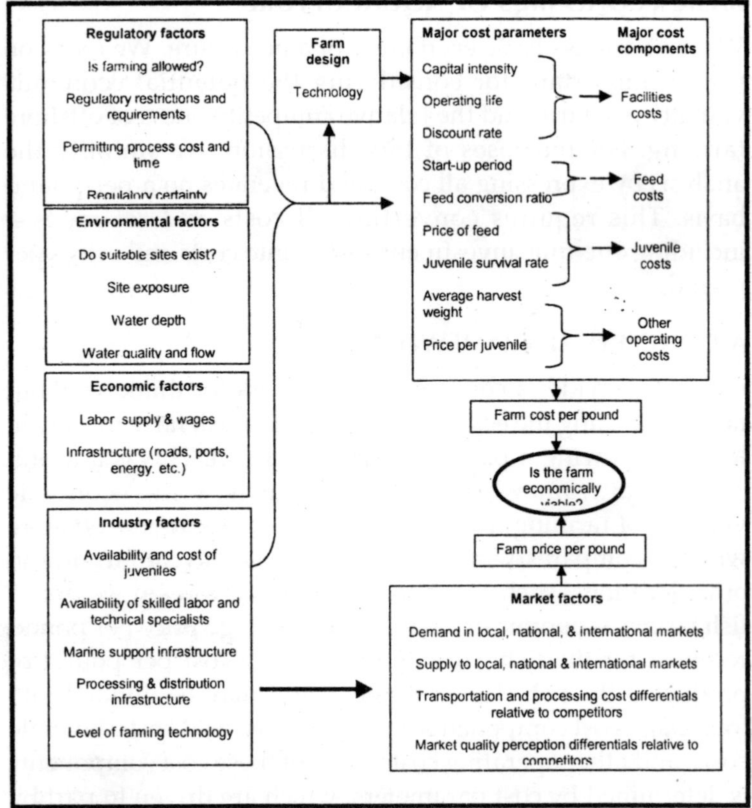

Figure 18: Major Factors Affecting the Economic Viability of a Fish Farm

feeding and monitoring systems, onshore facilities such as docks, storage facilities, and offices and initial project planning including design and permitting. The cost of these investments as a "facilities cost." any given total facilities cost of a fish farm may be converted into an equivalent annual facilities cost per year of production, which may be thought of as the annual equivalent payment that would be required to pay both principal and interest on a loan for the full cost of the investment over the lifetime of the investment. The facilities cost per pound is equal to: Equivalent annual facilities cost per year of production / Annual production in pounds

The most important factors affecting facilities cost per pound include:

- Capital intensity. For purposes of this analysis, we define "capital intensity" as the total initial investment per pound of annual production.
- Discount rate. This is the risk-adjusted opportunity cost of capital for the project. Depending on how the project is financed, this may be the interest rate which would be charged on a loan for the investment, or the rate of return which could be earned on an alternative investment of equivalent risk. For any given capital intensity, the higher the discount rate, the higher the facilities cost per pound.
- Operating life. This is the number of years with harvests to which facilities costs may be attributed. For any given capital intensity, the greater the number of years with harvests, the lower the facilities cost per pound.
- Start-up period. This is the period of time from when investments are made until harvests begin. For any given capital intensity, the longer the start-up period, the greater the facilities cost per pound.

Table 7 shows several examples of how the discount rate, operating life, and start-up period affect the facilities cost per pound for a fish farm with a hypothetical capital intensity of $1/lb. Note that for any given capital intensity of a fish farm, all three of these factors may significantly affect facilities costs per pound.

FEED COST

Feed cost is one of the largest components of finfish farming costs. The most important factors affecting feed cost per pound of fish production include:

- Price of feed. This is the price per pound of feed purchased by the farm.
- Feed conversion ratio (FCR). This is the ratio of the total weight of feed eaten by a crop of fish from the

time they are purchased as juveniles to the time they are harvested to the weight of the fish at harvest.

Feed cost per pound of fish is equal to: (Price of feed) x (Feed conversion ratio).

Table 8 shows feed costs per pound for various hypothetical combinations of the price of feed and the feed conversion ratio.

Table 7
Effects of Selected Factors on Facilities Cost Per Pound for a Hypothetical Fish Farm with a Capital Intensity of $1/1b

Example	*Discount Rate*	*Operating Life*	*Start-up Period*	*Total Years from Investment until Final Harvest*	*Facilities Cost Per Pound*
A	**10%**	10	0	10	$0.16
B	**15%**	10	0	10	$0.20
C	**20%**	10	0	10	$0.24
D	10%	**10**	0	10	$0.16
E	10%	**20**	0	20	$0.12
F	10%	**100**	0	100	$0.10
G	10%	10	**0**	10	$0.16
H	10%	10	**2**	12	$0.20
I	10%	10	**3**	15	$0.26

Note: All examples assume a capital intensity of $1/1b (a one-time investment of one dollar per pound of annual production).

Table 8
Fed Cost Per Pound of Fish: Effects of Price of Feed and Feed Conversion Ration

		Price of Feed ($/1b)				
		$0.30	$0.40	$0.50	$0.60	$0.70
Feed conversion ratio= pounds of feed per pound of fish	1.0	$0.30	$0.40	$0.50	$0.60	$0.70
	1.25	$0.38	$0.50	$0.63	$0.75	$0.88
	1.50	$0.45	$0.60	$0.75	$0.90	$1.05
	1.75	$0.53	$0.70	$0.88	$1.05	$1.23
	2.00	$0.60	$0.80	$1.00	$1.20	$1.40
	2.25	$0.68	$0.90	$1.13	$1.35	$1.58

Note: Feed Cost per Pound of Fish Produced = (Price of Feed) x (Feed Conversion Ratio).

Feed costs per pound of fish vary depending upon the type of feed, species, feeding technology, and other factors affecting growth and survival rates of fish, including water quality. In general, two opposing trends are likely to affect future feed costs per pound for marine aquaculture. The price of feed may increase as rising feed demand puts upward pressure on prices of fish meal and fish oil, which are major inputs to feed production. Rising prices of feed will increase farmers' incentives to reduce feed costs by improving feed conversion ratios. This may be done in a number of ways, such as reducing fish mortality, developing better feeds that fish are able to utilize more efficiently, improving the timing and method of feeding, utilizing more vegetable-based feeds, and shifting production from carnivorous species to noncarnivorous species. Future aquaculture feed costs per pound will depend on the relative strength of these opposing trends.

JUVENILE COST

Juvenile cost is another important component of marine aquaculture cost. The most important factors affecting juvenile cost are:

Price per juvenile. This is the delivered cost of individual juveniles purchased from a hatchery.

- Juvenile survival rate. This is the percentage of juveniles which survive to be harvested. It is equal to the inverse of the number of juveniles per harvested fish.
- Average harvest weight. This is the average weight of fish at harvest.

Juvenile cost per pound of fish harvested is equal to:

Price per juvenile * Juveniles per harvested fish / Average harvest weight

Price per juvenile / (Juvenile survival rate) * (Average harvest weight)

Table 9 shows juvenile costs per pound for various hypothetical combinations of price per juvenile, juvenile survival rate, and average harvest weight.

RELATIVE SCALE OF DIFFERENT COST COMPONENTS

Fish farming costs vary widely depending upon the species being farmed and where and how it is farmed. In general, however, feed and juveniles represent the largest cost components for most types of finfish farming, while operating costs and facilities costs tend to represent a much smaller share of total cost, even in offshore farms. This basic fact is important in considering the economics of offshore fish farming and its ability to compete with inshore farming, because while operating costs and facilities costs are likely to be higher offshore, feed and juvenile costs are likely to be the same—or potentially lower, if offshore water quality and water flow are better.

Table 9
Effects of Selected Factors on Fish Farm Juvenile Cost per Pound

		Price Per Juvenile							
Juvenile Survival Rate	*Avg. Harvest Weight (lbs)*	*$0.50*	*$0.75*	*$1.00*	*$1.25*	*$1.50*	*$2.00*	*$2.50*	*$3.00*
100%	2	$0.25	$0.38	$0.50	$0.63	$0.75	$1.00	$1.25	$1.50
	4	$0.13	$0.19	$0.25	$0.31	$0.38	$0.50	$0.63	$0.75
	6	$0.08	$0.13	$0.17	$0.21	$0.25	$0.33	$0.42	$0.50
	8	$0.06	$0.09	$0.13	$0.16	$0.19	$0.25	$0.31	$0.38
	10	$0.05	$0.08	$0.10	$0.13	$0.15	$0.20	$0.25	$0.30
90%	2	$0.28	$0.42	$0.56	$0.69	$0.83	$1.11	$1.39	$1.67
	4	$0.14	$0.21	$0.28	$0.35	$0.42	$0.56	$0.69	$0.83
	6	$0.09	$0.14	$0.19	$0.23	$0.28	$0.37	$0.46	$0.56
	8	$0.07	$0.10	$0.14	$0.17	$0.21	$0.28	$0.35	$0.42
	10	$0.06	$0.08	$0.11	$0.14	$0.17	$0.22	$0.28	$0.33
80%	2	$0.31	$0.47	$0.63	$0.78	$0.94	$1.25	$1.56	$1.88
	4	$0.16	$0.23	$0.31	$0.39	$0.47	$0.63	$0.78	$0.94
	6	$0.10	$0.16	$0.21	$0.26	$0.31	$0.42	$0.52	$0.63
	8	$0.08	$0.12	$0.16	$0.20	$0.23	$0.31	$0.39	$0.47
	10	$0.06	$0.09	$0.13	$0.16	$0.19	$0.25	$0.31	$0.38

Note: Juvenile cost per pound = (Cost per juvenile) / [(Juvenile survival rate) * (Average harvest weight)]

The smaller the share of total costs represented by a particular cost element—such as facilities—the less significant the effect of an increase in that cost element will be in its relative effect on total cost. This basic mathematical principle is illustrated in Table 10. For example, suppose facilities costs and feed costs account for 10% and 50% of the total cost of an inshore farming operation, respectively. If facilities costs are 100% higher for an offshore farm, they would result in only a

10% increase in total cost. Such an increase in facilities costs would be fully offset by a 20% decrease in feed costs.

Table 10
Percentage Increase in Total Cost Resulting from an Increase in One Cost Component

		Percentage of Cost Component in Total Cost				
		10%	*20%*	*30%*	*40%*	*50%*
Percentage increase in cost component	10%	1%	2%	3%	4%	5%
	20%	2%	4%	6%	8%	10%
	50%	5%	10%	15%	20%	25%
	100%	10%	20%	30%	40%	50%
	200%	20%	40%	60%	80%	100%
	300%	30%	60%	90%	120%	150%

FARM DESIGN

Some cost parameters are influenced by the farm design: the technology used by the farm and the scale of the farm . These cost parameters include capital intensity, operating life, feed conversion ratio, juvenile survival rate, and labor productivity. In general, as in other kinds of agriculture, fish farmers face a choice between capital intensity and other cost parameters. By increasing the capital intensity of the farm (which increases facility costs) farmers can achieve better feed conversion ratios, better juvenile survival rates, and higher labor productivity (which lowers feed costs, juvenile costs, and other operating costs). An important point to recognize is that cost-minimizing design choices for offshore farming may differ from those for inshore farming, and cost-minimizing design choices for offshore farms may differ from those for foreign offshore farms. For example, if labor costs more per hour for an offshore farm than for an inshore farm, an offshore farm is likely to use relatively less labor—thus reducing the extent to which higher labor costs represent a cost disadvantage.

REGULATORY FACTORS

Regulatory factors directly affect the economic viability of fish farming—most obviously by prescribing whether farming is allowed at all, but also in numerous other ways. Regulatory restrictions and requirements may limit farm design choices of scale and technology and may impose additional costs, such as environmental monitoring. The permitting process may represent a significant expense which increases with the time required for permitting and the uncertainty associated with the outcome. Regulatory certainty – the likelihood that regulations will stay the same over the life of the farm – affects the risk associated with farming investments and the discount rate for facilities investments. Taxes and royalties represent additional direct costs. Put simply, to a significant extent the costs and economic viability of fish farming depends on how it is regulated. Favorable regulation cannot make a fish farm economically viable if environmental, economic, industry, and market factors are unfavorable. But unfavorable regulation can keep a farm from being economically viable even if other factors are favorable.

ENVIRONMENTAL FACTORS

Key environmental factors affecting economic viability of a fish farm include site exposure, water depth, and water flow. Exposure to waves and wind directly determines what kinds of cages and other farm equipment will work, as well as the risks of farm damage and loss of fish. Water depth affects installation costs. Water depth, quality, and flow affect feed costs and juvenile costs by affecting fish growth rates and mortality rates. Water depth, quality, and flow also affect potential environmental effects of a farm and the extent to which these must be mitigated, either because it is in the farmer's own interest or in response to regulatory requirements.

ECONOMIC FACTORS

General economic conditions affect the costs and economic viability of a fish farm. Key economic factors include labor supply and wages, transportation infrastructure, and availability and cost of utilities. Another critical factor is political and economic stability, including protection of property and basic rule of law.

INDUSTRY FACTORS

The costs and economic viability of an individual fish farm are affected by a number of industry factors which depend on the scale and experience of the industry. As the scale of the fish farming industry within a region or nation grows, it creates a demand for specialized aquaculture support activities, such as hatcheries, veterinary services, fish transport, and processing. As the scale of these activities expands, it tends to lower costs and expand the types and scale of farming which are feasible. More generally, experience gained in farming drives technological change. Industry factors may be thought of as "feedback factors" affecting economic viability, in the sense that as an industry grows and gains experience, economies of scale and technological change help to lower costs and further expand the industry.

MARKET FACTORS

Price is as important as cost to the economic viability of a fish farm. The price per pound received by a farm is driven by a wide variety of market factors interacting in complex ways. The effects of these factors can generally be described within the supply and demand framework. Which market factors are most important depends on the size of the market and the relative scale of competition. If a fish farm is supplying a market or markets which are also supplied with comparable fish of comparable quality from competing sources, the volume of competing supply and the prices offered by competitors are key factors influencing the price received by the farm. Put differently, the price depends on whether the demand for the fish is local, national, or international, and whether the competing supply is local, national, or international.

Different factors also drive prices in the short term over the course of one or a few years than over the long term the expected period of operation of a fish farm. In the short term, prices are driven by the total supply available to the market, given current production. Over the longer term, prices are driven by the capacity of producers to expand or contract production in response to higher or lower prices. In national and international markets, competition typically occurs at the wholesale level, between fish which have undergone primary processing and been transported either to endmarket locations or locations where further processing occurs. The price paid to a fish farm is driven not only by the wholesale price, but also by the costs of processing and transportation, which must be subtracted from the wholesale price. Put differently, whether a fish farm can be competitive is determined not just by the cost of growing the fish, but also by the costs of processing the fish and transporting it to markets. In considering whether a particular farming operation can be competitive, an important factor is how both processing costs and transportation costs to markets compare with those of competitors. A higher-cost farm can be competitive if its products can be processed at a lower cost or shipped to markets at a lower cost than its competitors.

Both processing and transportation costs depend in part on the scale of the industry. A pioneer fish farm in one location may face relatively high processing and transportation costs if the fish processing industry and transportation infrastructure are not well developed. As the industry grows in scale, these costs may decline significantly, making fish farms relatively more competitive. Thus, some of the industry scale factors which affect the costs of a fish farm also affect the prices paid to a fish farm, through their effects on the costs of processing and transportation. A similarly important factor is the perceived quality of a farm's products compared with competing suppliers' products, as reflected in the relative prices that buyers are willing to pay. A higher-cost farm can be competitive if its products can command a higher price over those of competitors.

COMPETITIVE DISADVANTAGES OF OFFSHORE FARMING RELATIVE TO INSHORE FARMING

Exposure

Probably the greatest competitive disadvantages of offshore aquaculture derive from the technical challenges and costs of constructing, installing, operating, and maintaining cages and feeding and monitoring systems able to withstand wave and wind conditions in an exposed ocean environment. A more exposed environment also adds to the required sizes and construction and operating costs of support vessels. This cost disadvantage may be significantly reduced where there are synergies with existing or new offshore facilities built for other purposes, such as offshore oil platforms or as envisioned for the future wave power generation installations.

Support Transport Costs

Offshore farms are located farther from shore than onshore farms. In general, this will mean that fish, feed, and workers will need to be transported over greater distances, adding to fuel and labor costs. Note, however, that locating a farm farther offshore does not necessarily imply a greater transportation distance when compared to available inshore sites. Depending on terrain, infrastructure development, and the extent of the existing inshore farming industry, offshore facilities will not necessarily be farther from onshore support facilities such as docks and roads than are available protected inshore sites. Put simply, it may be shorter and quicker for a support vessel to travel three miles straight out to sea than five miles up the coast or around a cape to the next bay.

Water Depth

In general, water depth is greater for offshore farms, and may in some cases be much greater—adding to the costs of mooring systems.

Working Conditions

Offshore farms will likely need to pay higher wage rates for workers able and willing to work in a harsher and riskier offshore environment and able to work with the more complex technology of offshore farms. Note, however, that higher wage rates may be significantly offset by the use of more capital-intensive and labor-saving technology, such as remote feeding and monitoring systems.

Industry Economies of Scale

The costs of manufacturing cages and offshore feeding and monitoring systems depend upon the scale at which they are produced. Currently, far fewer cages and feeding and monitoring systems are being built for offshore farming than for inshore farming. Over time, as the scale of offshore investment expands, it will help to lower manufacturing costs for offshore cages and feeding and monitoring systems.

Operating Experience

For almost any economic activity, operating experience helps to identify better and cheaper ways of doing things. Worldwide, there has been far less experience in building and maintaining offshore farms than inshore farms. Over time, as more experience is gained with offshore farming, costs are likely to decline at a relatively greater rate.

Regulatory Experience

Experience with the regulation of offshore farming lags behind the regulation of inshore aquaculture. Regulatory frameworks and effective methods for offshore farm monitoring and regulatory enforcement may not be in place. Potential jurisdictional and legal issues may not have been resolved. This lack of experience is likely to increase the difficulty, time, costs, and risks associated with applying for offshore sites and meeting regulatory requirements. Over time, as more regulatory experience is gained, these offshore costs are likely to decline until they compare with those of inshore farming.

Competitive Advantages of Offshore Farming Relative to Inshore Farming

Water Quality

Water quality is critical to successful fish farming. In general, offshore farms will have more water flow than inshore farms. Offshore farms are also less likely to be affected by pollution from land-based sources, such as agricultural runoff. Better water quality contributes to better growing conditions for fish and is reflected in better feed conversion and survival rates, lowering the costs of feed, juveniles, and facilities and other costs on a per-pound basis.

Availability of Sites

For much of the world's coastlines, "inshore" farming is not an option because there are no protected waters in which to locate such farms. In areas with protected waters, inshore farming may still not be possible because available sites are already being used. In addition, the best inshore sites tend to be used first, so new inshore sites will be even less economically competitive, relatively speaking, with offshore sites. In contrast, available sites for offshore farming are almost limitless in comparison to the potential scale of offshore farming for the foreseeable future.

Conflicts with Other Activities

Because of their greater distance from shore, offshore farms are likely to experience fewer conflicts with other economic and recreational uses of the environment. This reduced potential for conflicts may result in fewer restrictions on farm size and greater economies of scale.

Environmental Impacts

Because of greater water flow and depth, the potential for fish feces, fish feed, or other farm residues to concentrate in the water or on the ocean bottom is comparatively less. The potential for interaction with species migrating close to shore or with concentrations of migrating anadromous fish is also less. Such reduced environmental impacts may result in fewer restrictions on farm size and greater economies of scale. Farm economies of scale Because of the greater availability of suitable large-scale farming sites and the potential for fewer regulatory restrictions on farm size, offshore farms have the potential to be larger, allowing for reduced costs through greater economies of scale.

Distance from Markets

Because of reduced conflicts with other activities and greater availability of sites, it may be possible to locate offshore farms closer to markets such as major cities, thus reducing transportation costs and making it possible for fresher products to be delivered to markets. This may, in turn, allow some offshore farms to capture higher prices than more distant, inshore farms.

OTHER CONSIDERATIONS FOR THE COMPETITIVENESS OF OFFSHORE FARMING WITH INSHORE FARMING

An uncertain factor affecting the relative economic viability of offshore aquaculture is its relative political viability: the choices of society—through the political process and legal, political, and regulatory institutions at local, state, and national levels—about whether to allow offshore aquaculture and how to regulate it. The relative political viability of offshore aquaculture may depend on the relative geographical distribution of perceived costs and benefits. Suppose inshore aquaculture is regulated by multiple local state-level or lower authorities, while offshore aquaculture is regulated by a single, national authority. A simple political theory would suggest that regulation of inshore aquaculture would reflect perceptions at local levels of the relative costs and benefits of inshore aquaculture, while regulation of offshore aquaculture would reflect national perceptions of these costs and benefits. The relative geographical distribution of perceived costs and benefits of inshore and offshore aquaculture is likely to differ for different regions and different types of farming. This may result in more economically favorable local regulation of inshore aquaculture in some areas, and less economically favorable regulation of inshore aquaculture in other areas—relative to national standards for offshore regulation.

ECONOMIC MODELING OF OFFSHORE AQUACULTURE

There is no single answer about the economic viability of offshore fish farming. The economic viability of offshore fish farms may vary widely depending upon where they are located, the species that are farmed, how they are regulated, how they are designed, and the scale of operation. Economic viability may also change over time as the scale of the industry changes and as markets change.

To move beyond these general conclusions to a more formal assessment of the prospects for a particular type of farm—or for offshore aquaculture in general—requires the development of models that explicitly consider both expected costs and prices. Such models may range from simple "back of the envelope" models based on rules-of-thumb for different types of costs, to complex systems of equations based on numerous, carefully researched assumptions. Table 5 provides an example of a relatively simple economic model of a hypothetical offshore fish farm for a hypothetical fish species. It is not intended to represent actual costs or prices for any particular fish species, or the economic viability of any particular kind of fish farming. It simply presents one potential approach to economic modeling of a fish farm. There are many other potential approaches. Which approach is best depends on the purpose for which the model is being developed and the reliability of the assumptions on which that model is based. In general, more complex models may be used to address more complex questions but require more assumptions and may be harder to understand.

THE ECONOMIC FEASIBILITY AND CONTRIBUTIONS OF SHELLFISH AQUACULTURE

The important shellfish species, blue mussels and sea scallops. Mussels will be grown on ropes suspended vertically from longline harness sets. Each harvest consists of a 120-meter-long horizontal longline held in place about seven meters below the surface by submerged flotation spheres and anchored to the bottom. Approximately 200 culture ropes are suspended from each longline to a depth of five meters above the seafloor. At full-scale operation, which is projected to be realized in three years, an offshore aquaculture plant will operate 120 longlines. Scallops will be grown using a seabed seeding technology. Scallops are to be seeded over a 143-acre site. The mussel operation is assessed over a 10-year period, and the scallop operation is assessed over a 20-year period.

BLUE MUSSEL (MYTILUS EDULIS)

The growth of blue mussels, as well as the growth of scallops and finfish, is estimated based on a discrete time version of the Beverton-Holt (1957) model, which relates growth to number of animals and weight of animals. The time period considered for the economic feasibility of producing blue mussels via offshore aquaculture can be determined by the useful life of longlines, which is ten years. The bio-economic assessment considers longline installation, spat collection, socking operation, maintenance, and harvesting. The assessment also includes purchase of a used vessel, which will be employed during the first three years, and then the purchase of a new vessel in the fourth year of the operation, which is the approximate time required to bring the operation up to full scale. All production activities are assumed to be equivalent to constant returns to scale; that is, a constant proportionate increase in all factors of production generates the same proportionate increase in outputs, or the production of mussels.

The up front investment cost for a mussel operation is approximately $1.1 million. This includes the purchase and installation of longlines, a used vessel, and other items essential to production. Additional costs include expendable supplies, vessel and equipment maintenance, and support for shore-side activities which in shown in (Table 1). The total constant dollar cost of the operation over the 10-year period equals $4.62 million. Over the 10-year period, it is projected that the mussel operation will generate, after deducting costs, a net present value of approximately $2.7 million which in shown in (Table 2). The average annual harvest will be approximately 892 metric tons, or 1.97 million pounds per year. Average annual revenue will approximate $1.2 million per year, with a product price of approximately $0.60 per pound. The break-even price is $0.35 per pound; that is, if prices received for scallops fall below $0.35 per pound, it will not long be financially feasible to operate the mussel operation, based on assumptions above.

One problem with the initial feasibility analysis is the assumption of constant returns to scale. It is, thus, not feasible to assess the potential economic impacts of mussel operations if expanded. There is no information to indicate the potential number of mussel operations, and thus, an assessment of the potential economic contributions can only be made in terms of either gross sales for a single plant, or on a per-$1-million-of-sales for mussel aquaculture basis. Based on the American aquaculture input/output model, it is estimated that an annual gross revenue of $1.2 million will generate a total of $6.49 million in total sales or output, $3.33 million in income, and 92 full- and part-time jobs for the U.S. economy as it is shown in Table 3). These impacts represent the impacts over all sectors, from the aquaculture operation to retail sales. The largest impacts are generated in the restaurant and primary producer i.e aquaculture operation sectors. Retail sales by grocers generate a total of $3.5 million in total sales or output, $2.03 million in income, and 62 full- and part-time jobs. The aquaculture-producing sector generates $2.67 million in total sales, $1.14 million in income, and 25 full- and part-time jobs.

Table 1
Basic Production and Cost Requirements, Blue Mussels

Description	*Unit*	*Value*
Longlines at full capacity	Number / farm	120
Longline installation cost[a]	$ / longline	10,000
Expendable supplies[b]	$ / longline / year	1,700
Used vessel acquisition	$ / vessel	70,000
Used vessel maintenance	$ / vessel / year	10,000
Used vessel upgrade & equipment[c]	$ / vessel	25,000
Equipment maintenance	$ / year	5,000
Used vessel variable and crew cost	$ / day	1,500
New custom vessel construction	$	800,000
New custom vessel maintenance	$ / year	30,000
New vessel variable and crew cost	$ / day	1,000
On shore cost[d]	$ / year	173,000
Annual discount rate		0.07

Notes:

a. Including 2 anchors ($2,000), 2 corner buoys ($2,000), rope and chain ($2,000), flotation ($2,000), and assembly and deployment ($2,000)

b. Including spat collectors, grow out ropes, socking material, bag, etc.

c. Including stripper / declumper / grader and continuous socking machine

d. Including CEO / captain salary ($100,000 / year) and vessel dockage, etc. ($20,000)

Table 2
Estimated Net Present Value, Investment, Harvest, and Cost, Blue Mussels

Description	*Unit*	*Value*
Net Present value	$ million	2.659
Investment [a]	$ million	1.114
Average fish harvest [b]	Metric ton / year	892
Total cost	$ million	4.624
Cost Share		
Longline installation	%	24.1
Expendable supplies	%	15.5
Vessel acquisition & maintenance	%	19.5
Vessel variable cost (fuel, crew, etc.)	%	13.4
Onshore and other	%	27.5
Total	%	100

Notes:
a. Longline system only
b. At full capacity annual output is 1,200 metric tons

Table 3
Economic Contributions of Single Blue Mussel Operation, $1.2 million in Sales

Impacts of Aquaculture Blue Mussels Offshore Shipments - Producers				
	Direct Impacts	*Indirect Impacts*	*Induced Impacts*	*Total Impacts*
Labor Income Impacts (millions of dollars)	0.50	0.18	0.45	1.14
Output Impacts (millions of dollars)	0.73	0.58	1.36	2.67
Employment Impacts (full-time and part-time jobs)	9.87	3.75	11.86	25.48
Impacts of Aquaculture Blue Mussels Offshore Shipments – Wholesalers				
	Direct Impacts	*Indirect Impacts*	*Induced Impacts*	*Total Impacts*
Labor Income Impacts (millions of dollars)	0.03	0.01	0.02	0.06
Output Impacts (millions of dollars)	0.03	0.02	0.07	0.12
Employment Impacts (full-time and part-time jobs)	0.54	0.11	0.60	1.25
Impacts of Aquaculture Blue Mussels Offshore Shipments - Grocers				
	Direct Impacts	*Indirect Impacts*	*Induced Impacts*	*Total Impacts*
Labor Income Impacts (millions of dollars)	0.06	0.01	0.05	0.11
Output Impacts (millions of dollars)	0.04	0.01	0.15	0.20
Employment Impacts (full-time and part-time jobs)	2.12	0.11	1.26	3.49
Impacts of Aquaculture Blue Mussels Offshore Shipments - Restaurants				
	Direct Impacts	*Indirect Impacts*	*Induced Impacts*	*Total Impacts*
Labor Income Impacts (millions of dollars)	1.06	0.10	0.87	2.03
Output Impacts (millions of dollars)	0.60	0.28	2.63	3.50
Employment Impacts (full-time and part-time jobs)	37.04	2.24	22.76	62.04

Contd.

Impacts of Aquaculture Blue Mussels Offshore Shipments – All Sectors				
	Direct Impacts	Indirect Impacts	Induced Impacts	Total Impacts
Labor Income Impacts (millions of dollars)	1.64	0.30	1.40	3.33
Output Impacts (millions of dollars)	1.40	0.89	4.21	6.49
Employment Impacts (full-time and part-time jobs)	49.57	6.22	36.48	92.27

SEA SCALLOPS (PLACOPECTEN MAGELLANICUS)

The economic feasibility of using aquaculture to produce sea scallops is based on a 20- year life cycle. A 20-year cycle permits ten, two-year cycles of harvesting and marketing scallops. The farming operation is scaled to produce 100,000 pounds of scallop meat every two years. Baseline production assumptions include the following: 1) the farming site is two hours by boat from port; 2) the site is surrounded by markers with annual maintenance requirements of three hours of boat time; 3) the juvenile scallop collecting/depositing time per cycle is 142 days; 4) the farm area seeded is 143 acres; 5) scallops are sold at dockside for $7 per pound of meat. The Potential Economic Ramifications of Offshore Aquaculture 146 the work day is 12 hours; and, vessels are capable of capturing and bringing to the farming site an average of 40,000 juvenile scallops in one day.

Although a two-year production cycle is assumed, the equivalent annual production is 22.7 metric tons, or 50 thousand pounds per year. At $7 per pound, the plant or production facility is projected to gross $350.3 thousand per year. The input requirements such as the number of buoys and moorings per farm, seeding density, etc. are summarized in Table 4. The up front investment is $52.7 thousand as shown in Table 5. The expected net present value, or net return over the 20-year cycle, equals $1.72 million. The total cost for one scallop operation over the 20-year period is $2.11 million. The annual economic contributions of the single scallop production facility equal $1.98 million in sales or output, $1.15 million in income, and 31 full- and part-time jobs. The production facility, itself, generates sales or output of $730 thousand, $430 thousand in income, and approximately 9 full- and part-time jobs. The largest contributions are generated by the restaurant sector—$1.14 million in sales or output, $670 thousand in income, and 21 full- and part-time jobs. Expanding the number of production facilities simply scales the magnitude of the impacts for example, two plants would be expected to generate $3.96 million in sales, $2.3 million in income, and 62 full- and part-time jobs.

Table 4
Basic Production and Cost Requirements, Sea Scallop

Description	*Unit*	*Value*
Marker buoys & moorings	Number / farm	14
Unit cost	$ / mooring set	3,000
Annual mooring maintenance	$ / mooring set / year	150
Total vessel cost	$ / day	2,000
Seeding density	1,000 scallops / acre	40
Mortality / loss rate to harvest	%	50
Average size at harvest	1bs (meat)	0.035
Onshore cost*	$ / year	20,000
Annual discount rate		0.07

Note: *Management and administration.

Table 5
Estimated Net Present Value, Investment, Harvest, and Cost, Sea Scallop

Description	*Unit*	*Value*
Cost		
Net Present value	$ million	1.723
Investment [a]	$	52,675
Average scallop harvest [b]	Metric ton / year	22.7
Total cost	$ million	2.110
Cost Share		
Marker buoys & moorings	%	2.5%
Annual mooring maintenance [c]	%	1.0%
Mooring maintenance [d]	%	5.4%
Collecting / depositing cost [d]	%	78.9%
Harvest cost	%	1.6%
Onshore cost	%	10.7%
Total	%	100%

Notes:
a. Marker buoys and moorings
b. Scallops are harvested every other year
c. Fix maintenance cost per year
d. Cost associated with vessel usage

THE ECONOMIC FEASIBILITY AND CONTRIBUTIONS OF FINFISH AQUACULTURE

Estimation and assessment of the economic feasibility and potential economic contributions of finfish aquaculture is considerably more complicated. A Beverton-Holt model is used to project growth, numbers abundance, and weight biomass of fish. In addition, various feed conversion ratios can be used to help estimate the cost of feed for various finfish species. Revenues can be estimated using price times quantity on a monthly basis, and subsequently aggregated to an annual basis. Costs and required investment levels will be obtained from a wide variety of sources. The economic feasibility and contributions of using aquaculture to produce the three species of finfish are examined here. The production technologies for all three finfish species involve large offshore cage farms utilizing high levels of automation. In addition, production of all three species relies upon purchasing fingerlings and subsequently stocking and growing them to marketable size. Except for salmon, the purchase of fingerlings accounts for the largest cost share—41.8 % of the total cost of producing cod, and 55.1% of the total cost of producing winter flounder. The purchase of salmon fingerlings accounts for 18.8 % of the total cost of producing salmon.

Table 6
Economic Contributions of Sea Scallop Operation, $350,300 in Sales

Impacts of Aquaculture Sea Scallops Offshore Shipments - Producers				
	Direct Impacts	*Indirect Impacts*	*Induced Impacts*	*Total Impacts*
Labor Income Impacts (millions of dollars)	0.22	0.02	0.19	0.43
Output Impacts (millions of dollars)	0.09	0.07	0.57	0.73
Employment Impacts (full-time and part-time jobs)	3.51	0.41	4.95	8.87
Impacts of Aquaculture Sea Scallops Offshore Shipments – Wholesalers				
	Direct Impacts	*Indirect Impacts*	*Induced Impacts*	*Total Impacts*
Labor Income Impacts (millions of dollars)	0.01	0.00	0.01	0.02
Output Impacts (millions of dollars)	0.02	0.00	0.02	0.05
Employment Impacts (full-time and part-time jobs)	0.16	0.03	0.17	0.36

Contd.

Impacts of Aquaculture Sea Scallops Offshore Shipments - Grocers

	Direct Impacts	Indirect Impacts	Induced Impacts	Total Impacts
Labor Income Impacts (millions of dollars)	0.02	0.00	0.01	0.03
Output Impacts (millions of dollars)	0.01	0.00	0.04	0.06
Employment Impacts (full-time and part-time jobs)	0.62	0.03	0.37	1.03

Impacts of Aquaculture Sea Scallops Offshore Shipments - Restaurants

	Direct Impacts	Indirect Impacts	Induced Impacts	Total Impacts
Labor Income Impacts (millions of dollars)	0.35	0.03	0.29	0.67
Output Impacts (millions of dollars)	0.18	0.08	0.88	1.14
Employment Impacts (full-time and part-time jobs)	12.57	0.65	7.62	20.85

Impacts of Aquaculture Sea Scallops Offshore Shipments – All Sectors

	Direct Impacts	Indirect Impacts	Induced Impacts	Total Impacts
Labor Income Impacts (millions of dollars)	0.60	0.05	0.50	1.15
Output Impacts (millions of dollars)	0.30	0.16	1.51	1.98
Employment Impacts (full-time and part-time jobs)	16.86	1.13	13.12	31.11

ATLANTIC COD (GADUS MORHUA)

Cod aquaculture assumes that stocking and harvesting will be done on a year-round basis. Although the actual economic assessment is based on monthly activity, the average annual price equaled $2.92 per pound. A 15-year period is used as the baseline assessment period. The baseline fixed cost per year is $100 thousand. Operating costs are $1,500 per day for fuel and other consumables, and personnel costs for a crew of four represent another $1,500 per day. Annual production cost equals $2.09/pound per year. Input requirements and associated costs involve purchasing cages, buying and installing moorings, acquiring fingerlings, supporting best management practices, and acquiring additional fixed and variable inputs please see Table 7.

The up front investment cost ranges between $2 and $3.1 million. The total cost of the project is between $35.9 and $59.9 million over the 15-year period. The variation is due to the possible production of baseline and high-end valued products. Expected production equals 177 metric tons, or 390.2 thousand pounds per month for a total of 4.7 million pounds per year. Gross revenue for the year is projected to equal $13.7 million per year. The net present value over the 15-year period equals

$10.6 million for the baseline product, but appears to be negative (-$13.4 million) for the high-end product. If the price falls below $0.91 per pound, the baseline farm is no longer economically viable. Revenues of $13.7 million received by the farm generate total sales for the producing sector of $38.8 million (Table 9). Of that total, the wholesale sector generates $2.23 million in totals sales; the grocery sector generates $2.96 million in total sales; and the restaurant sector generates $32.2 million in total sales. Total output generated by all sectors equals $76.3 million; total income equals $33.7 million; and total employment generated across all sectors equals 1,013 full- and part-time jobs. The largest levels of impact occur in the restaurant and producing sectors. Total employment generated in the restaurant sector equals 571 full- and part-time jobs, and total employment generated in the producing sector equals 367 full- and part-time jobs.

ATLANTIC SALMON (SALMO SALAR)

Cage culture is the primary method for culturing of salmon. Analysis of the economic feasibility of salmon culture is based on a 15-year cycle. The farm is assumed to produce salmon on a year-round basis. The expected harvest of salmon is 169 metric tons per month, or 4.5 million pounds per year. The assessment is based on a price of $1.81 per pound. It is anticipated that the salmon farm will generate revenues of $8.1 million per year. Both a baseline and a high-end product are considered in the assessment. The total cost over the 15-year period is between $31.3 (baseline product) and $46.5 million (high-end product). Up front investment equals $3.1 million. The input and cost requirements are summarized in Table 10; the economic performance and returns are summarized in Table 11. Overall, a salmon farm producing 4.5 million pounds per year is expected to yield a net return between $29.5 million baseline and $14.3 million high-end. The analysis also indicates that if the price falls below $0.91 per pound, the farm is not profitable.

Table 7
Basic Production and Cost Requirements, Atlantic Cod

Parameter	*Description*	*Unit*	*Baseline Value*	*High-end Value*
V	cage volume per cohort	m^3	5,000	5,000
acq	cage purchase cost[a]	$/ m^3	15.00	25
inst	cage mooring and installation cost	$/ m^3	3.00	3.00
cm	cage operation and maintenance cost[b]	$/ m^3 / year	1.00	6
stock	number of fingerlings stocked per cohort	1,000 fish	150	150
Sg	stocking weight	gram / fish	50	50
f	ratio of water weight to fingerling weight during transport to farm		5	5
Sp	fingerling cost	$ / fish	0.85	1.50
Fp	feed cost	$ / kg	0.60	0.73
bfix	vessel fixed cost	$ / year	100,000	150,000
bvar	vessel variable and crew cost[c]	$ day	3,000	3,000
Ld	vessel payload	MT	30	30
trip	round trips per day		3	3
Sh	on shore cost[d]	$ / year	150,000	250,000
ins	insurance cost[e]	$ / year	50,000	300,000
fmv	feed management variable cost	$ / cohort / month	0	33.32
scf	solid control BMP plan fixed cost	$ / farm	0	1615.20
scv	solid control BMP plan variable cost	$ / month	0	21.15
dcf	drug and chemical control BMP plan fixed cost	$ / farm	0	1615.20
dcv	drug and chemical control BMP plan variable cost	$ / month	0	21.15
Aff	active feed monitoring fixed cost	$ / farm	0	10,000
afv	active feed monitoring fixed cost	$ / cohort / month	0	33.32
d	annual discount rate		0.07	0.07

Notes:
a. Including feeder and other equipments
b. Including fuel, utilities, diving, repair, etc.
c. Including 4 crews (average $25/hour)
d. Including salaries for 1 manager and 2 office staff
e. Insurance covers fish and other capital

Table 8
Estimated Net Present Value, Investment, Harvest, and Cost, Atlantic Cod

Output Variable	*Description*	*Unit*	*Baseline Value*	*High-end Value*
NPV	net present value	$ million	10.620	-13.375
I	investment	$ million	2.010	3.139
X(T)	average fish harvest	metric ton / month	177	177
N(T)	average number of fish harvested	fish / month	120,535	120,535
W(T)	average harvest fish size	Kg	1.47	1.47
12-E[fq(t)]	average feed quantity	metric ton / year	2,765	2,765
Project Cost	total cost	$ million	35.871	59.867
Cost Share	cage installation	%	5.6	5.2
	cage maintenance	%	2.8	10.2
	boat and crew	%	6.0	4.4
	fingerlings	%	39.5	41.8
	feed	%	10.9	29.8
	onshore and other	%	5.2	8.5
	Total	%	100	100

Table 9
Economic Contributions of Cod Operation, $13.7 million in Annual Sales

Impacts of Aquaculture Cod Offshore Shipments - Producers				
	Direct Impacts	*Indirect Impacts*	*Induced Impacts*	*Total Impacts*
Labor Income Impacts (millions of dollars)	4.00	3.71	4.54	12.25
Output Impacts (millions of dollars)	11.69	13.50	13.64	38.83
Employment Impacts (full-time and part-time jobs)	148.61	99.04	118.99	366.65
Impacts of Aquaculture Cod Offshore Shipments - Wholesalers				
	Direct Impacts	*Indirect Impacts*	*Induced Impacts*	*Total Impacts*
Labor Income Impacts (millions of dollars)	0.55	0.10	0.44	1.09
Output Impacts (millions of dollars)	0.62	0.30	1.32	2.23
Employment Impacts (full-time and part-time jobs)	10.30	2.18	11.45	23.93
Impacts of Aquaculture Cod Offshore Shipments - Grocers				
	Direct Impacts	*Indirect Impacts*	*Induced Impacts*	*Total Impacts*
Labor Income Impacts (millions of dollars)	0.90	0.08	0.72	1.70
Output Impacts (millions of dollars)	0.56	0.22	2.18	2.96
Employment Impacts (full-time and part-time jobs)	31.85	1.67	18.91	52.43
Impacts of Aquaculture Cod Offshore Shipments - Restaurants				
	Direct Impacts	*Indirect Impacts*	*Induced Impacts*	*Total Impacts*
Labor Income Impacts (millions of dollars)	9.72	0.92	8.02	18.66
Output Impacts (millions of dollars)	5.54	2.53	24.16	32.23
Employment Impacts (full-time and part-time jobs)	340.59	20.61	209.33	570.53
Impacts of Aquaculture Cod Offshore Shipments – All Sectors				
	Direct Impacts	*Indirect Impacts*	*Induced Impacts*	*Total Impacts*
Labor Income Impacts (millions of dollars)	15.18	4.81	13.72	33.70
Output Impacts (millions of dollars)	18.41	16.54	41.30	76.25
Employment Impacts (full-time and part-time jobs)	531.36	123.51	358.68	1,013.54

The potential economic impacts of one offshore salmon farm are quite significant. The producing sector generates $18.7 million in total sales or output, $8.2 million in income, and approximately 189 full- and part-time jobs relative to producing sector activities (Table 12). Restaurant sales generate the second highest level of total output—at $17.2 million. The sale of salmon by restaurants, however, generates the highest level of income—approximately $10 million. The number of full- and part-time jobs generated by restaurant activity equals 304. Total sales or output, income, and employment of all

Table 10
Basic Production and Cost Requirements, Atlantic Salmon

Parameter	*Description*	*Unit*	*Baseline Value*	*High-end Value*
V	cage volume per cohort	m^3	5,000	5,000
acq	cage purchase cost[a]	$/ m^3	15.00	25
inst	cage mooring and installation cost	$/ m^3	3.00	3.00
cm	cage operation and maintenance cost[b]	$/ m^3 / year	1.00	6
stock	number of fingerlings stocked per cohort	1,000 fish	45	45
Sg	stocking weight	gram / fish	150	150
f	ratio of water weight to fingerling weight during transport to farm		5	5
Sp	fingerling cost	$ / fish	1.50	1.75
Fp	feed cost	$ / kg	0.73	0.9
bfix	vessel fixed cost	$ / year	100,000	150,000
bvar	vessel variable and crew cost[c]	$ day	3,000	3,000
Ld	vessel payload	MT	30	30
trip	round trips per day		3	3
Sh	on shore cost[d]	$ / year	150,000	250,000
ins	insurance cost[e]	$ / year	50,000	300,000
fmv	feed management variable cost	$ / cohort / month	0	33.32
scf	solid control BMP plan fixed cost	$ / farm	0	1615.20
scv	solid control BMP plan variable cost	$ / month	0	21.15
dcf	drug and chemical control BMP plan fixed cost	$ / farm	0	1615.20
dcv	drug and chemical control BMP plan variable cost	$ / month	0	21.15
aff	active feed monitoring fixed cost	$ / farm	0	10,000
afv	active feed monitoring fixed cost	$ / cohort / month	0	33.32
d	annual discount rate		0.07	0.07

Notes:

a. Including feeder and other equipments
b. Including fuel, utilities, diving, repair, etc.
c. Including 4 crews (average $25/hour)
d. Including salaries for 1 manager and 2 office staff
e. Insurance covers fish and other capital

Table 11

Output Variable	*Description*	*Unit*	*Baseline Value*	*High-end Value*
NPV	net present value	$ million	29.486	14.289
I	investment	$ million	2.010	3.139
x(T)	average fish harvest	metric ton / month	169	169
n(T)	average number of fish harvested	fish / month	37,446	37,446
w(T)	average harvest fish size	Kg	4.52	4.52
12-E[fq(t)]	average feed quantity	metric ton / year	2,619	2,619
Project Cost	total cost	$ million	31.315	46.512
Cost Share	cage installation	%	6.4	6.7
	cage maintenance	%	3.2	13.2
	boat and crew	%	6.0	5.0
	fingerlings	%	24.0	18.8
	feed	%	54.5	45.3
	onshore and other	%	5.9	11.0
	Total	%	100	100

sectors equal, respectively: $38.7 million, $19.6 million, and 534 full- and part-time jobs.

WINTER FLOUNDER (PSEUDOPLEURONECTES AMERICANUS)

Winter flounder is a highly valued flounder by New England and mid-Atlantic consumers. Domestic landings of winter flounder, however, have substantially declined over time. In the 1970s and 1980s, annual landings were typically between 25 and 40 million pounds. Between 1994 and 2004, annual total landings have ranged between 8 and 13 million pounds. Given its highly desirable characteristics, winter flounder is an excellent candidate for offshore aquaculture.

The economic feasibility of producing winter flounder is based on a cage operation and a 15-year period. Expected production is 125 metric tons per month, or 3.3 million pounds per year. The feasibility analysis assumes an average annual price of $4.60 per pound, which is considerably higher than previously observed ex-vessel prices for domestic wild product. The assessment is based on a monthly analysis and then aggregated up to an annual basis; then assessed relative to a 15-year production cycle.

Although the basic technology requires cages, actual production technology differs slightly for winter flounder than for cod and salmon. Stocking and harvesting are restricted to two-month periods per year; stocking occurs between March and April and harvesting occurs between November and December. Input and cost requirements are summarized in Table 13. The total cost of the operation over the 15-year period varies between $7.31 million baseline product and $8.8 million high-end product. See Table 14. The estimated net present value for the baseline product is $1.23 million over the 15-year period. The net present value for the high-end product is negative and equals -$0.3 million. Additional analysis indicates that the operation is no longer economically feasible if the price received falls below $1.59 per pound.

The farm operation is projected to produce 3.3 million pounds of flounder per year, while receiving approximately

$15.2 million is gross sales. The economic activity which might be generated from a flounder aquaculture operation is therefore quite significant. Total sales or output over all sectors is projected to be $81.8 million; total income is projected to be $37.9 million; and total employment is project to equal 1154.7 full- and part-time jobs (Table 15). The primary producing sector generates the highest level of sales or outputs, but the restaurant sector generates the highest levels of both income and employment.

Table 12

Impacts of Aquaculture Salmon Shipments - Producers

	Direct Impacts	*Indirect Impacts*	*Induced Impacts*	*Total Impacts*
Labor Income Impacts (millions of dollars)	3.71	1.16	3.31	8.18
Output Impacts (millions of dollars)	4.71	4.05	9.96	18.72
Employment Impacts (full-time and part-time jobs)	72.11	30.16	86.54	188.81

Impacts of Aquaculture Salmon Shipments – Wholesalers

	Direct Impacts	*Indirect Impacts*	*Induced Impacts*	*Total Impacts*
Labor Income Impacts (millions of dollars)	0.29	0.05	0.23	0.58
Output Impacts (millions of dollars)	0.33	0.16	0.70	1.19
Employment Impacts (full-time and part-time jobs)	5.49	1.16	6.10	12.75

Impacts of Aquaculture Salmon Shipments - Grocers

	Direct Impacts	*Indirect Impacts*	*Induced Impacts*	*Total Impacts*
Labor Income Impacts (millions of dollars)	0.48	0.04	0.39	0.91
Output Impacts (millions of dollars)	0.30	0.12	1.16	1.58
Employment Impacts (full-time and part-time jobs)	16.99	0.89	10.08	27.96

Impacts of Aquaculture Salmon Shipments - Restaurants

	Direct Impacts	*Indirect Impacts*	*Induced Impacts*	*Total Impacts*
Labor Income Impacts (millions of dollars)	5.18	0.49	4.27	9.95
Output Impacts (millions of dollars)	2.95	1.35	12.88	17.18
Employment Impacts (full-time and part-time jobs)	181.58	10.99	111.60	304.16

Impacts of Aquaculture Salmon Shipments – All Sectors

	Direct Impacts	*Indirect Impacts*	*Induced Impacts*	*Total Impacts*
Labor Income Impacts (millions of dollars)	9.67	1.74	8.20	19.62
Output Impacts (millions of dollars)	8.29	5.68	24.71	38.67
Employment Impacts (full-time and part-time jobs)	276.16	43.20	214.32	533.68

Table 13
Basic Production and Cost Requirements, Winter Flounder

Parameter	*Description*	*Unit*	*Baseline Value*	*High-end Value*
V	cage volume per cohort	m^3	5,000	5,000
acq	cage purchase cost[a]	$/ m^3	15.00	25
inst	cage mooring and installation cost	$/ m^3	3.00	3.00
cm	cage operation and maintenance cost[b]	$/ m^3 / year	1.00	6
stock	number of fingerlings stocked per cohort	1,000 fish	130	130
Sg	stocking weight	gram / fish	500	500
f	ratio of water weight to fingerling weight during transport to farm		5	5
Sp	fingerling cost	$ / fish	2.00	2.00
Fp	feed cost	$ / kg	0.65	0.73
bfix	vessel fixed cost	$ / year	20,000	30,000
bvar	vessel variable and crew cost[c]	$ day	3,000	3,000
Ld	vessel payload	MT	30	30
trip	round trips per day		3	3
Sh	on shore cost[d]	$ / year	40,000	70,000
ins	insurance cost[e]	$ / year	10,000	60,000
fmv	feed management variable cost	$ / cohort / month	0	33.32
scf	solid control BMP plan fixed cost	$ / farm	0	1615.20
scv	solid control BMP plan variable cost	$ / month	0	21.15
dcf	drug and chemical control BMP plan fixed cost	$ / farm	0	1615.20
dcv	drug and chemical control BMP plan variable cost	$ / month	0	21.15
Aff	active feed monitoring fixed cost	$ / farm	0	10,000
afv	active feed monitoring fixed cost	$ / cohort / month	0	33.32
d	annual discount rate		0.07	0.07

Notes:

a. Including feeder and other equipments
b. Including fuel, utilities, diving, repair, etc.
c. Including 4 crews (average $25/hour)
d. Including salaries for 1 manager and 2 office staff
e. Insurance covers fish and other capital

Table 14
Estimated Net Present Value, Investment, Harvest, and Cost, Winter Flounder

Output Variable	*Description*	*Unit*	*Baseline Value*	*High-end Value*
NPV	net present value	$ million	1.234	-0.303
I	investment	$ million	0.175	0.286
x(T)	average fish harvest*	metric ton / month	125	125
n(T)	average number of fish harvested*	fish / month	121,791	121,791
w(T)	average harvest fish size	Kg	1.03	1.03
12-E[fq(t)]	average feed quantity	metric ton / year	175	175
Project Cost	total cost	$ million	7.307	8.844
Cost Share	cage installation	%	2.4	3.2
	cage maintenance	%	1.2	6.3
	boat and crew	%	9.0	8.5
	fingerlings	%	66.7	55.1
	feed	%	14.3	13.3
	onshore and other	%	6.3	13.6
	Total	%	100	100

Note: *There are only two cohorts in a year (harvested in Nov. and Dec., respectively). Average annual harvest is the monthly figure times two.

Despite apparent evidence that offshore aquaculture is not only economically feasible but also capable of generating substantial contributions to the economy, there remain many obstacles which may hinder its development and adoption. There are potential uncertainties about obtaining loans, which will be necessary for satisfying up front investment costs. In all instances, these investment costs are quite high and will likely deter individuals or firms from investing in offshore aquaculture. There is considerable uncertainty about what constitutes best management practices.

Table 15

Impacts of Aquaculture Winter Flounder Offshore Shipments -Producers

	Direct Impacts	*Indirect Impacts*	*Induced Impacts*	*Total Impacts*
Labor Income Impacts (millions of dollars)	5.34	3.50	5.20	14.03
Output Impacts (millions of dollars)	13.20	11.37	15.60	40.17
Employment Impacts (full-time and part-time jobs)	219.29	80.04	136.10	435.44

Impacts of Aquaculture Winter Flounder Offshore Shipments – Wholesalers

	Direct Impacts	*Indirect Impacts*	*Induced Impacts*	*Total Impacts*
Labor Income Impacts (millions of dollars)	0.61	0.11	0.49	1.21
Output Impacts (millions of dollars)	0.69	0.33	1.47	2.48
Employment Impacts (full-time and part-time jobs)	11.46	2.42	12.73	26.61

Impacts of Aquaculture Winter Flounder Offshore Shipments - Grocers

	Direct Impacts	*Indirect Impacts*	*Induced Impacts*	*Total Impacts*
Labor Income Impacts (millions of dollars)	1.00	0.09	0.81	1.89
Output Impacts (millions of dollars)	0.62	0.24	2.42	3.29
Employment Impacts (full-time and part-time jobs)	35.41	1.86	21.02	58.30

Impacts of Aquaculture Winter Flounder Offshore Shipments - Restaurants

	Direct Impacts	*Indirect Impacts*	*Induced Impacts*	*Total Impacts*
Labor Income Impacts (millions of dollars)	10.81	1.03	8.92	20.75
Output Impacts (millions of dollars)	6.16	2.81	26.86	35.83
Employment Impacts (full-time and part-time jobs)	378.70	22.92	232.75	634.37

Impacts of Aquaculture Winter Flounder Offshore Shipments – All Sectors

	Direct Impacts	*Indirect Impacts*	*Induced Impacts*	*Total Impacts*
Labor Income Impacts (millions of dollars)	17.76	4.72	15.40	37.89
Output Impacts (millions of dollars)	20.67	14.76	46.35	81.78
Employment Impacts (full-time and part-time jobs)	644.87	107.24	402.61	1154.72

10

Economics of Biotechnology

BIOLOGICAL SCIENCES

There are three primary natural sciences– biology, chemistry and physics. Each breaks out into an ever widening range of sub-disciplines and cross-disciplines, e.g., biochemistry. In each there are distinct engineering specialties, e.g., chemical, genetic, mechanical and, electrical. It is from these that, today, most physical technology flows. Price argued that the relationship between Science and Technology is that of the research-front of one relating to the previous generation or archive of the other. Thus Science operates with the previous generation of Technology while Technology operates with the previous generation of Science. Knowledge in the Natural & Engineering Sciences (NES) is fact-based and subjected to objective, value-free testing in which replicability of results is the test. It is concerned with objective truth, understanding and manipulation of the physical world. It exhibits decreasing tolerance through Time for difference and error as old knowledge is progressively and reductively displaced by the new, i.e., NES knowledge progresses vertically up the ladder of Time. This assumes, however, 'normal science' within an established paradigm not a 'scientific revolution' leading to a quantum leap in understanding even with a 'Kuhnian loss'.

When applied for utilitarian purposes, NES knowledge generates physical technology, i.e., the ability to manipulate Matter/Energy to satisfy human want, needs and desires.

Using it in twenty-five generations we have literally enframed our planet with hundreds of artificial satellites enabling ourselves of planetary riches, making them ready at hand to serve our purpose, from the deepest oceans to the outer reaches of the solar system. Biological science is, however, different from physics and chemistry in a number of ways. These include: the nature of causality and the classification system used to order understanding of the world around us. First, causality in biology differs from that associated with physics. Aristotle identified four causes of things to be the way they are: (i) material cause: that out of which a thing is made, e.g., economic inputs; (ii) formal cause: the form or shape of the final thing, e.g., economic outputs; (iii) efficient cause: the initiating agent, e.g., the entrepreneur or firm; and, (iv) final cause: end purpose or teleos, e.g., satisfaction of consumer wants, needs & desires plus a normal profit. In effect, traditional 'Newtonian' physics relied upon only material and efficient causes. It generally ignored formal and explicitly excluded final causes. Among his many contributions Immanual Kant (1724–1804) established, as a law of nature, that the formal notion of the if-then relationship corresponds to the concept of cause and effect and that there is a single direction to causality, i.e., Time's Arrow only moves from cause to effect, from the past into the present and then out into the future by means of prediction. This law, however, was limited by Kant to matter defined as lifeless stuff objects pushed or pulled by measurable forces through Space/Time. This limitation was required because it was apparent to Kant that material and efficient causes cause and effect were insufficient to explain living things, i.e., biology.

For Kant all works of technological intelligence are finally caused by human purpose. Living things, however, do not require human or divine purpose but rather reflect a 'natural purpose'. Kant called this form of causality purposiveness. He was so convinced of the inherent complexity of living things that he claimed: it is absurd for human beings even to attempt it, or to hope that perhaps some day another Newton might arise who would explain to us, in terms of natural laws cause and effect unordered by any intention, how even a mere blade of grass is produced. This constraint, as we will see, began to loosen with the discovery by Watson and Cricks of the DNA double helix some fifty years ago. Their finding that it could split into complementary strands established the physical basis for the encoding and transmission of genetic information within an individual organism and between generations. In this regard, the New York Times on June 13, 1953 ran an article entitled "Clue to Chemistry of Heredity is Found" calling DNA "a substance as important to biologists as uranium is to nuclear physicists." Gathering momentum ever since, genomics achieved critical mass in 1980 with the U.S. Supreme Court decision in Diamond vs. Chakrabarty. The case involved a patent for a genetically engineered microorganism that breaks down crude oil. The Court observed that Congress had the power to limit such patents but by failing to legislate specifically about genetic patents it had, in effect, allowed gene patenting. The Court's rationale was based on the term 'manufacture' in Section 101 of the U.S. Patent Act: "the production of articles for use from raw materials prepared by giving to these materials new forms, qualities, properties, or combinations whether by hand labor or by machinery." Genes, the Court concluded, were material, i.e., they had tangible material form, even though invisible to the naked eye.

Second, biology uses distinct classification systems or taxonomies to order its subject matter. First, in theoretical biology the world is divided into three spheres: the geosphere of inanimate Matter/Energy; the biosphere of living things; and, the noösphere of human thought. Second, the biosphere itself is divided into kingdoms based on common forms morphology or on evolutionary DNA. There are five morphological kingdoms according to Whitaker including: Kingdom Monera which is made up of prokaryotes, i.e., cells without a nucleus including bacteria and archaea, i.e., organisms originally thought to live only in inhospitable conditions such as temperature, pH-extremes, and radiation. Archaea are considered by Woese to constitute a separate or sixth kingdom; Kingdom Protoctista which is made up of eukaryotes, i.e., cells with a nucleus, that cannot be classified in any of the other kingdoms as fungi, animals, or plants. In general they acquire their food by extending their cell wall around the food material to form a food vacuole; Kingdom Fungi which is made up of eukaryotes such as yeasts, molds and mushrooms which, along with bacteria, are the primary decomposers of organic matter; Kingdom Plantae which is made up of eukaryotes such as trees, flowers, herbs, bushes, grasses, vines, ferns, and mosses that feed by photosynthesis; and, Kingdom Animalia which is made up of eukaryotes that feed by consuming other organisms or parts of them. Kingdoms are, in turn, then progressively sub-divided into Phylum/Division, Class, Order, Family, Tribe, Genus and Species.

Morphological division has been traditional in biology since the time of Linnaeus in the 18th century. With the discovery of the DNA helix, however, a new method of classification has emerged based on genomics beginning in the 1980s. DNA is based on combinations of four nucleotides or a qubit made up of adenine (A), thymine (T), guanine (G) and cytosine (C). These are always paired A-T or C-G. A sequence of three pairs is called a codon encoding an amino acid. Amino acids, in turn, combine to form proteins "the molecular machines of life". The study and manipulation of proteins is called proteomics. Today, biotechnology involves the manipulation of the DNA code or the autobiography of a species. Traditionally and unknowingly, this was done through selective and cross-breeding of plants and animals. In this sense agriculture was the first biotechnology. Direct manipulation of genetic material, however, requires:

(a) the personal knowledge or 'know-how' of molecular biology/chemistry needed to effect a desired change;

(b) the codified knowledge documenting the code's norm state as well as the success or failure of previous manipulations; and,

(c) the tooled knowledge or instrumentation required to effect change in the living code.

Different sections of code generate specific proteins. It is production of specific proteins, their higher order constructs such as enzymes and the pathways of production that are the instrumental objectives of genomics realized in its sister science, proteomics, i.e., the science of proteins. Given the vast array of living things on planet Earth and the different proteins developed and coded by each in its evolutionary struggle for survival, there exists a veritable cornucopia of possible protein codes that may be transferred from one organism to another and/or between types of organisms transgenetic. This implies the ability to adapt every evolutionary success of every life form on the planet to the benefit of humanity.

Thus we can now inject or infect 'natural' with human purpose. We are arguably beginning the final chapter in human dominion over the Earth extending our grasp out from the geosphere to the living core of the biosphere, its DNA. One practical implication is that "it has become possible to think that biology can, for the first time, join physics and chemistry as a 'technoscience'". And this, of course, brings us to the question of biotechnology. And with it we must further distinguish between biotechnology as 'wetware' which is carbon-based artifacts such as genetically modified canola versus 'dryware' which is silicon-based such as current computer chips, bur perhaps not future ones.

TRANSFORMATIVE INNOVATION

In economics we can identify three classes of innovation. First, however, we must distinguish between invention and innovation. An invention is a new artifact or process to make an existing artifact. An innovation, however, is an invention that is successfully brought to market, i.e., it pays its way. Product innovation thus involves bringing a new product to market, e.g., the iPod. Process innovation involves a new and generally more cost-effective way of making an existing product, e.g., the Bessemer process in making steel. An enabling innovation or technology is a process innovation applicable in the production of a wide range of different goods or services in different industries. The printing press, telegraph, telephone, radio, television and the WWW Internet are examples of enabling technologies used across all sectors of the economy. As we can see biotechnology is an enabling technology with respect to existing goods and services but it also promises many product innovations, i.e., new goods and services. All three – product, process and enabling innovations- involve the impact of new knowledge on the economic process. The impact of new knowledge on the production function or a firm is called technological change. Why some things are invented and others are not and why some inventions are successfully innovated and others are not has been called 'the measure of our economic ignorance'. As we will see, advances in biotechnology, specifically bioinformatics, may in future aid economists in satisfying their ignorance which literally means 'want of knowledge'.

SUB-SECTORS

As an enabling innovation biotechnology is like a tidal wave fast approaching the coast line of modern society. The wake of its bow has already arrived and the contours of the economy are slowly eroding and reshaping. When the full crest hits sometime in the next decade it will sweep deep inland altering the landscape of human life forever. It has already reached a number of sectors including agriculture, art, defense, environment, health, informatics, justice and materials technology. Some sectors have already been altered dramatically. This is especially true in agriculture where generically modified food has become a cause célèbre in international trade disputes between the European Union and NAFTA. Even within agriculture, however, the impact of biotechnology is uneven with plant genomics having a greater immediate impact than animal genomics. The enabling nature of biotechnology, its very 'newness', the unevenness of its impact and the varying techniques and technologies used in different sectors presents a problem in the economics of biotechnology. In order to maintain an overview we will use the Industrial Organization Model. This is now a well accepted part of economics with its literature classified by the American Economic Association under category 'L-Industrial Organization''. At present this subject descriptor is formally available only with respect to agricultural biotechnology.

THE IO MODEL

Industrial Organization is the brain-child of the late Joe Bain. His seminal work - Industrial Organization - was published in 1959 (Bain 1968). Using IO, Bain began what has become an ongoing process within the economics profession of linking macroeconomics the study of the economy as a whole to microeconomics consumer, producer and market theory to better understand the way the 'real' world works. It can be called 'meso-economics' in contrast to micro- and macro-economics. The IO Model takes the industry as the basic unit of analysis. In effect it is a taxonomy or classification system with limited predictive power. Its essential prediction is that Basic Condition in an industry determines its Structure that in turn determines the Conduct of its firms that then dètermines the collective Performance of firms in the industry.

The IO schema (Exhibit 1) thus consists of four parts. First, basic conditions face an industry on the supply- production and demand-side consumption of the economic equation. Second, an industry has a Structure or organizational character, the primary elements of which are barriers to entry, the number and size distribution of firms, product differentiation, and the overall elasticity of demand. Third, firms in an industry tend to follow typical patterns of Conduct or behavior in adapting and adjusting to a specific but ever changing and evolving marketplace. Key variables in Conduct include pricing, advertising, capacity, legal tactics and quality of output. In policy terms, Conduct reflects the strategy of the firm in an industry. Fourth, an industry achieves varying levels of Performance with respect to contemporary socio-economic-political goals defined broadly to include social performance, allocative efficiency in terms of profitability, technical efficiency in terms of cost minimization, and innovativeness.

COST STRUCTURE

According to the Standard Model of economics - lternatively known as the Marshallian, Neoclassical or Perfect Competition Model - if at least one factor of production is fixed, i.e., we are in the 'short-run', then adding more and more of a variable input will eventually result in the diminishing marginal product of that variable factor, i.e., the addition to final output will decline and eventually turn negative. This produces the classic 'U'-shaped average cost curve with marginal cost intersecting at the minimum of average cost. With this curve and a given price the profit maximization point for the firm can be determined. Furthermore, when the price is just equal to the minimum point of the average variable cost curve where marginal cost intersects it we have what is called the 'shut-down' point of the firm. At the minimum point of the average total cost curve we have the 'break-even' point. Every point on the marginal cost curve above shut-down represents the supply curve for the firm. Profit maximization will occur where the going price is equal to the marginal cost of the last unit sold, i.e., where the marginal revenue earned equals the cost of the last unit produced. A profit is made on all previous units assuming a fixed price.

All of this became possible with the Marginalist Revolution of the 1870s with the integration into economics of second order differential calculus, specifically constrained maximization. It is important to note that this new calculus began with demand and Jeremy Betham's 'felicitous calculus', i.e., the calculus of human happiness. Unlike the other humanities & social sciences, economic epistemology, i.e., its theory of knowledge, is rooted not in Platonic or Aristotelian idealism but in Epicurean sensationalism. As noted by Alfred Marshall (1920), the most influential successor of Adam Smith (1723-1790) was not an economist but rather Jeremy Bentham (1748-1832), a radical reformer who formalized Utilitarianism as a comprehensive philosophy (Clough 1964).

The budget in terms of income and prices constrains maximization of pleasure by the individual consumer [U = f (x, y); $I = P_X X + P_Y Y$] yielding a demand curve while the cost constrained profit maximization of the firm [$Q = g(K, L)$; $C = P_K K + P_L L$] yields a supply curve. When put together in the 'Marshallian scissors' of supply and demand, a determinant geometric, mathematically precise equilibrium emerges. It is an ideology framed by an 'X' - the intersection of market supply and demand curves - marking the spot where human happiness is to be found, where, at one and the same time, consumers maximize their self-interest and producers their profits; everyone is happy here - if one accepts certain very strict assumptions.

In this situation three assumptions are relevant. First assume all consumers and producers have 'perfect knowledge' in which case, of course, there can be no market for knowledge since everyone has it freely and perfectly. Second assume that human beings are strictly rational, i.e., they are constantly calculating and weighing the relative probabilities of present and future pleasure against present and future pain. Third, while utiles cannot be physically measured let us assume they can be reified, i.e., an abstraction made concrete, in the form of money. The presence of money brings pleasure; its absence brings pain. It is ironic that the Standard Model in economics achieves what Plato, speaking about Art, feared most, that: "not law and the reason of mankind, which by common consent have ever been deemed best, but pleasure and pain will be the rulers in our State" Unlike the Standard Model in sub-atomic physics (Cottinham & Greenwood 1998), however, the economic model is not empirical, i.e., it does not reflect nor pretend to reflect observable reality. Furthermore, it is not experimental, i.e., controlled conditions cannot be maintained nor results replicated. Rather, the Standard Model in economics is normative, specifying conditions under which perfection can be attained, providing the benchmark against which economic reality can be judged, e.g., the cost of monopoly. It is therefore a 'theory of value' reflecting the origins of economics as a branch of moral philosophy. In this sense, the Standard Model of economics is indeed an ideology.

The cost structure of a knowledge-based economy including biotechnology is not the "U'-shaped average cost curve of manufacturing but rather is 'L'-shaped. Consider, hypothetically, that the first unit of Windows VISTA cost $500 million to develop but the second and all subsequent units cost a $1.99 once we have a CD/DVD burner. This highlights the economic significance of copyright and IPRs. Without State-sponsored and enforced IPRs the enormous initial investment required for many innovations would be unprofitable. There are implications to an 'L'-shaped average cost curve. The most obvious is that profit maximization cannot be geometrically specified and only with great difficulty and many assumptions can it be mathematically determined.

Biotechnology also exhibits an 'L'-shaped average cost curve. Consider the goat genetically engineered to produce spider silk in its milk. Much time and effort but relatively moderate cost was required to get the first goat but the second and all subsequent 'copies' is bred like any farm animal at minimal cost because of the 'natural purpose' of living things–to survive and reproduce. Given that it is primarily new knowledge in biotechnology rather than huge capital plant and equipment that plays the critical role of it should not be surprising that intellectual property rights also plays a major role in determining its cost structure of biotechnology.

ENTRY AND EXIT

Under perfect competition it is free entry and exit of consumers and firms from the marketplace allowing: a long run equilibrium with no excess profits: consumers and producer retaining all of their respective surplus; all firms operating at the same scale and using the same vintage of plant and equipment; and, attaining technical and economic efficiency. In this regard it is important to appreciate the difference between technical and economic efficiency. In general, efficiency refers to the ratio of outputs to inputs. To measure efficiency one must therefore be able to calculate both inputs and outputs. This is most easily done in the production of goods rather than services, especially in manufacturing, e.g. cars produced per worker. Technical efficiency is achieved when it is not possible to increase output without increasing inputs. Economic efficiency on the other hand is achieved when the cost of production of a given output is as low as possible. The final determining factor is 'price' or marginal revenue received for the output. Thus all economically efficient solutions are technically efficient but not all technically efficient solutions are economically efficient, that is, something may be technically possible but uneconomic. It does not pay its own way, e.g., space exploration and the military.

Finally, there is allocative efficiency resulting from perfect competition. Allocative efficiency implies all factors of production and all commodities demanded by consumers are in their best use and receive their opportunity cost. Further, it is assumed that there are no external costs or benefits, i.e. all external costs and benefits have been 'internalized' in market price. Three conditions must hold:

(i) Consumer Efficiency: when consumer cannot increase utility by reallocating budget;

(ii) Producer Efficiency: when firm cannot reduce cost by shifting input mix; and,

(iii) Exchange Efficiency: when all gains from trade have been exhausted. Gains from trade to consumer are called consumer surplus which measures the difference between what consumers are willing to pay and what they actually pay for a given quantity of a good or service at market price. Gains from trade to producers are called producer surplus which measures the difference between what producer are willing to accept and what they actually receive for providing a given quantity of output.

This 'efficient' outcome, however, cannot be achieved if there are barriers to entry/exit. Such barriers include economies of scale and of scope, possession of an exclusive input, IPRs or a government franchise. Economies of scale mean that the larger the scale of production, i.e., capital plant and equipment, the lower the cost per unit. At the extreme this leads to one firm, i.e., a natural monopoly, able to supply all market demand at the lowest possible cost. Any firm that enters the industry does so at a smaller scale of production and hence at a higher cost that allows the monopolist to price below any entrant's shutdown point. A monopolist can then raise price after the entrant has exited. The same outcome can occur under oligopoly when large firms attain scale economies and then, in collusion, use predatory pricing to drive entrants out of the market and then use price fixing to maintain excess profits. Economies of scope, unlike economies of scale that generally operate in the production of a single product, are associated with the marketing and distribution of different types of goods and services. Exclusive possession of a critical input to the production process can take two forms - physical and legal. Exclusive possession of a physical input is generally straight forward, e.g., a firm owns the only mine from which the input can be extracted. Without access to that input no competitor can enter the market. Exclusive possession of an intellectual property right is less straight forward. Such intellectual property is sometimes formally protected by copyrights, patents, registered industrial designs and trademarks which are grants of temporary monopoly made by the State.

CONDUCT

In Industrial Organization firms in a given industry tend to follow identifiable patterns of Conduct or behavior in adapting and adjusting to a changing and evolving marketplace. Key mainstream variables include pricing, advertising and product differentiation, capacity, legal tactics, quality of output as well as research & innovation. In policy terms, Conduct constitutes the strategy of the firm. Pricing strategy includes the choice between short-or long-run profit maximization as well as between single and tied goods, e.g., selling printers cheap but ink at a high price. Advertising is intended to persuade consumers–final or intermediary–to buy a particular brand.

ADVERTISING AND MARKETING

As previously noted, advertising is designed to persuade consumers – final or intermediate – to buy a particular brand. Some brands are technically similar but advertising can differentiate them in the consumer's mind, e.g., Tide vs. Cheer, effectively splitting off part of the industry demand curve as its 'owned' share. In the Standard Model of economics only factual product information qualifies as a legitimate expense. Attempting to 'persuade' or influence consumer taste is 'allocatively inefficient' betraying the principle of 'consumer sovereignty', i.e., human wants, needs and desires is the root of the economic process. This mainstream view connects with consumer behaviour research which calls this approach the 'information processing' model. A consumer has a problem, a producer has the solution and the advertiser brings them together. It is a calculatory process. An alternative consumer behavior school of thought, 'hedonics' argues that people buy products to fulfill fantasy, e.g., people do not buy a Rolls Royce for transportation but rather for show.

The 'advertising & marketing' of generically modified products, specifically food (Green) vs. medicine (Red), highlights these divergent approaches. In reaching out to the final consumer generically modified food advertising and marketing generally takes the form of well researched and well meaning 'risk assessments'. Such cost-benefit analyses are presented to a public that generally finds calculatory rationalism distasteful and the concept of probability unintelligible, e.g., everyone knows the odds of winning the lottery yet people keep on buying tickets. It would appear that the chances of winning are over-rated. By contrast the even lower probability of losing the generically modified 'cancer' sweepstakes are similarly over-rated. Attempts have been made to place this question within the context of known/unknown contingencies such as generically modified food safety within Kuhn's 'normal science'. The labeling debate also illustrates the 'information processing' view. At a minimum it would require all generically modified food products to be labeled as such. At a maximum it would require that all generically modified food products be traceable back to the actual field from which they grew. While attempts have been made to highlight the health and safety of generically modified foods little has been done to demonstrate that they 'taste' better. This may be the final hurdle, maybe not. Observers have noted, however, that the generically modified agrifood industry has been rather inept in its 'communication' with the general public. For whatever reasons, to this point in the industry's development, generically modified foods appear to feed nightmares, a.k.a., Franken food, not fantasies in the mind of the final consumer. Given that intermediate rather than final demand currently feeds the biotechnology sector one must also consider what might be called 'intermediate advertising & marketing'. Such activities are conducted by trade associations and lobbyists. The audience is not the consumer but rather decision makers in other industries and in government.

BIOPROSPECTING & PIRACY

While advances in analysis and sequencing now allow researchers and hence firms to experiment with known genetic command codes to build new drugs, enzymes, pathways, proteins et al, the reality is that the raw material for biotechnology is life itself–everywhere and every when. Nature is thus much older and more experienced in designing command codes under a wide range of environmental conditions than emergent biotechnology. Accordingly Nature has become the object of search by the biotech industry for novel code. This search is called 'bioprospecting' and takes two forms: ethnobiology and 'original research' which is self-explanatory. Ethnobiology is the interdisciplinary study of how human societies use or have used flora and fauna to serve human purpose, e.g., for medical or nutritional purposes. Its principal sub-disciplines include ethnobotany, ethnomycology, ethnolichenology, ethnozoology, ethnoecology, paleoethnobotany, and zooarchaeology. The Society of Ethnobiology publishes a journal documenting activities in these fields.

Ethnobiology draws heavily on the knowledge of historical, pre-modern and/or indigenous peoples of the Third and Fourth Worlds. Such knowledge is generally called 'traditional ecological knowledge' with the 1991 Convention on Biological Diversity (CBD) the principles of compensated bioprospecting were established globally with the notable exception of the United States which is not a member of the Convention. The convention recognizes ownership of biological forms like mineral deposits by the Nation-State in which they are found. Efforts by the World Intellectual Property Organization and UNESCO to cede traditional ecological knowledge rights to indigenous peoples themselves rather than the Nation-State in which they live have, so far, failed.

CONTEMPORARY 'RATIONALIZATION'

First, IPRs are created by the State as a protection of, and incentive to, creativity, a.k.a., new knowledge, which otherwise could be used freely by others. Without legislated rights knowledge suffers from the 'free-rider' problem associated with all public goods - one can get something for nothing. This problem is illustrated by the 'L'-shaped average cost curve in all knowledge-based industries. Second, in return the State expects creators to make works available and that a market is created in which such work may be bought and sold. Third, while the State wishes to encourage creativity it does not want to foster harmful market power. Accordingly it limits such rights - in time and space. Rights are generally granted only for:

- a fixed period of time, e.g., a specific number of years or life of the creator plus a fixed number of years; and,
- the 'fixation' of new knowledge in material form, i.e., it is not ideas but rather their expression fixed in material form sometimes called 'a matrix' that receives protection.

Fourth, all knowledge thus eventually enters 'the public domain' where it may be used by one and all without charge or limitation. This 'intellectual commons' is different from the physical commons, e.g., the atmosphere and oceans, which suffer from overuse. By nature and law, the public domain grows and increases with use. Or, in Isaac Newton's terms, 'We all stand on the shoulders of giants'. In law, IPRs are justified as a means to increase the public domain or 'learning'. The public domain plus works still under protection constitute the national knowledge-base. To paraphrase Rosenberg on science, the body of knowledge called the public domain consists of an immense pool to which small annual increments are made at the frontier. The true significance of the public domain is diminished, rather than enhanced, by extreme emphasis on the importance of the most recent increment to that pool, e.g., IPRs. First, as previously explained knowledge assumes three forms: personal & tacit, codified and tooled. In brief, the first is protected by 'know-how' and 'trade secrets'. The second is protected by copyright and trademarks. And the third is protected by patents and industrial design.

Second, what constitutes a matrix is problematic. For example, until 1988 under Canadian copyright recorded extemporaneous music, i.e., music improvised and simultaneously recorded, did not qualify for protection because it was not "reduced to writing or otherwise graphically produced or reproduced" The law, being inherently conservative, concluded that if the matrix was not perceptible by a human being then it was not possible to assess other requirements for protection, e.g., originality, non-obviousness, usefulness, etc. An electron might be a part of the physical world but if one could not see, touch or otherwise perceive it then it had no legal status. Patents are generally composed of an abstract, background of the invention, detailed description of the invention, various diagrams and figures, and the claim language. All these parts of the Patent are important but the actual Patent itself is described and defined in its claim language. The claims are the legal description of what the patent covers. Therefore to understand the patent is to understand its claims. Every patent affords a specific scope of protection unless it is found invalid or unenforceable. Scope is defined by the claims of the patent which are the numbered paragraphs at the end of the patent specification. They are the measure of exclusivity afforded by the patent.

Claim language is specific and has been carefully thought out by the inventor and the author and carefully reviewed and approved by a patent examiner. Each and every word in a claim has been specifically and carefully chosen to define the exact breadth and scope of that claim. This is why it is important to read a claim with no assumptions. Among this bundle of rights the scope and breadth of patents are major concerns in biotechnology: Not only are patents enforced more strongly, but they themselves are more broad and they frequently cover basic research tools. This is particularly the case in biotechnology where, for example, patents have been issued on all transgenic cotton, on biological receptors important in research on a broad category of pharmaceuticals, and on concentrated human stem-cell compositions useful for basic research on the immune system. For this type of situation, and there may be parallels in the computer software area, a patent cannot be analyzed in terms of the monopoly it confers on a single product. Its scope is broader, and the antitrust analysis must reflect this fact. Moreover, the existence of these very broad patents leads to a pattern of cross-licensing among the leading firms of a particular sector—and may be usable to prevent entry by others into that network. Again, there are significant, and novel, antitrust issues.

PATENTS AND DESIGNS

Patents are granted for new and useful compositions of matter e.g., chemical compounds, foods, and medicinal products, machines, manufactured products and industrial processes as well as to improvements to existing ones. In some jurisdictions, patents can also be granted to new plant and new animal forms developed through genetic engineering. Through case law and amendment, U.S. patents have, over time, extended to three basic types: patents of invention, design patents and plant patents. In all cases, registration is required and fees must be paid. To be patentable, an invention, design or plant must be novel, useful and, non-obvious "to one of ordinary skill in the art."

TRADE SECRETS AND KNOW-HOW

Trade secrets and know-how are the least protected form of intellectual property right. Know-how refers literally to knowing how to do something, e.g., how to run a construction project. It includes knowledge and experience of an administrative, commercial, financial or technical nature used in running a business or performing a profession. It is experiential in nature, i.e., it is acquired through practice and experience. It also tends to be 'tacit' rather than 'codified' (OECD 1996) and embodied in an individual rather than in an external matrix. In most countries, know-how is protected by contract binding employees and other agents to confidentiality. When a natural or legal person including a government discovers that know-how has been revealed by an agent without permission, legal recourse is available through breach of contract before the courts. No registration is required. Know-how can be protected without time limit.

Trade secrets can be defined as information of a technical or commercial nature that is not in the public domain nor generally available. It may be a formula, pattern, physical device, idea, process, compilation of information or other information that provides a competitive advantage in the marketplace. It is generally protected by contract binding employees and other agents to confidentiality. Normally the courts require that a trade secret be treated by its owner in such a manner that it can reasonably be expected to prevent the public or competitors from learning about it except by improper acquisition or theft. In the case of electronic data this includes using encryption and "password" technologies. The most famous trade secret is the formula for Coca-Cola. A trade secret may be fixed in written or other codified form or it may be tacit. No registration is required. There is no time limit on a trade secret as long as it remains secret. While know-how and trade secrets are often used as synonyms they need not be so. In the case of management and franchises, for example, know-how is usually accessible to third parties when being used. Single elements may be kept secret but the overall concept cannot be. Indirectly, trade secrets and know-how are protected in genomics by private contract enforceable in the courts. Where in a nation's judicial hierarchy such cases will be heard, however, varies, e.g., in the United States it is at the State level. Some international conventions, e.g., TRIPS and the Andean Pact Industrial Property Convention recognize infringement of both. In effect, when a senior executive moves from one 'major' in one country to one in another, an international form of 'legal' lobotomy is enforce; the executive and new employer may both be held liable. In William Gibson's future world of Neuromancer, corporations protect their know-how and trade secrets by implanting genomically designed "neural bombs" (Gibson 1984). If an employee's loyalty slips, the bomb goes off killing or mentally maiming: the bottom line, the knowledge is protected. Directly, know-how or 'lab bench knowledge' and team work in genomics is similar to that in the Arts. A group of highly talented and creative individuals generate what in economics are called 'economies of team production'. Division and specialization of labour combined with experience and growing trust generates know-how that leads to excellence. Such excellence, in turn, becomes embodied in the trademark of the team or firm together with the financial goodwill associated with it. In this sense, business goodwill is also a form of intellectual property.

SUI GENERIS

Sui generis in Latin means "of its own kind". There are two internationally recognized types of sui generis genomic-related intellectual property rights. These are:

- breeders' rights for 'lines' of plants and animals generated using pre-genomic 'selective breeding' technology; and,
- a special depository right for microorganisms in lieu of traditional patent requirements of a written description and drawings.

THE PANDA'S THUMB

Behind the façade of the contemporary rationalization lays their twisted legal evolution of IPRs. Historical, political and legal evolution is the source of the existing Anglosphere IPR regime, not rational planning and consideration. They are rooted in Common Law precedent creating 'path dependency' as in techno-economic regimes. Once a standard is set all subsequent developments must conform. Put another way, the intellectual property rights regime was not created "by any rational, consistent, social welfare-maximizing public agency". Economist Paul David thus characterizes the existing regime as 'a Panda's thumb', i.e., "a striking example of evolutionary improvisation yielding an appendage that is inelegant yet serviceable". The costs of administering such an awkward and ungainly creature have, however, grown dramatically. In the case of copyright this is due to, among other things, introduction of digitalization as fixation and the internet as publication. Similarly, even due diligence by patent officials is insufficient to cope with the flood of new genomic, nanotech and software patent claims. It is thus problematic if the existing IPR regime continues to inspire new knowledge or inhibit its creation and entry into the public domain. In what follows we examine three aspects of the Panda's Thumb: Statutory vs. Case Law; the Natural vs. the Legal Person; and, Predatory Practices. All affect the biotechnology industry.

STATUTORY Vs. CASE LAW

In the Anglosphere tradition IPRs are both statutory law enacted by a legislature and case law applying precedents set by judges. In general terms Common Law is rooted in precedent while the Civil Code is rooted in principle, i.e., judges are guided by principle not precedent. In this regard, the most important precedent in the development of copyright and arguably all forms of intangible property including 'good will' was Justice Yates' dissenting opinion in the 1769 case of Millar v. Taylor (Commons 1924). He argued, drawing on the Institutes of Justinian one of the sources of the European Civil

Code, that ideas are not the object of property rights because they are like wild animals or ferae naturae. Once set free they belong to no one and everyone at the same time, i.e., they are in the public domain. It is only their expression fixed in material form–commonly known as a work–that qualifies for protection.

NATURAL Vs. LEGAL PERSON

A Natural Person is a living human being; a Legal Person is a body corporate. The vast bulk of productive assets are owned by fictitious Legal Persons such as corporations, companies, sociétés, Gesellschaften. Such persons are birthed under incorporation statutes that allow them to engage in a wide variety of profit making and charitable activities. In the Anglosphere tradition, however, Legal and Natural Persons increasingly enjoy the same rights (Nace 2005) while under Civil Code they enjoy different rights especially with respect to IPRs.

PREDATORY PRACTICES

Another implication of State-sponsored IPRs is their predatory rather than defensive use. Beyond the Mercantilist tendencies of some Nation-States this includes 'patent wars' and 'copyright misuse'. In the case of patents, some corporations spend enormous sums of money on research projects that fail for one reason or another. Nonetheless, everything that can be patented is patented. These patents may be retained or sold to a patent holding company of one form or another. If a rival or competitor emerges who subsequently succeeds in making the technology work then that competitor may be charged with patent infringement. Whether the charge is valid or not, the rival faces enormous legal costs defending itself or settling out of court. Both ways, competition is restrained and innovation inhibited. Biotechnology, however, is also subject to other multilateral codes of conduct beyond IPRs. These, in general, impose specific obligations rather than 'national treatment'. Excluding multilateral agreements with tangential implications for biotechnology such as those covering the environment, e.g., Kyoto and the Law of the Seas, as well as health, e.g., communicable diseases,

PRESENT STATUS OF BIOTECHNOLOGY

Biotechnology today is used in primary production, health and industry. Platform technology such as genetic modification, DNA sequencing, bioinformatics and metabolic pathway engineering have commercial uses in several application fields. The main current uses of biotechnology in primary production are for plant and animal breeding and diagnostics, with a few applications in veterinary medicine. Human health applications include therapeutics, diagnostics, and pharmacokinetics to improve prescribing practices, functional foods and nutraceuticals, and some medial devices. Industrial applications include the use of biotechnological processes to produce chemicals, plastics, and enzymes, environmental applications such as bioremedication and biosensors, methods to reduce the environmental effects or costs of resource extraction, and the production of biofuels. Several applications, such as biopharmaceuticals, in vitro diagnostics, some types of genetically modified crops, and enzymes are comparatively "mature" technologies. Many other applications have limited commercial viability without government support e.g. biofuels and biomining or are still in the experimental stage, such as regenerative medicine and health therapies based on RNA interference.

BIOTECHNOLOGY IN 2015

What types of biotechnology applications are likely to reach the market by 2015? Regulatory requirements in agriculture and health provide data that can be used to estimate the types of genetically modified (GM) plant varieties and health therapies that will be available by then. There are far less data for other biotechnology applications, with estimates based on past trends in scientific discoveries, production, or employment.

Based on past trends, GM field trial data, and company reports, it is estimated that by 2015 approximately half of global production of the major food, feed and industrial feedstock crops is likely to come from plant varieties developed using one or more types of biotechnology. There biotechnologies include not only GM but also intragenics, gene shuffling and marker assisted selection. Several novel agronomic and product quality traits will reach the market for a growing number of crops. Biotechnologies, other than GM, will be used to improve livestock for dairy and meat. GM will increasingly used to develop animal varieties that can produce valuable pharmaceuticals or other compounds in milk. In health, biotechnological knowledge will play a role in the development of all types of therapies. It will no longer be meaningful to separate the pharmaceutical sector from the health biotechnology sector. Pharmacogenetics will develop rapidly, influencing the design of clinical trials and prescribing practices. The value of biochemicals other than pharmaceuticals could increase form 1.8% of all chemical production in 2005 to between 12% and 20% by 2015. biofuel production could partly shift form starch-based bioethanol to higher energy density fuels manufactured from sugar cane or to bioethanol from lignocellulosic feedstock such as grasses and wood.

EMERGING BIOECONOMY BUSINESS

Social, economic and technological factors will create new business opportunities for biotechnology, requiring new types of business models. The main business models to date have been the small, DEDICATED BIOTECHNOLOGY FIRM (DEDICATED BIOTECHNOLOGY FIRM) that specializes in research and sells knowledge to large firms, and the large integrated firm that performs R&D and manufactures and distributes products. This structure characterizes the health sector. In primary production, gene modification technology, as profitability depends on the ability to scale up production. This requires specialized engineering knowledge and large capital investment.

We identifie two business models that could emerge in the future: collaborative models for sharing knowledge and reducing research costs, and integrator models to create and maintain markets, collaborative models are relevant to all application areas. Their adoption, combined with new business opportunities for non-food biomass crops, could revitalize DEDICATED BIOTECHNOLOGY FIRMs in primary production and in industry. Integrator models could develop in health biotechnology to manage the complexity of predictive and preventive medicine, based on biomarkers, pharmacogenetics, shrinking markets for individual drugs, and the analysis of complex health databases.

BIOECONOMY IN 2030

What is the bioeconomy of 2030 likely to look? describe a "probable" bioeconomy in 2030 and develops two fictional scenarios that explore the interaction of different factors on possible futures. The 'probable' bioeconomy builds on the types of products that are likely to reach the market by 2015. Within the OECD region, biotechnology could contribute to 2.7% of GDP in 2030, with the largest economic contribution of biotechnology in industry and in primary production. The economic contribution of biotechnology could be even greater in developing countries, due to the importance of these two sectors to their economies.

The scenarios assume an increasingly multi-polar world, with no single country or region dominating world affairs. They include plausible events that could influence the emerging bioeconomy. The results highlight the importance of good governance, including international cooperation, and technology competitiveness in influencing the future. Complex scientific challenges and poorly designed renewable electricity combined with technical breakthroughs in battery technology could result in electrical vehicles out- competing biofuel transport systems. Public attitudes could result in electrical vehicles out-competing biofuel transport systems. Public attitudes could result in some biotechnology not reaching their potential. An example is predictive and preventive medicine, where the advance of this technology could be limited by public resistance to poorly planned and intrusive healthcare system.

BIO ECONOMIC POLICY

The social and economic benefits of the bioeconomic will depend on good policy decisions. The required mix of policies is linked to the potential economic impacts of biotechnology innovations on the wider economy. Each type of innovation can have incremental, disruptive or radical effects. In many but not all cases incremental innovations fit will within existing economic and regulatory structures. Disruptive and radical innovations can lead to the demise of firms and industrial structures, creating greater policy challenges, but they can also result in large improvements in productivity. We identifie policy options to address challenges in primary production, health and industrial biotechnology. It also looks at cross-cutting issues for intellectual property and for knowledge spillovers and integration, global challenges, and the need to develop policies over both the short and long term. Primary production provides a diverse range of policy challenges. Examples include the need to simplify regulation, encourage the use of biotechnology to improve the nutritional content of staple crops in developing countries, ensure unhindered trade in agriculture commodities, and manage a decline in the economic viability of cool-climate forestry resources for low value commodities such as pulp and paper.

The main challenges for health applications are to better align private incentives for developing health therapies with public health goals and to manage a transition to regenerative medicine and predictive and preventive medicine, both of which could disrupt current healthcare systems. Industrial biotechnology faces multiple futures due to competitive alternatives from both outside and within biotechnology. Policy needs to flexible adapt to different outcomes and prevent "lock-in" to inferior technological solutions. The role biotechnology could play in addressing what are considered the most serious challenges to world economies and societies over the next decades. These challenges include providing food, water, energy, healthcare and other resources and services to a world that will see its population increase by a third in the face of mounting environmental stresses over the next 20 years. The bioeconomy can have a major impact in many of these areas to ensure long term economic and environmental sustainability.

FOUNDATION OF BIO ECONOMY

Getting the most out of the bioeconomy will require identifying and preparing for a range of possible futures to prevent locking-in inferior technological solutions. To achieve this, broad approaches, such as creating and maintaining markets for environmentally sustainable products, funding basic and applied research, and investing in multi-purpose infrastructure and education, will need to be combined with shorter term policies, over the next five years, to establish a foundation for future applications. These foundational policies include:

1. In *agriculture*, encourage the application of biotechnology to improve plant and animal varieties through improving access to technologies for use in a wider range of plants, expanding the number of firms and research institutes that can use biotechnology particularly in developing countries, and fostering public dialogue.
2. In *health*, develop regulatory, research, and health record systems which can link prescribing histories, genetic and other information, to support long-term follow-up research into health outcomes.
3. In *industry*, increase support for the adoption and use of internationally accepted standards for life cycle analysis, along with other incentives to reward environmentally sustainable technologies (*e.g.* boosting research into high energy density biofuels).

The bioeconomy will be global, with heavy involvement especially in agricultural and industrial applications. Approximately 75 percent of the future economic contribution of biotechnology and large environmental benefits are likely to come from these two areas. Yet, over 80 percent of research investments in biotechnology by the private and public sectors go to health applications.

1. Boost research in agricultural and industrial biotechnologies by increasing public research investment, reducing regulatory burdens and encouraging private-public partnerships.

2. Encourage the use of biotechnology to address global environmental issues such as climate change and fishery depletion by supporting international agreements to create and sustain markets for environmentally sustainable biotechnology products.

BIOTECHNOLOGY IN HEALTH

As countries grapple with soaring health expenditures, the high cost of many health biotechnologies will be difficult to justify without commensurate health improvements in health outcomes. Furthermore, some emerging technologies, such as regenerative medicine and personalised and preventive medicine, could require far-reaching changes in healthcare delivery.

1. Ensure that private incentives for developing health therapies are better aligned with the public interest in accessible, effective and safe treatments.
2. Continue actively developing regulatory systems for healthcare products that incorporate pharmacogenetics.
3. Support long term research, using population-based medical databases, into health outcomes.
4. Analyse the long-term impacts of regenerative and personalised medicine on healthcare, including data confidentiality, new models for healthcare delivery, and new relationships between doctors and patients.
5. Examine the social, ethical and physical consequences of longer life spans.

BARRIERS TO APPLY TECHNOLOGY

Several biotechnologies that promise productivity improvements, better health, or environmental sustainability could disrupt current business models and economic structures. Many of these technologies will not reach their potential unless they can overcome economic and social barriers to their development.

1. Implement flexible policies that can adapt to and support socially and economically beneficial disruptive biotechnologies.

2. Fund foresight research to identify beneficial disruptive biotechnologies and the types of incentives, infrastructure, regulation, education, and business models that would support their development.

MEASURES TO REDUCE BARRIERS TO BIOTECHNOLOGY APPLICATION

High research costs, regulatory barriers, and market concentration can prevent new entrants, hindering biotechnological innovation, especially for small market applications.

1. Identify factors that can prevent the development of competitive and innovative markets for specific biotechnology applications.
2. Evaluate possible policy actions that could free up markets and access to knowledge, including encouraging public research institutions to adopt intellectual property guidelines that support rapid innovation and collaborative mechanisms for sharing knowledge.

PROMOTION OF BIOTECHNOLOGY RESEARCH

Knowledge spillovers across research disciplines and commercial applications can maximize the economic and social of the bioeconomy. Support for integration requires coordinated actions that draw on the expertise of numerous government ministries, including those responsible for agriculture, education, environment, health, industry, natural resources, and research.

1. Although coordinating policies across government ministries has always been a challenge, the benefits from promoting the integration of biotechnology and research should be worth the effort.

Many of the policies to support the bioeconomy will require the active participation of citizens and firms. Governments need to address some of the misconceptions around biotechnology and describe the different alternatives for managing sustainability.

1. Create an active and sustained dialogue with society and industry on the socio-economic and ethical implications, benefits, and requirements of biotechnologies.

Biotechnology offers technological solutions for many of the health and resource-based challenges facing the world. It can increase the supply and environmental sustainability of food, feed and fibre production, improve water quality, provide renewable energy, improve the health of animals and people, and help maintain biodiversity by detecting invasive species. Yet biotechnology is unlikely to fulfil its potential without appropriate regional, national and, in some cases, global policies to support its development and application. A bioeconomy can be thought of as a world where biotechnology contributes to a significant share of economic output. The emerging bioeconomy is likely to involve three elements: the use of advanced knowledge of genes and complex cell processes to develop new processes and products, the use of renewable biomass and efficient bioprocesses to support sustainable production, and the integration of biotechnology knowledge and applications across sectors.

There are three main sectors where biotechnology can be applied: agriculture, health, and industry. While primary production includes all living natural resources, such as forests, plant crops, livestock animals, insects, fish and other marine resources, the main current uses of biotechnology are for plant and animal breeding and diagnostics. Human health applications include therapeutics, diagnostics, pharmacogenetics to improve prescribing practices, functional foods and nutraceuticals, and some medical devices. Industrial applications include the use of biotechnological processes to produce chemicals, plastics, and enzymes, environmental applications such as bioremediation to clean up polluted soils, biosensors, methods to reduce the environmental effects or costs of resource extraction, and the production of biofuels. Several applications, such as biopharmaceuticals, *in vitro* diagnostics, some types of genetically modified crops, and enzymes are comparatively "mature" technologies. Many other applications have limited commercial viability without supportive policies such as *e.g.* biofuels and bioplastics or are still in the experimental stage, such as regenerative medicine and health therapies based on RNA interference.

The future bioeconomy will be global. Rapid income and population growth will ensure that the main markets for biotechnology in agriculture and industry will be in developing countries. Rising levels of educational achievement across the developing world, particularly at the tertiary level, will create centres of biotechnology research that can address some of the problems that are likely to develop in these countries, including a growing need for low carbon energy, clean water, and highyield agricultural crops that can tolerate drought, heat and other stresses.

What will the future bioeconomy look like? Two characteristics of biotechnology that are not shared by many other technologies improve our ability to predict the future applications of biotechnology. The first consists of regulatory requirements for some agricultural and health biotechnologies. These leave a data trail that can be used to predict what will possibly reach the market over the next five to seven years. The second characteristic is that biotechnology is frequently used as a process technology to make existing products such as fuels, plastics, and crop varieties. It can also be used to produce entirely new products such as medicines to treat cancer. For all of these examples, the problems that need to be solved are known in advance. These include the problem diseases, the types of crop traits that would improve agricultural output, and the types of industrial products that can be produced using biomass. In addition, the size of the potential market for products such as biofuels or anti-cancer drugs can be estimated with a reasonable degree of accuracy. Nevertheless, there are many unknowns, including the rate of technological advance and the ability of biotechnologies to compete with alternative technologies.

The use of biotechnology in agriculture is an evolving success story. By 2015, approximately half of global production of the major food, feed and industrial feedstock crops could come from plant varieties developed using one or more types of biotechnology. These biotechnologies include not only genetic modification (GM) but also intragenics, gene shuffling and marker assisted selection. Research into agronomic traits to improve yields and resistance to stresses such as drought, salinity and high temperatures has increased rapidly since the early 1990s, as shown by the increase in the number of GM field trials of agronomic traits by small and large firms and by public research institutions. A detailed analysis of this field trial data indicates that research will lead to improved crop varieties with agronomic traits reaching the market between 2010 and 2015, particularly for major food and feed crops such as maize and soybeans. Some of the agronomic traits will also be available for alfalfa, cotton, potato, rice, tomato and wheat varieties. Biotechnologies, other than GM, will be widely used to improve the quality and health of livestock for dairy and meat.

In health, biotechnological knowledge will play a role in the development of all therapies by 2015, including both small molecule pharmaceuticals and large molecule biopharmaceuticals. Pharmacogenetics will develop rapidly, influencing the design of clinical trials and prescribing practices. In industry, the value of biochemicals other than pharmaceuticals could increase from 1.8% of all chemical production in 2005 to between 12% and 20% by 2015. Biofuel production could partly shift from starch-based bioethanol to higher energy density fuels manufactured from sugar cane or to bioethanol from lignocellulosic feedstock such as grasses and wood. The development of the bioeconomy requires successful innovation. Biotechnology R&D must be performed, paid for, and result in commercially viable products and products. This process is influenced by many factors, including regulatory conditions, intellectual property, human resources, social acceptance, market structure, and business models.

Regulations to ensure the safety and efficacy of biotechnology products influence research costs and the types of research that are commercially viable. As shown in Table 1, pure regulatory costs are highest for genetically modified plant varieties ranging from USD 0.4 million to USD 13.5 million per variety and for the open release of genetically modified micro-organisms (approximately USD 3 million per release), such as for bioremediation to clean up polluted soils. In health, the future of regulation is not clear, with economic pressures and technical opportunities pushing the system in different directions. Increasing development costs could result in regulatory changes that increase the market for individual pharmaceuticals by extending the effective life of patents. Alternatively, technological developments could add to regulatory requirements and reduce the size of these markets.

Table 1
Indicative Regulatory Costs to Commercialise a Biotechnology Product

(USD thousands)

Agriculture	
Plant	
GM[2]	435-13 460
MAS crop[3]	5-11
Animal	
Vaccine[4]	242-469
Therapeutic[5]	176-329
Diagnostic[4]	9-189
Health	
Therapeutics[6]	1300
In vitro diagnostics	150-600
Industry	
GM open release[8]	1 200-3 00
GM in closed loop	Unknown

Intellectual property rights could be increasingly used by both firms and universities to encourage knowledge sharing through collaborative mechanisms such as patent pools or research consortia. Social attitudes to biotechnology will continue to influence market opportunities, but public opinion can change, for instance when biotechnology products provide significant benefits for consumers or the environment. Social, economic and technological factors will create new business opportunities for biotechnology, requiring new types of business models. The main business models to date have been the small, dedicated biotechnology firm that specialises in research and sells knowledge to large firms, and the large integrated firm that performs R&D and manufactures and distributes products. This structure characterises the health sector, where there are six times as many dedicated biotechnology firms than in agriculture and ten times as many as in industry. In agriculture, gene modification technology has created economies of scope and scale that have driven rapid corporate concentration. Only a few dedicated biotechnology firms have been active in industrial biotechnology, as profitability depends on the ability to scale up production. This requires specialised engineering knowledge and large capital investment. Both dedicated biotechnology firms and large integrated firms will continue to play a role in 2030.

Two business models could become increasingly important in the future: collaborative models for sharing knowledge between entities and reducing research costs, and integrator models that coordinate various disperate actors to create and maintain markets. Collaborative models are relevant to all application areas. Their adoption, combined with new business opportunities for non-food biomass crops, could revitalise dedicated biotechnology firms in agriculture and in industry. Integrator models could develop in health biotechnology to manage the complexity of predictive and preventive medicine, based on biomarkers, pharmacogenetics, shrinking markets for individual drugs, and the analysis of complex health databases.

The application of biotechnology to improve and manage food, feed and fibre crops is likely to increase substantially to 2030, driven by rising demand and increased agronomic stresses from climate change. In addition, the expectation of a long-term increase in the cost of fossil fuels from a decline in the supply of low-cost sources of petroleum; an increase in demand for energy; and restrictions on the production of greenhouse gases (GHGs) could create a growing market for biomass, including non-food crops such as grasses and trees, as a feedstock for biofuels, chemicals and plastics. Other potential biotechnology markets include the use of plants to produce valuable chemicals such as biopharmaceuticals and the production of nutraceuticals from plant and animal sources. All of these trends are likely to increase investment in agricultural technologies.

Some of the main challenges for agriculture are social and institutional factors, including public opposition to biotechnology, a lack of supportive regulation, and barriers to the use of biotechnology in developing countries. First, public opposition to GM food crops or GM or cloned animals is unlikely to halt the use of biotechnology, but it may drive firms to alter the *type* of biotechnology that they use. Second, the potential market for biomass is likely to be strongly dependent over the future on regulatory policies to shift economies towards zero- or low-carbon energy sources. Third, much of the future growth of agriculture will be in developing countries. These countries will need to increase their capacity to use biotechnology in order to develop improved food, feed and fibre crops that are adapted to local growing conditions.

Technological developments are creating both new opportunities and major challenges for existing business models in health. Regenerative medicine, pharmacogenetics, and predictive and preventive medicine will shrink markets for individual drugs, but pharmacogenetics could also reduce the share of new molecules that fail in clinical trials, reducing drug development costs. On the other hand, predictive and preventive medicine could be hugely expensive to develop, due to the cost of long-term trials to validate thousands of potential biomarkers.

Many social and institutional challenges will also arise in health applications. The ability to create and analyse large databases of genetic, phenotypic, prescribing, and health outcome information will be essential to predictive and preventive medicine. The construction of these databases will require solutions to confidentiality issues and the question of whether patients will be required to release information on risk factors to insurers. The increasing ability to discover adverse drug reactions or outcomes from analysing large longitudinal databases will increase risks for pharmaceutical firms and make it difficult to predict future sales. At the same time, these approaches could identify unknown health benefits, creating new markets.

In industry, the concept of a biorefinery that can use different types of biomass inputs to flexibly produce different products has elements of a new business model. The main challenges in the near term for biorefineries are logistical. Biorefineries need to be located close to sources of biomass because of high transport costs. In the longer term, the biorefinery business model will be challenged by technological developments in metabolic pathway engineering and synthetic biology. These two technologies have the potential to develop micro-organisms capable of producing a number of products, including carbon-based fuels and chemicals, with very little biomass feedstock. These production systems would draw energy from the sun and carbon from the atmosphere. If successful, the economic future of biorefineries could be limited to the production of high-weight and low-value products, such as biofuels, in regions with ample supplies of low-cost biomass. There can be three scenarios to examine the bioeconomy in 2030. The first scenario estimates the economic impact of the "probable" bioeconomy in 2030, assuming steady technological progress and a "business as usual" policy environment. The second two scenarios are fictional and examine how different drivers and events might shape the future bioeconomy.

The probable bioeconomy: Several biotechnologies with a high probability of reaching the market by 2030 are summarised in Table 2. The use of these biotechnologies in 2030 is estimated to contribute to 35% of the output of chemicals and other industrial products that can be manufactured using biotechnology, to 80% of pharmaceuticals and diagnostic production, and to approximately 50% of agricultural output. Given these figures, a "business as usual" estimate is that biotechnology could contribute up to approximately 2.7% of GDP in the OECD by 2030.

Biotechnology could account for an even higher share of GDP in non- OECD countries, due to the greater importance to GDP of primary and industrial production compared to OECD countries.

These figures underestimate the potential for biotechnology in 2030, as they exclude biofuels, new applications that are not currently imaginable, and impacts that are difficult to measure in monetary terms. Such impacts include the effect of health biotechnology on the length and quality of life and the environmental benefits of agricultural and industrial biotechnologies. Furthermore, they do not take into account increases in the output of each application, such as an increase in agricultural output in response to increasing demand for biomass as an industrial feedstock.

A striking implication of these estimates is that the economic contribution of biotechnology is potentially greatest in industrial applications, with 39% of the total output of biotechnology in this sector, followed by agriculture with 36% of the total and health applications at 25% of the total. These results are in marked contrast to an OECD estimate of the distribution of R&D expenditures by businesses in 2003, as shown in. The lion's share of private sector R&D investment, 87%, went to health applications in 2003, with only 2% of biotechnology R&D expenditures spent on industrial applications.

The mismatch between recent R&D investment and the potential economic contribution of biotechnology could partly reflect higher R&D productivity in agricultural and industrial biotechnology compared to health biotechnology. A lack of policy incentives, supporting regulations, skilled researchers, or complementary investment in public sector R&D could also play a role. The probable scenario describes a future bioeconomy with evolutionary advances from the use of biotechnology in agriculture, health, and industry, but the full potential of biotechnology is not realised. How biotechnology could result or not in more revolutionary changes are explored in the two fictional scenarios.

Table 2
Biotechnology with a High Probability of Reaching the Market by 2030

Agriculture	*Health*	*Industry*
Widespread use of marker assisted selection (MAS) in plant livestock fish and shellfish breeding	Many new pharmaceuticals and vaccines, based in part on biotechnological knowledge, receiving marketing approval each year.	Improved enzymes for a growing range of applications in the chemical sector.
Genetically modified (GM) varieties of major crops and trees with improved starch, oil, and lignin content to improve industrial processing and conversion yields.	Greater use of pharmacogenetics in clinical trials and in prescribing practice, with a fall in the percentage of patients eligible for treatment with a given therapeutic.	Improved micro-organisms that can produce an increasing number of chemical products in one step, some of which build on genes identified through bioprospecting
GM plants and animals for producing pharmaceuticals and other valuable compounds.	Improved safety and efficacy of therapeutic treatments due to linking pharmacogenetic date, prescribing data, and long-term health outcomes.	Biosensors for real-time monitoring of environmental pollutants and biometrics for identifying people
Improve varieties of major food and feed crops with higher yield, pest resistance and stress tolerance, developed through GM, MAS, intragenics or digenesis	Extensive screening for multiple genetic risk factors for common diseases such as arthritis where genetics is a contributing cause.	High energy density befouls produced from sugar cane and cellulosic sources of biomass.
More diagnostics for genetic traits and diseases of livestock, fish and shellfish.	Improved drug delivery systems from convergence between biotechnology and nanotechnology.	Greater market share for biomaterials such as bioplastics, especially in niche areas where they provide some advantage.
Cloning of high-value animal breeding stock	New nutraceuticals, some of which will be produced by GM micro-organisms and others form plant or marine extracts.	
Major staple crops of developing countries enhanced with vitamins or trace nutrients, using GM technology	Low-cost genetic testing of risk factors for chronic diseases such as arthritis, Type II diabetes, health diseases, and some cancers	
	Regenerative medicine providing better management of diabetes and replacement or repair of some types of damaged tissue.	

Up to 2030, the potential revolutionary effects of biotechnology will derive from both the *extent* to which specific biotechnologies are used and solutions to technical problems. The challenges are greatest in health and industry. In health, regenerative medicine and preventive and predictive medicine have the potential to revolutionize health care services and to significantly improve the quality of life. Some developments in both of these areas are possible by 2030, but both face major barriers that could limit both technical advances and the extent of use. In industry, biotechnology offers the means to manufacture a wide range of chemicals and high energy density biofuels, but this will require major technical breakthroughs and policies to ensure that these production systems are environmentally sustainable.

The two fictional scenarios extend technology trends to 2015 up to 2030, assume a multi-polar world, and include plausible natural and political events that could influence the bioeconomy. An analysis of the scenarios showed that two factors will be key in shaping the future bioeconomy: the quality of governance defined as the system of regulations and policies that influence the development of the bioeconomy and the economic competitiveness of biotechnological innovations.

The fictional scenarios describe how a change in the funding system for health therapies could encourage rapid innovation in regenerative medicine. In another fictional scenario, public attitudes result in some biotechnologies not reaching their potential. An example is predictive and preventive medicine, where the advance of this technology is limited by public resistance to poorly planned and intrusive healthcare systems. The fictional scenarios also explore different technological outcomes such as growing competition between biofuels derived from biomass, algal biofuels, and electrical transport systems. Problems with the competitiveness of environmentally sustainable technologies are exacerbated by insufficient long-term, credible support for promising technologies.

One lesson from the scenarios is that the future development of the bioeconomy will be shaped by how governments react to future crises such as those caused by finance, food scarcity or pandemics. The future will also be influenced by international co-operation, especially with developing countries, and incentive structures for research and markets. Incentives influence the types of biotechnologies that are commercially viable and the distribution of its benefits. The structure of incentives can also support environmentally sustainable technologies over less benign alternatives or the opposite.

POLICY ISSUES

Achieving the full promise of the bioeconomy by 2030 requires a policy framework that can address technological, economic and institutional challenges. Some biotechnology applications are only likely to require minor adjustments to current policies. Other areas of biotechnology will not develop their full potential without major policy interventions and new policy mechanisms. The required mix of policies is linked to the potential economic impacts of biotechnological innovations on the wider economy. Each type of innovation can have incremental, disruptive or radical effects. In many but not all cases incremental innovations fit well within existing economic and regulatory structures. Disruptive and radical technologies generally have a longer time horizon than incremental technologies and can lead to the demise of firms and industrial structures, creating greater policy challenges, but they can also result in large improvements in productivity. The challenge is to develop a policy framework that can flexibly support the economic and social benefits of each type of technology. Policy will need to be able to address challenges for the use of biotechnology in each of the three main application fields viz agriculture, health and industry, manage cross-cutting issues for intellectual property and integration across applications, and tackle global challenges.

Agriculture provides a diverse range of policy challenges. Examples include the need to simplify regulation, encourage the use of biotechnology to improve the nutritional content of staple crops in developing countries, ensure unhindered trade in agricultural commodities, and manage a decline in the economic viability of some sectors when faced with competition from more efficient producers. The main challenges for health applications are to better align private incentives for developing health therapies with public health goals and to manage a transition to regenerative medicine and predictive and preventive medicine, both of which could disrupt current healthcare systems. Industrial biotechnology faces multiple futures due to competitive alternatives from both outside and within biotechnology. Efficient policies to support many industrial biotechnologies will need to be linked to life cycle analysis standards to identify the most environmentally sustainable alternatives. Obtaining the full benefits of the bioeconomy will require purposive goaloriented policy. This will require leadership, primarily by governments but also by leading firms, to establish goals for the application of biotechnology to agriculture, industry and health; to put in place the structural conditions required to achieve success such as obtaining regional and international agreements; and to develop mechanisms to ensure that policy can flexibly adapt to new opportunities.

11

Sustainable Development

CONCEPT THEME

According J.Coomer, The sustainable society is one that lives within the self-perpetuating limits of its environment. That society... is not a "no growth" society... It is rather, a society that recognizes the limits of growth... and looks for alternative ways of growing. C. Howe, defines sustainable development in terms of activities should be considered that would be aimed at maintaining over time a constant effective natural resource base. This concept was proposed by Page and implies not an unchanging resource base but a set of resource reserves, technologies, and policy controls that maintain or expand the production possibilities of future generations. As per the views of IUCN and UNEP, sustainable development - means maintenance of essential ecological processes and life support systems, the preservation of genetic diversity, and the sustainable utilization of species and ecosystems. Sustainable development - development that is likely to achieve lasting satisfaction of human needs and improvement of the quality of human life.

According to Clark and R. Munn, sustainable development is a major challenge of the coming decades is to learn how long-term large-scale interactions between environment and development can be better managed to increase the prospects for ecologically sustainable improvements in human well-being. Repetto states that the core of the idea of sustainability, then, is the concept that current decisions should not impair the prospects for maintaining or improving future living standards... This implies that our economic systems should be managed so that we can live off the dividend of our resources, maintaining and improving the asset base. This principle also has much in common with the ideal concept of income that accountants seek to determine: the greatest amount that can be consumed in the current period without reducing prospects for consumption in the future. This does not mean that sustainable development demands the preservation of the current stock of natural resources or any particular mix of human, physical and natural assets. As development proceeds, the composition of the underlying asset base changes. There is broad agreement that pursuing policies that imperil the welfare of future generations, who are unrepresented in any political or economic forum, is unfair.

According World Commission on Environment and Development, sustainable development is the ability of humanity to ensure that it meets the needs of the present without compromising the ability of future generations to meet their own needs. Sustainable development is not a fixed state of harmony, but rather a process of change in which the exploitation of resources, the direction of investments, the orientation of technological development and institutional changes are made consistent with future as well as present needs. Barbier views that the concept of sustainable economic development as applied to the Third World... is therefore directly concerned with increasing the material standard of living of the poor at the "grassroots" level, which can be quantitatively measured in terms of increased food, real income, educational services, health care, sanitation and water supply, emergency stocks of food and cash, etc., and only indirectly concerned with economic growth at the aggregate, commonly national, level. In general terms, the primary objective is reducing the absolute poverty of the world's poor through providing lasting and secure livelihoods that minimize resource depletion, environmental degradation, cultural disruption and social instability.

Goodland and G. Ledoc hold the views that sustainable development as a pattern of social and structured economic transformations i.e. development which optimizes the economic and societal benefits available in the present, without jeopardizing the likely potential for similar benefits in the future. A primary goal of sustainable development is to achieve a reasonable however defined and equitably distributed level of economic well-being that can be perpetuated continually for many human generations. Sustainable development implies using renewable natural resources in a manner, which does not eliminate or degrade them, or otherwise diminish their usefulness for future generations... Sustainable development further implies using non-renewable mineral resources in a manner, which does not unnecessarily preclude easy access to them by future generations. Sustainable development also implies depleting non-renewable energy resources at a slow enough rate so as to ensure the high probability of an orderly society transition to renewable energy sources. According to Redclift the term "sustainable development" suggests that the lessons of ecology can, and should be applied to economic processes. It encompasses the ideas in the World Conservation Strategy, providing an environmental rationale through which the claims of development to improve the quality of life can be challenged and tested.

Mustafa Tolba opines that sustainable development encompasses:

1. Help for the very poor because they are left with no option other than to destroy their environment
2. The idea of self-reliant development, within natural resource constraints;
3. The idea of cost-effective development using differing economic criteria to the traditional approach; that is to say development should not degrade environmental quality, nor should it reduce productivity in the long run;
4. The great issues of health control, appropriate technologies, food self-reliance, clean water and shelter for all;

5. The notion that people-centered initiatives are needed; human beings, in other words, are the resources in the concept.

As per views of Allaby, M. sustainable development is an economic development that can continue indefinitely because it is based on the exploitation of renewable resources and causes insufficient environmental damage for this to pose an eventual limit. Brown, et al., state that sustainable development - to be the indefinite survival of the human species with a quality of life beyond mere biological survival through the maintenance of basic life support systems air, water, land, biota and the existence of infrastructures and institutions which distribute and protect the components of these systems. Markandya and Pearce view the basic idea of sustainable development that is simple in the context of natural resources excluding exhaustibles and environments: the use made of these inputs to the development process should be sustainable through time... If we now apply the idea to resources, sustainability ought to mean that a given stock of resources - trees, soil quality, water, and so on - should not decline. T. Meissari-Polsa states the following features of sustainable development: include environmental issues as an item on its agenda; give more attention to the concepts of "environment" and "sustainable development;"

- study in detail relationships between environment and development, and between growth and natural resource utilization. What are the effects of different development strategies on the environment: Is growth possible without severe exploitation of global natural resources? Can donor countries and international organizations make it a condition that future assistance not be used for activities that damage the environment?
- Introduce a new goal for development, a better environment, by using longer a perspective on development issues. Better use of natural resources are already an object of negotiation;

- take account of environmental requirements and sustainable development on every level of negotiations;
- establish a special committee or working group on environmental issues. Sustainable development can be discussed in all existent committees and working groups, especially in the Committee on Commodities;
- provide information to other international actors, initiate and co-ordinate international actions, and follow up implementation actions concerning environment and sustainable development.

David Pearce argues for development subject to a set of constraints which set resource harvest rates at levels no higher than managed or natural regeneration rates; and (2) use of the environment as a "waste sink" on the basis that waste disposal rates should not exceed rates of assimilation by the counter part ecosystems... There are self-evident problems in advocating sustainable rates for exhaustible resources, so that "sustainabilists" tend to think in terms of a resource set encompassing substitution between renewables and exhaustibles. Equally self-evident is the implicit assumption that sustainability is a "good thing" - that optimizing within sustainable use rates is a desirable objective. On these terms, sustainability could imply use of environmental services over very long time periods and, in theory, indefinitely.

David Pearce, Edward Barbier, Anil Markandya hold the view that sustainable development increases real income per capita; improvements in health and nutritional status; education achievement; access to resources; a "fairer" distribution of income; and increases in basic freedoms. Sustainable development is then a situation in which the development vector increases monotonically over time.

David pearce, Anil Markandya and Edward Barbier also state that sustainable development should be based on the following criteria. Economic growth means real GNP per capita which is increasing over time. But observation of such a trend does not mean that growth is sustainable. Sustainable economic growth means that real GNP per capita is increasing over time and the increase is not threatened by "feedback" from either biophysical impacts viz., pollution, resource problems or from social impacts viz., social disruption. Sustainable development means that per capita utility or well-being is increasing over time or Sustainable development means that a set of "development indicators" is increasing over time.

R.E. Munn states that O'Riordan as a contradiction in terms has criticized the phrase sustainable development, for example. If development is equated with economic growth, this criticism is indeed justified: Malthusian limits prevent sustained growth in a finite world... Ultimately, however, uncontrolled economic growth will cause the quality of the environment to deteriorate, economic development to decline and the standard of living to drop. Of course, the word development does not necessarily imply growth. It may convey the idea that the world, society or the biosphere is becoming "better" in some sense, perhaps producing more, or meeting more of the basic needs of the poor. The word therefore involves a value judgment. In principle, development could become sustainable through structural changes in economic, political, cultural or ecological or a succession of technological break-throughs. Hans Opschoor and Lucas Reijnders observed that sustainable development means maintenance of a steady state and it is one of the operational definitions of sustainable development. A steady state is a dynamic state in which changes tend to cancel each other out... Maintenance of a steady state in terms of resources, species and pollution would imply the following:

- Use of conditionally renewable resources should, within a specific area and time span, not exceed the formation of new stocks. Thus, for instance, yearly extraction of groundwater should not exceed the yearly addition to groundwater reserves coming from rain and surface water;
- Use of relatively rare nonrenewable resources, such as fossil carbon or rare metals, should be close to zero, unless future generations are compensated for current use by making available for future use an equivalent amount of renewable resources.

According to Maurice Strong, sustainable development involves a process of deep and profound change in the political, social, economic, institutional, and technological order, including redefinition of relations between developing and more developed countries. According to Schultink Sustainable development as the development and management of natural resources to ensure or enhance the long-term productive capacity of the resource base and improve the long-term wealth and well-being derived from alternative resource use systems, with acceptable environmental impacts. World Bank views sustainable development that it means basing developmental and environmental policies on a comparison of costs and benefits and on careful economic analysis that will strengthen environmental protection and lead to rising and sustainable levels of welfare.

According to one view Sustainable development means achieving a quality of life or standard of living that can be maintained for many generations because it is: 1. socially desirable, fulfilling people's cultural, material, and spiritual needs in equitable ways; 2. economically viable, paying for itself, with costs not exceeding income; 3. ecologically sustainable, maintaining the long-term viability of supporting ecosystems. According to Costanza sustainability an ecological system is healthy and free from 'distress syndrome' if it is stable and sustainable, that is, if it is active and maintains its structure viz., organization function viz., vigor and autonomy over time and is resilient to stress. According Kamal Hossain a sustainable society implicitly that is based on a long-term vision in that it must foresee the consequences of its diverse activities to ensure that they do not break the cycles of renewal; it has to be a society of conservation and generational concern. It must avoid the adoption of mutually irreconcilable objectives. Equally, it must be a society of social justice because great disparities of wealth or privilege will breed destructive disharmony. While there are now hundreds of operational definitions of sustainable development, most are variations of that put forward by the World Commission on Environment and Development. The concept of "needs", in particular the essential needs of the world's poor, to which overriding priority should be given; and

- the idea of limitations imposed by the state of technology and social organization on the environment's ability to meet present and future needs.

Thus the goals of economic and social development must be defined in terms of sustainability in all countries – developed or developing, market-oriented or centrally planned. Interpretations will vary, but must share certain general features and must flow from a consensus on the basic concept of sustainable development and on a broad strategic framework for achieving it. Development involves a progressive transformation of economy and society. A development path that is sustainable in a physical sense could theoretically be pursued even in a rigid social and political setting. But physical sustainability cannot be secured unless development policies pay attention to such considerations as changes in access to resources and in the distribution of costs and benefits. Even the narrow notion of physical sustainability implies a concern for social equity between generations, a concern that must logically be extended to equity within each generation." More specifically, sustainable development requires, the following attributes.

- a political system securing citizen participation in decision making,
- an economic system that is able to generate surpluses and technical knowledge on a self-reliant and sustained basis,
- a social system that provides for solutions for the tensions arising from disharmonious development,
- a production system that respects the obligation to preserve the ecological base for development,
- a technological system that can search continuously for new solutions,

– and an international system that fosters sustainable patterns of trade and finance, and a flexible and self correcting administrative system.

These requirements are more in the nature of goals that should underlie national and international action on development. What matters is the sincerity with which these goals are pursued and the effectiveness with which departure from them are corrected."

DIMENSIONS OF SUSTAINABLE DEVELOPMENT

Environmental Dimension

The natural-environmental constraint to (human) development is the main reason for any concern about sustainability. More precisely, the economic processes of production and consumption draw to a greater or lesser extent on services provided by resources of the natural-physical environment. These resources are of two broad types: natural resources and environmental resources. Natural resources of the conventional type - recognized by economists as crucial inputs to most production processes - include non-renewables such as minerals, renewables such as forests, and all forms of energy. They have been studied for a long time, so that policies dealing with them can build on a whole body of theoretical and empirical knowledge. Environmental resources have come under the purview of analysts more recently. Nevertheless, fairly well-developed tools are now available for their analysis. In general, environmental resources provide services not only for immediate human consumption but also for use in connection with production as well as consumption processes. The former services sustain the biological basis of human life and well-being as well as provide for enjoyment of natural resources by people. The latter services derive mainly from the absorptive capacities of the physical environment and as such contribute to human well-being.

Economic Dimension

The growth of economies and their structural transformation have always been recognized as being at the core of development. They still are the most important preconditions for the fulfillment of human needs and for any lasting improvements in living conditions. In addition to the quantitative economic aspects of development, an increasing number of qualitative aspects have come to be recognized too. The main argument is that neither economic growth in the aggregate nor growth of income at the personal level is sufficient to guarantee progress of an entire society. Accompanying qualitative changes are needed as well.

Social Dimension

Seen from a broad angle, development encompasses the strengthening of the material income base as well as the enhancement of capabilities and the enlargement of choices. Such a view of development clearly transcends the narrow concept of development-as-economic-growth and also emphasises the importance of social development in the context of sustainable development. There is one more argument for including social issues under the concept of sustainable development. This argument is part of the general discussion on sustainability and can be described in the following way: equity considerations are vital to the notion of sustainable development. More precisely, inter-generational or inter-temporal equity forms one of the cornerstones of the concept. As a consequence, the issue of intra-generational equity cannot be excluded from a comprehensive notion of sustainable development, because doing so would destroy the symmetry of the equity-argument on which the term 'sustainable' is built. Hence intra-generational equity – covering the whole gamut of social issues in development, such as regional and gender distribution – is rightly considered as an integral part of sustainable development.

SUSTAINABLE COMMUNITY

A sustainable community can persist over generations, enjoying a healthy environment, prosperous economy and vibrant civic life. It does not undermine its social or physical systems of support. Rather, it develops in harmony with the ecological patterns it thrives in. Sustainable development is an ambitious process in which a community develops attitudes and ongoing actions that strengthen its natural environment, economy and social well-being. Benefits include more livable communities, lower costs and an environment safe for future generations.

A growing number of communities have begun this process, gathering a number of local initiatives under the umbrella of sustainability. They are bringing preventive, integrative strategies to bear on crime, health, jobs, and land use and community values. Sustainable development means development that maintains or enhances economic opportunity and community well-being while protecting and restoring the natural environment upon which people and economies depend. Sustainable development meets the needs of the present without compromising the ability of future generations to meet their own needs.

A sustainable community is one that:

- *Acknowledges* that economic, environmental and social issues are interrelated and that these issues should be addressed "holistically."
- *Recognizes* the sensitive interface between the natural and built environments.
- *Understands* and begins to shift away from polluting and wasteful practices.
- *Considers* the full environmental, economic and social impacts and costs of development and community operations.
- *Understands* its natural, cultural, historical and human assets and resources and acts to protect and enhance them.
- *Fosters* multi-stakeholder collaboration and citizen participation.
- *Promotes* resource conservation and pollution prevention.

- *Focuses* on improving community health and quality of life.
- *Acts* to create value-added products and services in the local economy.

SUSTAINABLE DEVELOPMENT APPROACHES IN INDIA

This is the basic principle, which has to govern and guide developmental policies and programmes in all sectors. It implies systematic and planned utilization of all natural resources - land, water, air, flora and fauna - which constitute the basic life support systems, for development so as to satisfy the needs of the present without compromising the ability of future generations to meet their own needs. Sustainable development would call for increases in productivity and efficiency of the existing system. In general, renewable resources like water, forests, and fisheries can be made use of to the extent of their ability to renew themselves through natural growth. Sustainable economic development implies that the environmental capital stocks should be held constant over time. Their over-exploitation can cause loss of plant and animal species and corresponding genetic resources, which will then limit the options of future generation. There are certain ecological limits beyond which the exploitation of natural resources would not be sustainable. These limits determine the carrying capacity of the eco-system or the extent to which the natural resources could be exploited consistent with their sustained availability in the case of renewable resources. In the case of non-renewable resources like minerals, petroleum and natural gas, their utilization has to be done with necessary measures for safeguarding the ecology and environment.

India needs to adopt the strategy of conservation and sustainable development because the development process has jeopardized our basic life support systems. We have vast areas of wastelands drought prone areas, desert areas and flood affected areas; our major river systems are shrouded in atmospheric pollution; we have a very high rate of growth of human and livestock population creating rapidly growing demand for food, fuel and fodder; and our forests are getting denuded and degraded. The Core committee has, therefore, split out the following six major tasks of the policy of sustainable development.

(a) Stabilization of population growth

(b) Integrated land use and water management

(c) Conservation of biological diversity

(d) Sustainable energy and resource utilization

The main objectives of sustainable development could be stated to be environmental harmony; economic efficiency; equity with social justice; both intra and inter generation; conservation of resources; and local self-reliance. These objectives could be achieved only if the environmental dimension is added to the entire process of national development, and the development plans of all sectors are consistent with the concept of sustainable development outlined above.

THE POLICY ENVISAGES STEPS TO BE TAKEN TO:

Prevent pollution at source, encourage, develop and apply the best available practicable technical solutions, ensure that the polluter pays for the pollution control arrangements, focus protection on heavily polluted areas and river stretches and involve the public in decision making. Mechanisms will be evolved to reduce local concentration of pollutants in complex industrial sites. Setting up of industrial estates and clusters of small industrial units in rural areas will include pollution control measures as an essential component of infrastructure. Development and adoption of cleaner technologies by all industrial units will be promoted. While the large and medium industrial units will remain totally responsible for control of their pollution, subsidies will be provided to small scale industrial units, particularly those located in rural areas, to aid the implementation of pollution control measures.

The existing norms regarding pollutants in effluents and emissions would be revised setting specific limits to encourage the minimization of waste, promote recycling and reuse of materials, as well as conservation of natural resources, particularly water. New units will have to conform to more strict standards. Regulations for liability and compensation for damages will also b made to promote greater care and caution in the management of hazardous waste, and remedial action in case of contamination of soil and ground water. There are at present several fiscal incentives for installation of pollution control equipment and for shifting polluting industries from congested areas. The items for which excise and customs rebate are allowed will be reviewed to stimulate the advancement of abatement technologies and create increased demands for the products. Sectoral ministries, state governments, local bodies and agencies responsible for planning and implementation of development projects will be required to integrate environmental concerns more effectively in all policy areas. A long-term policy for pesticides use, including the introduction of environmentally acceptable pesticides, particularly non-persistent and bio-degradable ones, together with the phasing out of the proven harmful and toxic and persistent ones, would be formulated in consultations with the concerned ministries; and infrastructure evolved for its effective implementation.

Forest and vegetable cover would be increased wherever possible, specially on hill slopes, in catchment areas of rivers, lakes and reservoirs, ocean shores, semi-arid and arid tracts, in and around urban centres, industrial establishments and alongside roads, rail lines, canals and unutilized lands under state/corporate, institutional or private ownership. A system of environmental audit would be introduced for local bodies, statutory authorities and public limited companies by requiring them to prepare an annual environmental statement to evaluate the effect of their policies, operations and activities on the environment, particularly compliance with standards and the generation and recycling of wastes. The collection and integration of environmental, economic and health data will be done to develop a concise set up of environmental indicators for monitoring the effects of pollution. A system of certification of goods that are environmentally friendly will be introduced to encourage manufacturers to produce such goods. Consumer organizations would be involved in testing and dissemination of information relating to such products. Greater emphasis will be placed on promoting environmental awareness, understanding and competence in schools, colleges and training institutions. Professional and non-governmental bodies will be encouraged to be more active in environmental training and building awareness. Government of India has revised the National Forest Policy formulated in 1952. The objectives of the new policy adopted in 1988 are as follows.

Maintenance of environmental stability through preservation and where necessary, restoration of the ecological balances, conserving the natural heritage of the country checking soil erosion and denudation in the catchment areas of rivers, lakes reservoirs, checking the extension of sand-dunes in the desert areas of Rajasthan and along the coastal tracts, increasing substantially the forest/tree cover in the country through massive afforestation and social forestry programmes, meeting the requirements of fuelwood, fodder, minor forest produce and small timber of the rural and tribal populations, increasing the productivity of forests to meet national needs, encouraging efficient utilization of forest produce and maximizing substitution of wood and creating a massive people's movement with the involvement of women for achieving the objectives and to minimize pressure on existing forests.

The new forest policy stresses the need to fully protect the existing forests and forest lands and improve their productivity; provision of sufficient fodder, fuel and pasture specially in areas adjoining forests to prevent depletion of forests beyond the sustainable limit; increasing the production of minor forest produce which provides sustenance to tribals and other communities residing in and around the forests; and conservation of total biological diversity through a network of national parks, sanctuaries, biosphere reserves and other protected areas.

The national goal should be to have a minimum of one-third of the total land area of the country under forest or tree cover. In the hills and in mountainous regions the aim should be to maintain two-third of the area under such cover in order to prevent soil erosion and land degradation, and to ensure the stability of the fragile eco-system. The strategy visualized in the new forest policy includes a massive, need-based and time-bound afforestation programme, taking up of village and community lands, including those on the foreshores and environs of tanks, not required for other productive uses, for the development of tree crops and fodder resources; and modification of land laws to facilitate and motivate individuals and institutions to undertake tree-farming, and grow fodder plants, grasses and legumes on their own lands.

Diversion of forest land for any non-forest purpose should be subject to the most careful examination by specialists from the standpoint of social and environmental costs and benefits. Forest management should take special care of wildlife conservation and forest management plans should include prescriptions for this purpose. Efforts should be made to contain shifting cultivation within the area already affected. Area already damaged by such cultivation should rehabilitate through social forestry and energy plantation. There should be no regularization of existing encroachments on forest lands. Improved and modern management practices should be adopted to deal with forest fires. Grazing in forest areas should be regulated with the involvement of the community.

The environmental components of various sectoral policies, relating to housing, water, land use, industry and technology have been extracted in the report of the core committee, which are reproduced below. The objectives of the policy interalia include the following: To improve the environment of human settlement with a view to raising the quality of life through provision of drinking water, sanitation and other basic services; and to promote vernacular architecture and preserve the nation's rich heritage in the field of human settlement. The policy accords priority to shelter fro the houseless and disadvantaged groups and economic any weaker sections. For rural housing, special emphasis has been laid on (i) promotion of smokeless chulhas, built-in-latrines, renewable sources of energy and other measures that will improve the local environment and (ii) provision of potable water supply.

For informal sector housing and slums, the strategy includes (a) programmes for environmental improvement of slums through provision of a minimum level of basic services like potable water, sanitation, drainage etc. (b) relocating slum dwellers and squatters to the extent possible, wherever conferment of tenural rights in respect of the land occupied by them is not feasible (c) involvement of the slum dwellers in slum improvement and upgradation programmes by adopting a self-help and community approach in the maintenance and improvement of their settlement (d) promoting low-cost water supply and sanitation (e) use of smokeless chulhas and renewable energy sources; and (f) non-formal training for maintenance and improvement of dwelling units on self-help basis.

For protection of environment, specific measures that have been outlined in the policy are as follows:

- In the planning of human settlements, care will be taken to preserve, as far as possible, special natural features and historical monuments and integrate them into the environment of such settlements by suitable landscape planning.
- Necessary administrative and legal measures will be taken for ensuring a healthy environment in human settlements. Norms relating to the provision of open spaces, green belts, planting of trees etc., will be reviewed and enforced. Efforts will be made to ensure that buildings are designed and constructed to match with the environment. Planting of trees by individuals and their associations will be promoted.
- Efficient use of energy has become an important environmental need. Use of energy-efficient devices like smokeless chulhas will be promoted. Use of alternative sources of energy, like solar energy, biogas, etc. will be propagated. Designs and layouts will be reoriented to make maximum use of alternative sources of energy.

- The maintenance of purity and reliability of sources of drinking water and the installation of efficient wastes disposal systems and their proper maintenance will be given priority.
- Special care will be taken to locate hazardous industries at a safe distance from human settlements.

Recognising water as a natural resource, the policy embodies the nation's resolve that national perspectives would govern planning and development of water resources. The policy recognizes drainage basins as the basic functional unit of planning for water resource development and calls for proper measures to optimize utilization of these resources not only for the benefit of the people living in the basin but also for transfer of surplus water to meet the requirements of water short areas. Water is a scarce resource, therefore, it needs to be planned, developed and conserved as such, and on an integrated and environmentally sound basis. The issues that need to be tackled on the basis of common policies and strategies include the following:

- The planning and implementation of individual irrigation or multi-purpose projects, though done at the state level, involve a number of aspects and issues such as environmental protection, rehabilitation of project-affected people and livestock, public health, consequences of water impoundment, dam safety etc.
- Problems of water logging and soil salinity in some irrigation commands lead to the degradation of agricultural land.
- The development and exploitation of the ground water resources also give rise to questions of judicious and scientific resources management and conservation.
- Another important aspect is water quality. Improvements in existing strategies and innovation of new techniques resting on a science and technology base will be needed to eliminate the pollution of surface and ground water resources to improve water quality and step up the recycling and reuse of water.

- In the planning, implementation and operation of projects, the preservation of the quality of environment and the ecological balance should be a primary consideration. The adverse impact, if any, on the environment should be minimized and should be offset by adequate compensatory measures.
- There should be an integrated and multi-disciplinary approach to the planning, formulation, clearance and implementation of projects, including catchment treatment, environmental and ecological aspects, the rehabilitation of affected people and command area development.
- There should be proper organizational arrangements at the national and state levels for ensuring the safety to storage dams and other quality related structures.
- There should be periodical re-assessment on a scientific basis of the ground water potential taking into consideration the quality of the water available and economic viability.
- Both surface and ground water should be regularly monitored for quality. A phased programme should be undertaken for improvement in water quality.
- Conservation consciousness should be promoted through education, regulation, incentives and disincentives.
- Sound watershed management through extensive soil conservation, catchment-area treatment, preservation of forests and increasing the forest area and the construction of check dams should be promoted to reduce the intensity of floods.

The basic objectives of the national land use policy are as follows:

- To meet the consumption needs of a growing population by increasing productivity of the integrated land resource in the country.
- To prevent any further deterioration of ht eland resource by appropriate preventive measures.

- To restore the productivity of the degraded land by an appropriate package of practices.
- To involve the community for adoption of appropriate landuse for increased productivity by ensuring that the landuse policy provides adequacy for meeting their energy needs and generally improves their income levels and provides them a better quality of life.
- To restructure the livestock production programme in such a manner that the livestock population is gradually limited to economically productive stock; and to prevent degradation of grasslands by promoting measures for increasing stall-feeding of livestock in rural areas.
- To coordinate the formulation and implementation of water resource management policies, forest management policies and urban planning within the overall resource allocation needs dictated by a comprehensive national land use policy.

The following initiatives have been recommended.

- Urban planning must be restructured so as to ensure that highly productive land is not taken away. Town planning should also provide adequately for green belts so as to reduce congestion and pollution of environment.
- A special fodder development programme in selected blocks should be launched together with the livestock development programme which concentrates on the popularisation of stall feeding in rural areas.
- The policy of supplying forest raw material on subsidized basis to users other than the rural poor should be reviewed and raw material pricing should be suitably revised so as to obtain a higher price for raw material.
- The maximum shortage in the community's needs as predicted by the National Commission on Agriculture will be in respect of resources of fuel and fodder. A

massive campaign for increasing the land under productive use of fuel and fodder species needs to be launched.

- The entire policy of irrigation management needs to be reviewed with special reference to the inadequate investments made in the protection of the catchment and the drainage of the basin. The management of command areas should also be reviewed, restructured and revitalized within a specified time limit so that a scarce resource like water is used efficiently in a manner that will eliminate wasteful use of water, avoid damage to the soil and increase the productivity of the land. This alone will control water-logging and its deleterious effects in irrigated areas.
- Environmental protection cannot succeed unless there are heavy penalties imposed on any one who interferes with the land resource and its productivity. The laws, which relate to such acts as cutting trees should be made more stringent, and the growth of the appropriate species should be supported by incentives in favour of growing the recommended crops of trees and disincentives for departures from recommended land use. Such a package of incentives and disincentives should be carefully worked out.

The action points approved by the National Land Use & Waste Lands Development Council on 6 February, 1986 which are in the nature of policy guidelines and called National Land Use Policy Outline-Action Points are as follows:

- Land use boards at the state level should be revitalized. Wherever they do not exist, they must be created.
- Land use policy must be evolved by all users of land within government jointly and must be enforced on the basis of both legislation for enforcing land use as well as their promotional and preserving methods.
- Urban policy must be restructured so as to ensure that highly productive land is not taken away. Town planning should also provide for green belts.

- A national campaign should be launched for educating the farmers and government departments about the need to conform to an integrated land use policy.
- Cropping pattern should be reviewed specially in drought prone/desert areas, so that maximum advantage is taken of improved soil and water management practices.
- Land and soil surveys should be completed and inventory of land resources should be prepared in each state so that resource allocation is based on a reliable database.
- Heavy penalties should be imposed on those who interfere with land resources and its productivity. It must be recognized that environmental protection cannot succeed unless this is done.
- The problems of water logging, salinity and alkalinity must be brought under control by the use of appropriate technologies and by the adoption of proper water management practices.
- The management of command areas should be reviewed, restructured and revitalized within a specified time limit so that water is used efficiently. Necessary investments for treating the catchments must be made to prevent the collapse of irrigation system due to premature siltation.
- Technologies relating to dry farming, land shaping and water harvesting must be propagated and adopted in the interest of moisture conservation and optimal use.
- Special programmes of conservation and afforestation in the desert areas and of reclamation and rehabilitation in the ravine areas must be launched with greater vigour in order to prevent wind and water erosion.
- The practice of shifting cultivation should be controlled in order to protect valuable forests.
- Land use planning should be integrated with rural employment programmes in such a manner that loans

and subsidies are given only for those productive activities, which represent efficient land use.

- Rights of tribals and poorer sections on common land should be protected through legal and administrative structures.
- Stall feeding should be popularized, especially in such areas where grazing land is already degraded.

The main thrust in the context of environment protection and conservation is as follows:

- Energy-industry dovetailing: Until recently, little effort has not been made in dovetailing the industry and energy policies; nor has enough attention been paid to the effects of industrial growth on environment and pollution of air and water. Government has decided that such industrial processes and technologies as would aim at optimal utilization of energy or the exploitation of alternative sources of energy, would by given special assistance, including finance on concessional terms.
- Preserving ecological balance: Government is committed to preservation of ecological balance and for improving living conditions in the urban centres of the country. In pursuance of this policy and with a view to encouraging the dispersal of industry, steps have been taken to prevent the growth of industry in metropolitan cities and the large towns. Setting up of new industrial undertakings within the limits of such urban centres is not permitted.

The main approach of the National Policy on Education in the c1ontext of environment is as follows:

- The growth of our population needs to be brought down significantly over the coming decades. The largest single factor that could help achieve this is the spread of literacy and education among women.
- There is a paramount need to create a consciousness of the environment. It must permeate all ages and all

sections of society, beginning with the child. Environmental consciousness should inform teaching in schools and colleges. This aspect will be integrated in the entire educational process.

The basic aims of the Technology Policy Statement are to:

- Reduce demand on energy, particularly from non-renewable sources;
- Ensure harmony with the environment, preserve ecological balance and improve quality of the habitat; and
- Recycle waste material and make full utilization of byproducts. The technology policy statement gives priority to environment: Development should not upset the ecological balance for short as well as long-term considerations. Poorly planned efforts to achieve apparently rapid development, ignoring the long-term effect of many technologies on the environment, have resulted in serious ecological damage. It is, therefore, essential to analyze the environmental impact of the application of each technology. Due regard will be given to the preservation and enhancement of the environment in the choice of technology. Measures to improve environmental hygiene will be evolved.

In technology development, special emphasis will be laid on the following areas:

- Optimum use of water resources;
- Provision of drinking water in rural areas, improvement of nutrition and reduction in the incidence of major communicable diseases and population stabilization.
- Development and use of renewable non-conventional sources of energy.

The Election Manifesto of the Indian National Congress for the General Election 1991 has devoted one section to the subject environment and natural resources, which is reproduced below. Over the past 20 years, the congress has formulated and implemented a multi-pronged strategy for the protection, conservation and regeneration of natural resources and the environment. These policies are now contained in laws that congress governments have enacted. These will be reviewed and strengthened and new long-term and short-term schemes evolved and implemented. At the core of this strategy is our commitment to sustainable development, harmoniously integrating environmental concerns with the needs of economic development. We shall involve the people in environmental protection. One of the causes of air pollution leading to health hazards in the villages is smoke arising from fuel used for domestic cooking. This problem will be tackled through an intensified programme for smokeless Chulha cookers as well as the use of alternative sources of energy. Noise pollution is increasing with rapid industrialization, urbanization and mechanization. Effective steps will be taken to enforce pollution control regulations.

The flora and fauna in India have few parallels in the world. Yet these are under threat of depletion. The Congress will adopt specific strategies for their protection. Wildlife protection will be a priority area and stringent action will be taken against poaching. Ongoing projects will be implemented intensively and new ones taken up. India's genetic wealth is boundless. We will protect preserve and utilize it for the benefit of India and the world. The congress will increase financial outlays on environmental protection from current levels. Special attention will be paid to research on development. Emphasis will be laid on improved training and skills-enhancement of staff working in the field of environment.

Penalties and liability for compensation for pollution will be reviewed and modified to ensure that polluters are made to pay for the cost of mitigation. An integrated National Land Policy will be evolved and implemented covering land use, protection and rejuvenation. This holistic policy will integrate agricultural land, forest land, wasteland, desert land, coastal land, land used for human habitat as well as land needed and used for industrial development mining and irrigation. The project for cleaning the Ganga will be implemented with renewed vigour. Similar plans for the cleaning of other rivers in the country will be initiated. States do not generally have their own independent environment policy and adopt the policies formulated at the national level subject to such variations as may be necessary to suit local conditions. The central government has also been issuing guidelines to the states on various environmental matters. The sectoral policies and programmes pursued by the states are usually formulated within the framework of the national policies and guidelines.

12

Sustainable Society

It is undeniable that technological innovation has generated significant advances in human welfare. However, in retrospect, not all technologies have resulted in positive net improvements in human welfare. Nor have advanced technologies been managed responsibly. The most obvious cases of technologies without which humanity would be better off are the military technologies of mass destruction, such as nuclear and biochemical weapons, which society is struggling to ban. Additionally, it is possible to cite some nonmilitary technologies, such as nuclear energy, agricultural chemicals, and even the internal combustion engine, which have had large unintended negative environmental consequences. Certainly the final judgment of history has yet to be rendered on these technologies, but at the minimum, all but the most doctrinaire libertarians would concede that there is room for better management of these technologies. However, once these technologies are introduced, it is difficult to squeeze the genie back into the bottle. A reasonable inference to be drawn from experience is that lessons might be gained from history that can guide and manage the introduction of massive technological systems which potentially have far-reaching consequences for humanity.

Granted that the law of unintended consequences makes it impossible to anticipate all of the impacts for better or for worse of technology, this does not mean that it is totally impossible or undesirable to devise minimal guidelines in advance of introduction for assessing and managing technologies, especially those having global implications. While technological laissez faire may have been appropriate in a relatively empty world, now that humans have the capability of rendering the earth uninhabitable, we no longer can afford to let survival depend upon the benevolence and wisdom of naive technological enthusiasts.The shaping of policies and instruments for technology assessment is a difficult task requiring transdisciplinary research of a high order, but some minimal guidelines can be offered.

- Exceptional caution should be exercised before the introduction of high-entropy systems, such as fossil fuels and nuclear energy.
- Low-entropy systems, such as solar energy, are less irreversible and less damaging than high-entropy systems.
- Technologies that depend upon a high ratio of human intelligence and information to material and energy throughput have a higher probability of advancing human welfare than do high-entropy technologies.

Examples of low-entropy technologies depending upon high input ratios of intelligence and information to mass and energy include notably the telescope, the microscope, reading glasses, the compass, the sextant, the chronometer, and other navigational instruments that literally opened up new worlds to humanity. It remains to be seen whether the much higher entropy exploration of space will bring comparable benefits to humanity. Other examples of benevolent technologies are transistors and silicon chips, which have made possible the computer, yet save energy.

Obviously, any technology, even that characterized by lowest entropy can be applied to antisocial purposes of crime and warfare, so no guarantees of benevolence can be realistically expected, and the distinction must be made between the potential environmental impact of the technology and the purposes to which it is applied. What technology essentially does is to extend the power of humans to accomplish constructive or destructive ends. Thus the mastery of technology requires both its assessment before adoption and the responsible social control of its application as well as a realistic understanding of human motivation.

HABITAT PROTECTION, INTERGENERATIONAL TRANSFERS, AND EQUITY

Many options exist for habitat protection, including purchase, easements, and gifts, each having a role. Protection should begin as soon as possible, before adverse uses and property rights are established.

It could be noted that in selecting the stock of environmental resources to be passed along to future generations, emphasis should be given to such resources as large-scale living ecosystems containing species diversity, complex interrelationships between species, and, above all, the capability of supporting evolutionary processes over sufficiently long enough time frames that species can evolve and adapt to both man-made and natural changes in climate and other environmental conditions. They include rain forests, estuaries, wetlands, lakes, river basins, grasslands, polar regions, and coral reefs. However, the ultimate selection of the highest priorities for protection of sustainable ecosystems should be made by transdisciplinary teams including not only ecologists, but other representatives of life sciences, earth sciences, physical sciences, and social sciences preferably with insights also from the arts and humanities. After the identification of the scientific principles and priorities for selecting sustainable ecosystems for intergenerational transfer, the challenge of designing the most effective policy measures for acquiring and protecting these ecosystems will remain.

It is observed that serious intragenerational inequalities exist in the distribution of current income and wealth will make it difficult to achieve consensus on the need for intergenerational transfers and will complicate the problem of apportioning sacrifices. A related problem is that, in an uncertain future, the continuity of a commitment to pass on ecological resources cannot be guaranteed for future generations that are not parties to the agreement. Therefore, intermediate generations may be tempted to consume all or part of an inheritance that was intended for the more distant future. There is the danger of a prisoners' dilemma in which uncertainty about the action of intermediate generations could reduce the welfare of more distant future generations. However, as successful experience is gained in protecting intergenerational transfers, uncertainties could be reduced and welfare gains increased.

Well known public goods problems could pose additional difficulties in making intergenerational transfers, to the extent that future benefits will be shared by all regardless of which group made the sacrifice to provide them. In the case of global public goods like the atmosphere and oceans, those groups making current sacrifices to protect the resources could not reap the entire benefits. This free-rider problem could reduce incentives to sacrifice unless measures could be designed to spread the burden widely. Therefore, in choosing policy instruments for acquiring and protecting sustainable ecosystems, new courses must be charted utilizing what limited insights are available from the fields of public choice and poiicy science.

Given the fact that making bequests requires sacrifices and therefore involves scarcity problems, economic efficiency concepts can be helpful in achieving the maximum amount of resource protection for a given amount of resources available, or they can assist in achieving specified resource endowments at minimum total cost. The criteria for ecological bequests must be based upon good science which should emphasize protecting species diversity and minimizing entropy increase. Finally, in order to gain acceptance, policies for making intergenerational transfers must be realistically based upon acceptance by the major interest groups involved. Society has already begun the process of making intergenerational environmental transfers in the form of wilderness areas, wildlife sanctuaries, protected parts of the polar regions, and similar set-asides. These programs have been initiated not only by local, state, national, and international governmental organizations, but also by non-governmental organizations such as the Nature Conservancy. Significantly, many families and individuals have demonstrated the value they place upon intergenerational environmental transfers through their willingness to bear the opportunity cost of holding land and resources in their natural state. These public and private initiatives in protecting living ecosystems offer guideposts for the much greater future efforts that will be necessary for achieving sustainable global environments.

POLICY INSTRUMENTS

An important element in the evolution of ecological economics has been a serious concern not only with the goals, policies, and programs needed for environmental sustainability but also with the design of improved and innovative policy instruments needed for the successful accomplishment of these goals. Thus far, we have emphasized the basic principles of ecological economics and derived from them an agenda of programs that seem to us to be essential in changing our course from the current policy of looting the planet to that of protecting species diversity and of building a sustainable human society on earth with concern for equity among groups, regions, and generations.

However, one critical factor which is often given short shrift in discussions of environmental protection is analysis of the *policy instruments* which are fundamental to the achievement of program objectives. For example, Gore's *Earth in the Balance* provides a visionary set of programs which, if implemented, could advance us significantly toward the goal of a sustainable society. However, he gives much less attention to the policy instruments needed for achieving the admirable goals he enumerates. This is not intended as criticism, but as an observation that even some of the most serious and dedicated environmentalists, among whom Gore has certainly been in the forefront, are more comfortable in dealing with the large issues of goals and purposes than with the technical aspects of instruments for achieving them.

Although pollution is only one of the many causes of environmental damage, it is the one that best illustrates the evolution of policy instruments, and from which insights can be drawn for addressing related environmental issues. For controlling pollution, policy makers have devised a wide menu of instruments, ranging all the way from moral exhortation to imprisonment. Some of the most important include regulating emissions, taxing emissions, taxing products whose use pollutes, requiring permits to pollute, paying polluters to abate, labeling products as to contents, educating consumers, and imposing deposit-refund systems on polluting products. One useful way of classifying this wide range of options is to divide them into two general categories: conventionally defined as either regulatory or the incentive-based use of economic measures.

The regulatory approach is sometimes referred to, especially by those who disapprove of it, as the command-and-control or CAC approach. However, the CAC terminology is more appropriately applied to central planning for an entire economy, such as that of the former Soviet Union, rather than as a description of a subset of environmental policy instruments, which are entirely consistent as a correction to market failures in a predominantly market economy. Rather than casting the evaluation of policy instruments in terms of regulatory *versus* incentive systems, a more constructive approach is to investigate the conditions under which incentives yield better results as compared with conditions under which regulations make more sense.

Incentive systems are potentially more appropriate for the control of some pollutants rather than others. For example, regulation will continue to be the preferred instrument in the case of severe threats to human health, such as radionuclides and severely toxic carcinogens, where the optimal level of emission approaches zero. The prevalence of scientific uncertainty about all but the most simple damage functions is a powerful argument for explicitly recognizing the limitations on knowledge and for acknowledging them in formulating pollution control policies. Therefore environmental policies such as the precautionary principle and instruments such as assurance bonding, which are discussed further on, have been developed in order to preserve the advantages of economic incentives in the face of incomplete scientific knowledge about the effects of pollutants and about the interactions among them. In the face of uncertainty, appropriate public policy is to prevent emissions which is usually much cheaper than cleaning them up, and thus to limit exposure initially. This can be achieved by ending the assumption of safety for emissions unless damage has been proven and by shifting the burden of proof to emitters by requiring the demonstration of safety by the emitter before use, rather than the more costly procedure of requiring regulators to prove damage. Economic incentives can be effective instruments for this purpose, particularly when used in conjunction with regulations.

REGULATORY SYSTEMS

Environmental management in the U.S., as noted above, is based upon a federal regulatory system under which the Congress has enacted national guidelines for regulations, with implementation left largely to the states. This approach evolved from growing recognition in the second half of this century that serious environmental damage could not be prevented by relying exclusively upon state and local governments, whose competition for economic development was an impediment to effective local environmental management.

The regulatory approach has had only limited success in achieving the desired levels of environmental protection in the U.S. market economy and the system has failed disastrously in the centrally directed economies of the former USSR and Eastern Europe. In general, the regulatory system can work well where there are clear environmental goals with overwhelming political consensus, similar costs of abatement across all actors, relative certainty about what is being emitted, and easy and effective enforcement. These conditions hold in all too few cases and we have already identified and controlled many of them i.e., large industrial point sources and sewage treatment plants. Making further progress with only the regulatory system will be much more difficult.

The limits of the regulatory approach in achieving acceptable levels of environmental protection and the high cost of these traditional policies have led economists and others to propose less costly, more effective incentive-based management instruments, such as pollution charges, marketable emission permits, and performance and assurance bonds. The lack of widespread acceptance to date of alternatives to regulation suggests that current practices are viewed as possessing superior political and historical acceptability, or at least of not being as unacceptable as the proposed innovations.

1. Effective regulation requires a level of technical and proprietary information which is seldom available to regulators.
2. Successful enforcement of regulation requires high monitoring and enforcement costs.
3. The costly bureaucracies associated with regulation result in high expenditure per unit of pollution reduction.
4. Environmental regulations are easily evaded or avoided.
5. The lack of strong incentives to reduce pollution below the mandated level reduces motivation for technological advance and for preventing pollution before it is generated.
6. Polluters are permitted to ignore the costs their actions impose upon society *at the time decisions are made.*

In addition, the regulatory system, having its roots in the legal system, is based on a presumption of no damage on the part of polluters until they can be proven to have violated the regulations or to have caused demonstrable damages. Given the high degree of uncertainty about the fate and effects of pollutants, this presumption can lead to significant difficulties, especially in those cases where this uncertainty is high. Despite these limitations associated with regulatory systems, especially with respect to problems like pollution where incentives are significant, regulatory systems still have a major role to play in addressing the basic environmental problems of concern here: population, technology, habitat, and species diversity. Our point is that the efficiency of regulatory systems can be substantially enhanced by incorporating economic incentives within them.

INCENTIVE-BASED SYSTEMS: ALTERNATIVES TO REGULATORY CONTROL

The urgent need for alternative approaches to environmental management that are less costly and more efficient than traditional approaches has long been recognized. The major, but not only, alternatives suggested to the regulatory approach have been based on some form of economic incentives. The accumulating evidence suggests that the present regulatory approach to environmental management in the U.S. and throughout much of the earth, though leaving us better off than we would have been without any management system, does not inspire confidence in its adequacy for addressing the twin challenges of explosive global population growth coupled with growing expectations of exponential increases in per capita consumption by the growing billions of passengers on spaceship earth. We therefore emphasize that problems of achieving sustainable scale and distributional equity are basic to the human condition. Once these goals have been addressed, it becomes important to devise efficient instruments for accomplishing them. Unfortunately, it is inefficiency that characterizes most of the regulatory environmental control instruments now in place, though they have gained grudging acceptance. These shortcomings of the current regulatory approach are evident in the limited results from the excessive levels of bureaucracy and expenditures involved, compounded by the inadequate scientific basis for current programs. Reform efforts must therefore aim at improving both the efficiency of environmental protection programs and the scientific bases upon which they rest. We turn first to the role of economic efficiency, and to its limitations.

THE ROLE OF ECONOMIC EFFICIENCY

From the perspective of economic efficiency, the regulatory approach appears to be both cumbersome and costly. Indeed, now that most of the nations on earth have rejected command and control methods in favor of competitive markets for guiding economic policy, it seems anachronistic to rely so heavily upon regulatory techniques for organizing environmental policy rather than attempting to reap in the policy arena some of the efficiency advantages that economic incentives have demonstrated in the organization of markets. Proposals for economic incentive-based (IB) instruments for environmental management encompass a wide range of alternatives, including:

- taxes on pollution emissions (Pigouvian taxes or charges)
- product charges (levied on products whose use causes environmental damage, such as CFCs, carbon fuels, agricultural chemicals, and fertilizers)
- subsidies for pollution abatement (similar to taxes in concept but not in distributional consequences), especially for agriculture and sewage treatment
- marketable permits for pollution emissions
- creation of property rights for open access and other environmental resources
- creation of economic incentives for acting in the common interest

Several themes run through the literature that advocate more extensive use of these IB instruments as alternatives or supplements to current regulatory policies. The most important is the achievement of economic efficiency through correction of market failures such as:

- externalities, especially pollution
- open-access resources
- inadequate provision of public goods (because of nonexcludability and nondepletability)

- poorly defined property rights
- uncertainty and incomplete information
- myopic time discounting

IB instruments are designed to correct or offset these market failures as shown below.

POLLUTION FEES AND SUBSIDIES

The classic incentive-based alternative to regulation of pollution is a tax, fee, or charge per unit of pollution emitted, known as a Pigouvian tax after A. C. Pigou. However, the intellectual foundation for the incentive approach is Adam Smith's concept of the invisible hand operating in free, competitive markets. In this model, which emphasizes economic efficiency, rational utilitarian consumers attempting

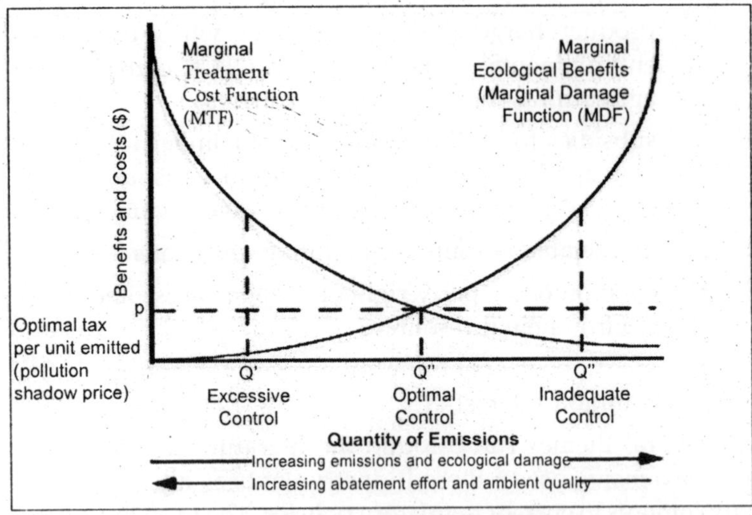

(*Source:* Costanza and Cumberland 1990)

Figure1: Optimal Pollution Control and Environmental Quality.

to maximize utility, and competitive producers attempting to maximize profits, will automatically generate optimal allocation of scarce resources. Thus free competitive markets are assumed to permit the pursuit of self-interest by producers and consumers to result in socially desirable outcomes, *except* where the rigorous conditions for competitive markets are not achieved and any of a number of well-defined market failures are present.

The significance of this approach for environmental management is that if markets existed, or could be created, for environmental goods and services, consumers could purchase the types and quantities of environmental quality and sustainability they desired relative to their means and their competing wants, just as they do now for marketed goods and services. Obviously, for the true believer the market approach is a compelling one since, if it could be made to work, it would effectively dispose of the environmental problem, which would then be reduced to a level of seriousness no greater than, say, of selecting one's household detergent. For readers interested in economic theory and graphics, a simple diagram typically found in texts on environmental economics (a version of which is presented and discussed in Figure 1) is provided.

The major problem with the strictly efficiency-based economic approach to environmental management is that even if all market failures could be corrected or offset by compensating countermeasures such as pollution taxes, the resulting outcomes, though economically efficient, would not necessarily be universally perceived as an improved state of affairs. Society does not exist for or by economic efficiency alone. Though economic efficiency is important, and should be an element in any successful management approach, society will also insist upon the protection of other crucial, deep-seated values such as fairness, equity, scientific validity, democratic pluralism, and political acceptability. Therefore one lesson that can be drawn from environmental management practices to date and from efforts to reform them, is that unidimensional approaches, whether regulatory, efficiency-based, or science-dominated, have a low probability of success as compared to more broadly based, multiobjective, eclectic, transdisciplinary approaches. It is for this reason that ecological economists have developed a range of policy instruments that meet all of the above criteria of equity, efficiency, scientific validity, and political acceptability.

THREE POLICIES TO ACHIEVE SUSTAINABILITY

Taken together they would go a long way toward achieving sustainability. The market incentive-based instruments suggested to implement the policies are intended to do the job with relatively high efficiency and effectiveness. They are not the only possible mechanisms to achieve these goals, but there is considerable evidence that they could work rather well in certain cultural and legal circumstances. By focusing on specific policies and instruments, we can also address the essential changes that need to be made in the system and begin to build a broad enough consensus to implement these changes. A consensus that is affirmed by opposing theoretical, religious, philosophical and moral doctrines is most likely to be fair and just, and is also most likely to be resilient and to survive over time.

In summary, the policies are:

- a broad natural capital depletion tax to assure that resource inputs from the environment to the economy are sustainable, while giving strong incentives to develop new technologies and processes to minimize impacts;
- application of the precautionary polluter pays principle to assure that the full costs of outputs from the economy to the environment are charged to the polluter in a way that adequately deals with the huge uncertainty about the impacts of pollution and encourages technological innovation; and
- a system of ecological tariffs as one way short of global agreements that are difficult to negotiate and enforce to allow countries to implement the first two proposals without putting themselves at an undue disadvantage at least on the import side relative to countries that have not yet implemented them.

NATURAL CAPITAL DEPLETION (NCD) TAX

One way to implement the sustainability constraint of no net depletion of natural capital is to hold throughput consumption of total natural capital constant at present levels or lower truly sustainable levels by taxing natural capital consumption, especially energy, very heavily. Nobel Laureate Robert Solow has emphasized the importance of replacing depleted natural capital by an amount of human-made capital sufficient to maintain the aggregate social capital intact in order to ensure sustainability and intergenerational equity. Not everyone would share Solow's optimism about the extent to which other forms of capital can be substituted for natural capital, but to the extent that this is feasible, a NCD tax would be an efficient instrument for achieving it. Society could raise most public revenue from such a natural capital depletion tax, and compensate by reducing the income tax, especially on the lower end of the income distribution, perhaps even financing a negative income tax at the very low end. Technological optimists who believe that efficiency can increase by a factor of ten should welcome this policy which raises natural resource prices considerably and would powerfully encourage just those technological advances in which they have so much faith. Skeptics who lack that technological faith will nevertheless be happy to see the throughput limited since that is their main imperative in order to conserve resources for the future. The skeptics are protected against their worst fears; the optimists are encouraged to pursue their fondest dreams. If the skeptics are proved wrong and the enormous increase in efficiency actually happens, then they will be even happier unless they are total misanthropists. They got what they wanted, but it just cost less than they expected and were willing to pay. The optimists, for their part, can hardly object to a policy that not only allows but offers strong incentives for the very technical progress on which their optimism is based. If they are proved wrong at least they should be glad that the rate of environmental destruction has been slowed.

Implementation of this policy does not hinge upon the *precise* measurement of natural capital, but the valuation issue remains relevant in the sense that the policy recommendation is based on the perception that we are at or beyond the optimal scale. The evidence for this perception consists of the greenhouse effect, ozone layer depletion, acid rain, and the general decline in many dimensions of the quality of life. It would be helpful to have better quantitative measures of these perceived costs, just as it would be helpful to carry along an altimeter when we jump out of an airplane. But we would all prefer a parachute to an altimeter if we could take only one thing. The consequences of an unarrested free fall are clear enough without a precise measure of our speed and acceleration. But we would need at least a ballpark estimate of the value of natural capital depletion in order to determine the magnitude of the suggested NCD tax. This, we think, is possible, especially if uncertainty about the value of natural capital is incorporated in the tax itself, using, for example, the refundable assurance bonding system discussed below. The political feasibility of this policy is an important and difficult question. It certainly represents a major shift in the way we view our relationship to natural capital and would have major social, economic, and political implications. But these implications are just the ones we need to expose and face squarely if we hope to achieve sustainability. Because of its logic, its conceptual simplicity, and its built-in market incentive structure leading to sustainability, the proposed NCD tax may be the most politically feasible of the possible alternatives to achieving sustainability.

THE PRECAUTIONARY POLLUTER PAYS PRINCIPLE (4P)

One of the primary reasons for the problems with current methods of environmental management is the issue of scientific uncertainty. At issue is not just its existence, but the radically different expectations and modes of operation that science and policy have developed to deal with it. If we are to solve this problem, we must understand and expose these differences about the nature of uncertainty and design better methods to incorporate it into the policy-making and management process. Problems arise when regulators ask scientists for answers to unanswerable questions. For example, the law may mandate that the regulatory agency come up with safety standards for all known toxins when little or no information is available on the impacts of these chemicals. When trying to enforce the regulations after they are drafted, the problem of true uncertainty about the impacts remains. It is not possible to determine with any certainty whether the local chemical company contributed to the death of some of the people in the vicinity of their toxic waste dump.

The "precautionary principle" is one way the environmental regulatory community has begun to deal with the problem of true uncertainty. The principle states that rather than await certainty, regulators should act in anticipation of any potential environmental harm in order to prevent it. The precautionary principle is so frequently invoked in international environmental resolutions that it has come to be seen by some as a basic normative principle of international environmental law.

Implementing this view of science requires a new approach to environmental protection that acknowledges the existence of true uncertainty rather than denying it, and includes mechanisms to safeguard against its potentially harmful effects, while at the same time encouraging development of lower impact technologies and the reduction of uncertainty about impacts. The precautionary principle sets the stage for this approach, but the real challenge is to develop scientific methods to determine the potential costs of uncertainty, and to adjust incentives so that the appropriate parties *pay* this cost of uncertainty and have appropriate incentives to reduce its detrimental effects. Without this adjustment, the full costs of environmental damage will continue to be left out of the accounting, and the hidden subsidies from society to those who profit from environmental degradation will continue to provide strong incentives to degrade the environment beyond sustainable levels. An innovative incentive-based instrument currently being researched to manage the environment for precaution under uncertainty is a *flexible environmental assurance bonding system*. This variation of the deposit–refund system is designed to incorporate *both* known and uncertain environmental costs into the incentive system and to induce positive environmental technological innovation.

By requiring the users of environmental resources to post a bond adequate to cover uncertain future environmental damages with the possibility for refunds, the burden of proof and the cost of the uncertainty is shifted from the public to the resource user. At the same time, agents are not charged in any final way for uncertain future damages and can recover portions of their bond with interest in proportion to how much better their performance is than the worst case. Deposit–refund systems, in general, are not a new concept. They have been successfully applied to a range of consumer, conservation, and environmental policy objectives. The most well-known examples are the systems for beverage containers and used lubricating oils that have both proven to be quite effective and efficient. Another precedent for environmental assurance bonds are the producer-paid performance bonds often required for federal, state, or local government construction work. Performance bonds provide a contractual guarantee that the principal the entity that is doing the work or providing the service will perform in a designated way. Bonds are frequently required for construction work done in the private sector as well.

Performance bonds are frequently posted in the form of corporate surety bonds, which are licensed under various insurance laws and, under their charter, have legal authority to act as financial guarantee for others. The unrecoverable cost of this service is usually 1–5% of the bond amount. Environmental assurance bonds would work in a similar manner by providing a contractual guarantee that the principal would perform in an environmentally benign manner but would be levied for the current best estimate of the *largest* probable potential future environmental damages. Funds in the bond would be invested and would produce interest that could be returned to the principal. An "environmentally benign" investment strategy would probably be most appropriate for a bond such as this.

MAKING TRADE SUSTAINABLE

If all countries in the world were to adopt and enforce the taxes there would be no problem at least from an ecological point of view in allowing "free" trade. Given recent commitments of the global community to the idea of sustainable development it does not seem totally out of the question that a global agreement along these lines could someday be worked out. But in the meantime, there are alternative instruments that could allow individual countries or trading blocks. It is within at least the spirit of the GATT guidelines to allow countervailing duties to be assessed to impose the same ecological costs on internally produced and imported products. The key is fairness. A country cannot impose duties on imports that it does not also impose on domestically produced products. But if a country chose to adopt the tax systems domestically, it could also adopt a system of ecologically based tariffs that would impose equivalent costs on imports. This is a different use for tariffs than the usual one. In the past, tariffs have been used to protect domestic industries from foreign competition. The mechanisms for imposing tariffs are well established. All that we are changing is the motive and the result. The proposed ecological tariffs would result in patterns of trade that do not endanger sustainability.

ECOLOGICAL TAX REFORM

Taken together, the three policy instruments suggested above [Natural Capital Depletion (NCD) taxes, the Precautionary Polluter Pays and Ecological Tariffs (ETs)] would go a long way toward assuring ecological sustainability, while at the same time taking advantage of market incentives to achieve this result at high efficiency. They represent components of what is coming to be called "ecological tax reform." There is a growing consensus among a broad range of stakeholder groups in the U.S., and even more so in Europe, concerning the need to reform tax systems to tax "bads" rather than "goods." Taxes have significant incentive effects which need to be considered and utilized more effectively. The most comprehensive proposed implementation of this idea is coming to be known under the general heading of "ecological tax reform".

The basic idea is to limit the throughput flow of resources to an ecologically sustainable level and composition, thus serving the goal of a sustainable scale of the economy relative to the ecosystem, a goal that was neglected until recently. The more traditional goal of efficient allocation of resources is also served by this instrument because it raises the tax on bads and lowers the tax on goods—it internalizes externalities in a blunt general way, without getting stuck in the informational tar baby of calculating Pigouvian taxes and fretting over "second best" problems. The third goal of distributive equity is both helped and hindered. Since the throughput tax is basically a capturing for public purposes of the scarcity rent to natural capital as economic and demographic growth increases its value, it has some of the equity appeal. However, like all consumption taxes it is regressive. This could be counteracted by retaining a zero tax bracket for very low incomes, and a progressive income tax structure for the rest of the population. Of the three major goals of economic policy sustainable scale, efficient allocation, and just distribution ecological tax reform serves the first two quite well, and the third partially, requiring some supplement from a progressive income tax structure.

The idea is to gradually shift much of the tax burden away from "goods" like income and labor, and toward "bads" like ecological damages and consumption of nonrenewable resources. Such a shift would have far-reaching implications, and should simultaneously encourage both employment and ecologically sustainability. There are three basic problems that need to be addressed: (1) *the research problem*: what would be the quantitative effects of various forms of ecological tax reform on the three policy goals discussed above? Would it significantly induce efficient resource-saving technologies? Would that raise or lower employment? What taxes would most effectively limit scale? How close can we come to the efficient and equitable ideal of taxing mainly rent? What are the implications for international trade of raising revenue by ecological taxes rather than income taxes? (2) *the communication problem*: how do we adequately develop and communicate with the relevant stakeholder groups the options for ecological tax reform and their implications? and (3) *the political problem*: how could such an idea be implemented in the current political climate? We believe that these three problems are best addressed in an integrated and coordinated manner, as described above.

The time for action is running short, but the political will to implement significant changes seems to be finally at hand. The tax reforms suggested embody the mix of environmental protection and economic development potential necessary to make them politically feasible.

TRANSDISCIPLINARY POLLUTION CONTROL POLICY INSTRUMENT

The proposed transdisciplinary framework, which supplements economic insights through a team approach by explicitly including concepts from ecology and the physical sciences as well as concerns for equity, distribution, and political feasibility, is illustrated in Figure 2.

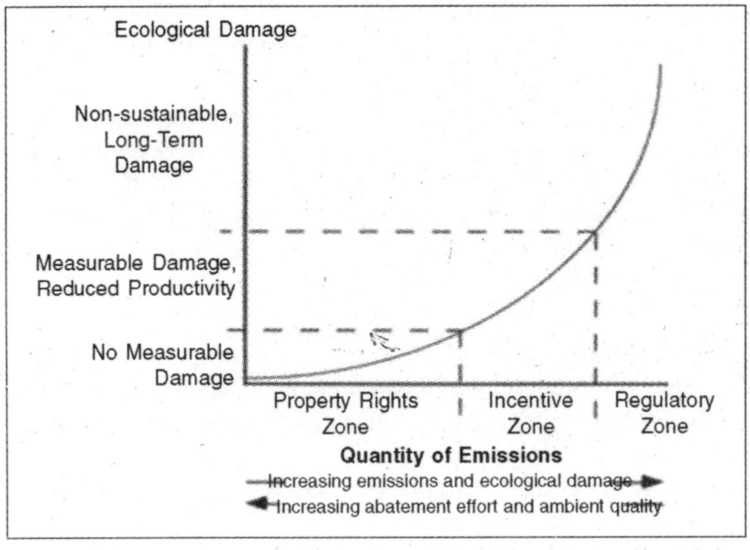

(*Source:* Cumberland 1994)

Figure 2: An Ecological Economic Approach to Pollution Control

This model is proposed as an alternative to the purely economic model, which is predicated upon marginal damage and treatment cost functions whose intersection yields a single uniquely efficient level of pollution tax, treatment, and environmental quality. In contrast, the proposed approach recognizes three separate ranges of environmental quality or levels of ecological health, each with its appropriate policy measure. The model allows for a range, band, or zone of low levels of emissions within which damage is too low to measure, or too low to reduce the productivity of the system. Until emissions and concentrations of pollutants reached a level at which damage could be detected, emitters would be permitted to release waste within legal limits without charge as under the present practice. This is termed the property right zone. For equity reasons, emitters are not taxed for emission levels below which (1) no damage occurs, (2) no accumulation results, and (3) ecological productivity is not impaired. Here emissions fall well within the assimilative capacity of the environment. Within this range or band of emissions, the marginal cost of monitoring and administration would probably exceed marginal ecological damage, and thus not justify the expense of administration costs.

The next level of policy concern is that at which ecological criteria indicate that pollution emissions and concentrations have measurably damaged the environment and threatened the productivity of the system. Within this emission range, a pollution charge, calibrated like the optimal tax and set at a level sufficient to prevent transgressing into the cumulative damage zone is imposed upon each additional unit of pollution emitted. This is termed the incentive range because the pollution tax is used as an economically efficient measure for confronting emitters with financial incentives to reduce pollution to efficient levels. Despite an understandable reluctance by regulators to place exclusive reliance on financial incentives, establishing an incentive range or band could serve the important goal of achieving the highest level of environmental safety per unit of social cost. The establishment of an incentive zone also creates a discrete threshold within which emitters are given the incentives to limit their emissions to nondamaging, assimilable levels. The central importance of the incentive zone here and of policies in general is that they apply the powerful forces of competition to the reduction of pollution through economic rewards to those who act in the public interest. Thus, they shift entrepreneurial talents away from regulatory evasion toward efficient, less entropic technical improvement. Within these first two management bands, the proposed instrument is similar to a Pigouvian tax.

However, even the ability and willingness to pay pollution taxes should not permit the privilege of purchasing rights to unconstrained emissions beyond ecologically acceptable limits. A third level of policy concern is therefore reached when pollution emissions and concentrations threaten to rise to the point that ecological criteria indicate irreversible, nonsustainable damage to the system. This is the regulatory zone, because at this threshold, the option of pollute-and-pay would be superseded by regulatory prohibition of any further increases in emissions. While an efficient pollution tax would have been designed to preclude taxed emissions from reaching an unsustainable level, back-up regulatory authority would serve as a safeguard against miscalculation and uncertainty.

There is an efficiency disadvantage in the proposed approach. Strict efficiency requires that each unit of emission be taxed at the same rate. However, in this proposal, those emitting within a no-damage range could continue to emit at initial levels even after new emissions pushed the total into the taxable incentive range. This equity–efficiency trade-off in the incentive zone is introduced in order to provide a measure of protection to existing firms against the possible impact of future entrants having greater market power. Also, the absolute cutoff of further emissions once the regulatory range has been reached would preclude the entry of new, more efficient firms.

Both the equity and efficiency goals, however, could be served by a variant of this tripartite approach, using tradable permits instead of charges. Provided that markets could be established for them, permits would be issued without charge in the property right range of no measurable damage. After the threshold of measurable damage was crossed, additional permits would be offered for sale on the open market, but their number would be limited to a level set by ecological criteria to prevent irreversible damage and transgression into the regulatory range. Therefore, additional emission permits would not be available at any price once the regulatory range had been reached. Economic efficiency would automatically result from the equilibrium price of permits set by bidders in the market.

Thus, limitations on sales of marketable permits to ecologically safe levels combine the best features of both regulation and economic incentives. The option of selling emission permits in competitive markets would automatically allow new and technologically efficient producers to emerge and to phase out those more pollution intensive producers, but only if the latter found this to be an attractive option. Resale of permits would also automatically adjust markets for inflation, unlike Pigouvian emission charges which would require administrative action for efficient response to price level changes. In fact, transferable permits for emissions in all ranges would have efficiency advantages over limiting charges to the incentive range by permitting new, efficient emitters to purchase permits and by requiring all emitters to pay the same price per unit of emission rather than merely cutting off all new emissions beyond the efficiency limit.

IMPLEMENTATION AND OPERATIONAL CONSIDERATIONS

Clearly, practical problems would have to be faced in implementing these proposals, depending upon local and other conditions. In deriving the damage and treatment cost functions, difficult decisions would have to be made concerning multiple pollutants, multiple species affected, and multiple spatial jurisdictions, depending upon the availability of data and knowledge. For example, Tietenberg has discussed techniques for dealing with multiple sources and multiple receptors of pollution damage. Fine tuning would require different tax levels appropriate spatially and temporally for different pollutants, again depending upon the state of data and knowledge. Given the limitations of scientific knowledge and the extent of uncertainty, a pragmatic approach could require simply proceeding on the basis of scientific consensus concerning the best current information. Given problems of assessing the differential impacts and synergisms among different pollutants, simple estimates of relative toxicity could serve as the basis for setting pollution charges or permit fees subject to the accumulation of additional data. Monitoring and enforcement would be essential. Nevertheless, it must be emphasized that these imperatives are just as compelling for all environmental management systems, including those now in place.

It should be noted that a variant of this approach has already been applied in the Netherlands. Farmers are permitted to discharge the manure equivalent of 125 kg of phosphate per hectare per year without charge. However, beyond that level, they are then charged the equivalent of 0.1 ECU ($0.11) per kg from 125 to 200 kg per hectare. Above 200 kg, the charge increases progressively to 0.2 ECU ($0.22) per kg per hectare per year, with a typical charge per farm of about 730 ECU ($810) annually.

DIFFERENT LEVELS OF SPATIAL AGGREGATION

The Local Level

Although the legal and institutional framework for environmental management is typically determined at the national level, and for some issues is shifting slowly to the international level, the individual events which in total determine environmental quality actually occur at the local level. Examples are the conversion of natural habitats to agriculture, subdivision of land for residential, commercial, or industrial development, and construction of a factory and the disposal of its waste. More generally, the most important decisions made at the local level are those dealing with land use. Land use decisions affect the full spectrum of environmental problems, from those of human habitat to those of habitat for protection of species diversity. The basic problem is that market processes do not necessarily result in land use densities that are consistent with local carrying capacity or with growth on a scale that is sustainable.

Just as most political issues are said ultimately to be local so are the sources of most environmental impacts. Therefore, although broad environmental policy issues should be coordinated at higher levels of governance, the struggle for ecological sustainability must ultimately be won or lost at the local level. A major obstacle to environmental protection that is readily verifiable through observation at the level of local government is the heavy bias of economic and political power toward growth and against ecological preservation. There are many reasons for this:

- Local economic growth decisions are typically based upon private cost and benefit, rather than upon total social cost and benefit.
- The economic benefits of particular development projects are immediately observable in quantifiable terms and measurable in monetary terms, while the benefits of ecological protection are often qualitative, future oriented, and therefore heavily discounted.
- The beneficiaries of development are sharply focused and can command the financial resources required to retain the top, politically connected legal talent which controls the development process and can persevere until they achieve their objectives. The economic and political power of the development establishment becomes institutionalized in the laws and procedures governing land use and environmental regulation.
- Local development establishments suboptimize by competing for growth with other jurisdictions and by subsidizing growth to inefficient, unsustainable levels.
- Though the total benefits of a decision to preserve an ecology may significantly outweigh the benefits of development, the beneficiaries of environmental protection are less sharply focused, are scattered throughout the general public and, unless they can rally thinly spread organized environmental associations to their cause, must rely upon part-time volunteers to protect their interests.

- The diffused nature of environmental benefits inclines many of the potential beneficiaries of ecological protection to become "free riders" on the activism of the minority, reducing their apparent total representation to below a socially warranted level.
- Subsidies from all levels of governance to transportation via cheap energy and infrastructure aggravate the bias toward excessive levels of local economic growth.

Together, these factors all contribute to the current dilemma of biases toward excessive, ecologically unsustainable rates of local economic growth. The problem is made particularly acute by the fact that the efforts of the local growth establishment to privatize the beneficial externalities of common property resources such as estuaries, public waterways, wetlands, forests, scenic areas, parklands, and other stocks of natural capital, too often target economic growth in the most sensitive ecological areas. Institutional biases toward local economic growth have resulted both in excessive aggregate levels of economic growth and economic growth concentrated in ecologically sensitive areas. Belated recognition of this problem has led to the emergence of policy instruments for its control, but these instruments are demonstrably not adequate to the task.

Improving the quality of local land use will depend most importantly upon giving appropriate weight to:

- assigning priority to net social welfare gains over net private gains;
- scientific evaluation, protection, and management of local ecological resources for sustainability;
- equitable participation in the decision process by all affected parties;
- oversight and review at higher levels of governance to prevent interregional competition for growth from degenerating into competitive sacrifice of natural capital and of critical areas.

Land Purchasing and Conservation Easements Before approving land for development it should be evaluated in terms of soil type, hydrology, habitat, archaeological significance, and other scientific criteria. Strengthening local land use authorities through strong transdisciplinary science input is essential to sustainable land use. Evaluation of land for development suitability prior to development could have saved. In terms of equity and Pareto fairness, when specific parcels of land are taken from owners or are subjected to prohibition from all uses because of ecological and other scientific or public purposes, compensation is a reasonable policy instrument to be considered. However, no such equity consideration is appropriate in the case of speculative pursuit of gain at public expense, since real estate activities should be recognized as subject to both profit and *loss* possibilities.

Full-Cost Pricing Local taxes, utility fees, and other services should reflect the full cost to society of additional residential, commercial, and industrial growth, both during the period of construction and throughout the life of the project. Among the unpriced social costs of residential, commercial, and industrial real estate development are environmental impacts from sewage disposal, storm water non-point-source runoff of silt and sediment, runoff of lawn and garden chemicals, and loss of open space. Unless local land prices and taxes fully reflect all of these costs, the resulting subsidization of the real estate and economic growth establishment causes excessive densities and misallocation of land resources.

The typical practice of avoiding full-cost pricing subsidizes new growth at the expense of current residents. The use of impact fees on new developments is a variant of this full-cost approach. In addition to these initial fees, continuing monthly fees should be set at levels sufficiently high to cover the full cost of sustainable environmental protection. The adoption of full-cost pricing may not be a sufficient policy instrument for achieving sustainability, but it is a necessary condition for confronting developers with the social cost of their actions and for sending proper signals to purchasers concerning the full social cost of moving to environmentally sensitive areas.

Economically efficient instruments of this type can assist in limiting population densities to the carrying capacity of the local environment.

Getting the prices right may seem to be a rather simplistic instrument for achieving the many important goals of good land use, and it obviously must be supplemented with other regulatory instruments such as regional planning for watersheds, air sheds, and life-support ecologies. However, incorporating full social and ecological costs into land prices is a potentially powerful instrument for achieving ecologically responsible development decisions. To the extent that consumer sovereignty can be preserved in free societies, getting the prices right is a necessary precondition for assisting markets to make decisions that serve the public interest. Most advanced societies found early on that rather than relying exclusively on markets to make land-use decisions, the introduction of planning and zoning was essential for capturing the benefits of positive externalities and avoiding the costs of negative externalities.

THE REGIONAL LEVEL: POLICY

The goal of national policy should be to assure that the means used by states and localities in interregional competition lead constructively toward improving the quality of development, and not merely toward the competitive subsidization of quantitative growth. Incentives to standards-lowering competition among states should be avoided, just as among nations. This problem is particularly egregious when states engage in competitive bidding wars to attract such facilities as factories, sports arenas, theme parks, industrial parks, housing developments, shopping centers, and industrial complexes. The now familiar give-away instruments used for such competition include tax relief, relaxation of zoning and environmental standards, subsidization of access roads and public facilities, and the disguised transfer of funds through the issuance of tax-free municipal bonds.

Although these types of subsidies to regional growth have become so widespread as to seem commonplace, it is important to recognize that they run against the public interest by violating the principles of efficiency, equity, and sustainability in numerous ways. They are inefficient because those projects that are economically viable would have been undertaken in any event without public subsidies. Therefore, from the national perspective, the subsidy is unnecessary and merely represents an unjustifiable transfer of publicly raised tax revenues from taxpayers to private developers in a zero-sum game. The bidding contest among states *may* influence where the project will actually be located, but it may not since fiscal subsidies are only one factor and usually a minor factor entering into the benefit–cost calculus of developers.

THE NATIONAL LEVEL

The hard-won democratic right to freedom of information can be especially valuable as an instrument for improving environmental management. In particular, the collection and public release of environmental data on emissions could, if more widely used, serve as a powerful management instrument. In the interest of truth in advertising, exciting opportunities exist for introducing ecological labeling, comparable to nutritional labeling, on a wide range of products, goods, and services. Some obvious candidates for information to be included in ecological labeling per unit of product are inputs per unit of energy, recycled vs. virgin materials, amounts and types of toxic and other wastes generated in both the product's production and consumption, amounts of nonrenewable vs. renewable resources used, and related information. Such ecolabeling could become a powerful instrument for informing consumers, persuading producers to improve products, and rewarding good practices. *Other National Policies* There are many instruments that combine features of both, as well as other altogether different types of options. Since government procurement is a major portion of many markets and products, government purchase directly and by example can influence environmental policy. Examples include:

- purchase of recycled paper and other products;
- purchase of vehicle fleets that operate on natural gas and other alternative fuels;
- construction and operation of energy-efficient public structures;
- management, cleanup, and prevention of wastes on military and civilian government installations.

In addition to using their procurement powers for green purposes, governments can take direct steps such as subsidizing the shift from use of nonrenewable to renewable energy sources and subsidizing research and development of sustainable technologies. Besides forging cost-effective new policies and instruments for environmental protection, national governments already have at their disposal efficient and virtually cost-free opportunities for making major environmental improvements by eliminating expensive subsidies and other obsolete programs which currently add to environmental damage. These perverse national policies have been referred to as "intervention failures" since they result from deliberately undertaken government actions which, whether purposely or inadvertently, cause environmental damage.

Examples include:

- underpricing the sale of publicly owned timber;
- underpricing the sale of public lands for mining;
- subsidizing the construction of roads for private harvesting of timber in national forests;
- subsidizing grazing and permitting overgrazing on public lands;
- subsidizing the sale of irrigation water to special-interest users;
- subsidizing the production of crops in excess supply e.g., sugar cane, or which damage human health (e.g., tobacco);
- subsidizing highly entropic technologies for which no generally acceptable method of waste management

has yet been found and which are regarded by the private insurance industry as too hazardous to qualify for commercial insurance (e.g., nuclear power);

- subsidizing the use of virgin materials and penalizing recycling by imposing uneconomically high transportation rates on the former;
- subsidizing the construction of costly environmentally damaging dams, levees, and irrigation projects.

Obviously, special interest groups, the subsidized polluters, benefit handsomely from the public largesse expended upon such programs, but continuation of such subsidies cannot be justified on public policy principles. Taxing citizens and using their money to pay the subsidized polluters to then damage these taxpayers is a double insult. A politically unlikely but perfectly rational alliance of conservatives concerned about downsizing government and liberal environmentalists concerned about governmentally sponsored environmental damage is emerging under the banner of "green scissors." They regard these and similar intervention failures as expensive self-inflicted ecological wounds whose early termination would permit immediate damage control and generate significant net public benefits. Intervention failures become particularly egregious at the regional level when they damage entire ecosystems such as estuaries.

THE INTERNATIONAL LEVEL

A modest international tax on carbon emissions, which would be an obvious candidate with which to begin, could have many advantages of the type. Positive financial incentives would accrue to nations and enterprises which reduced emissions, innovated cleaner technologies, and conserved resources. The charges would raise revenue that could be used for research, administration, and compensation in hardship cases. The global threat of climate change would be reduced, and equity adjustments could be made in hardship cases and for developing nations. Further recognition of the special needs of developing nations is embodied in the "debt-for-nature swaps." Unfortunately, many nations have borrowed so heavily that crushing pressures of servicing their debts are forcing them to deplete their environmental capital at rates that are causing problems not only internally, but which are of global concern. The discount at which this debt is traded in international capital markets, and which unfortunately provides de facto evidence of its excess, also fortunately provides low-cost opportunities for purchasing this debt economically and liquidating it in return for the debtor nations' agreements to undertake specific environmental projects.

Economic incentives can contribute positively to environmental protection in developing nations especially through the strengthening of property rights by making these rights explicit, enforceable, and marketable. A problem of developing nations that threatens all of the fundamental goals of sustainability, equity, and efficiency is the loss of rain forests and other habitats, which not only damages indigenous cultures, but destroys forever endangered species. In some cases, rain forests can yield higher economic returns if left in their natural state than if destroyed for timber cutting and grazing. Rain forests are now recognized as vast reservoirs of potential life-saving drugs and sustainable nontimber products. However, in the absence of property rights to these products, incentives are inadequate for their discovery and cultivation as contrasted to the clear-cutting of the forests.

Various policy instruments are available to mitigate this tragedy of the commons. One of the best ways to protect rain forests and other vital habitats is to create and protect property rights to the sustainable yields these resource systems can produce on a continuing basis in their natural state, rather than clear-cutting them for unsustainable short-run profits. The creation of property rights can be established in the form of patents, royalties, and discovery rights. These would be paid by developed nations to create incentives in the LDCs to protect and harvest these resources sustainably, rather than destroying them forever for short-term gain. Another promising approach is that pioneered in Costa Rica, which has negotiated a "prospecting fee" with Merck Pharmaceuticals, giving the company rights for two years to screen forest products for valuable drugs. In return, the nation has agreed to set aside and protect the extraordinary amount of one quarter of its total land. Potential benefits to both parties could be great, and Costa Rica has undertaken an action that makes it a world leader in the struggle for sustainable development. Other similarly situated nations could benefit from this and similar initiatives.

Innovative as this Costa Rica-Merck agreement is, Durning points out a major opportunity for improving such policies. Emphasizing the importance of secure property rights and tenure in the management of resources, it in noted that vesting these rights in central government agencies is one step toward correcting the tragedy of the commons. However, if it ignores the rights of indigenous tribes, in addition to being unfair to them, it results in a loss of their traditional knowledge of how to manage these resources for sustainable harvest of medicinal and other products. Thus, from the perspective of our approach, providing secure property rights to indigenous people in the management of forests, fisheries, and other environmental resources could provide significant improvements with respect to all of our criteria of scale, equity, efficiency, acceptability, and sustainability.

THE GLOBAL LEVEL

Increasingly, environmental and ecological problems are spilling over national borders and becoming not only transboundary phenomena, but, more seriously, threats to the global commons. Recognition of these increasingly serious global dimensions of the problem will require international solutions. One proposal, as noted above, has been to empower international agencies, such as OECD or the UN, to impose emission charges on transboundary pollutants with the proceeds used for monitoring, enforcement, and research.

One of the potentially most serious global environmental problems is that of greenhouse gases. Although much uncertainty remains concerning atmospheric science, there is considerable consensus that the growing concentration of carbon dioxide and other greenhouse gases in the atmosphere since the industrial revolution will, at current rates of accumulation, eventually raise global temperatures. The release of other gases, such as chlorofluorocarbons (CFCs) depletes the earth's protective atmospheric ozone, even causing periodic holes in this shield. Probable consequences include higher incidence of skin cancer, damage to human immune systems, to marine larvae, and to germinating crops. The accelerated melting of glaciers and polar ice caps could raise sea levels around the globe, inundating low-lying cities and coastal regions. Reducing damage to the atmosphere is even more difficult than dealing with transboundary problems because atmospheric emissions eventually encircle the globe, affecting all nations, not just two or several. Furthermore, the atmosphere is a truly global public good, because only a small fraction of the benefits from any efforts to protect or improve it can accrue to those nations taking individual action. This is a classical situation almost guaranteed to result in suboptimal control efforts unless international efforts are undertaken. As demonstrated by the 1992 UN Rio Conference, international efforts to protect the atmosphere are fraught with multiple problems. Among the most serious, in addition to scientific uncertainty, are those of national sovereignty, North–South value conflicts, and population issues. The Montreal Accords to control the emissions of CFCs was a step in the proper direction, establishing a program of phased future reductions for all parties. However, much greater efforts will be necessary in the future for a comprehensive approach to protect the ozone shield, atmosphere, and climate.

The UNEP proposal addresses equity by protecting the interests of all stakeholders in developing as well as industrial nations. It addresses the national sovereignty issue by making the program voluntary with a distribution of emission rights (ERs) to all signatories, recognizing the two fundamental realities of high current emissions by industrial nations and growing Third World populations. This would be accomplished by basing the ERs on the average per capita emissions of greenhouse gases of the five most advanced industrial nations and by allocating them to nations according to their current (but not future) populations. Economic efficiency would be achieved by making the ERs marketable. Developing nations would benefit by receiving large population-based allocations of currently unused permits, which they could choose either to hold for use in prospect of future industrialization or sell, using the proceeds in lieu of growth. These nations could also be awarded additional ERs in return for protecting forests and grasslands which offset greenhouse gases, benefiting themselves and other nations through incentives for managing population and growth. Each nation would thus have options for choosing its preferred development strategy. The marketable value of these permits would also reduce the temptation for the LDCs to attempt to reduce the initial distributions to levels that would create problems for industrialized nations.

Industrialized nations would benefit from having the alternative opportunities of reducing emissions and thus freeing permits for sale or purchasing permits from others if this appeared less costly in their particular situation. Choice and market incentives would encourage economic efficiency and technological advance. The incentives for industrial nations to press for high numbers of initial distributions would be tempered by awareness of the global danger from having excessive unused permits in existence, jeopardizing the planet in the event of their simultaneous future use. Ecological goals would be served under this scheme by phased proportional reductions in each nation's ERs. Scientific validity would be served by using the best current transdisciplinary scientific consensus as the basis for the periodic changes in the number of total allowable permits. Numerous refinements of this approach are possible, including a central banking feature under which the UN or other international organizations such as OECD could make a market for buying and selling the permits. Carrying this concept to the point of permitting nations to borrow permits from the future for current use, however, would create the potential for intergenerational inequity by letting current populations increase damage to the planet at the expense of as yet unborn future generations who would thus have no voice in the decision, despite its effects upon them.

NEW CONSUMERS SUSTAINABLE SOCIETY

The new consumers command sufficient income to buy household appliances of many sorts, notably fridges and freezers, washing machines and air conditioners, plus television sets and videos/DVD players—all the usual items that mark the "newly arrived". They are also shifting to a diet strongly based on meat, which they enjoy every day at least instead of once a week at most. Still more importantly, they are buying cars in large numbers. These three consumption activities have sizeable environmental impacts. First, the household appliances are almost always run off electricity generated by fossil fuels—with all that implies for build-up of carbon dioxide and other greenhouse gases in the global atmosphere, thus bringing on climate change. Secondly, meat is increasingly raised in major measure on grain, thus putting pressure on limited irrigation water and international grain supplies. Several countries import large amounts of grain for the primary purpose of feeding livestock rather than people, even though most of those countries feature many millions of malnourished people. Second, the new consumers possess one fifth of the global car fleet, a proportion that is rising rapidly. At least one seventh of CO_2 emissions worldwide comes from passenger cars—so to this extent the entire world community has an interest in all those new cars in new consumer countries just as the new consumer countries have an interest in the far larger numbers of cars in developed countries. Fortunately many new consumers can, if they feel inclined, purchase those cars that are more sparing in their CO_2 emissions, notably the Toyota Prius and the Honda Insight.

There are other downside repercussions of the burgeoning "car culture". In India there are an estimated five million premature deaths each year because of air pollution, up to 70% of which is due to motor vehicles. Some 40 million people suffer the effects of asthma. Fortunately there have been major efforts to improve air quality in New Delhi, as too in Beijing and

Mexico City. Bottom line: can we persuade the new consumers to enjoy their high-flying lifestyles in sustainable fashion? A first step in that direction is to recognize that consumption patterns will inevitably change in the future, if only by force of environmental circumstance which is becoming ever more forceful. Secondly, we must try to modify consumption patterns right around the world the new consumers are unlikely to alter their consumption until the rich-world consumers take solid steps to adapt their own consumption. Many observers believe that such patterns are set in concrete, but these may prove to be rather more malleable. For example, during a recent 20-year period, some 55 million Americans gave up smoking—a social earthquake, virtually overnight.

Most important of all is the need to establish sustainable consumption as a norm. This will not only foster far more efficient use of materials and energy. It will also seek to achieve an acceptable quality of life for all in perpetuity, and exemplify it throughout our lifestyles. How, for instance, can we attain a better balance between work and leisure, as between income and consumption? How can we prevent yesterday's luxuries from becoming today's necessities and tomorrow's relicts? How can we make fashion sustainable and sustainability fashionable? However hard it will be to live with the profound changes required, it will not be nearly so hard as to live in a world profoundly impoverished by the environmental injuries of current consumption.

The current economic textbook conviction is that income or wealth inequity is good for economic growth. The idea of incentive driven growth permeates the development and growth agenda so much that equity is rarely discussed in relation to economic growth. The works of Kaldor and Kuznets in the 1950s and 1960s seemed to help establish the idea that equity and growth could not be achieved simultaneously. Robert Solow's landmark work on growth theory added to the equity-blind growth agenda so ubiquitous today. The net result was the belief that 1) inequity induced growth, 2) growth would eventually reduce national inequity and 3) by pursuing growth all nations would converge to the same growth path, hence reducing international inequity.

For his part, Kuznets found that as Germany, the United Kingdom and the United States moved from agrarian to industrial societies the income gap increased at first, peaked several decades after industrialization began, and then decreased as full industrialization approached. His inverted U relationship between income growth and equality - eventually became known as the Kuznets Curve, and despite the fact that he warned his results were "speculative" this relationship has come to represent the traditional growth path of nations. Kaldor following similar assumptions formalized saving rates as an increasing function of real income, and the idea that profits largely outweighed workers' savings. Building on this assumption, Kaldor used empirical data to show that productivity growth in the 1950s and 1960s in Organization for Economic Co-operation and Development (OECD) countries was largely a function of investment behavior. The logic that capitalists and high-income earners had a greater marginal propensity to save, combined with the importance of investment for growth, led to the conclusion that inequality fostered growth.

Robert Solow's growth theory suggested that with low initial labor and capital productivity it was assumed that less developed countries (LDCs) would 'grow' at a faster rate and attract the bulk of international investment. The assumption remains today and is often invoked, along with the theory of comparative advantage, as the rational for liberalization policies. The long run assumption is a world without artificial barriers to trade, where both the developed countries and the LDCs would converge to the same growth path.

SOCIALLY SUSTAINABLE ECONOMIC DEGROWTH

Keynesianisms as triumphant in the 1960s, the era of very cheap oil Later, both short-run and long-run Keynesianisms were left aside. Neoliberal thought resurrected. The neoliberals, like Hayek, thought that markets knew much more than the state. But one unanswered objection to neo-liberalism raised by environmentalists was that the market did not value future, inter-generational scarcities. In the crisis of 2008-09, neoliberalism is suffering from ill health. Some bankers are asking for the State to take over their banks. Keynes has come back, reincarnated in Stiglitz and Krugman. As ecological economists we must ask, is this a short-run Keynes to get out of the worst aspects of the crisis, or also a long-run Keynes to get into a path of continuous economic growth?

Those who propose a short-run Green Keynesianism or a Green New Deal as a temporary measure, are close to ecological economics. If public investment must grow, as indeed it must to contain the rise in unemployment, it is better to channel it to the welfare of the citizens and to "green" energy production, than into motorways and airports. However, Green Keynesianism should not become a doctrine of continuous economic growth. Until now, growth has come with the use of energy from coal, oil and natural gas. In Green Keynesianism it seems desirable to increase public investment in energy conservation, photovoltaic installations, urban public transport, housing rehabilitation, organic agriculture. But it does not seem desirable to persevere in the faith of economic growth. In rich countries a slight economic decline is already taking place and it could easily be socially sustainable. We are not in the 1930s – in Europe we have economies with incomes per capita of over 25 000$. Going back ten per cent with a corresponding decrease in energy and material flows can be managed if institutions of redistribution are in place. Thus, we shall enter into a socio-ecological transition. There is already an agreement in Europe for the carbon dioxide emissions be cut by 20% compared to 1990. In fact, emissions and GDP are in early 2009 decreasing faster than required to reach this target.

The feminist movement made clear many decades ago that GDP does not value what is not in the market, like unpaid domestic work and voluntary work. A society rich in "relational goods and services" would have a lower GDP than an impossible society where personal relations would be exclusively mediated by the market. The sustainable degrowth movement insists on the non-chrematistic value of local, reciprocal services. Moreover, economists now agree that above a certain threshold GDP growth does not lead necessarily to greater happiness. This research updates the literature on the so-called Easterlin Paradox. Therefore, GDP should no longer have the dominant position in politics that it now has, to the detriment of environmental and social considerations.

However, degrowth might lead to social problems that we must face for the degrowth proposal to be socially accepted. If labor productivity (e.g. number of cars that a worker produces per year) grows by 2% annually, but the economy is not doing the same, this will lead to increased unemployment. The answer must be twofold. Increases in productivity are not well measured. If there is replacement of human energy by machines, does the price of energy take into account the depletion of resources and negative externalities? We know that it is not so. Furthermore, we should separate the right to receive remuneration from the fact of being employed. This separation already exists in many cases such as children and young people, pensioners, and persons receiving unemployment benefits, but it should be extended further. We have to redefine the meaning of 'job', taking into account the unpaid domestic services and the voluntary sector and we must introduce or expand the coverage of a universal Basic Income or Citizen Income. Another objection is raised. Who will pay the mountain of debts, mortgages and other debt if the economy does not grow? The answer must be that no-one will pay. We can not force the economy to grow at the rate of compound interest at which debts accumulate. The financial system must have rules different from today. In the United States and Europe what is new is not, therefore, Keynesianism, not even Green Keynesianism. What is new is a growing social movement for sustainable degrowth. The crisis opens up opportunities for new institutions and social habits.

THE PRICE OF OIL

The teaching of economics in universities is still based on an image of the economy as a merry-go-round between consumers and producers. They encounter each other in markets for consumer goods or in markets for the services of production factors like selling labour time for a wage. Prices are formed, quantities are exchanged. This is Chrematistics. Macroeconomic accounts (GDP) aggregate the quantities multiplied by the prices. The economy may be described however in a different way, as a system of transformation of exhaustible energy and materials including water into useful products and services, and finally into waste.

The critique of conventional economic accounting often emphasizes the forgotten current values of environmental services from ecosystems. The environmental services from coral reefs, mangroves, tropical rainforest may be given a notional money value per hectare per year, and then the lost hectares are translated into virtual economic losses. This approach is good in order to impress the public with the importance of environmental losses but it is certainly insufficient in order to grasp the relations between economy and environment because our economy depends on the photosynthesis of millions of years ago for our main energy sources. It depends on ancient biochemical cycles for other mineral resources that we are squandering without replacement. In the case of oil, the extraction peak in the Hubbert curve has perhaps been reached. In 2007 we were taking almost 87 mbd – in terms of calories, the world average was equivalent to about 20,000 kcal per person/day (ten times the food energy intake), and in the USA it was equivalent to 100,000 kcal per person/day. In exosomatic energy terms, oil is then far more important than biomass. In early 2009, extraction has decreased down to 84 mbd.

ECONOMIC DE-GROWTH AND CARBON DIOXIDE EMISSIONS

The economic crisis will mean a welcome change to the totally unsustainable increase of carbon dioxide emissions. The Kyoto objective of 1997 was generous with the rich countries because it gave them property rights on the carbon sinks and the atmosphere in exchange for the promise of a reduction of 5 per cent of their emissions relative to 1990. This modest Kyoto objective will be fulfilled more easily. One could easily foresee by October 2008 that the carbon trade would collapse unless lower caps were adopted. Air travel, housing starts, car sales decreased in the second half of 2008 in many European countries and the USA. Motorists in the USA were buying 9 per cent less gasoline in early October 2008 than in early October 2007, so that the figures released in February 2009 showing a 6 per cent decline in output of the USA economy in the last quarter of 2009 were not a surprise.

However, the apostles of growth are not willing to use the current crisis to shift the economy to a different technological and consumption pattern. On the contrary, they find reasons to think car sales would remain strong because, while the United States have nearly one car for every person of driving age, China has less than three cars for every 100 people and India fewer still. "Once people have a roof over their heads, meat on the table and a good job, the next thing they want is a set of wheels" - pontificates. The economy of India and also that of China propelled by internal demand might well continue to grow at rates of 4 or 5 per cent in 2009 and beyond. Provided the oil price remains low, the car industry will grow faster than the economy and will be an engine of economic growth together with the building industry. However, a world of 3 billion cars would require a much increased expenditure of energy. How will the real economy impact on the real-real economy? How will the cars be fueled? Electricity? Hydrogen? What will the energy cost be?

There is a historic trend towards increasing energy costs of obtaining energy. Brazil's recent discovery of 30,000 million barrels of oil one year of world consumption thousands of meters under the sea, might become a bottomless sink for energy and money. Coming down from the peak of the Hubbert curve will be politically and environmentally difficult. Conflicts arise in the Niger Delta and in the Amazonia of Peru and Ecuador against companies such as Shell, Repsol, oxy. Appeal to some other energy sources like agro-fuels, nuclear energy will compound the difficulties. Wind and photovoltaic energy are fortunately increasing. They will help to compensate for the dwindling supplies of oil over the next few decades. Coal supplies are increasing they already grew seven times in the 20th century but coal is noxious locally and also globally because of carbon dioxide emissions.

THE PEAK IN CARBON DIOXIDE EMISSIONS HAS BEEN REACHED

The world peak in carbon dioxide emissions has been reached because of the economic crisis. In May 2008 it was announced that carbon dioxide concentration in the atmosphere was at a record level of 387 parts per million (ppm) according to the measurements at the Mauna Loa observatory in Hawai. This meant an increase of 30 per cent above the level of 300 ppm that Svante Arrhenius used in his article of 1895, when he pointed out that burning coal would increase the concentration of carbon dioxide in the atmosphere and would increase temperatures. Between 1970 and 2000, the concentration had increased by 1.5 ppm per year, since 2001 and until 2007 growth in concentration reached 2.1 ppm. In early 2008 the world was still travelling at all speed towards 450 ppm to be reached in about thirty years. The great increase in the prices of oil, gas, and other commodities until July 2008, and the economic crisis in the second half of 2008 and in 2009, stopped economic growth and changed the trend in carbon dioxide emissions. From the point of view of climate change, the economic crisis should certainly be welcome.

Carbon dioxide concentration in the atmosphere will still increase, although not so quickly. Emissions are still much higher than the absorption capacity of the oceans, the soils and the new vegetation. The IPCC argues in its reports that emissions should go down by 60 per cent and not by the paltry 2 or 3 per cent likely to occur in 2009 that hopefully signals a permanent change in the trend. The objective of 60 per cent reduction is far from today's reality, and also from the Kyoto and likely post-Kyoto comittments. Nevertheless, the IPCC recommendation is today's closer to implementation than previously.

TOWARDS COPENHAGEN 2009

The GDP of the world will decrease by one or two per cent in 2009, while economic degrowth in the United States, the

European Union and Japan will be larger than this. Between August 2008 and March 2009, consumption of gasoline in the United States decreased not less than ten per cent. Emissions from these countries plus Russia will decrease by not less than 5 per cent. This is really high in comparison with the objectives that were admitted politically up to now. However, because of a problem of mental censorship, neither the IPCC nor Lord Stern's report, had contemplated a scenario of slight economic degrowth in the world economy followed by a period of non-growth in the European Union and the United States. This is the scenario that would convert the carbon dioxide emissions peak of 2007 into a unique historical event. The economies of South America, that in the neoliberal period "reprimarized" themselves and became again raw material exporting economies in greater amounts than ever before, now will pay an economic price. Their growth is stopping because of the economic crisis, and declining terms of trade.

Increased carbon dioxide emissions from China and India are expected, more or less in line with economic growth in India of about 5 per cent, and a little lower than economic growth in China. India's emissions are per capita much below the world average India has over 15 per cent of world population and about 4 per cent of emissions. China's emissions are per capita much closer to the world average. As a country it is now the largest emitter, a little bit over the USA. Increased emissions in India, China, Indonesia and a few other countries whose economies are growing in 2009 will not compensate for the decrease in the USA, the European Union, other European countries and Japan. There is a chance that 2007 was not an isolated peak, but on the contrary a historical peak, a unique event.

How will such developments be received in the climate change conference in Copenhagen in December 2009? Will the positive effects of the crisis be acknowledged? Will a slight economic degrowth and a socio-ecological transition towards a steady state in the rich economies be accepted as a plausible and beneficial scenario? Will raw material exporting countries change their tune and ask for exporting less and at higher prices, by introducing natural capital depletion taxes, and taxes that compensate for negative local externalities?

TOXIC ASSETS AND POISONOUS LIABILITIES

The assets that take the form of claims to debts that will remain unpaid, have been given the funny name of Toxic Assets. In the balance sheet of banks, the value of such assets will have to be downsized or written off. On the liability side of the balance sheet, our accounting conventions do not include damages to the environment. An enormous "carbon debt" is owed to future generations, and to the poor people of the world who have produced little greenhouse gases. Large environmental liabilities are also due by private firms. Chevron-Texaco is being asked to pay back 16 billion dollars in a court case in Ecuador. The Rio Tinto company left behind very large liabilities since 1888 in Andalusia where it got its name, also in Bougainville, in Namibia, in West Papua together with Freeport McMoran... debts to poor or indigenous peoples. Shell has very large liabilities in the Niger Delta. Don't worry. These poisonous debts are in the history books but not in the accounting books.

Look at the current case of Vedanta bauxite mining in the Niyamgiri hills in Orissa. The decline in the price of aluminium if the economic crisis deepens might save the Niyamgiri hills. It has dropped more than half in the last months of 2008. Therefore, bauxite is also cheaper. We may still ask: how many tons of bauxite is a tribe or a species on the edge of extinction worth? And how can you express such values in terms that a minister of finance or a Supreme Court judge can understand? Against the economic logic of euros and dollars, the peasant and tribal languages of valuation go unheeded. These include the language of territorial rights against external exploitation, the ILO convention 169 which guarantees prior consent for projects on indigenous land, or in India the protection of the adivasi by the Constitution and by court decisions. Appeal could be made also to ecological and aesthetic values.

FROM THE SOUTH: THE ENVIRONMENTALISM OF THE POOR

One may readily agree that conventional economic accounting is certainly misleading. The experience that Pavan Sukhdev with Haripriya Gundimeda and Pushpam Kumar gained in India trying to give economic values to non-timber products from forests, and to other environmental services such as carbon uptake, water and soil retention, has been an inspiration for the TEEB process (The Economics of Ecosystems and Biodiversity) sponsored by DG Environment of the European Commission and by the German Minister of Environment. As the TEEB team states, a monetary representation of the services provided by clean water, access to wood and pastures, and medicinal plants, does not really measure the essential dependence of poor people on such resources and services.

Decisions may indeed be improved by giving money values to environmental resources and services which are undervalued or not valued at all in conventional economic accounting. But there are other considerations. First, don't forget our uncertain knowledge about the working of ecosystems, and about the future impacts of new technologies. Second, do not exclude non-monetary values from decision making processes. Don't practice the fetishism of fictitious commodities. In National Income Accounting one could introduce valuations of ecosystem and biodiversity losses either in satellite accounts in terms of physical and monetary or in adjusted GDP accounts i.e. "Green Accounts". The economic valuation of losses might be low compared to the economic gains of projects that destroy biodiversity. However, which groups of people suffer most by such losses? In their project "Green Accounting for India", Sukhdev, Gundimeda and Kumar found that the most significant direct beneficiaries of forest biodiversity and ecosystem services are the poor, and the predominant impact of a loss or denial of these inputs is on the well-being of the poor. The poverty of the beneficiaries makes these losses more acute as a proportion of their "livelihood incomes" than is the case for the people of India at large. Hence the notion of "the GDP of the Poor": for instance, when water in the local river or aquifer is polluted because of mining, they cannot afford to buy water in plastic bottles. Therefore, when poor people see that their chances of livelihood are threatened because of mining projects, dams, tree plantations, or large industrial areas, they complain not because they are professional environmentalists but because they need the services of the environment for their immediate survival. This is the "environmentalism of the poor".

Glossary

Avoided Cost Methodology - An approach to estimate the economic value of environmental services from the cost of avoiding damages caused by lost services or the cost of providing substitute services.

Benefit-Cost Analysis - A method for comparing the benefits and costs of alternatives whose effects can be well represented in monetary terms.

Benefits Transfer - An approach to estimate economic values by borrowing estimates for environmental goods or services and applying them to the same goods or services in a new location or setting.

Bequest Value - The value derived through preserving a resource for future generations.

Consumer's Surplus - The aggregate of the net of what someone has to pay for a good or service and what he or she would be willing to pay.

Contingent Valuation - A method for estimating non-use values using a survey to determine what people would be willing to pay for specified changes in the quantity or quality of the resource—or, more rarely, what they would be willing to accept in compensation for a decline in the quantity or quality of the resource.

Cost-Benefit Analysis - See Benefit-Cost Analysis.

Cost-Effectiveness Analysis - A method for comparing alternatives to determine the most cost-effective means of producing a result of a specified type and level.

Direct Impact - The amount of the increased purchase of inputs used to manufacture or produce the final goods and services purchased by visitors.

Discounting - Adjusting values to account for time preference.

Discount Rate - The weighting factor applied to values to account for time preference.

Ecosystem Services - Services (such as filtering and purifying runoff water) provided by natural resources that are beneficial to people.

Existence Value - The value derived from knowing that resources exist in a certain state. It is the appreciation of something for its own sake, which does not require contact or proximity.

Externality - Benefits received (or costs paid) by someone who isn't directly involved in an economic transaction (such as the view that is enjoyed by those who live near a forest or the impacts of water pollution on the populations downstream from a factory).

IMPLAN - IMPLAN (Impact Analysis for Planning) is an economic impact modeling system that estimates the multiplier effect of a change in demand in order to derive the total economic impact to an economy (in terms of revenue, employment, income, and value added). IMPLAN was originally developed by the U.S. Department of Agriculture, Forest Service.

Incremental Analysis - A method for comparing alternatives that have similar outputs in order to rank them according to their cost-effectiveness.

Indirect Impact - The value of the inputs used by firms that are called upon to produce additional goods and services for those firms first impacted directly by spending.

Induced Impact - Result from the direct and indirect effects of spending. Induced effects are related to persons and businesses that receive added income as a result of local spending by employees and managers of the firms and plants that are impacted by the direct and indirect effects of direct spending. This added income results in increased demand for goods and services and, in turn, increased production and sales of inputs.

Inputs to Production - The resources used in producing goods and services, including land, labor, and capital.

Instrumental Value - Refers to something that is valued because of its usefulness, or because it provides a means to some other goal.

Intrinsic Value - Refers to something that is valued for its own sake.

Market Value - The net value (benefits minus price) of goods or services that are traded on the market.

Non-Market Value - The net value (benefits minus price) of goods, services, or states of nature not traded on the market (such as a day of fishing). The price is often approximated by looking at the cost of travel (see Travel Cost Method).

Non-Use Value - Economic value unrelated to use or consumption. Non-use values may include existence values, option values, quasi-option values, or bequest values.

Option Value - Values based on the option to use coastal resources in the future.

Quasi-Option Value - Values based on the potential option to use coastal resources in the future—even though the values may not yet have been identified. The value would be lost if the resource is diminished (or not preserved).

Time Preference - People's tendency to care more about today's consumption than tomorrow's and to believe that we will be better off in the future than we are today.

Total Economic Value - The sum of use and non-use values.

Travel Cost Method - A methodology that relies on travel-related costs as a proxy for price in a non-market valuation analysis in order to estimate net economic values.

Use Value - Economic value related to use or consumption. Use values may include both direct, consumptive uses (such as cutting a tree for firewood) and indirect, non-consumptive uses (such as viewing scenery).

Willingness to Accept - How much people say they would be willing to accept in exchange for foregoing an environmental improvement (or accepting a decrease in environmental quality). This is useful when trying to estimate non-market values.

Willingness to Pay - How much people say they would be willing to pay for an environmental improvement (or to avoid a decrease in environmental quality). This is useful when trying to estimate non-market values.

References

Akerlof, G. (1970), " The Market for Lemons: Quality, Uncertainty and the Market Mechanism", Quarterly Journal of Economics, 84, 488-500

Alderson, L. (1994), Rare Breeds, Laurence King Publishing, London

Aldrich, H.E. et al (2008), In Defence of Generalized Darwinism, Journal of Evolutionary Economics, Vol. 18, 577-596.

Anderson, J. L. (1985), 'Market Interaction between Aquaculture and the Common-property Commercial Fishery', Marine Resource Economics, 2, 1-24.

Apostolaki, P., Milner-Gulland, E.J., McAllister, M.K. and Kirkwood, G.P. (2002), Modelling the Effects of Establishing a Marine Reserve for Mobile Fish Species. Canadian Journal of Fisheries and Aquatic Sciences 59, 405-415.

Asche, F., Bjørndal, T. and Young, J.A. (2001), "Market Interactions for Aquaculture Products", Aquaculture Economics and Management, 5, 303-318.

Asgard, T., E. Austreng, I. Holmefjord, M. Hillestad, and K. Shearer (1999), Resource Efficiency in the Production of Various Species. Proceedings of the Second International Symposium on Sustainable Fish Farming. Oslo, Norway. Nov.2-5th 1997, Publ. A.A. Balkema, Rotterdam.

Ashby, W.R. (1956), Introduction to Cybernetics, John Wiley & Sons: New York.

Bain J. S. (1968), Industrial Organization, 2nd Edition, John Wiley, NYC.

Barataria-Terrebonne National Estuary Program (NEP). (1996), Economic Value Assessment for the Barataria-Terrebonne Estuarine System. Barataria-Terrebonne National Estuary Program. Thibodaux, LA

Barringer, G.I. Blanksten, R.W. Mack, eds., Social Change in Developing Areas: a Reinterpretation of Evolutionary Theory, Schenkman: Cambridge, Massachusetts. Reprinted 1969 in General Systems 14: 69-85.

Bauer, J. (2008), Das kooperative Gen – Abschied vom Darwinismus, Hoffmann und Campe.

Baumol, W., and W. Oates (1988), *The Theory of Environmental Policy: Second Edition*. Cambridge University Press. New York, NY.

Bennett, J., and M. Morrison (1999), "Valuing Wetland Rehabilitation." An International Perspective on Wetland Rehabilitation. Pages 217 to 224. Kluwer Academic Publishers. Dordrecht, the Netherlands

Berrill, M. (1997), The Plundered Seas: Can the World's Fish be saved? Greystone Books, Vancouver.

Beurton, P.J. (1995), Neo-Darwinism or Synthesis?, in: Wolters, G., Lennox, J.G. (eds.), Concpets, Theories, and Rationality in the Biological Sciences, Universitäts- Verlag Konstanz/Pittsburgh Press.

Beverton, R.J.H. and Holt, S.J. (1957), On the Dynamics of Exploited Fish Populations. Her Majesty's Stationary Office, London.

Bhat, M.G. (2003), Application of Non-Market Valuation to the Florida Keys Marine Reserve Management. Journal of Environmental Management 67, 315-325.

Botsford, L.W., Castilla, J.C. and Peterson, C.H. (1997), The Management of Fisheries and Marine Ecosystems. Science 277, 509.

Boulding, K., The Economics of the Coming Spaceship Earth, in H. Jarret et al, eds., Environmental Quality in a Growing Economy, John Hopkins Press, Baltimore, 1966.

Boyd, J., J. Sanchirico, and L. Shabman (2004), "Habitat Benefit Assessment and Decisionmaking: A Report to the National Marine Fisheries Service." Resources for the Future. Washington, D.C.

Brown, L.R. (2005), Outgrowing the Earth: The Food Security Challenge in and Age of Falling Water Tables and Rising Temperatures. NY: W.W Norton & Co., 2004.

Buenstorf, G. (2006), How Useful is Generalized Darwinism as a Framework to Study Competition and Industrial Evolution?, Journal of Evolutionary Economics, vol. 16, 511-527.

Bunge. Undated. http://www.bunge.com/US/en industry_information/afoa_slides.pdf

Caddy, J.F. and Gulland, J.A (1983), Historical Patterns of Fish Stocks. Marine Policy 7(4), 267-278.

Camazine, S., J.-L. Deneubourg, N.R. Franks, J. Sneyd, G. Theraulaz, E. Bonabeau (2001).

Campbell, D.T. (1965), "Variation, Selection and Retention in Sociocultural Evolution," in H.R.

Capra, F. (1996), The Web of Life: A New Synthesis of Mind and Matter, HarperCollins, New York.

Carroll, S.B. (2006), Endless Forms Most Beautiful. The New Science of Evo Devo and the Making of Animal Kingdom, Weidenfeld & Nicolson, London; German translation: Evo Devo - Das neue Bild der Evolution, Berlin University Press, 2008.

Carroll, S.B. (2005), Endless Forms Most Beautiful: The New Science of Evo Devo, W.W. Norton & Co.: New York and London.

Carroll, S.B., B. Prud'homme, N. Gompel (2008), "Regulating Evolution," Scientific American 298, No 5: 38-43.

Charles, A.T. (1995), The Atlantic Canadian Groundfishery: roots of collapse, Dalhousie Law Journal 18 (Spring), 65-83.

Chartrand, H.H. (2003), "The Future of Genomic IPRs", March, Saskatchewan Economics Journal, 4. 2003.

Chartrand, H.H. (2006), Ideological Evolution: The Competitiveness of Nations in a Global Knowledge-Based Economy, Doctoral Dissertation, University of Saskatchewan, July.

Chomsky, N. (1976), Reflections on Languages, Fontana Books: New York.

Chynoweth, D.P., J.M. Owens, and R. Legrand (2001), Renewable Methane from Anaerobic Digestion of Biomass. Renewable Energy 22:1-8.

Cicin-Sain, B., S. M. Bunsick, J. Corbin, M. R. DeVoe, T. Eichenberg, J. Ewart, J. Firestone, K. Fletcher, H.Halvorson, T. MacDonald, R. Rayburn, R. Rheault and B. Thorne-Miller. 2005. Recommendations For An Operational Framework For Offshore Aquaculture In U.S. Federal Waters. Gerard J. Mangone Center for Marine Policy, University of Delaware, Newark. Available at: http://darc.cms.udel.edu/sgeez/sgeez2final.pdf

Conrad, J.M. 1999. The bioeconomics of marine sanctuaries. Journal of Bioeconomics 1, 205-217.

Cordes, C. (2006), "Darwinism in Economics: From Analogy to Continuity," Journal of Evolutionary Economics 16: 529-541.

Cordes, C. (2006), Darwinism in Economics: From Analogy to Continuity, Journal of Evolutionary Economics, vol. 16, 529-541.

Cordes, C. (2007), "Can a Generalized Darwinism Be Criticized? A Rejoinder to Geoffrey Hodgson," Journal of Economic Issues 41: 277-281.

Cosmides, L. and J. Tooby (1997), Evolutionary Psychology: A Primer,http://www.psych.ucsb.edu/research/cep/primer.html, Santa Barbara: California.

Côté, I.M., Mosquiera, I. and Reynolds, J.D. 2001. Effects of marine reserve characteristics on the protection of fish populations: a meta-analysis. Journal of Fish Biology 59 (supp. A), 178-189.

Cowan, R., David P.A. & Foray, D.,"The Explicit Economics of Knowledge: Codifcation and Tacitness", Industrial and Corporate Change, 9 (2), 2000, 211-253.

Daly, H., Ecological economics and sustainable development, selected essays, Edward Elgar, Cheltenham, 2007.

Daly, H., On economics as a life science, Journal of Political Economy, 76, 3 (May - Jun., 1968), pp. 392-406.

Daly, H., Steady-State Economics: Second Edition with New Essays, Island Press, Washington, DC, 1991

Daly, H., The economic thought of Frederick Soddy, History of Political Economy, 12(4), 1980, pp. 469-488.

Darwin, C.R. (1859), On the Origin of Species by Means of Natural Selection, John Murray: London.

Dawkins, R. (1976), The Selfish Gene, Paladin: London.

Dawkins, R. (1982), The Extended Phenotype, W.H. Freeman and Company: Oxford and San Francisco.

Dawkins, R. (1996), The Blind Watchmaker, New York: W. W. Norton.

Delgado, Christopher L., Nikolas Wada, Mark W. Rosegrant, Siet Meijer, and Mahfuzuddin Ahmed. 2003. Fish to 2020, Supply and Demand in Changing Global Markets. International Food Policy Research Institute, Washington, D.C., 226 pp.

Department of Fisheries and Oceans (1981), Resource Prospects for Canada's Atlantic Fisheries 1981-1987. Supply and Services Canada, Ottawa.

Department of Fisheries and Oceans (2004a), Northern Cod (2J+3KL) Cod Stock Status Update. http://www.dfo-mpo.gc.ca/CSAS/CSAS/status/2004/SSR2004_011_E.pdf

Department of Fisheries and Oceans (2004b), A Recent Account of Canada's Atlantic Cod Fishery. http://www.dfo-mpo.gc.ca/kids-enfants/map-carte/map_e.htm

Diewert, W.E. (2002), Similarity and Dissimilarity Indexes: An Axiomatic Approach.

Discussion Paper 02-10, Department of Economics, University of British Columbia.

Doursat, R. (2008), "Organically Grown Architectures: Creating Decentralized, Autonomous Systems by Embryomorphic Engineering," in R.P. Würtz, ed., Organic Computing, Springer-Verlag: Heidelberg, New York, London.

Doyen, L. and Béné, C. (2003), Sustainability of Fisheries through Marine Reserves: A Robust Modelling Analysis. Journal of Environmental Management 69, 1-13.

English, D.B.K., W. Kriesel, V.R. Leeworthy, and P.C. Wiley (1996), "Economic Contributions of Recreating Visitors to the Florida Keys/Key West." National Oceanic and Atmospheric Administration. Silver Spring, MD.

EPA (Environmental Protection Agency) (2003), *National Pollutant Discharge Elimination System Permit Regulation and Effluent Limitation Guidelines and Standards for Concentrated Animal Feeding Operations (CAFOs).* Final Rule [68 FRL 74247, February 12, 2003].

EPA (Environmental Protection Agency). 2004. http://www.epa.gov/epaoswer/non-hw/muncpl/recycle.htm

European Environment Agency (2003), Europe's Environment: The Third Assessment. Copenhagen: European Environment Agency.

European Environment Agency (2004), Indicator: The North Sea Cod (Gadhus morhua) stock [2004.05]. http:themese.eea.eu.int/Sectors_and_activities/fishery/indicators/FISH01b,2004.05.

FAO (2005), The State of the World Fisheries and Aquaculture. PART 1: World review of fisheries and aquaculture, Overview. www.fao.org/docrep/007/y5600e/y5600e04.htm

FAO (2007), FishStat Plus: Universal Software for Fishery Statistical Time Series.

Field, B.C. (1994), *Environmental Economics: An Introduction*. McGraw-Hill [Publishers]. New York, NY.

Fischer-Kowalski, M. and Haberl, H. (eds) (2007), Socioecological Transitions and Global Change: Trajectories of Social Metabolism and Land Use . Edward Elgar, Cheltenham.

Food and Agriculture Organisation of the United Nations (FAO). (2000), State of World Fisheries and Aquaculture 2000. http://www.fao.org/docrep/003/x8002e/x8002e06.htm

Fox, K.J., Hill, R.J. and Diewert W.E. (2004), Identifying Outliers in Multi-Output Models. Journal of Productivity Analysis 22, 73-94.

Freeman, A. (1993), *The Measurement of Environmental and Resource Values: Theories and Methods.* Reasons for the Future. Washington, D.C.

Fuller, S. (2000), Thomas Kuhn: A Philosophical History of Our Times, University of Chicago Press.

Fullerton, D., and R. Stavins (1998), *How Do Economists Really Think About the Environment?* Resources for the Future. Washington. D.C.

Futuyma, D.J. (2005, 2007), Evolution, Sinauer Associates, Sunderland (USA), 2005; German Edition (in English) Elsevier München 2007.

Gaspar, J. and Judd, K.L. (1997), Solving Large-Scale Rational-expectations Models. Macroeconomic Dynamics 20, 45-75.

Geider, Richard J., et.al. (2001), Primary Productivity of Planet Earth: Biological Determinants and Physical Constraints in Terrestrial and Aquatic Habitats. Global Change Biology 7:849-882.

Gell, F.R. and Roberts, C.M. (2002), The Fishery Effects of Marine Reserves and Fishery Closures. World Wildlife Fund, United States, Washington DC.

Gell, F.R. and Roberts, C.M. (2003), Benefits beyond Boundaries: The Fishery Effects of Marine Reserves. TRENDS in Ecology and Evolution 18(9), 448-455.

Georgescu-Roegen, N. (1971), The Entropy Law and the Economic Process, Harvard U.P., Cambridge.

Georgescu-Roegen. N. (1966), Analytical Economics, Harvard U.P., Cambridge.

Gould, S.J. (1980), Is a New and General Theory of Evolution Emerging?, Paleobiology, no. 6, 119-130.

Gould, S.J. (2007), Punctuated Equilibrium, Harvard University Press: Cambridge, Massachusetts.

Gould, S.J., Eldredge, N. (1972), Punctuated Equilibria: An Alternative to Phyletic

Gould, S.J., Eldredge, N. (1977), Punctuated Equilibria: The Tempo and Mode of Evolution Reconsidered, Paleobiology, vol. 3, 115-151.

Government Accountability Office (2005), Livestock Grazing. http://www.gao.gov/new.items/d05869.pdf

Gradualism, in: Schopt, T.J.M. (ed.), Models in Paleobiology, San Francisco, 82- 115.

Grafton, R.Q., Sandal, L.K. and Steinshamn, S.I. (2000), How to Improve the Management of Renewable Resources: The Case of Canada's Northern cod Fishery. American Journal of Agricultural Economics 82, 570-580.

Greeley-Polhemus Group, Inc. (1991), *National Economic Development Procedures Manual – Overview Manual for Conducting Economic Development Analysis.* U.S. Army Corps of Engineers. Fort Belvoir, VA.

Grene M.,& Depew, D. (2004), The Philosophy of Biology: An Episodic History, Cambridge University Press.

Grinevald, J., Rens, I. eds, La Décroissance : Entropie, écologie, économie, Sang de la Terre, Paris, 1995 (a selection of writings by N. Georgescu-Roegen, first publ. 1979).

Hanley, N., J. Shogren, and B. White (1997), *Environmental Economics: In Theory and Practice.* Macmillan. London, UK.

Hartwick, J., and N. Olewiler (1998), *The Economics of Natural Resource Use: Second Edition.* Addison Wesley Longman. New York, NY.

Hayek, F.A. (1967), "The Evolution of the Rules of Conduct," Studies in Philosophy, Politics and Economics, The University of Chicago Press: Chicago.

Heidegger, M, "The Question Concerning Technology" [1955], in W. Lovitt (trans.), The Question Concerning Technology and Other Essays, Harper Tourchbooks, 1977, 3-35.

Hirshleifer, Jack (1982), "Evolutionary Models in Economics and Law: Cooperation versus Conflict Strategies", Research in Law and Economics, Vol. 4: 1-60.

Hirshleifer, Jack (1985), "The Expanding Domain of Economics", American Economic Review, 75: 53-75.

Hodgson, G.M. (2002), "Darwinism in Economics: from Analogy to Ontology," Journal of Evolutionary Economics 12: 259-281.

Hodgson, G.M. (2004), "Darwinism, Causality and the Social Sciences," Journal of Economic Methodology 11: 175-194.

Hodgson, G.M. and T. Knudsen (2006), "Dismantling Lamarckism: Why Descriptions of Socioeconomic Evolution as Lamarckian are Misleading," Journal of Evolutionary Economics 16: 343-366.

Hodgson, Geoffrey M. (1999), Evolution and Institutions. On Evolutionqry Economics and the Evolution of Economics, Cheltenham, Edward Elgar.

Hodgson, Geoffrey M. (2002), "Darwin, Veblen and the Problem of Causality in Economics", History and Philosophy of the Life Sciences, 23: 383-422.

Hodgson, Geoffrey M. (2003a), "Darwinism and Institutional Economics", Journal of Economic Issues, 37: 85-97.

Hodgson, Geoffrey M. (2003 b), "Hayekian Evolution Reconsidered", Cambridge Journal of Economics (forthcoming).

Hodgson, Geoffrey M. (2003c), "Social Darwinism in Anglophone Academia: A Brief History of the Term", mimeo.

Hofstadter, Richard 1992 [1944]. Social Darwinism in American Thought, Boston, Beacon Press.

Holbrook, Stewart (1953), The Age of the Moguls, Garden City, Doubleday.

Holland, J.H. (1995), Hidden Order: How Adaptation Builds Complexity, Reading, Massachusetts: Helix Books.

Hood, L. (2002), "A Personal View of Molecular Technology and How It Has Changed Biology", Journal of Proteome Research, 1 (5), 399-409.

Hornborg, A. (1998), Towards an Ecological Theory of Unequal Exchange: Articulating World System Theory and Ecological Economics, Ecological Economics, 25(1) April, pp. 127-136.

Huesemann, M.H. (2006), Can Advances in Science and Technology Prevent Global Warming? A Critical Review of Limitations and Challenges. Mitigation and Adaptation for Global Change 11(1).

Hull, D.L. (1980), "The Units of Evolution: A Metaphysical Essay," in U.J. Jensen and R. Harré, eds., Studies in the Concept of Evolution, Harvester Press: Brighton.

Huxley, A. (1942), Evolution: The Modern Synthesis, Allen & Unwin: London.

Ihde, D. (1991), Instrumental Realism: The Interface between Philosophy of Science and Philosophy of Technology, Indiana University Press, Bloomington.

ISSN 0194-4088: No. 121. http://www-formal.stanford.edu/jmc nature/nature.html

Jones, L.B. (1989), Schumpeter versus Darwin : In re Malthus, Southern Economic Journal, 56, pp. 410-422.

Kauffman, S.A. (1993), Origins of Order: Self-Organization and Selection in Evolution, Oxford, Oxford University Press.

Kauffman, S.A. (1993), The Origins of Order: Self-Organization and Selection in Evolution, Oxford University Press: Oxford and New York.

Kaye, Howard L. (1986), The Social Meaning of Modern Biology. From Social Darwinism to Sociobiology, New Heaven, Yale University Press.

Kimura, M. (1983), The Neutral Theory of Molecular Evolution, CUP, Cambridge.

King, D. (1998), "The Dollar Value of Wetlands: Trap Set, Bait Taken, Don't Swallow." National Wetlands Newsletter. Volume 20. Number 4. Pages 7 to 11

Kirkley, J., J. Duberg, and J. Ward. (2005), A User's Guide to the U.S. National Offshore Aquaculture Model for Assessing Economic Impacts, prepared for NOAA Fisheries.

Kirschner, M.W., Gerhart, J.C. (2005), The Plausability of Life, Yale University Press, New Haven; German translation: Die Lösung von Darwins Dilemma (2007), Rowohlt Reinbek.

Kneese A. and Ayres, R.U. (1969), Production, Consumption and Externalities, American Economic Review, 59, pp. 282-97.

Knudsen, T. (2004), "General Selection Theory and Economic Evolution: The Price Equation and the Replicator/interactor distinction," Journal of Economic Methodology 11: 147-173.

Krutilla, J.V. (1967), "Conservation Reconsidered." The American Economic Review. Volume 57. Pages 777 to 786.

Kuhn, T.S., The Structure of Scientific Revolutions, Third Edition, University of Chicago Press, Chicago, [1962, 1970] 1996.

Kutschera, U. (2008), Evolutionsbiologie, 3. Aufl., Eugen Ulmer, Stuttgart.

Latouche, S., Le Pari de la Décroissance, Fayard, Paris, 2006.

Lippman, Walter, Public Opinion, [1922] Macmillan, NYC, 1960.

Lutz, C.G. (2001), Practical Genetics for Aquaculture, Blackwell Science, Osney Mead, Oxford.

Lutz, W., Sanderson, W.C. and Scherbov, S. (2001), The End of World Population Growth in the 21st Century. New Challenges for Human Capital Formation and Sustainable Development, Earthscan, London.

Manier, Edouard (1978), The Young Darwin and His Cultural Circle: A Study of Influences which Helped Shape the Language and Logic of the First Draft of the Theory of Natural Selection, Dordrecht: Reidel.

Marciano, Alain and Maud Pélisser (2000), "The Influence of Scottish Enlightenment on Darwin's Theory of Cultural Evolution", Journal of the History of Economic Thought, 22: 239-249.

Marciano, Alain and Maud Pélisser (2003), "La théorie de l'évolution culturelle de Hayek à la lumière de La Descendance de l'homme de Darwin", Economies et Sociétés, 12, pp. 2121-2143.

Marschak, J. (1954), "Towards an Economic Theory of Organization and Information" in Thrall et al., eds, Decision Processes, John Wiley: New York, and Chapman & Hall: London.

Martinez-Alier and L. Temper (2007), Oil and Climate Change: Voices from the South, Ecological and Political Weekly, 15 Dec.

Martinez-Alier, J. (1987), Ecological Economics. Energy, Environment and Society. Blackwell, Oxford.

Masjuan, E. (2000), La ecología humana en el anarquismo ibérico, Iberia, Barcelona.

Mattick, J.S. (2004), "The Hidden Genetic Program of Complex Organisms," Scientific American 291, No 4: 30-37.

Maynard Smith, J. (1964), Group Selection and Kin Selection, Nature, Vol. 201, 1145–1147.

Maynard Smith, J. et.al. (1985), Development Constraints and Evolution, Quarterly Review of Biology, vol. 60, 265-287.

Mc Cannaughy, Gloria (1950), "Darwin and Social Darwinism", Osiris, 9, pp. 397-412.

Mitchell, R.C., and R.T. Carson (1989), Using Surveys to Value Public Goods: The Contingent Valuation Method. Resources for the Future. Washington, D.C.

Müller, G.B. (1994), Evolutionäre Entwicklungsbiologie: Grundlagen einer neuen Synthese, in: Wieser, W. (ed.), Die Evolution der Evolutionstheorie–Von Darwin zur DNA, Spektrum Akademischer Verlag, Heidelberg, 155-193.

Müller, G.B. (2005), Evolutionary Developmental Biology, in: Wuketits, F.M., Ayala, F.J. (eds.) (2005), Handbook of Evolution, Wiley VCH, 87-115.

Müller, G.B., Newman, S.A. (2003), Origination of Organismal Form: The Forgotten Cause in Evolutionary Theory, in: Müller, G. B., Newman, S. A. (eds.), Origination of Organismal Form – Beyond the Gene in Developmental and Evolutionary Biology, MIT Press, 3-10.

National Marine Fisheries Service (NMFS). (1996), Fisheries of the United States 1995. U.S. Department of Commerce, National Oceanic and Atmospheric Administration, National Marine Fisheries Service, Office of Science and Technology, Fisheries Statistics Division.

National Marine Fisheries Service (NMFS) (1997), Fisheries of the United States 1996. U.S. Department of Commerce, National Oceanic and Atmospheric Administration, National Marine Fisheries Service, Office of Science and Technology, Fisheries Statistics Division.

National Marine Fisheries Service (NMFS) (2007), Fisheries of the United States 2005. U.S. Department of Commerce, National Oceanic and Atmospheric Administration, National Marine Fisheries Service, Office of Science and Technology, Fisheries Statistics Division.

Naylor, R. et.al. (2000), Effects of Aquaculture on World Fish Supplies. Nature 405, 1017-1024.

Nelson, R.R. and S.G. Winter (1982), An Evolutionary Theory of Economic Change, Harvard University Press: Cambridge, Massachusetts.

Nelson, Richard R. And Sidney G. Winter (1982). An Evolutionary Theory of Economic Change, Cambridge, Harvard University Press.

NOAA. 2007. NOAA 10-Year Plan for Marine Aquaculture. Available at http://aquaculture.noaa.gov/pdf/finalnoaa10yrrweb.pdf

North, D.C. (1990), Institutions, Institutional Change, and Economic Performance, Cambridge University Press: Cambridge and New York.

North, D.C. (2005), Understanding the Process of Economic Change, Princeton University Press: Princeton and Oxford.

North, D.C. and R.P. Thomas (1973), The Rise of the Western World, Cambridge University Press: Cambridge.

OECD (1996), The Knowledge-Based Economy, Paris.

Orr, H.A. (2009), Selektion im Test, Spektrum der Wissenschaft Spezial, no.1, 12-19.

Osborn, Henry. F. (1894), From the Greeks to Darwin. An Outline of the Development of the Evolution Idea, New-York, Macmillan.

Overbye, D. (2003), "For the History of Science, the First Draft Is Often Late", New York Times On-Line, February 25.

Paul, Diane B. (2003). "Darwin, Social Darwinism and Eugenics", in Jonhatan Hodge and Gregory Radick (eds), The Cambridge Companion to DARWIN, Cambridge, Cambridge University Press, pp. 214-239.

Pearce, D.W., and R.K. Turner (1990), *Economics of Natural Resources and the Environment*. Harvester Wheatsheaf. London, UK.

Pearce, D.W., and R.K. Turner (1990), Economics of Natural Resources and the Environment. The Johns Hopkins University Press. Baltimore.

Pelikan, P. (1988), "Can the Imperfect Innovation System of Capitalism be Outperformed," in G. Dosi et al., eds., Technical Change and Economic Theory, Pinter Publishers: London and New York.

Pelikan, P. (1992), "The Dynamics of Economic Systems, or How to Transform a Failed Socialist Economy", Journal of Evolutionary Economics 2, 39-63; reprinted in H.J. Wagener, ed., On the Theory and Policy of Systemic Change, Physica-Verlag: Heidelberg, and Springer-Verlag: New York.

Pelikan, P. (2003a), "Why Economic Policies Require Comprehensive Evolutionary Analysis," in P. Pelikan and G. Wegner, eds., The Evolutionary Analysis of Economic Policy, Edward Elgar: Cheltenham and Northampton.

Pelikan, P. (2003c), "Bringing Institutions into Evolutionary Economics: Another View with Links to Changes in Physical and Social Technologies," Journal of Evolutionary Economics 13: 237-258.

Pennisi, E. (2007), Jumping Genes Hop Into the Evolutionary Limelight, Science, vol. 317, 984-895.

Pennisi, E. (2008), Modernizing the Modern Synthesis, Science, vol. 321, 196-197.

Penrose, Edith T. (1952), "Biological Analogies in the Theory of the Firm", American Economic Review, December, 42: 804-819.

Penrose, Edith T. (1953), "Rejoinder", American Economic Review, 43: 603-609.

Pinker, S. (2001), The Blank Slate: The Modern Denial of Human Nature, Penguin Books: London.

Potter, Van R. (1962), "Bridge to the Future: The Concept of Human Progress", Land Economics, 38 (1), pp. 1-8.

Pribram, Karl (1953), "Patterns of Economic Reasoning", The American Economic Review, 43 (2), pp. 243-258.

Price, D. de S., "Is Technology Historically Independent of Science? A Study in Statistical Historiography", Technology & Culture, VI (4), Fall 1965, 553-568

Prigogine, I. and I. Stengers (1984), Order out of Chaos, Bantam Books: New York.

Rapoport, Anatol (1960), Figths, Games and Debates, Ann Arbor, University of Michigan Press.

Redlich, Fritz (1951), "Sanctions and Freedom of Enterprise", The Journal of Economic History, 11 (3), Part 1, pp. 266-272.

Ridley, M. (2003), Nature via Nurture: Genes, Experience, & What Makes Us Human, HarperCollins: New York.

Ridley, M., Genome (1999), The Autobiography of a Species in 23 Chapters: Preface and Chapter 1: Life, HarperCollins, NYC.

Riedl, R. (1975), Die Ordnung des Lebendigen, Parey, Hamburg, Berlin.

Roger, James (1972), "Darwinism and Social Darwinism", Journal of the History of Ideas, 33,

Ronsin, F., La grève des ventres; propagande malthusienne et baisse de la natalité en France, XIXe-XXe siècles, Aubier, Paris, 1980.

Rosenberg, N. and L.E. Birdzell (1986), How the West Grew Rich, Basic Books: New York.

Rubin, Paul (2000), "Group Selection and the Limits to Altruism", Journal of Bioeconomics, 2 (1): 9-23.

Ruse, M. (1986), Taking Darwin Seriously, Oxford, Basil Blackwell.

Rust, M.B. (2002), Nutritional Physiology. Chapter 7 in R. W. Hardy and J. H. Halver (ed.), Fish Nutrition, 3rd ed., San Diego: Elsevier Science. pp 367-452. Stickney, R.R., B. Costa-Pierce, D.M. Baltz, M. Drawbridge, C. Grimes, S. Phillips and D.L. Swann. 2006. Toward Sustainable Open Ocean Aquaculture in the United States. Fisheries 31 (12):607-610

Sagan, C. (1977), The Dragons of Eden, Balantine, NYC.

Samuelson, P. & S. Scotchmer (2002), "The Law and Economics of Reverse Engineering," Yale Law Journal, 111.

Scherer, F.M. (1971), Industrial Market Structure and Economic Performance, Rand McNally, Chicago.

Schumpeter, J.A. (1954), History of Economic Analysis, New York, Oxford University Press.

Schumpeter, J.A. (1912/1934), The Theory of Economic Development, Harvard University Press: Cambridge, Massachusetts.

Schweber, Silvan S. (1977), "The Origin of the Origin Revisited", Journal of the History of Biology, 10: 229-316.

Schweber, Silvan S. (1980), "Darwin and the Political Economists: Divergence of Character", Journal of the History of Biology, 13: 195-289.

Self-Organization in Biological Systems, Princeton University Press: Princeton and London.

Senglaub, K. (1998), Neue Auseinandersetzungen mit dem Darwinismus, in: Jahn, I. (ed.), Geschichte der Biologie, 3. ed., Spektrum Akademischer Verlag, Heidelberg, 558-579.

Shannon, C.E. and W. Weaver (1949), The Mathematical Theory of Communication, University of Illinois Press: Urbana.

Singer, E. (2009), A Comeback of Lamarckian Evolution?, Technology Review (MIT), February 4.

Smith, Adam. 1759 [1976], The Theory of Moral Sentiments, Indianapolis, Liberty Press.

Smith, Adam. 1776 [1979], An Inquiry into the Nature and Causes of the Wealth of Nations, Oxford, Clarendon.

Soddy, F. (1933), Wealth, Virtual Wealth and Debt, Allen & Unwin, London 1926, 2nd ed.

Soddy. F. (1922), Cartesian Economics: the Bearing of Physical Sciences upon State Stewardship, Hendersons, London.

Solow, Robert (1954), "The Survival of Mathematics", Review of Economics and Statistics, 36 (4), pp. 327-374.

Spencer, Herbert (1855), The Principles of Psychology, London: Longmans.

Spencer, Herbert (1857), "Progess: Its Law and Causes", The Westminster Review, 67 (April 1857), pp 445-465.

Spencer, Herbert (1862), First Principles, London: Williams and Norgate.

Spurgeon, J. (1999), "The Socio-Economic Costs and Benefits of Coastal Habitat Rehabilitation and Creation." *Marine Pollution Bulletin* Volume 37, Number 8-12, Pages 373 to 382.

Swanson, T. M. (1994). The International Regulation of Extinction, New York University Press, New York.

Tacon, Albert (2005), State of Information on Salmon Aquaculture Feed and the Environment. World Wildlife Federation, special publication.

Theil, H. (1967), Economics and Information Theory, American Elsevier: New York, and North-Holland: Amsterdam.

Trivers, Robert (1971), "The Evolution of Reciprocal Altruism", Quarterly Review of Biology, 46: 36-57.

Tullock, Gordon (1970), "Switching in General Predators: Comment", Bulletin Ecological Society of America, 51: 21-24

U.S. Army Corps of Engineers (USACE) (2008), "Economic and Environmental Principles and Guidelines for Water and Related

Land Resources Implementation Studies." Accessed April 27, 2009, at www.usace.army.mil/CECW/Documents/pgr/pg_draft.doc.

U.S. Commission on Ocean Policy (2004), An Ocean Blueprint for the 21st Century. Final Report. Washington, D.C.

UN Millennium Environmental Assessment (2005).

Vanberg, V.J. (1992), "Innovation, Cultural Evolution and Economic Growth," in U. Witt, ed., Explaining Process and Change: Approaches to Evolutionary Economics, The University of Michigan Press: Ann Arbor.

Vanberg, V.J. (2004), "The Rationality Postulate in Economics: Its Ambiguity, Its Deficiency and Its Evolutionary Alternative," Journal of Economic Methodology 11: 1-29.

Vrba, E., Eldredge, N. (1984), "Individuals, Hierarchies and Processes: Towards a More Complete Evolutionary Theory", Paleobiology, Vol. 10, 146-171.

Waggoner (1994), How Much Land Can Ten Billion People Spare for Nature? Task Force Report.

Washington State. General Administration (2007), "Capitol Lake Adaptive Management Plan." Accessed May 12, 2009, at www.ga.wa.gov/CLAMP/Plan.htm.

Whitehead, J.C., P.A. Groothuis, R. Southwick, and P. Foster-Turley. (2006), "The Economic Values of Saginaw Bay Coastal Marshes." Department of Economics. Working Papers 06-10. Appalachian State University. Boone, NC

Wieser, W. (1994), Gentheorien und Systemtheorien: Wege und Wandlungen der Evolutionstheorie im 20. Jahrhundert, in: Wieser, W. (ed.), Die Evolution der Evolutionstheorie - Von Darwin zur DNA, Spektrum Akademischer Verlag, Heidelberg, 15-48.

Wild, Ruedi (1997), Snapshot of the World Feed Industry: Global Perspective. Feed Management 48(7):10-13.

Witt, U. (2003), The Evolving Economy: Essays on the Evolutionary Approach to Economics, Edward Elgar: Cheltenham and Northampton.

Witt, U. (2004), On the Proper Interpretation of 'Evolution' in Economics and Its Implications for the Production Theory, Journal of Economic Methodology, vol. 11, 125-146.

Witt, U. (2004), "On the Proper Interpretation of 'Evolution' in Economics and its Implications for Production Theory," Journal of Economic Methodology 11: 125-146.

Witt, U. (2008), What is Specific About Evolutionary Economics?, Journal of Evolutionary Economics, vol. 18, 547-575.

Zimmerli, W.C. (1990), Grenzen des evolutionären Paradigmas– Metakritische Bemerkungen zu einer auslaufenden Denkmode, in: Jüdes, U., Eulefeld, G., Kapune, T. (eds.), Evolution der Biosphäre, Hirzel, Stuttgart, 137-152.